SOCIAL RESEARCH

FOURTH EDITION

SOCIAL RESEARCH

Issues, methods and process

FOURTH EDITION

Tim May

McGraw Hill

Open University Press

Open University Press
McGraw-Hill Education
McGraw-Hill House
Shoppenhangers Road
Maidenhead
Berkshire
England
SL6 2QL

email: enquiries@openup.co.uk
world wide web: www.openup.co.uk

and Two Penn Plaza, New York, NY 10121-2289, USA

First published 1993
Second edition published 1997
Third edition published 2001
Reprinted 2003, 2004, 2005, 2006 (twice), 2007, 2008, 2010
First published in this fourth edition 2011

A catalogue record of this book is available from the British Library

ISBN-13: 978-0-33-523567-4
ISBN-10: 0-33-523567-0
e-ISBN: 978-0-33-523998-6

Library of Congress Cataloging-in-Publication Data
CIP data applied for

Typeset by RefineCatch Limited, Bungay, Suffolk
Printed and bound by CPI Group (UK) Ltd, Croydon, CR0 4YY

Fictitious names of companies, products, people, characters and/or data that may
be used herein (in case studies or in examples) are not intended to represent any
real individual, company, product or event.

The McGraw·Hill Companies

Contents

Acknowledgements

There are a number of people I would like to thank who have been sources of friendship and support during the writing process.

At SURF, my thanks go to Simon Marvin and Mike Hodson for the support and to Matt Thompson and Vicky Simpson for their assistance. Beth Perry and I have worked together on many projects that have involved comparative research and case studies. It thus made perfect sense to ask Beth to co-author those chapters. My thanks to her for that and for reading the entire manuscript and suggesting positive change to its content.

Cian, Calum, Alex, Nick and Lewis remind me that there are many other things beside the world of work to preoccupy my time in so many different ways and their lives are a never-ending source of change, insight, experience and hope. My love and gratitude to Vikki for her support and for so many good times and for many more to come in our lives together.

Malcolm Williams, whom I asked in the production of the second edition to join me in writing the questionnaire chapter, took on new responsibilities which prevented him from contributing to this edition. I was, however, fortunate that Carole Sutton, who is an experienced quantitative researcher and author, agreed to co-author that chapter and my thanks to her.

Finally, my thanks to Ken Parsons for his friendship and the editorial and production teams at Open University Press/McGraw-Hill and to Christine Firth for her excellent copy-editing skills.

Preface to the second edition

I was very pleased to learn that this book has been so successful as to warrant a second edition. Many people have been very supportive in their comments and letters regarding its aims, structure, style and content. Students, lecturers and researchers alike found the book to be accessible and comprehensive. It was therefore with some trepidation that I approached the writing of a second edition.

This book, as with all books, has its limitations, as well as strengths. However, when it came to taking critical comments onboard in an attempt to rectify any shortcomings, published reviews, while complimentary, were mixed in relation to its intended audience. All agreed that it was aimed at undergraduates, but noted that it was suitable for postgraduates. I also found that while lecturers were defining it as a 'textbook', they were often consulting it in order to update themselves on current thinking, as well as quoting from it to justify or expand upon their own investigations.

With these messages in mind, where was I to start? In the end I decided that the structure of the book should remain intact and it can be read at different levels. What I thought was required were additions to the content of each chapter in order to render further justice to ideas on the research process in general, as well as aspects of its practice in particular. Given this decision, all chapters have been revised and expanded and I have added suggested further readings to the end of each chapter.

When it came to the chapter on questionnaires, it is now five years since I have undertaken, first-hand, survey research through the stages of design, administration and analysis. This does not reflect so much a methodological preference, but the ebbs and flows to which one is subjected in the first years of an academic career, as well as the costs associated with large-scale survey research. Quite simply, you are not in a position to refuse opportunities that come your way and these have involved more qualitative aspects of research practice. Thus, although I have acted in an advisory capacity on survey research projects, Malcolm Williams, an experienced quantitative researcher and friend with whom I have worked on several occasions, kindly agreed to assist me in expanding and updating that chapter.

Overall, the end result is a new edition which takes into consideration recent developments in the field of social research. In so doing it is hoped that readers find it as accessible and comprehensive as the first edition and it renders further justice to a rich and varied field of perspectives and practices. Its basic philosophy, however, remains the same: that is, reflexive researchers will produce the most insightful research into the social worlds which we inhabit, while the social sciences are central for understanding social relations and explaining the workings of societies in general.

Preface to the third edition

When this book was first published in 1993, it was my belief that it could fill a gap in the literature on social research. It aimed to do this by bringing together, in one volume, a discussion of the issues, methods and processes of social research. While it could never be exhaustive and I was very uncertain whether it would be successful it was, contrary to the expectations of those few persons who sought to support my endeavours by telling me that there were 'plenty of books' already on the market, a success. Then, with the publication of a second edition and following substantial revision, sales increased even further and I received communications from people who were very complimentary and supportive of the book. Now, as I write the third edition, I am delighted that people still find it a book worth reading.

As with the second edition, I approached the revision of this book with some trepidation. After all, the structure and content clearly appeal to a wide audience, with varying degrees of research experience, across a range of disciplines. At the same time, it is necessary that its content reflects the developments that have occurred within the interdisciplinary field of social research. Given this, I have undertaken a number of revisions to reflect these changes.

In the first part of the book, revisions and additions have been made in order to reflect new ways of thinking about the relationship between theory and research and values and ethics in the research process. This takes onboard advances in post-empiricist thinking, as well as the relations between values, objectivity and data collection. Also, where necessary, recommended readings have been updated, as well as references to studies that form the basis of discussions throughout the book. With the valuable help of my friend and colleague, Malcolm Williams, additions have been made to the chapter on questionnaires (a method that, since the second edition, I have again utilized in employing what is known as

Delphi-style questionnaires), while discussions on research on the internet, narratives, case studies and new technologies, among others, have been introduced in the second part of the book. The reader will also detect many other changes, the intention of which is to aid understanding by keeping up-to-date with the latest innovations in social research.

In making these changes, I hope that you find a third edition that is richer in insight, but retains the original philosophy that motivated me to write the book in the first place: that is, to further our understanding of ourselves and each other and explain the relations and dynamics that are generated in and through societies, we need to produce and maintain reflexive and disciplined practices in the social sciences. The overall purpose of this is to enable an engagement with social issues in order that people are better able to understand one another within improved conditions for all.

Preface to the fourth edition

I started work on this book in 1992, along with a co-edited collection on ethnography. That was two years after I had completed my PhD and published it as a book on organizational change in the probation service, based on a multi-method, action research study. In those first two years I taught modules across two campuses that were 50 miles apart. To say that was an 'interesting start' to an academic career disguises as much as it illuminates, but I genuinely felt privileged to have obtained the work.

My own experiences of being an undergraduate and graduate at university led me to write a short book on study skills. I then wrote a series of modules on research methods, both of which were to provide the content for a qualification in the design and development of open learning materials. Some of this material found its way into the first edition of this book.

It was a bewildering period as I sought to grapple with the expectations of a new career. I had spent, including my two years at night school, nine years accumulating the understanding and qualifications necessary to enter the world of academia. My prior experiences of being an agricultural engineer and working in different places, as well as those gained since becoming an academic, still inform my practices. For these and other reasons, I have become very attached to this book over the years.

The previous editions appeared at four year intervals (1993, 1997 and 2001). This one now appears ten years later. Why? I have been working in a research centre in Manchester, the Centre for Sustainable Urban and Regional Futures (SURF: please see www.surf.salford.ac.uk), which requires the generation of external income to meet its salaries, rent and overheads. We operate a mixed-economy of funding between research council and public and private clients at city, regional, national and international levels.

The idea that the source of income should dictate the integrity of social inquiry, in a way that means you move frenetically from one project to another, had to be properly thought through and a resistance built into our practices that allowed the space and time to inform a value base which keeps our critical faculties intact. That means we have to work at being different in both the university sector and in public and commercial life in general. We have to make spaces of reflection in places of contradictory expectations. Overall, this is important for the future of research contexts as a whole, but it receives little systematic attention.

We learnt about new areas of work while liaising with external clients, working to tight deadlines and producing lengthy research reports in short time periods. We have sought clarification through the production of many journal articles and book chapters as a matter of routine and are highly successful in the UK 'research assessment exercise' as part of a 'built environment' research grouping. We engage in dissemination activities according to the idea of knowledge being a public good and seek to balance the attraction of expertise within a cooperative spirit of inquiry.

Those experiences have informed the writing of this new edition, along with those obtained by working in interdisciplinary research teams. New chapters have been added and all chapters modified and brought up-to-date in order to reflect changes and new modes of thinking. I hope, however, I have retained the spirit of the original book. This is not a manual for methods. While they have their place, the actual practice of research is a great deal more than is contained within such pages. Here, I hope, you will find insight and inspiration if you are conducting research for the first time, as well as food for thought if you are more experienced in its craft.

Introduction

Research methods are core to scientific activity. They constitute an important part of scientific curricula and provide a means through which intellectual development and understanding of phenomena are enhanced. The status as a 'science' is justified by alluding to the technical aspects of research methods, while the very term carries with it ideas of areas of study that are accessible only to those who have undergone lengthy training processes in order to understand the inner workings of disciplines.

At the same time there are also those within disciplines who characterize themselves as 'theorists' rather than 'researchers'. The latter tend to concentrate on the process of research, while the former might argue that they gain an advantage in having a distance from the empirical world in order to reflect upon those processes and their products, as well as raise issues for subsequent research.

There is merit in both of these views. Innovative thinking and meticulous attention to the details of data gathering inform the practice of social research. Theory, methodology and methods are all part of the issues that surround and inform a field of activity that is populated by different disciplines. These differences, however, frequently lead to disputes, as well as confusions, over the nature of research and the methods that it should employ in pursuance of its aims. For this reason Chapters 1–3 of this book examine the ways in which we gain our knowledge of the social world, the relationships that exist between theory and research, and the place of values and ethics in research practice.

While these issues may appear complicated, they are fundamental to an understanding of research methods. Without this, issues and methods become separated and practitioners are left with the impression that they simply have to learn various techniques in order to undertake research. The purpose of Part I of this book is thus one of clarification.

A narrow attitude to research practice perpetuates the idea that theory, ethics, values and methods of social research are distinct topics that researchers, despite living and participating in the societies that they study, are somehow distinct from the social world which is the object of their investigations. A distance between them and the subjects of their study permits a limited notion of value-freedom to be maintained. As will become evident, our very membership of society is a necessary condition for understanding the social world of which we are a part, as well as being a fact of life from which we cannot escape. Indeed, such participation is a prerequisite of objectivity.

In having an understanding of these debates and the applicability of different methods of research, improved practice and more inquiring and confident researchers will be the end result. To this extent, it is important to be aware of not only the strengths of particular methods of social research, but also their limitations.

AIM AND CONTENT

A discussion of issues forms the starting-point for the philosophy which underlies this book: that is, issues and methods cannot be simply separated and that we, as researchers, will produce more systematic understandings of the social world by recognizing these in our practices, as well as how those practices raise issues for consideration. That noted, this book is also written for those who do not have a working knowledge of social research and its practices. Issues are thus presented in a way that does not assume a detailed prior knowledge on the part of the reader, with additional readings being provided for those who have the time and disposition to pursue matters in greater depth.

The book itself is divided into three parts. Part I examines the issues, Part II discusses the methods and Part III is devoted to reflections on the process of research. Because the aim is to produce an accessible text, there is a limit to which connections between the different parts can be developed. For this reason, different perspectives are presented and parallels are drawn between Part II and the earlier discussions in Part I. Nevertheless, all too often reading can be a passive exercise in which we, as the readers, act as the recipients of the text, but do not engage with it by criticizing, analysing and cross-referencing the materials covered (May 1999a). To assist in this process, questions appear at the end of each chapter that are intended to help you in reflecting upon its content individually, within a group, or in a workshop or seminar.

PART I: AN OVERVIEW

Part I introduces the perspectives involved in and around the research process. This part of the book is based on the observation that values, prejudices and prior beliefs affect the way we all think about an event, object, place, person, thing or subject. An awareness and consideration of how these relate to the research process is then taken to sharpen and focus the decisions and choices in our work.

Chapter 1 covers the different perspectives which exist on social research by examining their arguments and intellectual foundations. To use a building analogy, if we do not understand the foundations of our work, then we are likely to end up with a shaky structure! Chapter 2 develops the points raised in the previous one by examining the relationship between social theory and social research, with Chapter 3 devoted to a discussion of the place of values and ethics in social research.

The topics covered are often thought to present such intractable problems for the researcher that they move to a backstage position in the research process. That, however, can lead to subsequent issues in the research process as they are a necessary part of its practice and an intellectual sharpening of its place in society. Thus, for example, ethics are a fundamental component of the idea of a 'discipline' and the confidence which people have in the actions of its members. As I hope will become evident, ignoring these issues does not mean that they no longer exert an influence, for they routinely inform and have consequence for, research.

PART II: AN OVERVIEW

The first chapter in Part II (Chapter 4) begins by considering the main sources of official statistics that researchers use, followed by an account of their strengths and weaknesses. By tracing the issues which surround the production of statistics, the questions regarding their place and use in social research can be considered.

Chapters 5–9 examine the process and methods of analyses involved in major techniques used in social research. These cover questionnaire design, interviewing, participant observation, documentary research and case studies. In order to provide for ease of comparison between these different methods, each of the chapters follows a similar structure. Each one begins with a discussion of the place of the method in social research which makes links with the discussions in Part I. That is followed by an examination of the process of undertaking research and an overview of techniques that may be deployed for data analysis.

The intention in following the above structure is to enable you to consider the different ways of approaching your data and to direct you to specific sources for further investigation of the topics. Therefore, should you decide to utilize a method, or combination of methods, you will be aware of the ways in which the data are collected and the means employed for their analysis. Finally, each of these chapters ends with a discussion of the method within the field of social research as a whole.

Chapter 10 is concerned with comparative research. The idea of comparison has long been used in the social and natural sciences and so there is a discussion of experimental and quasi-experimental methods. In relation to cross-national comparisons, the process of globalization coupled with a growth in information technology, has led to much interest in comparative research which has a long history. As such, there are important developments taking place in this field. Awareness of both the potential and issues involved in these developments is thus an important part of social research.

PART III: AN OVERVIEW

Chapter 11 is the third part of the book. I wrote this in order to offer the reader some reflections on the practice of social research. I have learnt these either directly or through acquaintance with other researchers, as well as through written accounts of the research process and reading across a number of disciplines.

Throughout the text you will find extensive references to contemporary and other important works in and around social research. The bibliography is thus a resource for you to use in exploring themes and topics in greater depth. I hope by the end of the book you will have gained a sense that research is an exciting field of endeavour that is central to understanding human relations and the environments that we inhabit and rely upon.

Part I   Issues in social research

Perspectives on social scientific research

1

The world and experience
  The objective world
  The experienced world
  Bridge-building
Knowledge and difference
  Exclusions
  Inclusions
Summary
Suggested further reading

This first chapter provides an outline on perspectives that assist in understanding the aims and practices of social research. These do not determine the nature of the research process itself, for there is a constant interaction between ideas about the social world and the data collected on it, as well as the influences of factors such as power and values. However, an understanding of these issues is important for the actual practice of research to enable the practitioner to understand the influence of wider social forces on the process of research, as well as the arguments and the assumptions that are made about the world and the dynamics and properties it contains. These may then be linked with Part II where we discuss the actual practice of research methods.

THE WORLD AND EXPERIENCE

Social research falls under the general heading of 'social science'. A science is thought of as being a coherent body of thought about a topic over which there is a broad consensus among its practitioners as to its properties, causes and effects. A view of science is that it is based on 'what we see, hear and touch rather than on personal opinions or speculative imaginings' (Chalmers 1999: 1). However, the actual practice of science shows that there are not only different perspectives on a given phenomenon, but also alternative methods of gathering and analysing data. Disagreements do exist between practitioners, but these are not thought to somehow undermine a collective search for better ways of explaining phenomena.

We are concerned here with the history and practice of the social sciences (see M. Williams 2000). To have differences of perspective in a site of activity such as social research may, at first glance, appear to be problematic. After all, if there is no one established way of working then surely that undermines the idea of a scientific discipline? Yet if we shift our focus we might say that, as with the physical sciences, disciplines are contested in both justification and application because there are important political and value considerations that relate to how we live. These are not within the power of science to alter, nor in any democracy should they be (Fuller 2000). The role is to understand and explain social phenomena and to focus attention on particular issues. We shall also find theories that challenge our understanding of the social world as part of social research practice.

So the practices of the physical sciences and social sciences are more complicated and interesting than any single definition of their activities might encompass. To understand this further, we need to understand the main ideas that inform social research before moving on (in Chapter 2) to examine the relationship between social theory and social research.

The objective world

Objectivity, along with generalization and explanation, is a fundamental characteristic of a science. If we are to hold to the view that social science research offers us knowledge about the social world which is not necessarily available by other means, then we are making some privileged claims about its work. Research thus becomes more than a reflection of our opinions and prejudices: it substantiates, refutes, organizes or generates our thinking and produces evidence that may challenge not only our own beliefs, but also those of groups and societies in general.

It is at this point that objectivity in the social sciences becomes of importance. It is often assumed that if our values do not enter into our research, it is objective in the sense of being beyond criticism. Objectivity is therefore defined as:

the basic conviction that there is or must be some permanent, ahistorical matrix or framework to which we can ultimately appeal in determining the nature of rationality, knowledge, truth, reality, goodness, or rightness.

(Bernstein 1983: 8)

While many accept that what scientists say is the 'truth', there are fundamental differences of opinion concerning what science can and cannot
pronounce upon: the most obvious example being the existence of a deity
among those with religious beliefs. Within social research people constitute social life and so the question is now raised as to whether social
researchers, as members of society, can suspend their sense of belonging
to turn it into an object of study?

Positivism

A sense of belonging may be a secondary consideration if we hold that
social facts exist independently of people's perceptions. It may be held that
people react to their environment much as molecules which become 'excited'
when heat is applied to a liquid. Science does not have to ask molecules
what they think. So is it necessary that social scientists ask people? We may,
of course, be interested in people's opinions in terms of their reactions to
events that affect their lives, but only in so far as they are reacting to events,
processes and conditions and we wish to explain and predict their behaviour accordingly. However, what of free-will? That is, we can control our
destinies rather than have them controlled by a change in our environment.
We can 'act on', as well as behave in 'reaction to', our social environments.

Experiments in the natural sciences take the form of altering the environment and observing subsequent reactions. The issue is one of controlling the inputs into experimental situations in order to see what factors
cause particular changes. There are problems with this approach: it
assumes that the criteria that are used for scientific selection and elimination do not vary according to changes in local circumstances. Because of
this issue and the myriad of influences that exist in social life, the idea of
'quasi-experimentation' has arisen as an approximation of this idea of a
particular research method. In some approaches to research, for example,
a group is selected who will be subject to the programme that is to be
evaluated. The treatment group will then be compared to those who have
not been subject to the programme in order that any differences may be
argued to be a result of the intervention itself. Nevertheless, if we create
artificial conditions they may satisfy the desire to apply a method, but
they say nothing about the complications, conditions, decisions and
contradictions that are actually part of our social lives.

If we believe ourselves to be the product of our environment – created
by it – then we are the mirror image of it. It defines our nature, or our
being. We do not have to ask people themselves because we can predict
how they will behave through reference to environmental factors alone.
Simply expressed, this is the position of two schools of thought in social
research: behaviourism and positivism. It should be noted, however, that
positivism refers to varied traditions of social and philosophical thought
and given that the term is often used in a pejorative sense in social science

without due regard to its history, it runs the risk of being devoid of any specific meaning (C. Bryant 1985).

For one social scientist, often characterized as being inclined toward positivism, the social scientist must study social phenomena 'in the same state of mind as the physicist, chemist or physiologist when he probes into a still unexplored region of the scientific domain' (Durkheim 1964: xiv). Objectivity is defined according to particular depictions of the natural scientific method and social life may be explained in the same way as natural phenomena. This tradition may therefore be characterized in terms of the prediction and explanation of phenomena and the pursuit of objectivity, which is defined as the researcher's 'detachment' from the topic under investigation. The results of research using this method of investigation are then said to produce a set of 'true', precise and wide-ranging 'laws' (known as covering laws). We would then be able to generalize from our observations on social phenomena to make statements about the population as a whole. Positivism thus explains human behaviour in terms of cause and effect (in our example above, heat is the cause and the effect is the molecules becoming excited as the temperature increases) and 'data' are collected on the social environment and people's reactions to it.

Empiricism

If the aim of positivism is to collect and assemble data on the social world from which we can generalize and explain human behaviour through the use of our theories, then it shares with empiricism the belief that there are 'facts' which we can gather on the social world, *independently* of how people interpret them. As researchers, we need to refine our instruments of data collection in order that they are neutral recording instruments much as the ruler measures distance and the clock, time. The fundamental difference between empiricism and positivism, however, lies in the realm of theory. As will be developed in Chapter 2, positivism is theory driven and data test the accuracy of the theory. Empiricism, on the other hand, is a perspective on research which does not refer explicitly to the theory guiding its data collection procedures. It is thus characterized 'by the catchphrase "the facts speak for themselves"' (Bulmer 1982: 31).

It is important, as happens all too often, not to confuse the words empirical and empiricism. The word empirical refers to the collection of data on the social world to test, generate or interact with the propositions of social science, while the empiricist school of thought believes that the facts speak for themselves and require no explanation via theoretical engagement. Although there are differences between positivism and empiricism, the former relies on the methods of the latter. They both assert that there are facts about the social world which we can gather –

independent of interpretive variations. Objectivity is thereby defined in terms of detachment from the social world, as well as the accuracy and neutrality of data collection instruments. Quite simply, there is a world out there that we can record and analyse independently of people's interpretations of it. There is a strong affinity, therefore, with the 'correspondence theory of reality' which holds that a belief, statement or sentence is true as long as there is an external fact that corresponds to it.

Realism

Realism shares with positivism the aim of explanation. Beyond that, the parallels end. A branch of realism, known as 'critical realism' (the two are frequently and incorrectly conflated), has enjoyed a particular boost in the social sciences with the works of the philosopher Roy Bhaskar (1998; Archer et al. 1998). He writes that:

> to be a realist in philosophy is to be committed to the existence of some disputed kind of being (e.g. material objects, universals, causal laws; propositions, numbers, probabilities; efficacious reasons, social structures, moral facts).
>
> (Bhaskar 1993: 308)

The critical element of realism has a long history and may be associated with the works of Karl Marx and Sigmund Freud (see M. Williams and May 1996: 81–8), but has also been associated with the ideas of Foucault (Pearce and Woodiwiss 2001) and Durkheim (Pearce 1989). Marx, for example, constructed his typology (a method of classification) of capitalism on the basis that there are certain essential features which distinguish it from other economic and political systems. Within this economic system there exist 'central structural mechanisms' and the task of researchers are 'to organize one's concepts so as to grasp *its* essential features successfully' (Keat and Urry 1975: 112, original emphasis).

In referring to underlying structural mechanisms, an important argument is being employed. If researchers simply content themselves with studying everyday social life, such as conversations and interactions between people, this will distract them from an investigation of the underlying mechanisms which make those possible in the first instance (Collier 1994; Sayer 2000). The task of researchers within this tradition is to uncover the structures of social relations in order to understand why we then have the policies and practices that we do. Similarly, Sigmund Freud argued that our consciousness was determined by our subconscious. Thus people's neuroses are the visible manifestations of their sexual and aggressive desires that are repressed in their subconscious. Freud's single contribution to social thought may thus be said to lie 'in the idea that culture is reproduced through a repressive structuring of unconscious passions' (Elliott 1994: 41). While people may not be directly aware of the causes of these experiences, they still affect their actions.

Realism in general argues that the knowledge people have of their social world affects their behaviour and, unlike the propositions of positivism and empiricism, the social world does not simply 'exist' independently of this knowledge. Given this, causes are not simply determining of actions, but must be seen as 'tendencies' that produce particular effects. Yet people's knowledge may be partial or incomplete. The task of social research, therefore, is not simply to collect observations on the social world, but to explain these within theoretical frameworks which examine the underlying mechanisms that inform people's actions and prevent their choices from reaching fruition: for example, how schools function to reproduce a workforce for capitalism despite the resistance that may take place in the classroom (P. Willis 1977). As Bob Carter (2000) puts it in his examination of the relationship between realism and racism, 'realism is resolutely post-empiricist in its stress on the theory-driven nature of social scientific knowledge' (Carter 2000: 171).

The aim of examining and explaining underlying mechanisms cannot use the methods of empiricism as these simply reflect the everyday world, not the conditions which make it possible. Therefore, along with others in this tradition (Sayer 1992; Carter and New 2004), Keat and Urry (1975) argue that realism must utilize a different definition of science to positivism. In particular, a realist conception of social science would not necessarily assume that we can 'know' the world out there independently of the ways in which we describe it. That is not to say, however, that social reality is not stratified: for example, into individual, interactive and institutional levels.

Access to these different layers of reality is the task of a realist research programme and brings to the attention of persons how they affect their actions in a situation of dialogue and cooperation. It is this, in contrast to other approaches to evaluation (see Clarke 1999; Brandon and Lombardi 2005), that underlies recommendations for programme evaluation (Pawson and Tilley 1997) or evidence-based policy (Pawson 2006). As one researcher puts it in his exposition of complexity theory and its parallels with the tradition of critical realism, we see in both an 'insistence on the emergent material character of understanding in particular and social action in general' (Byrne 1998: 51).

Given the above, there are those within this tradition who have built bridges between the idea that there is a world out there independent of our interpretation of it (empiricism and positivism) with the need for researchers to understand the process by which people interpret the world by, for example, focusing upon the role of reflexivity in social life (Archer 2007). Before discussing those who have attempted this, I shall first examine the perspectives which argue, contrary to positivism and empiricism, that there is no social world 'beyond' people's perceptions and interpretations.

The experienced world

Up to now, we have spoken of the ways in which our environment or its underlying structures – of which we are not necessarily aware – structure us, or create us as objects (positivism) or subjects and objects (realism). At the same time we like to believe that we exercise free-will and make judgements which alter the courses of our lives. Positivism does not pay much attention to the detail of people's inner mental states except in so far as it reflects a conformity to pre-existing states of affairs. Realism, on the other hand, refers to people's consciousness in so far as it reflects the conditions under which they live, how structures are reproduced and how their desires and needs are constructed.

When we refer to people's consciousness we are concerned with what takes place – in terms of thinking and acting – within each of us. These subjective states refer to our 'inner' world of experiences, rather than the world 'out there'. To concentrate on subjectivity we focus on the *meanings* that people give to their environment, not the environment itself. As researchers, we cannot know the world independently of people's interpretations. The only thing that we can know with certainty is how people interpret the world around them. A core focus is now upon people's understandings and interpretations of their social environments, part of which has been termed a 'phenomenological' approach to researching the social world (see Moustakas 1994).

Idealism

Some schools of thought emphasize our creation of the social world through the realm of ideas, rather than material relations. They would argue that our actions are governed not by cause and effect, as in the case of molecules in a test tube, but by the rules and norms which we use to interpret the world. As the physical sciences deal with matter which is not 'conscious', researchers of this persuasion argue that its methods cannot deal with social life and should be discarded from its study. To speak of determinate causes is not applicable to researching social life as people contemplate, interpret and act within their environments. For these reasons, the methods of the social sciences are fundamentally different from, but *not* inferior to, the natural sciences. It is the world of ideas in which we are interested as social researchers: 'Such a viewpoint suggests that human activity is not behaviour (an adaption to material conditions), but an expression of meaning that humans give (via language) to their conduct' (Johnson et al. 1990: 14).

Rules exist in social action through which we produce society and understand and recognize each other. Rules, of course, are often broken and also subject to different interpretations. For that reason, we cannot predict human behaviour but people still act as if they were following rules and this makes their actions intelligible. People are constantly engaged in the process of interpretation and it is this which we should seek to understand. In other words, researchers should concentrate upon *how* people produce social life. Social life can be understood only through an examination of people's selection and interpretation of events and actions. Understanding these processes and what makes them possible is the aim of research for those influenced by this tradition. It is not explaining why people behave in certain ways by reference to their subconscious states or environmental conditions, but how people interpret the world and interact with each other. This is known as *intersubjectivity*. The idea of an external social 'reality' has now been abandoned because the meanings which we attach to the world are not static, nor universal, but always multiple and variable and constantly subject to modification and change in our relations with each others. Our accounts of the social world must therefore be 'internalist': that is, arising from within the cultures that are studied. As one advocate of this view puts it in relation to meaning and language use: 'To give an account of the meaning of a word is to describe how it is used; and to describe how it is used is to describe the social intercourse into which it enters' (Winch 1990: 123).

There are those within this tradition who argue that researchers need to employ 'hermeneutic principles' – hermeneutics referring to the theory and practice of interpretation. We are no longer proclaiming our 'disengagement' from our subject matter as a condition of science (positivism), but our 'commitment' and 'engagement' as a condition of understanding social life. Our sense of belonging to a society and the techniques which we use for understanding are not impediments to our studies. The procedures through which we understand and interpret our social world are now necessary conditions for us to undertake research. In the process we both utilize and challenge our understandings in doing social science research and the social researcher stands at the centre of the research process as a requirement of interpreting social life. The idea of social scientific work is now very different from positivism and empiricism. For these reasons, as will be noted in Part II, there is a tendency to prefer methods of research such as participant observation and focused interviewing.

Bridge-building

There are those who have attempted to synthesize some aspects of these major perspectives. The social theorist Anthony Giddens, in particular, has argued that our everyday actions are meaningful to us, but they also reproduce structures which both enable and constrain our actions (Giddens 1984) and he has taken such insights into the realms of climate change (Giddens 2009). Such a position is also shared by Roy Bhaskar, noted earlier, while Pierre Bourdieu was a social scientist and public intellectual whose work was driven by empirical interests. In the process he developed a series of 'tools' for researching and thinking about the social world (Bourdieu and Wacquant 1992; Bourdieu 1993) that includes studies of education (Bourdieu 1995), everyday suffering in social life (Bourdieu et al. 1999), the social organization of scientific knowledge (Bourdieu 2004) and housing markets (Bourdieu 2005). The insights of psychoanalysis and linguistics have also been employed to argue that while human actions are meaningful and variable, this does not mean that we cannot then agree on what is valid or 'true' about the social world. This bridge-building attempt fuses the twin aims of 'how' (understanding) and 'why' (explanation) in social research (Habermas 1984, 1987, 1989, 1990, 2003).

There is also the school of 'poststructuralism', which includes the influences of Jacques Derrida (see Kamuf 1991), as well as Michel Foucault. Foucault's thought, in particular, evolved in reaction to both the subjectivism of some social science perspectives and the naive empiricism imported from the natural sciences (Foucault 1977, 1980). His work is thus characterized as moving beyond structuralism and hermeneutics, towards an 'interpretive analytics' (Dreyfus and Rabinow 1982). In the process, Foucault considered knowledge and power to be constructed within a set of social practices. The result is to question the concept of truth as separable from the exercise of power (May and Powell 2007).

As interesting and provocative as these ideas are, they have often been discussed at a socio-theoretical and philosophical level. Yet Foucault himself was a social researcher and while he used his research sources in particular ways, his work has been deployed in research methods in general (Kendall and Wickham 1999) and governance studies (Dean 2007), management and organizations (McKinlay and Starkey 1998) and geography (Crampton and Elden 2007). While an exposition of these ideas is a task in itself, I have deliberately included them so you can refer directly to their works, or studies about their works (see Morrow 1994; Dean 1999; May and Powell 2008). They demonstrate the ingenuity with which social thinkers have attempted to tackle issues that are part of the social research endeavour.

In considering all of the above perspectives, the waters are far muddier than suggested. For instance, Durkheim is often termed a positivist but would not simply deny the place of subjectivity in social life, nor would an idealist necessarily deny objectivity defined as 'detachment' from the social world, while Foucault in discussing the implications of his work noted that if these meant 'one is a positivist, then I am happy to be one' (Foucault 1972: 125).

There do remain important differences; in particular whether the social sciences are the same or different from the physical sciences and whether human actions, unlike the observed effects of phenomena in the physical world, are meaningful and intentional. In addition to this, there has also been an increasing tendency among the public to challenge scientific findings in situations where both risk and trust are significant factors, along with a greater access to varying forms of information upon which to base judgements. Alongside this, but not necessarily related, are arguments that we have entered a new era in which any claim to universal knowledge is challenged and there are no standards beyond particular contexts through which we may judge truth or falsity. At this point we enter the terrain of relativism.

Such a viewpoint has been bolstered by a movement called 'postmodernism' which refers to a cultural perspective and/or epistemology, while postmodernization relates to a process that is said to lead to the historical period known as postmodernity (see Lyon 1999; Delanty 2000). Therefore, it is important to note that one does not necessarily have to become a postmodernist in order to accept some of its insights regarding the changing times through which we are living. Indeed, 'postmodernism' is often used as a convenient label around which to base a series of observations on contemporary issues (Bauman 1997, 2000, 2008).

What we see within this movement is an anti-foundationalism. Whether talking about implosions of meaning with the consequence that the world becomes devoid of any meaning (Baudrillard 1983a), or of the computer age and the severing of the link between knowledge and legitimacy (Lyotard 1984), or of the potential for dialogue within a liberal consensus in which scientific claims to truth about the social and natural worlds have little place (Rorty 1989), postmodernists have exhibited the same underlying tendency: that is, that there are no universal standards against which science may lay claim in order to validate its standards. Quite simply, objectivity gives way to relativism with the result that not only science, but also truth, goodness, justice, rationality, and so on, are concepts relative to time and place: 'Since every act of cognition necessarily occurs within a particular perspective, relativism claims that no rational basis exists for judging one perspective better than any other' (Fay 1996: 2). The 'repressed rivals' of science – religion, folk knowledge, narrative and myth – are now returning to challenge how it is that a particular group of people claimed their ideas were universal. The aim is to enter into a conversation without the presupposition of accumulating knowledge or building a science of society (Seidman 2008).

It is significant that it is within the humanities and the area of cultural studies that these views have found their greatest legitimacy. Yet how this translates into a practical research programme, without contradiction and retaining the relevance of research, is a matter of some considerable difficulty, let alone dispute concerning its insights (B. Williams 2002). Take, for example, the idea of truth which underlies research. Must not all communities, including those conducting research, assume a truth which lies beyond that which they propagate in order to legitimize their beliefs and practices in the first instance? If so, relativism must presuppose the existence of something beyond itself to legitimize its own position.

For the purposes of actually conducting social research, it is helpful to see these differences between those who hold that knowledge is a social product and those who hold that it is distinct from the social realm (Hacking 1999). Throughout the book, I shall return to issues in order to render these debates more intelligible.

KNOWLEDGE AND DIFFERENCE

An important question emerges from the above discussions: that is, the extent to which the knowledge produced by one group is applicable to different groups? All of the thinkers whom I have discussed so far have been men. Is this important? If men have produced valid ideas and research results that have enabled us to understand social relations, it would remain a matter of concern if more women wished to become theorists and researchers, but were prevented from doing so because men, either intentionally or otherwise, stood in the way of their aspirations. Yet, what if the ideas and practices of men reflected a bias that defines society and science in terms of particular values? Not only would research then be incomplete, but also its results would be a distortion of the world. What we take to be science would then reflect this state of affairs and so perpetuate certain views of women by providing a 'scientistic cloak' which is no more than prejudice.

Exclusions

These contentions form the starting-point of a feminist critique of science. Perhaps the first point which should be made is that, like the social sciences in general, feminist perspectives are not simply a unified body of thought and it is more accurate to talk of 'feminisms'. However, in the following discussions it should be borne in mind that they do share several beliefs. First, women and their fundamental contributions to social and cultural life have been marginalized and this is reflected in research practice. Second, the norms of science perpetuate and disguise the myth of the superiority of men over women and reflect a desire to control the social and natural worlds. Third, gender, as a significant social category, has been absent from our understandings and explanations of social phenomena in favour of categories such as social class. Clearly, these characterizations do not convey the depth and sophistication of arguments employed by different schools of feminism (see Meyers 1997; Kourany et al. 1999), that includes bringing in important issues of class (Skeggs 1997, 2004). At the same time, these cogent criticisms cannot be ignored. Therefore, in order to add to our understanding of social life in general and research methods in particular, it must occupy a centre-stage position in any discussion of research perspectives.

Our notions of the roles, relations and forces within society are built upon unexamined assumptions about the characteristics of people that are reproduced in our theories about society. When the roles of women are considered in social life, they are characterized as passive and emotional. Although this assumption has long been challenged by groups of women, a selective reading of historical events lost their voices (Spender 1982). In particular, there is the reference to something called 'human nature': that is, a belief in the fundamental characteristics of people regardless of their history or social context. Social thinkers have provided many a justification for the belief that social roles are natural, rather than the product of social and political manipulation by men over women. An influential philosopher, John Locke (1632–1704), for example, believed people to be innately 'reasonable' (a view of human nature). At the same time he saw a need for a 'social contract' so that order could be brought to what would otherwise be a chaotic social and political world (Jaggar 1983).

From these positions of 'reasonableness' and the need for a social contract, he then took a leap to argue that because of their reproductive capacity, women were 'emotional' and were also unable to provide for themselves so were 'naturally' dependent on men. As in contemporary western societies, property rights were crucial in Locke's ideas and due to women's natural dependence, he argued that they do not then possess such rights. Marriage was a contract they entered into in order to produce sons who can then inherit property. The contract of marriage thus ensures that property rights are stable within society and men have sons in order to perpetuate their lineage.

As feminist scholars have noted (Sydie 1987), Locke equated 'rights' with the capacity to be reasonable, which he then argued that women did not possess. This splitting of so-called natural differences, feminists argue, occurs throughout western thought and provides the foundation upon which we base our thinking and scientific practice. Buried within these assumptions are not scientific statements, but deep-rooted biases against women by male thinkers. The German philosopher Hegel (1770–1831) believed that women's position in the family, as subordinate to men, was the natural realm for their 'ethical disposition'. Similarly,

Darwin (1809–82) believed he had found a scientific basis for traditional assumptions about the division of labour between the sexes. Again, we are led to believe that these are natural differences. If we believe them to be natural, then tampering with them would upset the 'natural order of social life'. However, this is precisely the point of contention. Feminists argue that women's position within society is not a natural phenomenon, but a social, political and economic product. Sandra Harding, for example, is influenced not only by feminism, but also by postcolonial perspectives that lead her investigations to see a bias in scientific activity. While not abandoning the idea of a world 'out there', it is interpretations that are at stake and to make those more meaningful means the inclusion of voices that have been excluded from scientific practice because 'Our methodological and epistemological choices are always also ethical and political choices' (Harding 2006: 156).

Economics, politics, sociology, anthropology, urban studies, planning, geography, social policy, psychology, philosophy, history, like the natural sciences, perpetuated this myth during the course of their history (for example, see J. Dale and Foster 1986; Sydie 1987; Gibson-Graham 1996; Henriques et al. 1998). For instance, in the earlier studies on the family and work, before feminist research had some impact on dominant practices, women were 'wives', 'mothers' or 'housewives', but not people in their own right. The American sociologist Talcott Parsons (1902–79) appeared to believe that the major 'status' of an urban, adult woman was that of a housewife. Her status in this domestic sphere was, in turn, determined by the status of the husband or, as he is also commonly referred to, head of household. Emile Durkheim, who so adhered to the idea of a natural science of society, did not in fact produce a scientific account of society, but a moralizing one hidden behind the guise of science. His views on the family were, according to what is probably the most authoritative study of his life and work, an 'alliance of sociological acumen with strict Victorian morality' (Lukes 1981: 533). The use of the term 'family' in social policy research is also problematic for omitting women's interests (McKie 2005).

If claims to theorize about social life simply function to disguise such moralizing, they will be distortions of the social world. In the separation of the 'public' from 'private' social worlds, men have become the people of action in the public realm, while women are subordinated to the private realm of the family and their status determined accordingly. For feminists, perspectives on social life have either reflected this political phenomenon or attempted to justify it as a natural state of affairs.

This silencing through exclusion of voices perpetuates particular and narrow ideas of science and thereby limits our understandings. In the public realm it is apparently men who paint pictures, men who think about the world, men who make money and men who shape destinies. If the contribution of women is acknowledged, it is in terms of being the 'power behind the throne', 'the boss in the house' or what has been described as 'drawing-room manipulation'. In research on the world of work, for example, we operate according to definitions which remain unchallenged and the supposed benefits of a global economy rest upon a division of labour between the rich and poor expressed in pay and conditions of work and variable skills. In these secondary labour markets, women form a majority:

> This is because skills distribution is often differentiated by sex. On a global scale, most subcontracted, labour intensive work is carried out by women, who have historically been marginalized from skill development and training. It is important, therefore, to recognize that the continuous-flow infrastructure of the 24-hour global economy is driven by a reservoir of female labour.
>
> (Odih 2007: 159–60)

Inclusions

Not only have researchers provided evidence for some changes to this dominant model of work (Hörning et al. 1995), but also its gendered nature and relationship with sexuality is of central importance (Adkins 1995). Theories of the social world and practices of research are thus argued to be *androcentric*. What we call science is not based upon universal criteria which are value free, but upon male norms and, in particular, the mythical separation of reason (men) and emotion (women) which can result in extreme forms of androcentricity such as 'gynopia (female invisibility) and misogyny (hatred of women)' (Eichler 1988: 5).

In the conclusion to her study on gender and work in capitalist economies, Pam Odih notes that enthusiastic advocates of globalization and decentralization are mostly impervious to the inequities it generates along the lines of class, gender and race (Odih 2007: 184). Feminisms, while correcting the class-based accounts of research, have faced similar criticisms for neglecting the issues of race and class. Researchers have documented the ways in which sexual and racial stereotypes cut across each other (Ackers 1993). An exclusive concentration on gender and class within research, however, is to the detriment of differences which exist between women on ethnic and racial lines: 'To deal with one without ever alluding to the other is to distort our commonality as well as our difference' (Lorde 1992: 139).

Studies have documented racial bias in the early women's movement with its assumptions concerning the intellectual inferiority of black men and women (Davis 1981). Class-based accounts of society, on the other hand, have been criticized for being economically determinist and ignorant of the political dimensions of gender and race. In the research process and within the limits of our power, we should be aware of these issues (Phoenix 1994; Reynolds 2002), along with those of poverty and exclusion in general. What is most important to frame in the context of these criticisms is the interaction between these elements without the assumption that one simply speaks in the name of *the* truth. Instead, recognition of the partiality and situated nature of knowledges can provide for the possibility of enhancing understanding by challenging what are dominant ways of thinking. As Patricia Hill Collins (2000) puts it:

> Alternative knowledge claims in and of themselves are rarely threatening to conventional knowledge . . . Much more threatening is the challenge that alternative epistemologies offer to the basic process used by the powerful to legitimate knowledge claims that in turn justify their right to rule. If the epistemology used to validate knowledge comes into question, then all prior knowledge claims validated under the dominant model become suspect.
>
> (Collins 2000: 270–1)

The idea that 'rigorous research' involves the separation of researchers from the subject of their research simply reflects the idea that reason and emotion must be separated. Instead of seeing people in the research process as simply sources of data, here we move to research being a two-way process aimed at inclusion and dialogue that examines, for example, how particular meanings reproduce social hierarchies (Jordan-Zachery 2009). Frequently, however, textbooks speak of not becoming 'over-involved' with participants. Over-identifying with the 'subject' of the research is said to prevent 'good' research. The researcher should be detached and hence assumed to be objective. This is not only a mythical aim, but also an undesirable one which disguises the myriad of ways in which the researcher is affected by the context of the research or the people who are a part of it, as well as the productive nature of the research enterprise itself.

In much the same way as the ideas of disengagement and objectivity are challenged, so too is the idea that a researcher's biography is not important or relevant to the research process. Both the researcher and those people who are part of the research carry with them a history, a sense of themselves and the importance of their experiences. However, personal experience is frequently devalued as being too subjective, while science is objective. Such critique has opened up the range of methodological approaches to include biographical research (B. Roberts 2002).

There is much to be gained from exploring the lives and experiences of marginalized people in understanding society and correcting the silence that has surrounded women's voices (Griffiths 1995). Different forms of knowledge are brought to recognition in order that we may all learn for the future. Thus, an exploration into how women in rural Bangladesh had accumulated knowledge, over generations, on how to relate to and live from their environments produced clear economic, social and environmental consequences for how to live in a more sustainable way (Akhter 2008). As will be apparent in Part II, an exploration of this experiential dimension is central to the field of social research. In the process, researchers should be aware of the ways in which their own experiences are a fundamental part of the process itself. It is both the experiences of the researched *and* researchers which are important. Despite this, it is a subject in social research frequently reserved for separate publications (see C. Bell and Newby 1977; C. Bell and Roberts 1984; Roberts 1990; D. Bell et al. 1993; Hobbs and May 1993; Davies et al. 2010). However, we should remember that social research is important for what it tells us about the world, not just those who are studying it.

We now have the critique of disengagement, the critique of the absence of gender as a significant social category in social research and the critique of the nature and methods through which science is constructed based upon a male perspective and limited ideas of what constitutes reason. These add up to a considerable indictment of the practice of science. We have examined the epistemologies and ontologies of positivism, empiricism, realism and idealism. In order to produce a more complete practice for social research, those who have been critical of science for its exclusion of voices, have developed a variety of means to address its inadequacies.

Standpoint feminism developed in contrast to many of the dominant ways of viewing knowledge (Hartsock 1987; Smith 1993, 1999, 2002, 2005). Its basis lies in taking the disadvantage of women's exclusion from the public realm by men and turning that into a research advantage. Because women are 'strangers' to the public realm and excluded from it, this provides them with a unique opportunity for undertaking research: 'The stranger brings to her research just the combination of nearness and remoteness, concern and indifference, that are central to maximizing objectivity' (Harding 1991: 124). A female researcher is thus able to operate from both an oppressed position as a woman and a privileged position as a scholar (Cook and Fonow 1990).

Biography and experience become central to the production of un-biased accounts of the social world. However, it is not experience itself which provides the basis of claims to objectivity by standpoint feminists. While experience is a fundamental starting-point, experiences themselves are reflections of dominant social relationships. Experience is a beginning point to research, but for standpoint feminists this must then be situated within the wider context of women's lives in general. However, dominant views override experience. Thus, in order that the theorist does not then become the expert on people's lives, as is the usual hierarchical way in which scientism proceeds, any thinking about lives by the researcher must take place in a democratic and participatory way through involving others.

Two emphases are apparent from this discussion. First, marginalized experiences are an excellent starting-point upon which to base research because of a position that enables the person to 'look in' as the stranger might to a new social scene. As Sandra Harding puts it, the aim 'is not so much one of the right to claim a label as it is of the prerequisites for producing less partial and distorted descriptions, explanations, and understandings' (Harding 1987: 12). Second, there is an emphasis on the scientific study of society whose aim is to place marginalized experiences within a wider theory of location in society. For this reason, there are parallels between feminist standpoint epistemologies and realism (Cain 1990). Although the idea of science is maintained, its norms have changed. It becomes a stance which does not marginalize, but promotes the cause of women and the marginalized in general.

These two contentions form the starting-point for the differences with approaches that reject any influence of the idea of science along two lines. First, to introduce an idea of science is just another way in which experiences of the marginalized are sequestrated by those who claim to be experts. Second, a rejection of the view that knowledge about general positions in society, whether informed by such issues as race, class, gender or sexuality, is possible. Instead there are many versions of social reality, all of which are equally valid.

To impose some theoretical idea on the social world conspires with this suppression of difference. Women's experiences and feelings are not limited in this perspective, but are valid in themselves. The means by which research is undertaken should then be made available for all to see as part of this process of validating experiences. However, are all experiences equally valid and not limited and/or biased? Is the opinion of the middle-class woman who says women are not oppressed, the same as the working-class woman who says they are?

With the tension between difference and essentialism, relativism and objectivism, and idealism and realism in mind, particularly when it comes to the actual practice of feminist research (Acker et al. 1991), there are those who argue for a 'fractured foundationalism' (Stanley and Wise 1993), a 'strategic essentialism' (Grosz 1994), an 'interactive universalism' (Benhabib 1992) and a return to 'middle range' theory (Maynard 1998). Recognizing that there is both a material reality to the social world, along with different views of those realities, does not mean that the researcher is then in a privileged position to judge reality. At the same time, of course, there is still a need for a grounding of such a position which, for some, comes in the form of a methodology that is analytically reflexive in orientation and deploys retrievable data upon which to base its insights (Stanley and Wise 2006).

There are also those who 'see themselves as primarily following more rigorously the existing rules and principles of the sciences' (Harding 1991: 111). In this spirit Margrit Eichler (1988, 1997) has provided a series of technical steps that the researcher should avoid in order to produce research which does not fall into the four 'traps' of malestream research. These include: androcentric practices; an overgeneralization of research findings based solely on particular experiences; an absence of explanations for the social and economic influences of gender relations, and finally, the use of 'double standards', for example, in terms of language through the use of 'man' and 'wife', rather than 'man' and 'woman'. The aim is to produce less partial and more accurate accounts of social life. In other words, its criticism is focused not so much on the *foundations* of science, but upon its *practice*. For this reason, it has been criticized for replicating male norms of scientific inquiry which, according to other feminist epistemologies, should be both challenged and changed.

As with research perspectives in general, there are a number of viewpoints from which feminists approach issues in social research. Nevertheless, we can take the following lessons for research practice. As researchers, we should seek to avoid the age-old fallacy of a woman's reproductive capacity as being a hindrance to her participation in society. The important questions are, first, how the fact of women's reproduction is manipulated in the organization of social life. Second, how women and other groups are marginalized in the public sphere. Third, a greater understanding of the fundamental contribution that women and marginal groups make to cultural, political and economic life. Fourth, the implications of feminist analysis for research in particular and social life in general in exploring the experiential dimension of social life. Fifth, a general challenging not only of androcentric thought, but also of assumptions in general that perpetuate hierarchies within our societies.

SUMMARY

This chapter has provided an overview of major perspectives in social research. We have moved from the idea that social science should reflect the aims and methods of natural science, through a critique of these methods as inapplicable to social research, to feminist criticisms of the foundations and aims of science as being male-centred and hierarchical, finishing on a critique of research practice as ethnocentric and racist.

The debates themselves may appear complicated, but are no less important for that. Yet we should note that these perspectives do not simply dictate the nature of research itself, or how it is conducted; although the issues will inform how the aims, methods and process of social research are considered with methodology being informed by a number of considerations (Platt 1996). Research that is aware of the issues surrounding and informing its practice and then acts reflexively upon those is more likely to produce enhanced and systematic studies of the world.

Questions for your reflection

1 What are the differences between idealism and realism?

2 What is a 'positivist' approach to the practice of social research and what are its strengths and limitations?

3 Why have feminist researchers been critical of science?

4 After reading this chapter, what issues would now inform your practice as a researcher?

SUGGESTED FURTHER READING

Alvesson, M. and Sköldberg, K. (2009) *Reflexive Methodology: New Vistas for Qualitative Research*, 2nd edn. London: Sage.

Hesse-Biber, S. N. and Yaiser, M. L. (eds) (2004) *Feminist Perspectives on Social Research*. New York: Oxford University Press.

May, T. with Perry, B. (2011) *Social Research and Reflexivity: Content, Consequences and Context*. London: Sage.

Williams, M. and May, T. (1996) *Introduction to the Philosophy of Social Research*. London: UCL Press.

2   Social theory and social research

The interactions of social theory and social research
  Linking issues
Making the links
Summary
Suggested further reading

Let me start this chapter with a simple statement: data are not collected, but produced. Facts do not exist independently of the medium through which they are interpreted, whether that is an explicit theoretical model, a set of assumptions, or pre-existing interests. These observations, however, beg the question about the role of theory in social research. Is it a neutral medium through which we interpret our findings? Should it be a critical endeavour that challenges our dominant ways of thinking about social phenomena in order to recognize and produce alternative ways of seeing the world? Should the data we produce about the social world and its relations refute, organize or generate theories? As we discuss these issues, questions will be raised concerning the place of values and ethics in social research; this is the subject of Chapter 3.

Let me first ask a core question: what can we expect of social theory? Social theory, along with social research, is of central importance in the social sciences. Social theory is deployed for the interpretation of empirical data. However, it also enables a more general orientation in relation to political, historical, economic and social issues, as well as providing a basis for critical reflection on the process of research itself and social life and social systems as a whole. What we see here is a two-way relationship between ideas and practices. Given this, social theory should fall under our gaze in order that its presuppositions are open to scrutiny.

From this point of view, to gain the most from socio-theoretical explanations requires an open and inquiring attitude. The study of social theory and social research is a reflexive endeavour in which to assume that one theoretical paradigm, as an enclosed system of thought, is capable of fully explaining the social world is rendered problematic.

Monolithic social theories and one-dimensional approaches to research cannot fully explain the workings of societies or understand social relations. Instead, we have a constant relationship between social theory and social research in which both are modified through combinations of reflection, experience and systematic interrogation.

A social scientist requires insights into both theory and research. Some would deny any orientation towards theory on the grounds of a 'without prejudice to the facts' orientation. There are also those self-proclaimed 'theorists' who regard data as a distraction from the purity of their efforts. This book is not written with either of these positions in mind. Nevertheless, as noted in the Introduction, there is often a problematic dichotomy between areas of activity. Practically speaking, it is difficult enough just to keep up with trends in research methods, let alone those in methodology, the philosophies of social and natural sciences and social theory. The chapter recognizes this and seeks to provide an account of the main issues that should be considered in examining the relations between social theory and social research. In so doing, the reader's attention is drawn to references that take issues in particular directions in the realization that: 'Real learning always entails a struggle to understand the unknown' (D. Harvey 2010a: 1).

THE INTERACTIONS OF SOCIAL THEORY AND SOCIAL RESEARCH

The idea of theory, or the ability to explain and understand the findings of research within frameworks that make 'sense' of data, is the mark of a mature discipline whose aim is the systematic study of particular phenomena. In our case, as social researchers, these phenomena are the dynamics, content, context and structure of social relations. We aim, with our training and experiences of doing research in mind, together with the perspectives that guide our thinking, to understand the social world. This requires the development, application, testing and even falsification of social theory.

Social theory informs our understanding of issues which, in turn, assists us in making research decisions and sense of the world around us: for example, and following the discussion in Chapter 1, whether in approaching a research topic we consider meaning generation or the relationship between 'social facts' as being central to our focus and why? What we might call this sensitizing and orienting function to social theory is not one way. Our experiences of conducting research and generating findings also influence our theorizing. In other words, there is a constant relationship that exists between social research and social theory. The issue for us as researchers is not simply *what* we produce, but *how* we produce it, and these are inseparable issues in the process of social research. An understanding of the relationship between theory and research is part of a reflexive project that focuses upon our abilities not only to apply techniques of data collection, but also to examine the nature and presuppositions of the research process and the audiences we wish to reach. In this way we can sharpen the practice of our craft and develop insights into the place of social research in contemporary society.

Social theory is often thought to be a grand enterprise. Nevertheless, the concerns of theorists are not so different from those that occupy so-called 'non-theorists' and some writers argue that theory and practice are simply two sides of the same coin. This may be expressed in the following ways:

> Theory aims at the production of thoughts which accord with reality. Practice aims at the production of realities which accord with thought. Therefore common to theory and practice is an aspiration to establish congruity between thought and reality.
>
> (G. A. Cohen 1984: 339)

Theoretical considerations can appear to be abstract in order to connect thought with the nature of reality. The question here is whether this is a necessary endeavour to capture the dynamics of society in order to situate concerns and issues within a more general framework of understanding? We might suggest that a theory should be judged by its ability to inform practice, but this might leave factors that inform and influence practice, that are not seen by that practice, out of the frames of reference. However, it is very possible for whole groups of scholars to become seduced by the beauty of their models of reality and confuse that with the reality of their models. We need to be sensitive to such possibilities and recognize that theories, while often abstract, need to be both interrogated and 'open our eyes to dilemmas that we can't avoid and for which we have to prepare ourselves' (Habermas 1994: 116–17).

What is different is the approach of theorists to those questions that concern us. Some appear to float over the social landscape as if unfettered by the problems and realities of everyday life. The ability to transcend or abstract theories from everyday life allows us to have a perspective on our social universe which breaks free from our everyday actions and attitudes with which we are, understandably, preoccupied. Such formal theories allow us to make links from our own specific fields of interest where substantive theories have been formulated to those of other researchers, as well as locate our research findings within the general workings of society. As such, there is more to assessing social theory than its empirical utility. It might also be assessed in terms of its logical coherency, the kinds of problems that it generates and the insights that it offers; insights and issues that empirical researchers may have overlooked (Anthony Giddens, in Mullan 1987: 102). To this we should add that bodies of social theory may be constituted and developed in order to give representation and a research agenda for those issues that other forms of theorizing have overlooked. Postcolonial and multicultural theories may be seen in these terms, for they give representation to historical and contemporary identities and experiences which have been ignored by invoking heterogeneity among different peoples (Clough 1994; Brooks 2007).

Theories enable us to break free from everyday thinking to consider issues beyond our normal frames of reference (Bauman and May 2001). Equally, we should recognize that their level of generality may be of little use in researching particular areas of social life, as well as reflecting limited perspectives. There have been those who are disparaging of the inability of 'grand theorists' to grasp the social problems which are important to specific 'historical and structural contexts' (C. W. Mills 1959: 42). Critiques of this type have been aimed at different theoretical schools of thought from the critical theory of the Frankfurt School to contemporary postmodernist claims.

An alternative to such abstraction or generality is, in the words of one book on this subject, to 'ground' social theories in our observations of everyday life (Glaser and Strauss 1967). As researchers, we should seek to render the attachment between theory and data as close as possible (unlike grand theory that is stated at such a general level we could not possibly match data to theory). Instead of descending upon the social world armed with a body of theoretical propositions about how and why social relations exist and work as they do, we should first observe those relations, collect data on them, and then proceed to generate our theoretical propositions thereby enabling 'imaginative engagement with data that simple application of a string of procedures precludes' (A. Bryant and Charmaz 2010: 25).

In such a call there is a focus upon generating rather than verifying theory. The aim would then be to undertake detailed data collection alongside the generation of concepts to explain the data. To choose this course of action does not mean our research is then more 'relevant' (a term often used to mean how research meets the ends of predetermined, dominant interests). It simply means that our presuppositions about social life remain more hidden, but still influence decisions and interpretations. To add to this there is an argument which suggests that involvement in present problems, divorced from theory, is a sign of 'immaturity' as it severs the link which exists between the present and the development of humanity across time (Elias 1987). It is for such reasons that Michel Foucault (1980) not only spoke of a 'history of the present', but also emphasized the importance of what he called 'eventalization' as a method in order to avoid the problem of reading events from patterns in history to breach the 'self-evidences on which our knowledges, acquiescences and practices rest' (Foucault 1991a: 76).

We now return to the same issue – except at a different end of the spectrum from which we left grand theory. If we assume that we can neutrally observe the social world, or read off events according to pre-existing theoretical ideas, we shall simply either reproduce the assumptions and stereotypes of everyday actions and conventions, or miss the importance of practices, events and processes that do not accord with general, formal theories. We need to understand and acknowledge these influences in our own thinking and that of society in general. Facts, in other words, do not speak for themselves, nor should theories saturate data. Thus, for social research to intellectually develop and to be of use in understanding or explaining the social world, we need theory and theory needs research. There is a 'mutual interdependence' between the two (Bulmer 1986a: 208). It is argued that for a discipline to be conferred the status of a 'science' the assumption that there is an object world beyond the descriptions that it employs to understand and explain it, must hold. In realist terms this can be expressed in terms of the object world necessarily existing independently of our theories, but that they can be known only under certain conditions. Science then becomes 'the systematic attempt to express in thought the structures and ways of acting of things that exist and act independently of thought' (Bhaskar 1975: 250).

Linking issues

In the process of research, we embark on empirical work and collect data that initiate, refute or organize our theories and enable us to understand or explain our observations. Bearing in mind the above references to 'grounded' and 'grand' theories, we may achieve this by using one of two routes. First, we might consider a general picture of social life and then research a particular aspect of it to test the strength of our theories. This is known as *deduction* where theorizing comes before research. Research then functions to produce empirical evidence to test or refute theories. On the other hand, we might examine a particular aspect of social life and derive our theories from the resultant data. This is known as *induction*. Research comes before theory and we seek to generate theoretical propositions on social life from our data. Let us examine both induction and deduction and their relationship to theory.

Induction has a long history in the philosophy of science. It is based on the belief, as with empiricism, that we can proceed from a collection of facts concerning social life and then make links between these to arrive at our theories. The first point of consideration in this process refers to the relationship between theory and data in order to demonstrate that the 'facts' can speak for themselves and are distinct from interpretation by researchers. An example will help to explain this.

Consider the proposition, maintained some time ago by the results of psephological research (D. Butler and Stokes 1969), that 'more manual workers vote labour than they do conservative'. This is an empirical generalization about the voting behaviour of a particular group within society. Note, however, that it is not a theory or explanation for the pattern of behaviour observed, but a statement of observation on voting behaviour collected by asking people, via surveys, about their voting intentions. For the purposes of explanation (in other words, *why* manual workers vote Labour) we need a theory. The form for this might explain voting behaviour in terms of the different primary and secondary socialization processes that manual workers undergo in comparison to non-manual workers. Alternatively, we might say that manual workers tend to vote Labour because they believe that party best represents their interests in maintaining material securities such as housing, employment prospects, and so on.

The connection between class position and voting behaviour has been argued to have diminished since Butler and Stokes's research (Dunleavy and Husbands 1985; Inglehart 1997). Nevertheless, this is a highly contestable proposition. Comparative empirical work on voting behaviour which is sensitive to clear and defensible definitions of class, aside simply from those that might predict voting patterns, illutrates that the connection remains, but has been complicated in its relations (Evans 1999). Class is correlated with levels of turn-out for elections (Rallings and Thrasher 2009) and while there is evidence of a decline of the connection among particular parties, it does not result from an increased individualism, thereby showing the continuing importance of contextual factors on behaviour (R. Anderson and Heath 2000). This illustrates that we require not only rigorous approaches to method and measurement, but also refined theoretical approaches in order to inform the process and interpretation of research. As social researchers, our findings on the social world are devoid of meaning until situated within frameworks of understanding.

A question still remains: why do researchers decide to collect data in the first place? They might be representing particular interests who are funding the research, or are personally interested in this area and have access to resources to test ideas which they have on the relationship between class membership and voting behaviour. Whether the research is 'pure' or 'applied' in this sense, interests have guided our decisions *before* the research itself is conducted. It cannot be maintained that research is a neutral recording instrument, whatever form it might take. The very construction of a field of interest is itself a matter of academic convention that should be open to scrutiny (Bourdieu and Wacquant 1992; Bourdieu 2000):

> This interest may consist, as it does everywhere else, in the desire to be the first to make a discovery and to appropriate all the associated rights, or in a moral indignation or revolt against certain forms of domination and against those who defend them within the scientific world. In short, there is no immaculate conception.
>
> (Bourdieu 1993: 11)

This is not a situation from which researchers can escape, for their interpretations are an inevitable part of the research process. An alternative to induction is thus to make the theories or hypotheses which guide our research explicit.

Deduction rejects the idea that we can produce research on the basis of initially rejecting theory or, to put it another way, that there is a simple distinction to be made between the language of theory and the language of observation. It seeks to fuse the empiricist idea that there are a set of rules of method by which we proceed as researchers, with the ideas of deductive reasoning which hold that if our hypothesis or ideas about social life are 'true', they will be substantiated by the data produced. In order for this to take place, data collection is driven by theoretical interests, not the other way round. The question then remains as to how we know when we have arrived at the truth of our propositions?

Such are the difficulties of constituting a final resting place, is the best that science can hope for is to render such concepts testable and open to falsification? We then arrive not at this final destination, but an increased confidence about what it is not by developing theories that can be falsified. Thus, according to the leading exponent of this tradition: 'scientists try to express their theories in such a form that they can be tested, i.e., refuted (or else corroborated) by such experience' (Popper 1970: 654–5). A theory concerning social life must not only be based upon empirical evidence, but also be capable of being *falsified* by such evidence: '*it must be possible for an empirical scientific system to be refuted by experience*' (Popper 1959: 41, original emphasis).

The above acknowledges that data are theory driven. It also sustains social theory only in so far as it is corroborated by empirical evidence. Therefore, it proceeds on the same basis as the methods of natural scientific inquiry to enable the production of a 'science of society'. Attractive as this may appear, we are still left with some issues. First, if our empirical evidence falsifies a theory, is this a sufficient reason for rejecting it? We might simply assert that we have found a deviant or exceptional piece of evidence which does not falsify our theory as such. Second, there is a pragmatic point for us to consider as researchers. Until a new theory comes along to explain our research findings, we are unlikely to abandon existing theories which still assist us in understanding or explaining social life. Scientists, in general, are likely to hold on to core elements in their theoretical armoury that are not open to the process of falsification (Lakatos and Musgrave 1970). Finally, deductivism still, like inductivism, assumes that we can derive theories of the social world independent of our preconceptions or values, due to its adherence to a particularly limited idea of scientific method.

The idea that we might derive our theories on the social world, independent of our preconceptions, is highly problematic. Theorists, for instance, take for granted certain aspects of the social world which are not subjected to empirical falsification (the assumptions concerning the 'natural' roles of women in society for instance). As noted in Chapter 1, we research a social world which people are already interpreting and acting within. To assume that we can separate these activities from scientific fact may be not only an impossibility, but also undesirable for the production and practice of social science itself. In accepting this, our focus of attention is now transferred away from the procedures of generating or testing theories, to the influences which inform theorizing and research. This provides us with a starting-point for examining a seminal contribution on the way in which science has developed – as opposed to how it should develop according to the rules of deduction and induction.

Thomas Kuhn's (1970) work was a historical study of scientific progression. Kuhn argued that science does not progress according to the criteria of falsifying theories, as Popper would maintain. On the contrary, evidence which does not support theories is regarded as only a temporary problem to which future research is directed. In this way theories are not falsified, but become the subject of continuous research. It is this that Kuhn calls 'normal science':

> 'normal science' means research firmly based upon one or more past scientific achievements; achievements that some particular scientific community acknowledges for a time as supplying the foundation for its further practice.
>
> (Kuhn, quoted in B. Barnes 1991: 87)

Given that any deviant data serve as the basis for future research, the theory is never falsified because there will always be evidence which both supports and refutes it. Kuhn therefore refers to scientific *paradigms* as characterizing the practice of science. These paradigms do not, unlike deductivism and inductivism, provide rules which the methods of research must slavishly follow, but provide only examples

> of good practice . . . And scientists must themselves determine how the model is to be used . . . Thus, scientists doing normal science do not merely have to agree upon what should serve as the basis of their work; they also have to agree upon how it should serve that purpose

in every particular case. They are obliged to employ a paradigm much as a judge employs an accepted judicial decision.

(B. Barnes 1991: 88)

Science develops according to the culture that scientists inhabit and this, not the rules of deduction and induction, determines their practices and choices of theories. If an example of counter-evidence is found to falsify a theory, it will be the competence of the individual researcher which is called into question, not the theory. Scientists do not attempt to falsify a theory as such: 'Instead, they attempt to extend and exploit it in a variety of ways' (Kuhn 1972: 91). However, unlike other commentators who see some method to the practice of science, but argue that other forms of knowledge should not be undermined by its supposed rigorous presuppositions (Feyerabend 1978), Kuhn views science as a conservative endeavour which is challenged only by what he calls 'scientific revolutions'. At this point, a new paradigm replaces the old. This does not result from mounting empirical evidence which refutes the old paradigm but, for instance, is due to younger scientists entering the field and bringing with them a new set of ideas and problems upon which they too can research and make their names. In the scientific field, therefore, we see a struggle in which 'the dominant players are those who manage to impose the definition of science that says that the most accomplished realization of science consists in having, being and doing what they have, are and do' (Bourdieu 2004: 63). Despite the change of personnel, the conclusions of the discipline would depend on 'the scientist's theoretical preferences rather than the empirical evidence' (Papineau 1978: 36).

We have travelled from the problems of inductivism and its atheoretical stance, through deductivism with its concentration on rules to which no science can, or arguably should, live up to, to arrive at the idea of Kuhn's paradigms that are argued to reflect the actual practices of science. To express it another way, we have moved from the idea that there is an object world which science describes in a neutral manner, via an examination of the means of description that is employed in relation to that world, to a focus upon the means of description themselves. The social and physical worlds are then seen to be constructed according to these descriptions and so it is the social practice of science that becomes of interest.

At this point in our discussions recognition of the role of social elements in the production of science allows different ideas to develop and go off at what are complete tangents to each other. The idealism of ethnomethodology permits it to focus upon the intersubjective construction of the object world, while postmodernists argue that science is nothing more than rhetoric or, to express it another way, as the 'real' cannot be represented, then the process of representation itself is examined. An absence of a basis upon which to justify these insights then leads to issues of relativism whereby the only findings that science and social science can justify are those relative to time and place. In the process generalization and explanation, key characteristics of scientific practice, are rendered redundant. Parallels are also found with Jacques Derrida's deconstructionist project whereby language does not refer to an independent reality, but is self-referring. Therefore, meanings within language are derived 'not from their correspondence to a world they purport to represent but only in terms of their internal relations of "difference"' (Agger 1998: 57). However, it should not be forgotten that Derrida was clear on this matter:

> the value of truth (and all those values associated with it) is never contested nor destroyed in my writings, but only reinscribed in more powerful, larger, more stratified contexts . . . And within those contexts . . . it should be possible to invoke rules of competence, criteria of discussion and of consensus, good faith, lucidity, rigour, criticism, and pedagogy.
>
> (Derrida, quoted in Norris 1993: 300)

These debates, while complicated, have a productive potential in that they prompt a continual reflection upon the relationship between theory and research and the manner and means under which its practice takes place. They may also be limited in their attempts to understand and explain the social world for they represent the triumph of speculation over a detailed understanding and explanation of the events, circumstances and experiences that are part of our everyday lives. Social theory then moves from a regulative to constitutive function in which it seeks to speak in the name of reality – even if that means a denial of reality itself! In the next section, therefore, I wish to examine the ways in which different researchers and theorists have attempted to tackle the problems raised in the above discussions.

MAKING THE LINKS

Kuhn's concept of the practice of science raises several questions for us as social researchers (and, it should not be forgotten, for those in the natural sciences as well). In particular, the attempt to separate *what* we do, from *how* we do it, as considered by both inductivism and deductivism, is problematic. The ways in which we conduct our research is inevitably affected by the social context in which it takes place (Knorr-Cetina 1999). In describing a lecture given by a Nobel Prize winning chemist on the scientific method to students on a biology and society module, Davydd Greenwood and Morten Levin wrote of the students' reactions to the actual reality of the process within the laboratory: 'Most had not considered the matrix of ideas, experiences, organizational structures, and histories that provide the context in which scientists ask questions' (Greenwood and Levin 1998: 59).

Within our disciplines (as noted in Chapter 1) there are different ways of viewing how we gain knowledge of social phenomena in the first instance. Disciplines, therefore, are characterized not by a single paradigm, but divisions with regard to the aims and methods of social research. These do not simply reflect schisms within the disciplines themselves, but the subject matter with which we are concerned. Social life itself is characterized by divisions and is not a unified phenomenon while all sciences, not just social sciences, are directly influenced and affected by factors that exist 'externally' to the discipline: for example, the values and interests of sponsors of research or the ways of working within the discipline itself which may exclude, for instance, the reception of critical ideas. Yet we are able to sever ourselves from particular interests at particular points in time through attention to an understanding of those factors and the varying degrees to which our practices are isolated from certain influences. This adds to our more fully understanding the dimensions of production and reception in the research process (May with Perry 2011).

Paradigms are not closed systems of thought hermetically sealed off from one another and this gives us an advantage. There is a constant process in the practice of social science which enables us to compare one paradigm with another and to see the strengths and weaknesses of each. A process of clarification and mediation of theories within the practice of social research is then able to occur: 'The process of learning a paradigm or language-game as the expression of a form of life is also a process of learning what a paradigm is not' (Giddens 1976: 144).

Social sciences are dynamic disciplines within which, depending upon the disposition and position of the researcher within an academic field, other paradigms can be considered. This enables an understanding and explanation of empirical inquiries, while also adding to the challenging of assumptions about social life as an important part of research practice. It is this 'openness' to engage in reflection upon which the idea of a 'discipline' depends (May 2010). The very objects that the social sciences study concern events, process and conditions that are themselves the subjects of power struggles over who control the rules, relations and resources that constitute them in the first instance. To ignore those is not scientific; it is simply to be ignorant of their existence and consequences.

Apart from an ability to penetrate that which is taken for granted, there are a set of core issues which need to be borne in mind when conducting research. First, social researchers deal with social phenomena which people have already endowed with meaning before they arrive on the 'real' or 'virtual' terrain with their notebooks, questionnaires or interview schedules. Research, therefore, involves the interpretation of social settings, events or processes by taking account of the meanings which people have already given to those settings or processes. While such observations have tended to produce a simple separation between the social and the natural sciences, this is problematic. Our environments, for instance, produce risks which we take account of in our daily lives (see Lash et al. 1996; Adam et al. 2000). In this way our understandings, once again, become a precondition of the production of the research itself.

Second, the results and practices of social research also feed back into social life; people engage in the interpretation of its findings and are co-participants in its process. Take, for instance, the writings of nineteenth-century economists. They may well have been describing changes in society at that time, yet

> The discourse of economics entered constitutively into what industrial society is. Industrial society could not exist if everyday actors hadn't mastered concepts of investment, risk, cost, even the meaning of economics.
>
> (Giddens 1996: 77)

Here we should not forget the power of ideas in terms of their ability to be taken up according to dominant material conditions and the implications they have for people's lives. Economic policies, based on false ideas, have led to dire consequences for our well-being, leading to a need for new ways to understand the world that do not repeat these mistakes (D. Harvey 2010b).

Given this 'feedback' of ideas and research into social life, researchers have to make connections between the language which is used in social theory and the methods of interpretation which people already use in attributing meaning to their social environment. Research practice, in other words, must take account of people's everyday understandings and how and why those are constituted. This has been referred to as the 'double hermeneutic' (Giddens 1984), in which it is suggested that it would not be unusual to find a coroner who has read Durkheim's (1952) classic study on suicide (Giddens 1990: 42).

Such formulations acknowledge that there is a constant slippage between the language which we use as researchers to understand and explain social life and the meanings which people already employ to get on with the business of everyday life, leading to the question: how do translations between lay and professional frames of meaning occur and how are they negotiated and acted upon and with what consequences? Here we find an interpretative space in which trust 'is at least heavily qualified by the experience of dependency, possible alienation, and lack of agency, though there are of course many areas of experience where relationships between expert and lay publics are well integrated and non-alienated' (Wynne 1996: 52). How these situations arise, for what reasons and with what consequences are important topics for understanding the place of social research in society.

The issue is now raised as to whether we can have a theory of social life which does not take full account of people's experiences and understandings in everyday life. We have already seen (in Chapter 1) how standpoint feminism regarded experiences as a starting but not finishing point for research. Theory is then deployed to situate the experiences of women within a wider context and the production of knowledge is regarded as a social activity. If a certain type of knowledge predominates in a society, this is not necessarily because it is scientific, but due to the power that certain groups have to define what is right or wrong, or true and false. Theorizing about this state of affairs must take place within a democratic and participatory situation, otherwise it will become, like the practice of science itself, another way of regarding the experiences of particular people as 'faulty'. The production of theory and research then become 'critical projects' which go hand in hand in challenging oppression in society – whether on gender, race, ethnic, class, disability or other lines. This brings us round to a discussion of the relationship between critical theory and an understanding of everyday life.

Critical theory has a long tradition in the work of the Frankfurt School with the ideas of Adorno, Horkheimer and Marcuse who were influenced by Marx and Freud (see Held 1990; May 2004). It does not assume, unlike positivism, that the differences between facts and values can be sustained. It is also in opposition to the idea that the world cannot be changed. The interests of the researcher towards this end are not then bracketed by a concentration on 'fact-gathering' or neutrality, nor the development of hypotheses to be tested. Routes to theory such as these become reflections of the status quo, leaving questions of the constitution of reality, power and its effects upon different segments of the population, unexamined. As Horkheimer (1972: 232) wrote: 'Those who profit from the status quo entertain a general suspicion of any intellectual independence'.

For critical theory there is a constant interaction between theory and facts and the theorist seeks to recognize the relationship between the constitution of their propositions and the social context in which they find themselves. This form of reflexivity, upon the conditions of production of theoretical propositions, distinguishes traditional from critical theory. Further, the question of the relationship between people's everyday meanings and the generation of social theory does not entail a resort to the idea that there is a truth that we can reach as researchers by simply concentrating on the techniques of social research (as with positivism and empiricism). Thus, the issue of research results feeding back into social life is not a 'problem' for researchers. On the contrary, in the works of Karl Marx, the adequacy of social theory was not its ability to discover social facts as such, but its value 'in informing actions, and in particular, political actions' (Johnson et al. 1990: 144). The Italian social theorist Antonio Gramsci (1891–1937) produced a social theory which was 'designed primarily to analyze capitalist relations in order to point out the strategic lessons for the socialist movement' (Hall 1988: 57). In the works of Jürgen Habermas, theory is considered by its ability to diagnose the ills of society and form part of the process of understanding and explanation that has implications for transformation of existing relations (see Outhwaite 1996), while its insights have also been deployed in such areas as recognition and respect (Honneth 1996, 2007) and studies of globalization (Hayden and El-Ojeili 2006). Despite the differences in their work, Michel Foucault (1991b: 117) wrote how 'the Frankfurt people had tried ahead of time to assert things that I too had been working on for years to sustain'.

Research based on critical theory is then measured by its ability to reveal the relations of domination which exist in society:

> At the heart of critical social research is the idea that knowledge is structured by existing sets of social relations. The aim of a critical methodology is to provide knowledge which engages the prevailing social structures. These social structures are seen by critical social researchers, in one way or another, as oppressive structures.
>
> (L. Harvey 1990: 2)

Aspects of critical theory have been considerably modified with the advent of post-empiricism, postmodernism and poststructuralism (see, for example, Laclau and Mouffe 1985; Heller and Fehér 1988; Fraser 1989; Agger 1991, 1998; Benhabib 1992; Calhoun 1995; Honneth 1996; Fraser and Honneth 2003; Mouffe 2005). Despite this, critical theory might be argued to be claiming to know the 'wishes and struggles of the age' regardless of whether people are conscious of this or not. Its theories would not then represent the everyday understandings which people have of their social environments and we would still be left with a gap between social theory and people's interpretations of social life. Perhaps, therefore, we should abandon the idea of attempting to invent a theory which aims to achieve anything else than describe people's everyday understandings.

With this in mind we now turn to the 'interpretative paradigm' of social theory and social research and an underlying drift away from realism, towards idealism. This was most clearly represented by the works of the German theorist Max Weber (1949), for whom subjective meanings used by people in social interaction are a starting-point for the objective analysis of society. As Weber wrote of action, it 'is social in so far as, by virtue of the subjective meaning attached to it by the acting individual (or individuals), it takes account of the behaviour of others and is thereby orientated in its course'. From here a science of society then seeks 'the interpretive understanding of social action in order thereby to arrive at a causal explanation of its course and effects' (Weber 1964: 88).

Weber leaves us with an issue: how to bridge the gap between a beginning point of understanding everyday subjective meanings in the social world and an end-point in which causality is employed to explain the social world. Some theorists, while influenced by Weber, have thus argued that the theoretical constructs of research should simply reflect the same everyday constructs which people use to interpret social life in order to bridge this gap. The topic of investigation for researchers then becomes the common-sense methods that people employ in interpreting and interacting within their social environments.

Broadly speaking, this was the position of the phenomenologist Alfred Schutz (1899–1959), who argued for the 'postulate of adequacy' for social theory. This simply means that our theoretical constructs of the social world must be compatible 'with the constructs of everyday life' (Schutz 1979: 35). Our research would then focus on people's subjective experiences and not treat these as 'faulty' in terms of the theoreticians' categories. The focus would be on how people 'make up' the social world by sharing meanings and how they 'get on' with each other (intersubjectivity). In contrast to Weber, Schutz argues that we are not then able to theorize beyond this world of common-sense understandings about social life towards the realm of causal explanation. In other words, the gap is closed by regarding any attempt to causally explain the social world as unfounded.

Unlike critical theory, that emphasizes the way in which we are constrained by society so stifling our creativity, this method of theorizing examines how we create the social world through an intersubjective process. We could take this even further to make a link between data and social theory in two ways. First, we should not even presuppose, as Schutz does, that there are shared meanings in the social world through which people interact with each other. Second, we should cease to try and uncover meanings behind appearances and instead take those appearances at face value. As a result, all social interactions should be treated as skilled performances by people and it is argued, our presuppositions about social life would then be open to full scrutiny. We do not, therefore, seek to find 'motives' behind people's actions. Our topic of inquiry is the way in which people view society and render it comprehensible to each other using a 'documentary method of interpretation' (Garfinkel 1967). Common sense itself is a topic of research. We assume little about social life and dispel the idea that we can have access to an objective world beyond people's interpretations. Our research results are now assumed to be fully grounded in people's everyday understandings.

This particular form of closing the gap between theory and data has, its exponents would argue, a very different aim in mind to conventional research and theorizing (Sharrock and Watson 1988; Silverman 1998; Hutchinson et al. 2008). Despite this, we are back to the same issue raised by critical theory and, in particular, the work of the Italian theorist, Antonio Gramsci. He argued that common sense resulted from the operation of political and economic power within society. If we study the operation of common sense then we are studying the product of these relations. Critical theorists, on the other hand, would argue that we should be interested in the process through which it is constituted so it might be changed for more individual and collective benefit. However, it is still necessary to start with common sense, because 'it is not a question of introducing from scratch a scientific form of thought into everyone's individual life, but of renovating and making "critical" an already existing activity' (Gramsci 2010: 330–1). Researchers influenced by ethnomethodology often write as if unfettered by the cultures that are the objects of their inquiry, thereby replicating the error of empiricism. For this reason, these types of approach to studying social life are criticized as being empiricist and conservative.

Another way of characterizing the differences between the above approaches is that between micro and macro theory. Micro theory is more concerned with understanding face-to-face interactions between people in everyday life whereas macro theory is concerned with the behaviour of collections of people and the analysis of social systems or structures. How these two strands of theory might be examined and deployed has been addressed by researchers and theorists (see Knorr-Cetina and Cicourel 1981; N. Fielding and J. Fielding 1986; Hage 1994; Archer 1998, 2003). There are also those who have advocated middle-range theories (Merton 1957) which should situate themselves between grand theory and empiricism. Research would then be left with a series of testable propositions on particular aspects of people's behaviour which would, in the case of feminist research, relate to the experiences of women (Maynard 1998).

In addition to the above is the strategy of retroduction which is associated with critical realism. Retroduction refers to the process of building models of the mechanisms and structures that generate empirical phenomena through using a process of description, explanation and redescription. As Roy Bhaskar puts it, this requires the construction of models which

> *if* it were to exist and act in the postulated way would account for the phenomena in question (a movement of thought which may be styled 'retroduction'). The reality of the postulated explanation must then, of course, be subjected to empirical scrutiny.
>
> (Bhaskar 1998: 12, original emphasis)

The basis of this move lies within what is taken to be the stratified nature of reality as divided into the real, actual and empirical. The former is not taken to be a statement of a privileged position from which the researcher speaks, but is taken to be the realm of objects, along with their structures and powers. The realm of the actual then refers to what occurs when those powers are activated, while the empirical is the domain of experience (Sayer 2000: 11–12). Some powers may remain inactivated, while this emphasis upon the discovery of necessity also raises possibilities in terms of changing those structures and powers. However, in order to explain these relationships within the social world, a retroductive strategy is required in contrast to the others we have examined in this chapter.

In the above formulation we see matters of ontology (about what exist) tending to take primary place to those of epistemology (how we know it). Within the general realm of realist theory we have seen those who have argued that each have their place, along with a rejection of positivist and empiricist approaches. Bringing both subjective and objective features of social life into theoretical perspectives for social research examines how systemic phenomena (power and money, for example) condition and influence actions which, in turn, may transform or reproduce and sustain those features of the world. The result is an 'adaptive theory' that is responsive to new data and ways of understanding evidence through its attempts:

> to map some of the lifeworld-system interlocks that form a synthesis of subjective and objective aspects of social life. As such, the form of theory is both descriptive and explanatory and relies on concepts, networks and conceptual models of the social world which both shape and are shaped by that world.
>
> (Layder 1998: 175)

Other underlying issues that we have dealt with include not only those related to epistemology or realism versus positivism or interpretivism, but also scientific authority and the status of knowledge in relation to individuals, groups, communities and those who pay for the research itself. The idea that social science simply 'knows better' than the persons it studies concerning the reasons for their actions is something of a dead-end which every perspective we have covered so far takes seriously. We might think about this in terms of a product–process relation. Very often, the results of research are the dull thud of the report, leaving those who were 'researched' to absorb the findings. If, on the other hand, we take an approach that involves people in the process through an ongoing dialogue, in the recognition that action is the only way to generate and test knowledge, then we have a situation in which 'cooperative inquiry' (Heron 1996) takes place. We can see the same impetus in approaches to action research, across a broad range of scientific disciplines which have a commitment to democratization and community development (Greenwood and Levin 1998; Reason and Bradbury 2001), as well as calls for the social sciences to contribute to practical wisdom (Flyvbjerg 2001; Schram and Caterino 2006).

In examining the relationship between social theory and social research, we have moved from critical theory to an interest in the practical usage of common sense, towards approaches to social inquiry which seek to engage with the issues we have discussed through participatory means. However, it is important to recognize that wider and more powerful social forces may be at work rendering some problems intractable at certain levels of action. Instead they require action at a scale between nation-states because, for example, of the power of finance capital to move around the world.

SUMMARY

The basis of theory has been examined in several ways: first, in terms of its needing to be based solely in fact (inductivism); second, by its being subject to empirical falsification (deductivism); third, by its reflecting the dominant trends of the discipline – as not being based upon rules of method, but the preferences of its scientists (Kuhn's paradigms); fourth, by its ability to diagnose and inform change (critical theory and realism); fifth, by being grounded in the same constructs as people use in interpreting their social environments in everyday life (Schutz and Garfinkel), and finally, through a process of inquiry that takes into account the spirit of learning and knowing in action.

Each of the above has been subjected to examination in terms of its relationship to research. We have views that suggest social research describes the facts of social life – however they may be conceived – in what is taken to be an unproblematic and atheoretical manner. As we have seen, this assumes that there is a separation between theory and data that is impossible to maintain. There is also the argument that there is a difference of perspective from the practical logic exhibited in everyday life and the scholastic position which turns that logic into an object of scientific curiosity. In the end, researchers need to guard against the inclination that they can unproblematically reflect social reality by producing data without theory and the idea that theory without data can speak in the name of reality.

Both approaches commit a 'scholastic fallacy' (Bourdieu 2000). Such a position is exemplified by the beliefs that there are no presuppositions in the thought of researchers, or that there is no chance of speaking of reality because we have only biases that cannot be addressed and examined through systematic research. One leads to complacency and the other to retreat. Admitting of the inevitability of the relationship between theory and data, therefore, requires a reflexive practice in order that its implications for knowing the social world are understood and the craft of social research can produce better understandings.

These are complicated but practical discussions. In the process, a simple distinction between social facts and social values is often exhibited. It is commonly thought that if values enter the research process, this renders its findings void. However, it has also been argued that values should enter our theories as a condition of research which is capable of critically evaluating how knowledge is produced and why some groups, more than others, are able to perpetuate their beliefs within society. The adequacy of such a theory focuses on not only the ability to understand and explain social life, but also the potential to change it.

How does this leave us as researchers? We are left with the observation that the practice of science, natural or social, is not simply a choice between facts and theory, as there is 'no longer a reliable difference between theory construction and empirical work' (Baldamus 1984: 292). Further, social life itself is diverse and complicated and not amenable to understanding through the use of ideas that seek to close down that reality by concentrating on selected facets of social life. These issues should not deter us. On the contrary, they provide food for conceptual thought by producing new ideas about the process of validating our inquiries and the concept of objectivity itself. Instead of seeing these as a problem, perhaps we should be subjecting our own values and practices and those of others to critical scrutiny in the pursuance of social science? As Charles Taylor notes:

> There is nothing to stop us making the greatest attempts to avoid bias and achieve objectivity. Of course, it is hard, almost impossible, and precisely because our values are also at stake. But it helps, rather than hinders, the cause to be aware of this.
>
> (C. Taylor 1994: 569)

In considering this question, how values enter the research process and affect the product of research is of central concern. To understand the ways in which this occurs and its effects on the research process requires, as noted at the beginning, a reflexivity on the part of researchers or, to express it another way, a consideration of the practice of research, our place within it and the construction of our fields of inquiry themselves. It also necessitates a further understanding of the issues involved in research practice: in particular, the relationship between values, ethics and social research. It is to these subjects that I now turn.

Questions for your reflection

1 What issues do you think are significant in thinking about the relationship between social theory and social research?

2 How can the aims of a critical theory be justified according to the canons of scientific inquiry?

3 What does Anthony Giddens mean by the 'double hermeneutic'? How does this relate to the practice of social research?

4 Do we produce, reproduce, or are we made by society?

SUGGESTED FURTHER READING

Bryant, A. and Charmaz, K. (eds) (2010) *The Sage Handbook of Grounded Theory*, paperback edn. London: Sage.

Fielding, N. (ed.) (1988) *Actions and Structure: Research Methods and Social Theory*. London: Sage.

May, T. and Powell, J. (2008) *Situating Social Theory*. 2nd edn. Maidenhead: Open University Press/McGraw-Hill.

Morrow, R. A. with Brown, D. D. (1994) *Critical Theory and Methodology*. London: Sage.

3   Values and ethics in the research process

I have examined issues that inform the practice of social research in order to stimulate a 'problem consciousness'. To be aware of our strengths in terms of what we can achieve as social researchers, as well as our limitations, enables us to reflect in a productive fashion and take those into our practices and, in turn, allow our practices to inform our thinking. Some issues remain beyond our control to resolve, but that does not mean we should not seek clarification, nor do what we can within the spheres of influence that we possess.

It is often only after undertaking research that a period of reflection enables this to occur, for research is increasingly driven by particular interests that demand results in ever shorter time periods. There is also a need to be aware that what we do is not simply explicable in terms of prior, rational deliberations that are then taken forward in our actions, but is informed by a wider set of issues, including our social contexts and conditions. Reflexive practices need to take account of these issues (May 2005, 2006a).

Such considerations bring us into the realm of understanding the relationship between research and values. This chapter thus examines values, how they enter the research process and the different perspectives that exist on their influence in the process of research. In the second section, I move on to examine the place of ethics in social research. Given that values and interests may guide the process in what may be unanticipated or unrecognized ways, ethics are fundamental in maintaining the integrity and legitimacy of research in society and in protecting practitioners and participants in its practices.

VALUES AND SOCIAL RESEARCH

My purpose in this section is not to review the literature on the relationship between values and scientific practice, but to assist in understanding in what ways values and research practice interact. I shall first consider what is meant by value judgements and then move on to examine in what ways values are part of the research process. These discussions will then provide a basis from which arguments on the relationship between values and research can be considered.

What are value judgements?

In our everyday conversations and judgements, we tend to make statements of two kinds: *positive* and *normative*. One idea of science prides itself on the ability to separate statements of what does happen (positive) with statements concerning what scientists would like to happen (normative):

> In philosophy it is often said that facts correspond to 'is' statements, whereas values correspond to 'ought' statements. In other words, to state a fact is to describe the way something is. Ought statements ascribe a value to something, or prescribe how someone should act. For example, if we know the following to be true we can say it is a fact (an 'is' statement): 'Garfield has three houses, six cars and £2 million in the bank'. On the other hand 'Garfield is a miser' can be seen as an 'ought' statement.
>
> (M. Williams and May 1996: 109)

According to this distinction, science should strive to make positive judgements free from values. The content of science is thereby taken to be value free and so beyond reproach for how and why it produces knowledge. While this appears to separate questions about 'what is' from 'what ought to be', is this desirable, let alone feasible?

In terms of addressing this question, such a separation is rendered doubtful by an absence of clear ways in which we can separate 'is' and 'ought' statements or beliefs within society and ideas within science. For instance, some religious groups in the nineteenth century believed that the world was only a few thousand years old. Subsequent geological advances demonstrated that some rocks were a million years old and others considerably older. In the face of such findings these religious groups had several choices. First, they could deny the validity of the scientific findings. Second, they could modify their convictions to account for such findings. Indeed, one writer on the relationship between theology and philosophy sees this as an important part of the intellectual development of those who are firmly committed to a set of beliefs (McPherson 1974).

Finally, a situation of ambivalence might hold in which beliefs remain unmodified and evidence is accepted. In this instance a 'positive' scientific finding has apparently countered a religiously held belief. Yet positive scientific findings might be accommodated within belief systems. Arguing that God was responsible for the initial occurrence, for instance, can incorporate the 'Big Bang' theory of the origin of the universe. Such beliefs, however, are argued to be without scientific warrant and counter to a truth-seeking disposition (Dawkins 2008).

This short discussion demonstrates that the social or natural world is not as clear cut as a strict separation between fact and value, or positive and normative statements, would seem to suggest. Instead, there appears to be a constant interaction between scientific practice and societal beliefs with resulting effects upon research practice, as well as those beliefs themselves. Scientists, for example, debate among themselves the relative merits of renewable energy sources to mitigate the effects of global warming; the relationship between the amount of sugar a person consumes and the health of their teeth and the relationship between inequalities of income and the overall happiness of people within capitalist societies – to say nothing of the origins of the universe, or the meaning of life!

In the social sciences we routinely deal with phenomena that people are already busily interpreting and endowing with meaning and value. That appears to make our task as researchers a different one from that of the physical scientist. Nevertheless, let us exercise caution in overextending this argument. To allow for the possibility that the social sciences have a hermeneutic, or interpretative, dimension to their activities does not necessarily mean they then simply reflect and cannot explain the origins and effects of such values through rigorous and systematic inquiry. Seeking explanations of this type are in response to 'why' questions – in this case, why people hold particular values? It is also noteworthy that the natural environment is not only a contested arena, for instance, in relation to the most effective forms of conservation, but also a strict separation of the social and natural worlds is not, as it might appear at first glance, a simple and unproblematic matter (Latour 2004).

We now need to ask what exactly are value judgements? We may define these as expressions that contain either disapproval or approval and carry 'the implication that what is approved of should not be done if the expression is used in circumstances where action is called for' (D. Emmet 1966: 39). To consider the implications of this definition, let us take some examples (from E. R. Emmet 1981). In the first one, two people are asked to say which is the longer of two sticks by looking at and touching them (using their senses). We can then measure them with instruments to apparently solve any debate over which is the longer. This is said to be a matter of fact. However, is it that simple? Say the sticks were made of metal. At one temperature one may be longer than another (they have different coefficients of linear expansion). Which can we then say is the longer? Similarly, I place one in water and the other on a table. Which is then the longer? If I ask someone to tell me by looking at them, the way in which the light is reflected back to the person's eyes will be distorted by the medium. Which is the longer now depends on their temperature, their coefficients of expansion, the accuracy of the measuring instruments and the conditions under which they are observed. We might then be able to say which is the longer by adding these 'clauses' to our conclusions.

Consider a second example. Someone asks you which of two runners is the 'better one'. As a researcher who seeks clarification before accepting definitions as self-evident, you ask what the questioner means by 'better'. Such questions take the form of 'it depends what you mean by X'. You may know that runner A is better than runner B over 400 metres, but runner B is better than runner A over 1500 metres. So you need clarification before you can answer because you are being asked to make a *comparative assessment* between the runners. There is not a 'correct' answer, because each is faster than the other at certain distances. Your answer will depend on which is preferred and why.

We can extend this by considering asking two people to sit in a chair and express an opinion on its comfort. One person says it is comfortable; the other says it is the most uncomfortable chair she has ever sat in! They are expressing an opinion that they hold about the comfort of a chair. It is not a matter of fact capable of being verified, but one of personal taste. In between so-called matters of fact and matters of taste, we have a whole realm of judgements – simply called value judgements with which we, as social researchers, are constantly dealing.

Many people find the idea of value judgements uncomfortable – why can they not be factual? As a methodological problematic, this would require a strict separation of the language of observation from a theoretical description of what is being observed – a characteristic of logical positivism that, in practice, is impossible to maintain (see M. Williams and May 1996: Chapter 2). Instead of this route we might say that values are a fundamental part of the human condition and we should pose the question in a different way and thus seek a different answer. We should not seek the impossible – the elimination of values – but ask the more important question: what types of values are the judgements based upon and how do these affect the judgements themselves?

Value judgements are dependent on beliefs and experiences in everyday life. They also concern what we would like our experience to be. This may arise from a bad experience in circumstances which we thought would be more pleasant. For example, we join an organization and find that everyone is not as friendly as we were told and hoped they would be. We went with an expectation of, say, participatory dialogue within a supportive atmosphere aimed at the achievement of understanding and the taking of appropriate action. However, we found a narrowness of opinion and a defensive attitude concerning the positions of established employees whose only logic was to preserve the status quo. Expectations were not met by experiences which itself can be of value in understanding organizations (see Fineman and Gabriel 1996). Nevertheless, we might emerge with ideas of how the organization should be run along more cooperative, efficient and pleasant lines. Given this, we are not seeking to eliminate values because they inform and relate to the very reasons why we hold our beliefs, as well as the things to which we aspire. Instead, we might seek to change the values which guided the way in which the organization was run. We would then need to understand the ways in which values entered this process and in what contexts, to say nothing of the nature and dynamics of power and its relationship to positions within the organization (May 2006b).

Values in the research process

Because of the sums of money involved, most large-scale social research projects are sponsored by governments, or other private or voluntary organizations or agencies. It might reasonably be suggested that they have a vested interest in any results. Nevertheless, this does not suggest that the conclusions are invalid because the work is 'interested' as opposed to 'disinterested' (a characteristic of objectivism). A link between 'interest' and the pursuit of 'truth' is often made, but if a social scientist succeeds in producing the truth, they do so because they have an interest in doing so, 'which is the exact opposite of the usual somewhat fatuous discourse about "neutrality"' (Bourdieu 1993: 11).

The idea that social scientific research ought to be conducted with particular interests in mind is not one that simply evaporates with the force of the more reasonable argument. As government funds research with particular aims in mind, there are periodic attacks upon the legitimacy of research that run counter to governmental expectations – from all points on the political spectrum. Ultimately, we are dealing with the idea of a democracy being one in which research may be produced that runs counter to the expectations of funders and thus challenges and does not simply reflect, presuppositions. Those that challenge might be dismissed as 'unscientific', while research conducted by private corporations may not even reach the public domain to be criticized or subject to scrutiny. At this point our critical intellectual faculties should come to the fore and ask what definition of 'science' is being invoked, who is paying for it, for what reasons and with what effects?

It is important to be aware of the issues which surround the production of a piece of work and the place and influence of values within it. As a matter of routine the following questions can be asked of any piece of research: who funded it and why? How was it conducted and by whom? What were the problems associated with its design and process and how were the subsequent results interpreted and deployed? This enables an understanding of the context in which research takes place and the influences upon it, as well as countering the tendency to see the production and design of research as a technical issue simply uncontaminated by 'outside' influences. All research, implicitly or explicitly, contains issues of this sort. That does not render the research invalid but, on the contrary, recognition of such issues heightens our awareness of the research process itself and sharpens our insights into the influences upon its work. Table 1 illustrates the stages in which values enter the research process.

As we are all aware, different groups within society have different interests. Those interests may not be recognized when coming from the powerless and disproportionately influential when arising from a powerful minority. An ability to define a problem or issue according to values will, in its turn, affect all stages of the research process but, in the first instance, its design and aim. In such instances, social researchers should be cautious in accepting that a problem exists for which there must be a solution. How a problem is defined will depend on several factors, all of which either influence values, or enable some values to predominate over others.

The call for 'relevant' research is frequently heard, despite an ambiguity over what this actually means (Eldridge 1986; Perry and May 2010). It is usually taken as that which serves the ends of particular interests. In such cases, the social researcher should ask the questions 'relevant for whom and why'? These interests may be constantly fed information

Table 1 Values in the research process

---

1 Interests leading to research
2 Aims, objectives and design of research project
3 Data collection process
4 Interpretation of the data
5 The use made (or not) of the research findings

---

by a whole army of social scientists. It is these social scientists that Bourdieu describes as social engineers, 'whose function is to supply recipes to the leaders of private companies and government departments' (Bourdieu 1993: 13).

Here it is helpful to distinguish between different types of research in terms of the dimension of excellence and relevance to understand the influence of values. From research we have conducted for different types of funders at different scales of activity, we have mapped an excellence–relevance continuum against degrees of contextualization of the research (from global to local). As a result we have found the following forms (see Perry and May 2006, 2010; May with Perry 2011). First, a *disembedded excellence*, which may be seen as non-spatial and operating according to global 'logics' and divorced from the context in which it is produced and governed by scientific peer review processes. Second, a *competitive relevance* that is not so concerned with place because of an emphasis upon the application of science, technology and innovation to specific economic issues as a precondition for global competitive success. A focus on biotechnology, nano-technology or genomics, for instance, does not necessarily accrue benefit to any specific community or group, but the commercialization of technologies may lead to economic advantage for individuals or firms.

We then move onto *relevant excellence* which places a greater emphasis on the indirect benefits of science and technology to particular places. There is no underlying challenge to scientific investment, but an acceptance of a spatial dimension to excellence. It does not confront the processes of knowledge production, therefore, but rather seeks to exploit knowledge products for territorial benefit. Policies focusing on the attraction of 'world-class' facilities and expertise are based on assumptions of indirect benefits and the mobility of researchers. A partner to this research emphasis can be characterized as *excellent relevance*. Here we see a concern with what is produced in scientific establishments in terms of the generation of co-produced research priorities and agendas through a linking of content with context. The emphasis is as much on the processes of knowledge production as exploiting particular products. Policies then emphasize how to connect the research base, both public and private, with industry as well as issues of social inclusion or economic opportunity. While this appears as the polar opposite of disembedded excellence, quality is still deemed to be important, but judged according to a wider set of scientific, social, economic and political values.

In each of these cases different forms of values enter into the research process at different scales of governance from the local to the national and international. Even if researchers were given a free rein to design research in any way they decide, or to undertake a research project into any social area they wish, it does not follow that it is then immune from values as, in each case, these are of different types. Further, we should remember that while the production of research findings may be invested in as a means of persuading people to pursue particular ends, there are other, often more effective, methods available. Here is where culture, history and power enter our discussions.

First, different cultures have different values. Because the values of different groups vary, what may be a problem to one group is not a problem to another. Heterosexual marriage is a value which found its way into law. However, the idea that this is the only acceptable form of two people living together is challenged not only by other cultures, but also by groups within our own society and with that struggle may come an increasing recognition of such differences. The Lele tribe of East Africa, for instance, practise polyandry (one woman may marry two or more men), while in the United Kingdom heterosexism has been increasingly challenged by lesbian and gay groups who wish to possess the right to live in a way accepted as equally legitimate; this took a step forward with the Civil Partnership Act (2004). Quite simply, to be different is not necessarily to be deviant. As values vary within and between societies, research cannot assume that they are characterized by something called 'value-consensus'.

Second, history changes and with it the way we perceive social problems. As time moves on, so attitudes towards events and groups can alter. What is considered wrong or deviant at one point in time can be considered normal at another time: for example, the suffragette movement was considered subversive in the earlier part of the twentieth century. While attitudes to women's liberation still, in the main, range from support to suspicion and hostility, it is clear that the position of women in society has altered to some extent – particularly in the case of voting rights. Here, also, caution should be exercised in accepting nostalgic versions of bygone days in which the problems of today did not exist. Careful historical research tends not to support such narratives (for example, on hooliganism see Pearson 1983). As a result, awareness of the changing values that define social problems is required and to paraphrase the Czech novelist Milan Kundera: 'the struggle against power is the struggle of memory against forgetting'.

Third, social power is not evenly distributed between groups. A definition that there exists a problem will depend on the power that the people who define the problem have over those who are categorized in that way: for instance, those with access to the media may possess more power in the construction of social problems than those with limited access. In these cases different methods of social research may be required if the powerful prevent access (see Bourdieu 1995). It may be easier to gain access to social groups who cannot so easily mobilize their resources to prevent or control access. Given these factors, rather than simply accepting given definitions, it is possible to examine the process through which a phenomenon became defined as a problem. In this way the idea that there exists a problem (product) is abandoned in favour of researching how it became constructed (process). This is a subtle but profound difference in research technique whereby social values may be subject to critical scrutiny in the realization that classification has consequences (Hacking 1999; Bowker and Star 2002).

In considering the values that inform the decisions of researchers in the course of their practice, feminists argue that the androcentric values of male researchers affect all aspects of their research practice from design, through data collection to interpretation and application. Similarly, a racist attitude can affect the way in which research is conducted, while social researchers may be heterosexist in their methods and interpretation, believing and perpetuating, for example, that a 'normal' and 'legitimate' family is one man and one woman who are married under law and have children. To invoke any sense of 'normality' in this instance is a value term. The use of such a term assumes that people living together who do not meet these criteria are then 'deviant' or 'abnormal'.

In the process of data collection itself, there are decisions to be made over the strengths and weaknesses of particular methods in relation to the aims and objectives of the research project. The decision as to which method to use may be based upon the researcher's own preferences, as opposed to applicability for the task at hand. For instance, a difference between a technical and epistemological (theory of knowledge) decision when considering qualitative or quantitative methods (Bryman 1988a, 1998; Gorard 2004). Additionally, within the data collection process itself, there are a number of ethical and political decisions to be made. Researchers may wish to concentrate on one group of people rather than another, reflecting their own bias towards that group. More practically, they may concentrate on one group because it is easier to study that group. Indeed, a frequent criticism of social research is its concentration on less powerful groups. As such, we know relatively little about 'elite' groups who may possess the power to prevent research being conducted in the first place (Hertz and Imber 1995).

The anticipation of the needs of a sponsor throughout the research process can also lead to the selection of data and the interpretation of those aspects of the research findings which 'prove' the sponsors' prejudices. Alternatively, the provision of findings that do not accord with those prejudices can lead to attacks on the validity of the research itself by interested parties, leading to the possible absence of future funding from those sources. These issues are becoming more important as academics and contract researchers are under increasing pressures to publish and acquire research monies from funding agencies that follow particular agendas.

Here we enter the terrain of *selectivity*. In being selective, a number of interesting findings can be dismissed which could aid understanding and explanation. In addition, researchers may not only anticipate the needs of the sponsors, but also interpret what they consider 'society at large' would find acceptable. Take two examples to illustrate this point.

In the first example, a criminologist is examining crime statistics. Society may be concerned about youth crime and single parent families. However, in the process of undertaking the investigations the researcher discovers that a large percentage of violence takes place against women in domestic situations and the majority of perpetrators are men. Evidence of this type would clearly question the values of not only the researcher, but also society in general who exhibit a reluctance to intervene in what is taken to be the sanctity and security associated with the ideal of 'normal' family life.

In the second example, a team of economists are undertaking work on the economic impact of a city upon its region's prosperity. The assumption, made by the city's leaders, is that the city benefits the region in general and therefore should receive more national government finance to support its economic agenda. During the process of research the investigators draw a 'travel to work' boundary at ten miles from the city centre as they discover that beyond this point only a minority of people commute to work in the city itself, so its economic influence is diminished. However, the researchers then come under considerable pressure from city leaders to draw the same boundary at 20 miles from the city centre because at this distance people could, if they chose, still travel to work in the city centre. What we have here is a difference between 'actual' and 'potential' influence and a clash between political agendas and social scientific judgements.

In research design, data collection and interpretation the researcher will, depending on the circumstances, influence the conduct of the research. This is not necessarily a disadvantage, bearing in mind that having a point of view is a starting-point to research, but not its end-point. It does mean that from the first stage (interests leading to research), through the second stage (aims, objectives and design of research project), right through to the fourth stage (interpretation of findings), the researcher must be aware of the place of values in the research process. What is more difficult to account for are the wider influences of values and how they affect research. As the second example above described, this can be an issue in the process of research, but can also become a particular problem when the results reach a wider audience (the use made of research findings).

In this last stage political circumstances can take over regardless of the good will or intentions of the researcher. The research results may then be used for purposes for which they were not intended (known as the 'unintended consequences' of social action). For instance, during the Vietnam War, social scientists asked the people in rural areas of Indo-China questions which were designed to elicit or discover their moral and political allegiances. Despite the researchers being told that it was for scientific purposes, the information was allegedly used by the military to select bombing targets (J. Barnes 1979: 17). This brings us round to the section on ethics and a discussion of means and ends in social research. Before this, however, I wish to conclude this section of the chapter by examining perspectives on the relationship between values and research.

Connecting values and research

For those who adhere to the idea of 'value neutrality' throughout the research process, there are insurmountable problems in mounting a defence for this position. Most scientists would not, if asked, attempt to maintain this in the face of overwhelming arguments to the contrary. However, there are those who would adhere to the *values* of science and objectivity.

Ernest Nagel (1961) was aware of the arguments that social science cannot be value free, but critics of their value presuppositions failed to take account of different types of value judgements. Nagel thus made a distinction between two types of value judgements: *characterizing* and *appraising* (Nagel 1961: 492–5). When scientists make a characterizing value judgement, they are expressing an estimate of the degree to which something is present, such as dissent among protesters against road building through the countryside or attitudes to the use of cars and lorries and their effects on global warming. On the other hand, appraising value judgements express approval or disapproval of some moral or social ideal: for example, the attitude of mainstream political parties in the west to those arguments that see capitalism and ecology as fundamentally incompatible.

In drawing this distinction, Nagel (1961) notes how the two are often indistinguishable. We make statements which contain both character-izing and appraising value judgements. Nevertheless, he argues that their separation is a practical task and not an insoluble one. If we succeed in separating the two, we are left with characterizing judgements as a routine part of both the social and natural sciences. The possibility of a value-free social science (in terms of appraising judgements) is therefore a technical matter and not a theoretical impossibility.

Max Weber (1949), unlike Nagel, argued that the subject matter of the social sciences is fundamentally different from the natural sciences. In trying to understand people, we are obviously dealing with specifically human characteristics, and these include 'meaning' and also phenomena such as 'spirituality'. However, despite our goal being an understanding of the subjective meanings that people attribute to their world, alongside that of explanation, Weber does share Nagel's belief that social science can be objective. It is, he argued, logically impossible for the social sciences to establish in a scientific manner the truth of ideals which people believe in – the normative or 'what ought to be' statements. What social science allows for is the determination of the suitability of a given range of means for the attainment of specified ends. In other words, if people desire a particular goal, social science can assist them in finding the best way to achieve that goal. Social science cannot, however, tell people that they should accept a given end as a value, or tell them what they ought to believe in. In this way, the role of the social scientist is to demonstrate the pros and cons of different means and perhaps the social, economic and political costs involved, but not tell people what they should desire as ends. That, as Weber argues, is for the 'contemplation of sages and philosophers about the meaning of the universe' (Weber, quoted in Gerth and Mills 1948: 152). The issue for a social scientist, as Weber puts it, is the absolute separation between two problems in the conduct of their research:

> first, the statement of empirical facts (including facts established by him about the 'evaluative' behaviour of the empirical human beings whom he is studying); and secondly, his own practical value position, that is, his judgement and, in this sense, 'evaluation' of these facts (including possible 'value-judgements' made by empirical human beings, which themselves have become an object of investigation) as satisfactory or unsatisfactory.
>
> (Weber 1949: 78)

Why does Weber believe this? Quite simply, absolute values are a matter of faith and not of scientific knowledge. As social scientists we may be sufficiently committed to choose a particular area of study and so make a value judgement, yet from this point on, our work can be objective. Thus, values enter into research only in the problem selection stage.

In a similar vein, in his discussion of social theory and social policy, Robert Pinker (1971) argues that social theory should be based upon what the members of society actually believe, not what the theorist tells them they ought to believe. Beyond this, the researcher may seek 'to inform or change public opinion, and to help create consciousness of problems where this consciousness is absent' (Pinker 1971: 131). The overt nature of the role of values in social research is therefore recognized in this formulation, but values must not determine the final product: 'the first function of scientific theory is . . . to help us distinguish correct from incorrect knowledge' (Pinker 1971: 130).

Weber, Nagel and Pinker all share, to one extent or another, a belief in the possibility of fact-gathering, while recognizing the crucial role which values play in the research process (noting that objectivity is a value position). What are at issue are the places, roles and types of values in social research. According to critics of these positions, social research is not a neutral medium for generating information on social realities (Gouldner 1962). Instead it is

> an activity recognized by many as not just unveiling the facts but as constructing them, and the researcher plays a major role in this. Thus enters the question of values in research activities as well, and a fuller discussion of what is good – that is, what values should guide the researcher in her studies and interventions – is required.
>
> (Ravn 1991: 112)

Once we accept that values enter the process of research at all stages, then it can be argued that the above accounts of Weber, Nagel and Pinker are based on certain versions of objectivity. Values do not simply affect *some* aspects of research, but *all* aspects. Furthermore, the idea of objectivity as detachment was criticized in Chapter 1 as being based upon a limited idea of science through its separation of reason and emotion. Instead of the attempt to separate the researcher from the researched, there are those who argue for the taking of sides in the research process (Becker 1967).

Others, influenced by feminist-based research, argue for 'dialogic retrospection' which is defined as 'an open and active exchange between the researcher and participant in a partnership of co-research' (Humm 1995: 63). This formulation of active partnership is said to recognize that feelings and experiences are a routine part of the research process. In order to address this issue, rather than attempt to distinguish correct from incorrect knowledge (Pinker) or subjective realities from objective analysis (Weber), research must be a cooperative endeavour in which the researchers and participants share information and experiences. 'Correct' knowledge does not then come from detachment based on a limited concept of reason, as we saw in Chapter 1. Further, it is important to note that in questioning the relationship between research and objectivity as 'detachment', it does not follow that research cannot produce accurate knowledge.

For Jürgen Habermas (1990), the strive towards what he calls 'objectivism' comes from bracketing the hermeneutic, or interpretative, dimension of the research process thus failing to see the historical influences upon our consciousness. If the social sciences are concerned with the explication of meaning then, by necessity, the interpretation of that meaning by the researcher must be included within the objects of its inquiries. It is at this point that a great deal of confusion arises concerning value-freedom. Because a researcher must explicate the meaning of an event, then values are clearly part of that process. For postmodernists, those values are specific to a given community and thus relative, thereby negating the scientific desire to generalize from specific instances. However, it does not follow that the means through which we interpret events are not themselves open to rational inquiry (see Habermas 1992, 1996, 2003). To this extent, Weber's argument that ultimate values are beyond rational justification, and therefore the province of the social sciences, is mistaken.

Those thinkers who argue for value-freedom, in whatever form, are viewed as inheriting a mythical distinction between reason and emotion so characteristic of the scientific claims which feminists seek to debunk. The consequences are that the researcher is expected to act in a role which no individual could possibly perform. To translate this into a feminist methodology, the research process should become 'a dialogue between the researcher and researched, an effort to explore and clarify the topic under discussion, to clarify and expand understanding' (Acker et al. 1991: 140).

To examine these modes of dialogue between researcher and researched we could say that there is a distinction to be made between the different types of value judgements in the community in general and the social scientific community in particular. Thus, Helen Longino (1992) speaks of constitutive and contextual values. The former are internal to science and 'are the source of the rules determining what constitutes acceptable scientific practice or scientific method'. The latter, on the other hand, refer to social and cultural values that concern 'groups of individual preferences about what ought to be' (Longino 1992: 206). For Longino, the eradication of contextual values is an impossible project. Furthermore, scientists must make assumptions in their work that often remain untestable and so there is no way in which they can be ruled out of scientific work. Given this, there is no basis to argue that the place of such values in science is indicative of 'bad science'. Constitutive values cannot rule out contextual ones and this opens up 'the possibility that one can make explicit value commitments and still do "good" science' (Longino 1992: 208).

These debates take place against the background that we cannot proceed from facts to values, from 'is' to 'ought' statements. However, one should bear in mind that a commitment to the production of truth is a value position in the first instance and it 'is not only a condition of moral discourse, it is a condition of any discourse at all' (Bhaskar 1998: 63). From here we would not seek the elimination of value judgements, but an understanding of their constitution and consequences; there is no seeking to detach them from research, but an understanding of their place and experiences within social research as a central part of its process and product. This focus places researchers in their research which enables an understanding of the social world, but this is to *inform* research in the name of better explanations but should not *saturate* its insights. It is a starting and not finishing point.

To separate the means and ends of research, in the manner Weber suggests, could not be sustained by the commitments of a feminist or critical research programme. Research which assumes 'facts' can be collected on the social world simply reflects and perpetuates unequal power relations that already exist within society. Weber's position would preclude the researcher from making any analysis and critique of the ends which any society, organization or group pursues. Richard Titmuss (1974), who placed values such as social justice at the forefront of his work on social policy, recognized this: 'There is no escape from values in welfare systems . . . Not only is "policy" all about values but those who discuss problems of policy have their own values (some would call them prejudices)' (Titmuss 1974: 132).

The above view does not lead to an 'anything goes' view of research. Certain standards are still needed in the conduct of research, particularly if the idea of a 'discipline' is to be maintained. Martyn Hammersley (1995), in a neo-Weberian defence of value neutrality, argues that the most effective way of achieving objectivity, which is no guarantee in itself, is via the institutionalization of research communities who produce knowledge. For him, there is no principle underlying research other than value neutrality:

> Taking sides *within* research is effectively to take sides *against* it. It involves either an appeal to a false harmony of values, or a systematic deception whereby political activists work under the cover of research and thereby undermine it.
>
> (Hammersley 2000: 34, original emphases)

As values cannot be derived from facts, researchers have no special expertise to judge what is good and bad about a particular situation (Hammersley 2009). Now the ways in which a community of researchers is constructed and conducts itself is of the utmost importance. This is an 'internalist' question regarding the ethics of a research community. At the same time, researchers, whatever their perspective, are routinely faced with choices about what is right or wrong in the conduct of their research on a given subject while, as noted, Longino (1992) does not think a community of scholars can insulate themselves from outside influences. We are now faced with another set of issues concerned with the relationship between researchers and the subjects of their research.

ETHICS AND SOCIAL RESEARCH

Continuing with the theme of reflexivity in the research process, this section is divided into two. The first subsection asks the question 'What is ethics?' The second subsection then looks at the actual place of ethics in social research by considering the relationship between means and ends and the main ethical issues raised in the research process.

What is ethics?

Ethics is concerned with the attempt to formulate codes and principles of moral behaviour. Our focus here is with the capacity for ethical inquiry to inform reasons for action in the conduct of social research and to protect participants and the integrity of inquiry. In so far as researchers critically reflect upon their own views or those of others, or consider the justification for their actions in comparison to others, they enter the realm of philosophical ethics. Such considerations are known as 'second order' questions: they are questions 'about things', rather than simply taking them at face value.

A definition of ethical problems as they apply to social research is given by John Barnes (1979). He defines ethical decisions in research as those which 'arise when we try to decide between one course of action and another not in terms of expediency or efficiency but by reference to stand-ards of what is morally right or wrong' (J. Barnes 1979: 16). He is making a distinction here by basing ethical decisions upon *principles* rather than *expediency*. This is an important point for researchers do not have a fundamental right to conduct their work. Therefore ethical decisions are not being defined in terms of what is advantageous to the researcher or the project upon which they are working. They are concerned with what is right or just, in the interests of not only the project, its sponsors or workers, but also others who are the participants in the research and the role of research in society.

At the same time the particular interests that govern a research project can influence those decisions that subsequently take place. Knowledge is not a politically neutral product as would be maintained by positivism and empiricism. Therefore, ethical decisions will depend upon the values of the researchers and their communities and will inform the negotiations which take place between the researcher, sponsors, research participants and those who control access to the information which the researcher seeks ('gatekeepers'). The amount of control the researcher can exercise over the research process will also influence the exercise of ethical decisions themselves.

For the above reasons the relationship between ethics and social research is a complicated one. While the development of a code of ethics for social research is a laudable aim, many argue that it must also recog-nize those factors which influence the conduct of research. Thus, Warwick and Pettigrew (1983) attempt a set of guidelines, but still note that there are problems that lie outside of social scientific communities: 'the spon-sors of research and the mass media of communication. Repeatedly, our discussion has shown how these influences contribute to ethical problems in policy research' (Warwick and Pettigrew 1983: 368). In addition, the growth of ethical regulation in organizations and institutions, such as universities, are not without their issues (see Shea 2000; Israel and Hay 2006: Chapter 4).

Given such a state of affairs, there are two ways in which approaches to ethics and social research have proceeded. These may not accurately reflect all the ethical decisions which are made, but are useful 'heuristic' devices (which means helping to study or discover, as in Weber's 'ideal types'). They are known as *deontology* and *consequentialism*.

Deontological approaches to morality are associated with the work of Immanuel Kant (1724–1804). Quite simply, ethical judgements in social research would, from this point of view, follow a set of principles which guide the conduct of research itself. Research ethics takes on a universal form and should be followed regardless of the place and circumstances in which researchers find themselves. One such doctrine is that of 'informed consent'. This refers to a freely given agreement on the part of the researched to become a subject of the research process. However, this not only is based on a complete understanding of the aims and processes of the research itself, but also may assume to encompass any consequences that follow from its publication in the public domain. A researcher might, and in many cases ought, to take all possible steps to protect the identity of any person in the anticipation of any information being used for purposes other than those intended.

Practical problems can arise in these circumstances. Take, for example, research on the internet. Not only do the boundaries between the public and private aspects of life have the potential to become somewhat blurred, but also in seeking consent from respondents, from whom should this be obtained? If a group is 'virtual' and subject to routine changes in its composition this creates problems for those seeking to follow such a doctrine. Hence those undertaking research within the field of 'internet research ethics' may take an approach extending from uncloaked, through to minimum, medium and maximum cloaking. In the former the researcher might use the online pseudonym or real name of the participants, while in the latter fictive details might be introduced to ensure the protection of participants against harmful impacts (Kozinets 2010: 154–5).

While individual researchers may seek to disguise the identities of respondents, can they reasonably guarantee this outcome when much of what they do is beyond their individual control? At the same time, the actions they observe or accounts they receive may themselves transgress laws, morals or ethical codes. We should also note that an observance of formal ethical requirements may operate to exclude particular groups. For instance, in the case of interviews with those under 18, parental consent may be required. Barriers imposed by adults may then prevent the voices of young people being heard. In this case, as long as the research is respectful of the interests of this group, the research may be justified without formal parental consent (Alderson 1999).

With these scenarios in mind consequentialism is not so concerned with following a set of inviolate rules, but with the situation in which researchers may find themselves and with the consequences of their acts. According to this view, a set of doctrinal rules for the conduct of social research does not take account of context. Thus, the British Sociological Association (BSA) code of ethics states: 'Guarantees of confidentiality and anonymity given to research participants must be honoured, *unless there are clear and overriding reasons to do otherwise*' (BSA 1996: 3, emphasis added).

It might be argued that adherence to deontological ethical codes would entail undue restrictions on the researcher's activities and creativity, as well as preventing the representation of marginalized voices. In this sense, action may be justified if it prevents harm or offence to a person. The dilemmas that the researcher encounters are therefore not so different from those which we all face in everyday life. The difference is that those with whom the researcher interacts are not normally intimate friends. Yet in the case of online interviews in real time there are cultural and geographical differences that create issues that are difficult to anticipate in advance (Salmons 2010).

We find in the history of writing about ethics and social research a view concerning participants along the following lines: 'Since they are not intimates, we are under less social obligations to keep secrets about them. And we can normally deal with almost all our problems of privacy by maintaining the anonymity of the people we write about' (Douglas 1979: 29). Douglas is not ruling out those who believe in professional ethics, simply those who believe that ethical rules of research must be applied rigorously in all settings. In particular, he notes that the development of professional ethics provides something of a safeguard against encroachments on freedom of speech and research (Douglas 1979: 32). They also serve to remind social researchers about their obligations in the conduct of their work. Equally, however, their existence may prevent discussions concerning ethical issues and lead the researcher to believe that simple adherence discharges them from having moral responsibility in the conduct of their work (Homan 1991).

Overall, rigid and inflexible sets of ethical rules for social research (deontology) could leave us with undesirable consequences. Going so far down this particular ethical road, we might also conclude that 'the only safe way to avoid violating principles of professional ethics is to refrain from doing social research altogether' (Urie Bronfenbrenner, quoted in J. Barnes 1979: Preface). On the other hand, a loose and flexible system involving 'anything goes' so easily opens the research door to the unscrupulous; to those who regard such considerations as a luxury or irrelevance in the face of the assertion of a self-interested pursuit of ends. As a result, there are those who feel that both sides have their merits and weaknesses (Plummer 1990: 141). If research is to be viewed as a credible endeavour, then perhaps the relations that are established with all those party to the research must utilize some ethical basis which provides guidelines for, but not simply constraints on, the researcher?

With a huge growth in information technology and the potential for a routine invasion of people's privacy, it becomes more likely that they may refuse to cooperate with research. Despite this, people may also be increasingly unaware of how their behaviour is routinely monitored by information technology (see Lyon 2001) with liberty and surveillance lying in a delicate balance. The formulation and adherence to a set of ethical guidelines then enable the researcher continually to reflect on the expectations which they make of people and their relationships with participants, as well as form part of public discourse about the desirability of new forms of knowledge acquisition. That not only assists in preventing social research becoming a mouthpiece of powerful vested interests, but also assists in maintaining public cooperation and trust in social research (Bulmer 1979b). Here, the 'internalist' concept of ethics comes into play. The ways in which a centre or department concerned with the production of social research conducts itself, including how it treats its members of staff and discusses its ideas in an open and inquiring manner, is a fundamental part of the research process itself.

Relations between ethics and social research

In comparing ethical issues in the social and natural sciences, John Barnes (1979) notes that those in the natural sciences relate more to the application than to the gathering of information. However, the use of animals for experimentation and the ethical issues surrounding nuclear energy and genetic engineering, for example, make this distinction less tenable. This difference, therefore, as Barnes (1979: 17) speculated, is now much less apparent, particularly as studies of natural science have made clear the role of social factors in the data gathering process itself, leading to the so-called 'science wars' (see G. Cooper 1999; Ashman and Baringer 2001).

I have deliberately raised the question of ethics and natural science research. When reading about ethics in social sciences, there is a tendency to believe that ethical issues are not so important in the conduct of natural, as opposed to social science research. In addition, the use of the term 'science' often carries with it a justification of using various means of collecting information in pursuance of 'truth'. There are also those for whom the end may be justified in terms of the furtherance of a political cause or the heightening of a particular issue in the public conscience.

This relationship between the means and ends of research has provided the focus for much debate.

Max Weber refers to the 'ethic of ultimate ends'. Under the banner of scientific inquiry in the search of truth, some would argue that it is possible to justify their actions. However, whatever the merit of their ends: 'From no ethics in the world can it be concluded when and to what extent the ethically good purpose "justifies" the ethically dangerous means and ramifications' (Weber, quoted in Gerth and Mills 1948: 121). The means, in other words, cannot justify the ends. Yet in our current climate, research is highly dependent on government and agency funding. These bodies have a vested interest in the conduct and findings of research. They may even explicitly impose their own conditions on the research process or, more commonly, their political expectations may govern the decisions which can be made during the research: for example, research on poorer sections of the community for the purposes of determining their 'eligibility' for state support. Should such information be gathered at any cost to the dignity of the individuals concerned, in order to try to save the government of the day money? If the government of the day justifies its actions by reference to democracy and the 'wishes of the majority', would this be satisfactory? Researchers would then have to ask themselves a number of questions to justify ethically being part of such a project.

First, if we are talking about what a majority might wish, then this would work in a 'direct democracy' where all people have a channel of communication to all political decisions made in their interest. Such a condition does not hold in any country that claims to be a democracy. Second, even if the majority 'willed' it, as one of the greatest advocates of democracy Alexis de Tocqueville (1805–59) was only too aware, the exercise of the 'tyranny of the majority' may predominate. Minority rights may then be ignored and we do not have to look deep into history, or glance at modern times, to see the disastrous consequences of such a course of action. Third, the researchers might ask themselves what autonomy from the sponsors they would have in the project in order to exercise some discretion in the design, collection and analysis of data; to say nothing of anticipating how the results might be used.

If researchers ignored the ends for which their research is intended and there are those who do by invoking various justifications, they could still provide the means for dubious ends. Claims of ignorance or lack of control may be justified in some instances, but 'collusion' can occur whether the researchers intended it or not. In addition, a refusal to undertake a piece of research hardly means that the research will not take place. As Homan (1991: 182) puts it: 'Professionals can undercut one another with their moralities as they can with their ethics'. Alternatively, what moral questions can be reconstructed as being morally neutral, thus apparently freeing the researcher from what are held to be the burdens of such considerations. Such a process has been noted with respect to marketing practices, business ethics and moral indifference (Desmond 1998).

For Weber, social science can provide only the means, but not tell people the ends to which it should be employed. Researchers may even advise on the best means to pursue given ends, but again may not comment, as a social scientist, on the ends themselves. This is problematic. As noted, Habermas would challenge, from a rational viewpoint, the values which govern the ends to which research is used. More generally, it might be argued that means are inextricably related to ends. The relationship in research is a problematic one to which there are no simple answers. It is further clouded by a number of factors. Most importantly, there is the extent to which a scientific community organizes itself in a manner that promotes free and rational inquiry and recognizes and works against, and not with, underlying power relations. I have in mind, for example, relations between younger and older members of staff, women and men, black and white, those who defend and those who are seen to threaten an established order and those on permanent and temporary contracts. Without this awareness in place, dubious practices are likely to flourish.

We are still left with a question: 'should the production of knowledge be pursued at any cost?' If so, we can then justify our means in terms of our ends. There is no simple answer to this. Once research reaches the public domain, as Warwick and Pettigrew (1983) noted, the control that the researcher can exercise over it changes. With a growth in information technology and the use to which research findings can be put, in the face of mass communication researchers find their power limited. However, this is not simply a one-way relationship. A wide dissemination of information can also work to undermine vested interests, as the use of coded information on the internet for those fighting totalitarian regimes has made clear. Therefore, researchers can make tactical decisions in the process of research which have an ethical content in relation to possible consequences. In this balance between people's privacy and the generation of knowledge, one of the classic debates centred around a research project undertaken by Laud Humphreys (1970). Although this work is dated, it is often misunderstood and still illustrates the dilemmas that social research faces.

Humphreys conducted his doctoral dissertation as a covert participant observer (observation conducted without the knowledge of those being observed). He focused upon a number of homosexual acts in what were known as 'tearooms' (public rest-rooms). He became a familiar part of the social scene. This was assisted by his pastoral experiences in a part of Chicago known as 'queen parish', by making the 'rounds of ten gay bars then operating in the metropolitan area' and by attending 'private gatherings and the annual ball' (Humphreys 1970: 25). As a result, he was then able to adopt the role of 'watch-queen', the function of which was to act as a look-out, but who was also recognized as deriving pleasure from watching homosexual encounters. In this role, which he termed the 'sociologist as voyeur', Humphreys was able to record the events he witnessed.

During the period of his observations, Humphreys made a note of 134 licence plate numbers of the cars belonging to the men. By pretending to be a market researcher and making use of friendly contacts in the police force, he collected their names and addresses. Approximately one year later, after changing his appearance and now being employed on a social health survey of men, he sought the permission of the project director to add 100 of those original names to the health survey. He did this in order to collect further data on the participants. Most of the men in his study were married and not overt members of the gay community – often considering themselves neither bisexual nor homosexual. He then called on their homes, under the guise of the health survey, to conduct his additional research. Their names were kept in a safe deposit box, no means of identification appeared on the questionnaires and the interview cards were destroyed after completion of the schedule (Humphreys 1970: 42).

Reactions to the publication of Humphreys' study were variable. As he notes in a postscript to the book: 'several have suggested to me that I should have avoided this research subject altogether' (Humphreys 1970: 168). He was accused of deceit, the invasion of privacy and increasing the likelihood of the sample's detection by the police force. One account suggests that some faculty members at Washington University were so outraged 'that they demanded (unsuccessfully) that Humphreys' doctoral degree be revoked' (Kimmel 1988: 23). On the other hand, some social scientists and those in the gay community thought that the research shed 'light on a little-known segment of our society' and that it dispelled 'stereotypes and myths' (Kimmel 1988: 23).

In this sense, the means could be said to justify the end. Humphreys brought into the public domain an understanding of an issue which American society had done so much to repress. To his critics, however, the means can never justify the ends for practices of manipulation and deception 'ultimately helps produce a society of cynics, liars and manipulators, and undermines the trust which is essential to a just social order' (Warwick 1982: 58). Yet, for those who have used such methods, they may be justified according to the nature of the research materials which they produce in relation to the power that one group may hold over another.

Rosenhan's (1982) research involved eight sane people gaining admission as 'pseudopatients' to mental hospitals. This followed their display of certain 'symptoms'. This process may be argued to have gained information on psychiatric diagnoses not available by other means. It became apparent that, despite the 'science' of psychiatry, 'we cannot distinguish the sane from the insane in psychiatric hospitals' (Rosenhan 1982: 36). As he notes, this was a general criticism of the psychiatric system and was not aimed at the individuals who treated these pseudo-patients. Indeed, he notes that these staff were committed to and cared for their patients (Rosenhan 1982: 37). This research thereby constituted how knowledge can be employed to good effect: 'by the benign use of deception and where the use of deception on obtaining information increases rather than decreases its credibility' (J. Barnes 1979: 125).

Similarly, Nigel Fielding's (1981) reflection on his work on the National Front saw him adopt the role of interpreter between the inner workings of this organization and society in general. His hope was that the end result assisted people outside of the organization to 'understand its appeal' and that in a more political vein, this enabled the National Front's opponents 'to persuade those susceptible to membership that the answers to our problems do not lie in racist politics' (N. Fielding 1982: 104).

The relationship between means and ends in social research, and the ethical decisions, power and disposition of the researchers themselves, are clearly difficult issues. Any debate tends to focus upon the use of covert participant observation because it seems to raise the central issues of knowledge production and its relationship to privacy. Yet in an information society where so many data are routinely stored on individuals (Poster 1990; Lyon 2001; Lash 2002), invasions of privacy are more likely to become a routine part of our lives. This does not give social research licence to conduct itself without due consideration to privacy. It does, however, widen the scope of ethics and social research to incorporate quasi experiments, online methods, documentary research and also surveys and evaluation research (for example, see Bulmer 1979a; McKie 2002). In survey research, for example, reporting correlations as causal may not be a valid means of conducting research, while the type of indicators that are constructed and deployed have ethical significance for research practice (K. Jones 2000).

Such issues are fundamental to practice but we should also remember the form and content of institutional processes that govern research ethics. Here we may find a less critical attitude through an undue focus upon certain research techniques by those who draw upon unexamined views of what is assumed to count as 'legitimate procedures'. Such practices underlie Homan's comments concerning critics of covert methods who might helpfully demonstrate why such practices 'should be expected to conform to standards not honoured elsewhere' (Homan 1991: 114). It also focuses our attention on the relationship between funding research, its process and the contexts in which it is produced and the use, or not, to which it is subsequently put.

SUMMARY

From our discussions on values and ethics, it is evident that the idea of research free from values is problematic. Indeed, value-freedom is itself a value position! Social research takes place within a context in which many of its rules of procedures are taken for granted. These 'background assumptions' (Gouldner 1971), upon which research decisions and analysis are based, should be open to scrutiny. Without this in place, social research can so easily reflect the prejudices of society in general, or a research community in particular. At the same time, it is worth remembering that social life, while illuminated by social research, does not ultimately depend upon it. Decisions are constantly made which directly affect our lives and which are not based upon systematic research. We should remember not only that social life does not wait for social research to catch up with it (Shipman 1988), but also that it is valuable for what it tells us about the world and that comes through what we can show for our efforts, not just our methodological or philosophical arguments (Fay 2009).

As those with a more critical disposition have pointed out, simply 'knowing about' the issues of values and ethics is not a sufficient basis upon which to conduct research; they need to form part of research practice itself. Values and experiences are not something to be bracketed away as if ashamed by their entry into the process. On the contrary, many now argue that an examination of the basis of values and their relationship to decisions and stages in research is required in order to provide justifications for systematic and valid social research. The aim is not their elimination, for this is impossible. Instead, these criticisms acknowledge that research takes place within a context where certain interests and values often predominate to the exclusion of others. 'Objective' research is not achieved by uncritically accepting these as self-evident. Such a position can perpetuate discriminatory practices. At the same time, social researchers may have to acknowledge that their individual power may be limited in acting on this state of affairs. Despite their best efforts, they cannot guarantee to control the use to which research might be put, nor expect to exercise full control over the process and that is why where research is conducted and how it is organized and discussed and supported is fundamental to its practice.

Social researchers need to recognize that there are limits to counteracting the wider societies of which we are all a part. That recognition, however, does not license acquiescence, nor relieve a research community from a responsibility for drawing up and conforming to a set of ethical guidelines which are, at least, a beginning. The development, application and discussion of research ethics across the full range of disciplines is required not only to maintain public confidence and to try to protect individuals and groups from the illegitimate use of research findings, but also to ensure its status as a legitimate and important undertaking.

Questions for your reflection

1 What issues does research on the internet raise for the relationship between ethics and social research?

2 Should social research challenge power relations in society?

3 Can values be justified scientifically?

4 You have been awarded £100,000 by your government to conduct research into the characteristics of young people who commit crime and you are asked to use both quantitative and qualitative approaches. You are told that the results of your research will be used to inform crime prevention strategies and 'tackle' patterns of offending. What value and ethical issues do you face if you chose to conduct this research?

SUGGESTED FURTHER READING

Hammersley, M. (2000) *Taking Sides in Social Research: Essays in Partisanship and Bias*. London: Routledge.

Israel, M. and Hay, I. (2006) *Research Ethics for Social Scientists*. London: Sage.

O'Neill, J., Holland, A. and Light, A. (2008) *Environmental Values*. London: Routledge.

Simons, H. and Usher, R. (eds) (2000) *Situated Ethics in Educational Research*. London: Routledge.

Part II Methods of social research

4   Official statistics: topic and resource

Sources
Issues in construction
Official statistics: the debates
Summary
Suggested further reading

There is an ever-increasing volume of information available on the demographic characteristics of the population and their opinions, values and consumption patterns. The amount of material routinely collected by the government and its agencies provides a rich source of data for the social researcher. With access to data sets via the internet now available, technology has afforded researchers greater access to information and with that, more opportunities for secondary data analysis.

Given the above, in the first section of this chapter I examine the common types of official statistics that researchers may utilize. Nevertheless, there is a temptation to use such data without due consideration being paid to their weaknesses, as well as their strengths. Those collecting official statistics, as with the practice of social research in general, may employ unexamined assumptions about social life which, if due caution is not exercised, will be inherited and reproduced in studies. Therefore, we should view them not simply as 'social facts', but social, political and economic constructions which may be based upon the interests of those who commissioned the research in the first instance. From this point of view the researcher needs to understand how they were constructed and for what purpose. In order to assist in this process, the second section of this chapter considers the construction of official statistics. A third section then outlines various perspectives on the use of official statistics for the purpose of conducting social research in order to sharpen a reflexive practice.

SOURCES

The term 'official statistics' is normally used to refer to data collected by the state and its agencies, but may also include larger areas such as the European Union and Eurostat. Eurostat (the Statistical Office of the European Communities) produces data covering a number of areas, including the labour market, migration, standards of living, money and finance and services such as transport and tourism. Its tasks are to provide statistical information for 'devising, managing and assessing common policies'; to set up a 'European statistical system using a common language linking the national statistical systems'; to supply 'the general public with statistical information, including the use of new electronic media' and offer 'technical co-operation with the rest of the world' (Franchet 2000).

Countries vary in the collection of official data in terms of their capacity, quality and the fluctuations of political decision-making. In the UK, the General Register Office was established in 1837, with registration of deaths placed on the political agenda. During the 1840s regular statistical reports were then produced on subjects such as births, deaths and crimes, while in the United States, the US Census of Population began in 1790 and Eurostat celebrated its fiftieth anniversary in 2003.

Official statistics cover the economy, crime, employment, age, education and health – to name but a few. This heading would include the UK ten-year Census which began in 1801 with government concerns over the growth of the population exceeding its available resources, as well as the Family Expenditure Survey, which ran continuously from 1957 to 2001 and was utilized for constructing the Retail Price Index as a cost of living indicator. The data for the survey were collected from, approximately, 7000 households, but response rates of 70 per cent led to questions over validity. Then, as if to illustrate how changes can occur that may affect comparison over time, it was combined with the National Food Survey in 2001 to become the Expenditure and Food Survey and is now known as the Living Costs and Food Survey, based on 12,000 people deploying postcode addresses.

Included also are the General Household Survey (GHS, now called the General Lifestyle Survey) and British Social Attitudes Survey (BSAS). The GHS began in the 1970s covering household, family and individual issues such as employment, consumption, education, leisure and health; the BSAS began in 1983 and now includes an international component allowing for comparisons between countries. Both of these were introduced with the intention of being employed for secondary analysis (see Kent 1981; A. Dale et al. 1988). This may be broadly defined as using data for a different purpose from the one that originally motivated its collection. In short, there are enormous ranges of official statistics and guides to these sources are published annually by agencies in different countries.

Official statistics represent an extensive source of data on changing attitudes to particular social issues and the composition and incomes of households which are then available for analysis. The Worldwatch Institute's *State of the World* reports draw on such sources as the United National Population Division in order to produce annual progress reports on sustainable futures across the world (e.g. Worldwatch Institute 2010). Drawing upon statistics can be a powerful means of illustrating the significance of particular trends for the future of our planet:

> In 2006, people around the world spent $30.5 trillion on goods and services (in 2008 dollars). These expenditures included basic necessities like food and shelter, but as discretionary incomes rose, people spent more on consumer goods – from richer foods and larger homes to televisions, cars, computers, and air travel. In 2008 alone, people around the world purchased 68 million vehicles, 85 million refrigerators, 297 million computers, and 1.2 billion mobile (cell) phones.
> (Assadourian 2010: 4)

While official statistics represent rich data sets, it has also been argued that they represent only what is seen as of importance to officialdom (A. Dale et al. 1988: 18) and issues continue to exist in terms of the relations between government secrecy and confidentiality (A. Dale 1999). These are fundamental political issues as many governments seek to cloud their activities in the presentation of favourable and restricted measures of so-called 'success'. For social researchers in terms of their validity and reliability, there are also concerns regarding 'an absence of consistency in definitions, data sources and measures, as well as changes over time in census and administrative geography' (Fahmy et al. 2008: 10), which can frustrate, for example, the measurement of poverty over time. For this reason, as we shall see in the third section of this chapter, there is a debate over their use for social research.

There is now an enormous volume and range of data which are produced or sponsored by the state, government and its agencies that are accessible via the internet, with sets of issues to consider in their use (Owen 1999; Stein 1999). We are overwhelmed by information, but intelligence may be in shorter supply. It is also important to remember that internet access is not at all evenly distributed and varies widely between and within countries with just under 11 per cent of people in Africa having access. The Office for National Statistics in the UK, on the other hand, reports that in 2010:

> 30.1 million adults in the UK (60 per cent) accessed the Internet every day or almost every day . . . Internet use is linked to various socio-economic and demographic indicators, such as age, location,

marital status and education. For example, the majority of those aged 65 and over (60 per cent) had never accessed the Internet, compared with just 1 per cent of those aged 16 to 24. While 97 per cent of adults educated to degree level had accessed the Internet, 45 per cent without any formal qualifications had done so.

(source: www.statistics.gov.uk)

The United Nations, UNESCO, World Health Organization and World Bank, among others, publish extensive data. To these we could add what are referred to as ad hoc or one-off surveys. These studies

usually relate to a specific topic that is of current policy interest. They are commissioned not just for the purposes of providing background data but also with the aim of increasing understanding within the area of concern.

(A. Dale et al. 1988: 9)

Statistics such as these enable us to understand the dynamics of society – perhaps along race, class, age and gender lines – as well as charting trends within society (hence the title for one of the most detailed UK government statistical publications, *Social Trends*). This information provides government and social policy formulators with data upon which to base their decisions, as the Eurostat foreword indicated, as well as the means to forecast and evaluate the impact of new social policy provisions (Berridge and Thom 1996). In short, enormous amounts of information are collected, stored and used about individuals in society. Market researchers who, for commercial reasons, are interested in the tastes, habits and opinions of the population also use this information. Such is the interest in consumption patterns, that studies are even conducted on the relationship between purchasing decisions and the types of music played in, for example, supermarkets.

Both the production of official statistics and their secondary analysis are not unproblematic enterprises. It is at this point that the different theoretical schools of thought and their approaches to research become apparent. Each of these considers the use of official statistics in a different way. Therefore, it is helpful to frame this discussion by using examples. I have chosen those relating to crime, but the reader should be aware that any limitations should not be uncritically applied to other areas of statistical compilation.

While wishing to introduce a critical awareness of the process of data collection and analysis, one should be sensitive to the types of data which are being spoken of and not necessarily resort to bland and general condemnation. Nevertheless, this discussion does demonstrate the process through which official statistics are produced and how that affects the final product. As we shall see in the third section, there are those who believe the product is useful for social research and those who reject their utility and concentrate only upon the process of their construction. There are also those who see the links between process and product in terms of their effects upon how we then view the social world and how this informs our actions and impressions.

ISSUES IN CONSTRUCTION

Crime statistics are often published by governments on an annual basis. In the United States the Federal Bureau of Investigation (FBI) publishes data, while the Bureau of Justice Statistics publishes the National Crime Victimization Survey. *Criminal Statistics* appears in the UK providing policy-makers and researchers with an indicator of the types of crimes being committed and the extent to which crime is increasing or decreasing according to the impact of particular criminal justice policies. In addition, there are statistics on probation, as well as prisons that include not only the population, but forms of escape and rates of overcrowding.

It is not uncommon for us to read in newspapers of a 'new crime wave'. That, in turn, contributes to a fear of crime which alters the habits of society's vulnerable groups: for example, elderly people locking their doors, not going out at night and avoiding certain areas. Researchers have also shown that women's fear of crime, in particular, is real enough and should not be dismissed as simply 'false' as it represents concerns over wider social issues (Farrall et al. 2009). In terms of those issues, there is a clear gendered component to interpretation:

> Women tend to view violence with greater abhorrence than men, but it is a grotesque masculinism to suggest that because they worry more about violence, they are suffering from a form of irrationality which necessitates an expert unravelling their 'real' causes of discontent.
> (J. Young 1999: 74)

Can we be sure that official statistics are an accurate picture of the extent and nature of crime in the UK? If not, then the decisions of policy-makers and media presentations of crime, at least those based upon this information, will be limited and in some instances entirely wrong. In order to understand this question we need to examine the ways in which an initial act becomes officially defined as criminal.

To have confidence in using official statistics on crime, we must be sure that they fulfil the criteria of *validity* and *reliability*. For these purposes the conclusions of research should produce true knowledge, on the one hand, and be repeatable, on the other. The following conditions must hold in order to sustain the validity and reliability of official statistics on crime. First, those responsible for compiling the crime statistics must categorize a similar incident or act of breaking the law in the same manner. We must assume, therefore, that there is little room for the discretion of, say, different police forces and individual officers, to enter the recording of such information and if it should, it is exercised in a manner that produces the same final classification. If this is not the case, then similar incidents will be categorized in different ways.

Second, our statistics must be mutually exclusive so that two different occurrences cannot be categorized in the same way. If two different incidents can be categorized in the same way, then our statistics cannot be reliable: that is, accurate and repeatable. Third, it follows that the categorization of criminal acts must be exhaustive in that all criminal acts committed are categorized under a particular heading and included in the official statistics. For instance, the police record all burglaries committed on a daily basis. To consider how official statistics on crime measure up to these criteria, I shall examine the process through which a criminal act becomes a crime statistic.

In the first place an act is defined as being criminal. At this point there are two important aspects to bear in mind. For an act to be 'criminal' it must be defined as such by the criminal law (and we make a distinction between criminal and civil law). In addition, someone, aside from the perpetrator, must know that a criminal act took place, otherwise, quite simply, it will not be detected except in cases of self-confession, or the perpetrator is caught for another act and asks for others to be 'taken into consideration' (TICs). Even at this first stage we face two issues in the compilation of crime statistics: the *definition* of an act as criminal and the *detection* of that act.

While the idea of 'definition' may seem non-problematic, it is important to remember that what is criminal in one society may not be in another, while the definition of criminal varies across time. As with the discussion on social problems in Chapter 3, the idea of what is criminal changes in societies with history, culture and the power that particular groups have to frame social definitions. In other words, the idea of a 'criminal' is not a static definition, but changes with time: it is a *diachronic*, not *synchronic* concept.

The issue of detection is also problematic. The decision to report a crime by a member of the public will depend on a number of factors. These include a sense of obligation that a crime ought to be reported, or that the crime was of a serious nature, or that by reporting the crime it lessens the risk to others. Further, the individual may benefit through the possibility of recovering their property, reducing their risk of further incidences of victimization, or that it is a requirement of an insurance company. A calculation concerning overall loss and severity may also be accompanied by a wish to see an offender caught, as well as the belief that it is a private matter, rather than one for the police (Flatley et al. 2010: 27).

At the same time we are often faced with the spectre of the 'anonymous attacker' on our streets. Such events do occur. However, it is not necessarily the public arena where women, for example, are threatened. Instead, the greatest threat has been found to come from those who are 'intimates, acquaintances, authorities and service providers' (Stanko 1990: 175). Given this, will a woman who is the victim of domestic violence perpetrated by her partner necessarily report it to the police according to the criteria listed above? Studies have shown that women tend to conceal such experiences from the police, as well as from researchers (Radford and Stanko 1996), and this will vary with cultures and religious practices. As Linda McKie puts it:

> Silences can present the survivor with a situation of double jeopardy, namely of suffering ongoing physical or psychological harm, coupled with inhibitions on speaking out for fear of further indignities, violations and even death.
>
> (McKie 2005: 130)

The overall assessment of domestic and 'non-stranger' violence will be affected as a result because the detection of the crime of domestic violence depends upon the possibility of the victim reporting it without fear of repercussions – physical, emotional and material, thereby affecting an initial willingness to report an incident to the police (Flatley et al. 2010: 56). In addition, it depends upon police practices and their predisposition to see an incident as a legitimate part of their normal duties. As one researcher concluded from her earlier work on violence against women, it may be the routinization of harassment and assault, despite its evident consequences, that may lead women not to report the incident to the police in the first instance (Radford 1990).

Although very different in form, crimes at work are often not reported for fear of losing jobs, or companies not wishing to attract adverse publicity, or simply that there is a lack of confidence in the capabilities of official agencies to tackle the crime effectively (Croall 1992; Nichols 1999). For these reasons, crime statistics tend to reflect so-called street crimes which are visible, rather than white-collar and domestic crimes which are difficult to detect and take place within conventional working environments or domestic spheres. Criminology, as a discipline, reflects this trend in being more concerned with 'conventional' crimes as are the media and politicians (Minkes and Minkes 2008).

In terms of the types of offences that official statistics reflect, *criminal statistics* comprise the following offences recorded by the police. First, they include most indictable offences (defined as those that will be tried by a judge and jury at Crown Court). Second, they contain summary offences which mean those offences which, if reaching the trial stage, are heard at a magistrates court, and third, they comprise 'either way' offences. These final categories, as the name implies, may be tried in either court. Overall, this range is frequently assumed to reflect more 'serious' offences recorded by the police. However,

> many minor offences are included; all thefts are included, even though the property stolen may be some sweets or a bottle of milk from a doorstep. By contrast, no statistics are provided on the incidence of most summary *offences*, although some information is given about *persons processed* for such offences in the statistics about offenders.
>
> (Coleman and Moynihan 1996: 27, original emphases)

Matters of detection, definition and police practices thus affect the production of crime statistics. In turning our attention to these issues, we have examined the initial process through which a crime statistic is produced. The compilation of official statistics on crime is now dependent upon two criteria which directly influence their validity and reliability. First, a set of *discretionary procedures*, for example, the decision of individuals to report an incident to the police and the decision of police officers to record an incident and take the matter seriously. Second, *institutional practices*, which include the policies of the police force and the government in tackling certain offences. In practice, these two are very difficult to separate. Thus, what a police officer decides to do will depend not only on the circumstances of the incident and how sympathetic or otherwise the officer may be towards the person(s) or act(s) itself, but also on the organizational policies which the officer is instructed to follow and the culture of the police organization itself. It is this latter aspect that may come to predominate in the performance of duties. The process of socialization of new recruits leads them to focus upon 'not what the job is for, but how it is and ought to be done' (N. Fielding 1988b: 50). Examining police cultures and their corresponding interpretative procedures therefore tells us more about how statistics are compiled, than taking official crime statistics at face value.

In focusing upon the organizational culture of the police, we are beginning to see that 'criminal facts' do not simply speak for themselves, but possibly tell us more about organizational practices and power relations within society. If an incident occurs where the police are faced with a case of violence in the home and their organizational and discretionary definitions of domestic violence are not capable of categorizing this, we cannot then say it did not happen! In addition, even if the police do act in such circumstances, the courts may categorize such incidents as 'trivial' in comparison to other crimes – despite the severity of the offence (Edwards 1990). Quite simply, if a crime act does not enter the statistics then, officially at least, it did not occur. For these reasons official statistics on crime are criticized by researchers for revealing little about violence against women, in particular (Kelly and Radford 1987), and more generally, for their sexist nature (Oakley and Oakley 1979; Ginn and Duggard 1994).

Officially, the procedures and ideas through which an act becomes a crime statistic look like the stages shown in Table 2.

If we move away from the formal definition in Table 2 to one which reflects the situations we have described so far, we end up not with 'facts' about crime, but the result of a series of decisions and practices which do not produce either valid or reliable outcomes. The process then becomes more like Table 3.

It appears that we cannot assume that the law applies equally to all incidents as this depends upon the initial detection of the act and the way in which the police then deal with the matter and how the criminal justice process as a whole then works (see Ashworth and Redmayne 2010). Holding aside the question as to whether the law is biased in the first instance, it was noted that this will depend on whether the incident is reported and what action is taken as a result. From surveys conducted by interviewing a random sample of the general public, estimates show that, over time, between 36 and just under 49 per cent of crimes committed on

Table 2 The stages in the process of compiling official statistics – the official version

---

The law is democratically arrived at and applied equally to all
people at all times
↓
A criminal act takes place and the law is broken
↓
The crime is known to a member of the public who reports it to
the police
↓
The police react and all similar incidents are treated in a similar
way without prejudice
↓
The offender is detected, apprehended and charged with the offence
↓
The offender is, without prejudice, subject to sanctions by the
criminal courts
↓
The initial act becomes a crime statistic

Table 3 The stages in the process of compiling official statistics – an alternative version

The law changes over time. Further, it does not apply equally to all people at all times
↓
A crime is committed, but is it reported?
↓
If reported, will the decisions of the police apply to all similar incidents in the same way?
↓
The crime may be reported, but not recorded
↓
If recorded, not all offences are included in the statistics
↓
If recorded, the perpetrator may not be apprehended by the police
↓
If detected, not all people are treated in the same way by officials in the criminal justice system, even when they have committed similar crimes
↓
Official statistics are compiled which are neither valid nor reliable

a daily basis are reported to the police (Hough and Mayhew 1983; Mirrlees-Black et al. 1998; Flatley et al. 2010). Thus, according to these estimates, between half and two-thirds of all crimes committed, on a daily basis, never even reach the attention of the police as gatekeepers of the official crime statistics.

The key elements in the alternative process as constructed in Table 3 are *interpretation*, *discretion* and differential *application* and *enforcement*. Between the construction of the law, someone breaking that law and being sanctioned for the original act, there stands the interpretation of the victim, police and other officials in the criminal justice system. Will all officials act in a similar way so we can say that they are both valid (a true picture) and reliable (always recorded in the same way)? If different people record the same incident in different ways and people are treated differently for the same crime, how can the statistics be valid? As we have seen, the decision to report a crime in the first instance, the decision to pursue a particular case and how its outcome will be determined are not neutral products applying to all people at all times. As a final example to clarify these issues, I shall consider the link between crime statistics and race.

Men from black or black British groups form approximately 1.2 per cent of the total population in the UK. In the British prison population as a whole they comprise 15 per cent (K. Jones et al. 2007). In other words, many more people from this group end up in jail in comparison with their percentage in the general population. An immediate conclusion from these statistics would seem to indicate that they are more criminal than other ethnic groups. Nevertheless, let us look at the criminal justice process to see if this is an 'objective' indicator of criminality, or the result of discriminatory decision-making.

We start, once again, with the decision to report a crime. The police are reliant upon the general population to report crimes to them. Yet evidence has shown that if an assailant is thought to be black, white people are more likely to report an offence to the police than if the same offence were committed by a white person (Carr-Hill and Drew 1988), while indirect discrimination is also evident in the criminal justice process as a whole (Webster 2007). Further, when it comes to the police detecting crime themselves, past research conducted at two London police stations found that young black males, aged 16 to 24, were ten times more likely to be stopped by the police under stop-and-search powers (C. Willis 1983); such findings remain relevant with black people being stopped and searched at six times the rate of their white counterparts (Equality and Human Rights Commission 2010). Further, even if arrested for the same offence, there are variations in the use of caution, noting of course that rates of caution depend on such thing as the severity of offence and preparedness to admit guilt (Riley et al. 2009). If then processed through the criminal courts, black people have found to be dealt with in a different way by the courts (Shallice and Gordon 1990). Of course, this might be accounted for in the differences in the offences committed. However, even where the severity of offences is controlled for, studies have found significant differences in the custody rate for black offenders over their white counterparts (Hood 1992). While the UK has not reached the problems that are evident in the United States, there remains a 'stubborn reluctance to acknowledge serious problems' (Ratcliffe 2004: 120).

What exactly is going on here? Is it a neutral process of reporting, detecting and processing criminals regardless of their race? Research into the actual process of criminal justice appears to show that statistics which link race and crime are not neutral, but the product of a series of discriminatory decisions. Following an examination of UK government policies over time and their effects upon ethnic inequality, one study concludes that with respect to the criminal justice system there has been 'minimal progress towards the aim of increasing trust and confidence among minority ethnic groups' (Phillips 2009: 195). The creation of racial stereotypes within the criminal justice system has an indirect impact on attitudes and actions which, in turn, construct the crime statistics. For this reason, a consortium representing some 31 organizations associated with criminal justice pointed in the mid-1990s to the need for programmes which aimed 'to combat discrimination in the criminal justice process'

(Penal Affairs Consortium 1996: 8). It is important to bear in mind that issues of race, while of clear significance in the interpretation of these findings, also interact with other variables: for example, those of class, age, gender and belief systems.

We have seen the problems associated with the construction of criminal statistics. From the decision to report a crime, through the police decision to pursue an investigation, to the courts' decision to sanction offenders – if they are caught – a number of different practices leads to a variable outcome. For these reasons, we should treat official statistics on crime with considerable caution. Nevertheless, these issues are not so clear cut and, as we shall see in the next section, there exists a debate on the use of official statistics as a resource for conducting social research.

OFFICIAL STATISTICS: THE DEBATES

We have considered the means by which one of the most contentious sources of official statistics are compiled. However, in order to enable the reader to consider the issues surrounding their use, it is important to bear in mind two points. First, what *type* of official statistics are we talking about? Second, what is the *aim* of the research which is either compiling or examining these statistics? Official statistics will vary in terms of not only their accuracy – statistics of birth rates compared, for example, with crime statistics – but also the way in which they are compiled. Thus, these considerations will affect our judgements about their utility for analysis. Further, what are the statistics being used for? You may wish to examine statistics on crime as an indicator of the incidence of drug taking. On the other hand, perhaps the police are concentrating on drug taking and while this will mean an increase in the statistics, you decide not to examine the accuracy of the statistics themselves, but use them as an indicator of police practices. The aim of this project would be very different from one wishing to discover the incidence of drug use in the population as distinct from interpretative procedures. Having made these points, attention will now be turned to the debates between schools of thought on official statistics.

For the sake of illustration, we can divide perspectives on official statistics into three broad schools of thought. First, the *realist* school, second, the *institutionalist* school, and finally, the *radical* school of thought. What do these three terms mean? The realist school is not to be confused with realism as covered in the first part of the book. Broadly speaking this school is characterized as taking official statistics to be objective indicators of the phenomena to which they refer. As a result, they may be characterized as drawing their inspiration from positivism and empiricism.

The institutionalist school of thought rejects the idea that official statistics are objective indicators of the social conditions they seek to describe. Instead, it considers official statistics as neither valid nor reliable indicators of objective phenomena. For the institutionalists, official statistics will tell us more about an organization's behaviour or the discretionary actions of individuals within them, rather than the phenomenon itself. In the above example on drug use, the institutionalists would argue that statistics on drug use tell us more about an organization's priorities and the actions of its representatives, than about the amount of drugs which the population are taking at any one time. This is why people refer to the 'iceberg phenomenon' when it comes to crime statistics: that is, all we ever see is the tip of the iceberg and most crime is out of sight and undetected. This school of thought therefore parallels idealism, in terms of its emphasis upon the social construction of statistics, as discussed in Chapter 1.

Finally, there is the radical perspective. While agreeing with the institutionalists that such statistics represent an organization's priorities or are the product of discretionary practices, the radical perspective would locate these within a wider theory of the dynamics and structure of society. For instance, the government compiles social statistics on the health and income of the nation which itself could be argued to facilitate the order and regulation of the population (Foucault 1980; Squires 1990):

> Central to the possibility of modern forms of government, we argue, are the associations formed between entities constituted as 'political' and the projects, plans and practices of those authorities – economic, legal, spiritual, medical, and technical – who endeavour to administer the lives of others in the light of conceptions of what is good, healthy, normal, virtuous, efficient or profitable. Knowledge is thus central to these activities of government and to the very formation of its objects, for government is a domain of cognition, calculation, experimentation and evaluation.
>
> (N. Rose and Miller 2008: 55)

From a perspective more informed by critical theory, to this group we could add the ways in which the police concentrate on and process more working-class crime because this group are relatively less powerful and their crimes more visible compared to middle-class groups (Hall et al. 1978). Thus, we should note that those whom I have placed in this school of thought might not necessarily 'read off' official statistics as indicative of underlying structures of power: for example, along the dimensions of race, class and gender. Michel Foucault's pluralist theory of power, for instance, does not lend itself to such a mode of analysis (see May and

Powell 2008: Chapter 10). Statistics are also analysed in terms of their effects as *products* as well as in terms of being *constructions*, 'because the definitions used are determined by organizations and are usually imposed upon the subjects of statistics irrespective of the meaningfulness of these categorizations to the subject' (Thomas 1996: 32).

What are the effects of this production and construction of official statistics in practice? Take the example of child abuse. Who are the people who sexually abuse children? They are typified to us through the newspapers, television and other media in particular ways. So what is our *typical* offender? The impression is often of someone who lurks in an old raincoat near children's playgrounds and school playing fields; they are isolated and inadequate individuals whose inadequacies constitute a danger to children. The police, in their turn, police public areas, not the private homes of individuals. They seek those individuals who may fit this stereotype and act on it by using grounds of 'reasonable suspicion'. Some individuals are apprehended who reflect this stereotype and it appears that its 'truth' has been established. However, as one writer on child abuse has noted: 'The closer to home the abuse, the more ambivalent the legal and indeed the popular response' (Viinikka 1989: 132).

The accounts of incest survivors, coupled with the work of the feminist movement, have brought such issues more into the public arena. This has resulted in changes in the practices of the police and other agencies, such as social services. The question remains, however, as to whether this is but an act of trying to maintain the legitimacy of the family as a 'safe' institution. More critical accounts of this process suggest that the compilation of these statistics reflects the notion of an ideal family and that 'every man's home is his castle'. To this extent, changes do not challenge underlying relations of patriarchy concerning the power that men exercise over women and children (Radford and Stanko 1996).

Considering this issue we can say that the more private and invisible from the gaze of agents of social control (including social services), the less the chance of detection of child abuse (the feminist criticism of the public/private dichotomy). Indeed, evidence suggests that such abuse is far more widespread than the statistics would have us believe (Driver 1989; Coleman and Moynihan 1996). If child abuse takes place in families or those institutions that seek to protect particular ideas of their status among the public and their followers, its rates of detection may be lower and related, as noted earlier, by class, cultural and religious factors (McKie 2005). Thus, the stranger may constitute a risk to children, but the abuser may be a close relative, friend or acquaintance.

Given this state of affairs, it is argued by critics of official statistics that they help to generate myths by reflecting power relations and ideologies within society – in this case the 'familial' ideology of the harmonious and secure institution of the family. Of course, this is not to suggest that an abuser may not be a 'stranger', simply that official definitions distort the idea of those who are mostly responsible for this offence, as well as its underlying causes (Hester et al. 1996).

Earlier on I quoted a statistic noting how many crimes committed are actually reported to the police. If the official statistics are so inadequate, how did I know this? At regular intervals since 1982 (see Hough and Mayhew 1983, 1985; Mirrlees-Black et al. 1998; Flatley et al. 2010), the Home Office has undertaken random surveys of the population in England, Wales and Scotland (from 1993 Scotland had its own survey). By asking people questions about their experiences of crime, a picture is formed of the number of crimes committed in England and Wales, but which are not reported to the police for various reasons. The results of this self-report study have been used in comparison with official statistics as recorded by the police. It is then possible to compensate for deficiencies in validity and reliability using these data. Therefore, what seems to be needed is the employment of more accurate methods in order to account, objectively, for certain patterns of behaviour in society.

The above point noted, the *British Crime Survey* (BCS) still has its limitations. For instance, going back to the example of domestic violence, if a woman is interviewed with a male partner present, will she admit to being a victim of domestic violence when the perpetrator is in such close proximity? As the authors of these reports note, some violent incidents, such as domestic violence and sexual violence, are issues that may be too sensitive for people to admit to interviewers (Mirrlees-Black et al. 1996: 27). On the other hand, the BCS is argued to correct for a lack of validity and reliability in police statistics, while the researchers themselves are aware of these issues and seek to compensate accordingly. Thus, a new method of computerized self-completion questionnaire has been introduced in subsequent surveys to address this issue.

In terms of thinking about different forms of offence, the BCS allows researchers to note that, approximately 90 per cent of thefts of vehicles are reported to the police (Flatley et al. 2010). Researchers could then use official records upon which to base a sample of people to interview, bearing in mind this high rate of reporting (May 1986). However, if researchers wished to conduct a study on the incidence of thefts *from*, as opposed to thefts *of* cars, it is estimated that only 43 per cent are reported to the police (Flatley et al. 2010: 85). Thus, realists would argue that official statistics do have their uses, as long as one is aware of the limitations and types of data that are being utilized.

In the history of approaches to official statistics, contributors to one volume regarded them as in need of 'demolition' and 'demystification' (Irvine et al. 1979), while there are those who utilize such data for the purposes of exposing the ways in which they reflect power relations (see Dorling and Simpson 1999). This requires an understanding of the modes in which they are constructed and it is the institutionalists who focus on these social practices. Within this research tradition there are classic studies: for example, Max Atkinson (1978) on the social organization of suicide and Aaron Cicourel (1976) on juvenile justice. Atkinson's work on the topic of suicide is particularly interesting because it charts his change of research focus from the influence of Durkheim (1952) to a focus influenced by the work of Garfinkel (1967).

This latter approach abandons the idea that suicide statistics represent facts about a certain type of behaviour (what has been termed the 'realist' position). Additionally, they are not simply regarded as indicative of wider power relations and structures in society (the radical position) and are examined as 'accomplishments'. In Atkinson's (1978) study, he focuses on the methods by which coroners formulate judgements and categorize deaths as suicide. This does not assume that there is a 'shared definition' which coroners employ which, as noted in the discussion on crime statistics, is problematic. As soon as the idea that officials do not simply share definitions from which their practices can be 'read off' is abandoned, the aim of the research changes. This avoids the problems that come from trying to reconcile the theoretical categories of the researcher with the organizational and legal definitions themselves.

Instead of assuming the prior existence of a definition – theoretical or legal – that could explain the decisions of coroners, Atkinson (1978) turned his attention to an investigation of the factors which surrounded the circumstances of the death in relation to the coroners' judgements of it as suicide: for example, the presence of suicide notes, previous threats of suicide, the mode, location and circumstances of the death and the biography of the deceased. He therefore examined the methods that coroners used in categorizing sudden death. We have now moved away from facts, to the method of their construction. As John Heritage (1984) notes, social research now considers

> what counts as 'reasonable fact' in a casual conversation, in a court-room, a scientific laboratory, a news interview, a police interroga-tion, a medical consultation or a social security office? What is the nature of the social organization within which these facts find support? To what vicissitudes, exigencies and considerations are the formulation of these facts responsive?
>
> (Heritage 1984: 178)

An examination of the process, not the product, is the institutionalist approach to official statistics. The methods that officials who are respon-sible for their compilation employ become the topics of research. Unlike the radical approach, the analysis does not fit within a more general theory of social and political organization: for example, a Marxist approach to the processing of the working classes by the criminal justice system as symptomatic of wider capitalist relations (I. Taylor et al. 1973).

SUMMARY

Social research has become increasingly dominated by the government and its agencies (Bulmer 1986b). Within the UK researchers may enjoy access to some of what has been described as the 'best official statistics available anywhere', but 'they have been reduced in scope' (Bechhofer and Paterson 2000: 61) and government cuts in spending led to even less. Thus, although social researchers enjoy some discretion in the design and execution of such research, there is also a need to be concerned over government control of official information in what may be characterized as the 'surveillance society' (Lyon 2001).

It is not difficult to find controversies between statisticians and their political pay masters over the validity of procedures, or the consequences of decisions to cut particular surveys for our understanding of societies, trends and the impacts of policies. For these reasons we find that the production of accurate information has been the subject of routine questioning and critique (Dorling and Simpson 1999), as well as how social scientists can end up providing sets of justifications for government policies and practices that are not legitimate (Allen and Imrie 2010). The sources of criticism are not simply from those who are dismissive about their utility. The concern focuses upon how they may be rendered problematic for the purposes of conducting research into a number of important issues. Take, for instance, the measurement of poverty. A series of reports by the Department of Social Security entitled *Households below Average Income* did not even accept, or employ, a meaningful definition of poverty (Townsend 1996). This shows, as a Government Statisticians' Collective have written, that

> statistics do not, in some mysterious way, emanate directly from the social conditions they appear to describe, but that between the two lie the assumptions, conceptions and priorities of the state and the social order, a large, complex and imperfectly functioning bureaucracy, tonnes of paper and computing machinery, and – last but not least – millions of hours of human grind.
>
> (Government Statisticians' Collective 1993: 163)

It is the last part of this quote that indicates that there may be something positive to gain from the use of official statistics. Researchers have long argued that while they have their problems, they are still useful for research purposes. Contrary to some critics, official statistics are said to produce interesting findings on contemporary society which, despite their shortcomings, have been used by radical and realist researchers alike. The conceptual issues faced by those who compile official statistics are not dissimilar to those faced by social researchers in general and they provide useful empirical data for the production of knowledge about society and social relations (Bulmer 1984b).

If researchers become more aware of how these errors occur, they can correct for shortfalls, but there is good reason to be concerned over their accuracy and potential for political manipulation, but this does not prevent researchers from taking imaginative approaches to their use through the use of supplementary data and approaches (for example, see Bhat et al. 1988; Levitas 1996; Dorling and Simpson 1999; Fahmy et al. 2008). Official statistics can be useful, but that is not to suggest that you cannot still 'lie with statistics' (Huff 1993).

We should also be aware that particular statistics reflect sets of practices whose rationale for compilation may be outdated. One notable source of contention is in the area of economic data where narrow measures of supposed 'success' say nothing about levels of inequality within a society that, in turn, relates to the general health of a population (Wilkinson and Pickett 2010). They also say nothing about what are unsustainable practices in the face of depleting natural resources and climate change. As Tim Jackson (2009) writes about Gross Domestic Product (GDP), as a measure of total household, government spending and investment, it fails

> to account properly for changes in the asset base; to incorporate the real welfare losses from having an unequal distribution of income; to adjust for the depletion of material resources and other forms of natural capital; to capture the external costs of pollution and long-term environmental damage; to account for the costs of crime, car accidents, industrial accidents, family breakdown and others social costs; to correct for 'defensive' expenditures and positional consumption or to account for non-market services such as domestic labour and voluntary care.
>
> (Jackson 2009: 179)

Due to their susceptibility to political manipulation, the debate will continue and rightly so if researchers are to remain sensitive to their advantages and pitfalls. The realist will look for more accurate techniques for generating such information; the radical will criticize and use such information as indicative of more immediate or wider power inequalities in society, while the institutionalist will concentrate on the process of their production.

In practice, such neat theoretical divisions may often break down when it comes to the work of understanding for the purposes of policy intervention. Each of these approaches, therefore, is not as incommensurable as is sometimes suggested. We should also note that official statistics do not simply exist independently of the actions of those who compile them, they also feed back into everyday practices. It is not simply the process (the institutionalists) or the product (the realists) which should be part of the research focus, but the ways in which the process affects the product and vice versa. After all, official statistics are formulated by the actions of individuals within organizational settings and by governmental policies. Organizational statistics can then generate a view of the world which feeds back into those practices and constructs particular images of individuals and their actions. This much is evident from research in organizations (du Gay 1996; May 2006b, 2007). A circle is then formed, rather than the straight lines of examining construction or uncritically utilizing the final product. From this point of view we investigate how people are 'made up' by statistics. In the process we could discover how a particular category is produced for their classification and its effects, *alongside* their emergence as a distinct group (Hacking 1986; Bowker and Star 2002).

As described in the first section of this chapter, official statistics are mainly based upon the use of surveys which are a central method of social research. As a main aim of this book is to examine the place and use of particular methods in social research, Chapter 5 is devoted to this topic.

Questions for your reflection

1 What are the different types of official statistics that are available to the social researcher?

2 Bearing in mind your answer to the first question, why do you think they are produced and what are they are used for?

3 In what ways are criminal statistics both similar to and different from other forms of official statistics and why?

4 What is your perspective on the use of official statistics? Consider this question with reference to issues associated with the economy and climate change and resource constraint.

SUGGESTED FURTHER READING

Dorling, D. and Simpson, S. (eds) (1999) *Statistics in Society: The Arithmetic of Politics*. London: Arnold.

Government Statisticians' Collective (1993) How official statistics are produced: Views from the inside [originally published 1979], in M. Hammersley (ed.) *Social Research: Philosophy, Politics and Practice*. London: Sage.

Levitas, R. and Guy, W. (eds) (1996) *Interpreting Official Statistics*. London: Routledge.

Worldwatch Institute (2010) *State of the World: Transforming Cultures from Consumerism to Sustainability*. New York: W.W. Norton.

5 Social surveys: design to analysis
With Carole Sutton

This chapter provides an introduction to survey method and specifically offers practical guidance on how to conduct a survey. First, it looks at types of surveys. Second, it considers the logic of survey method. Third, it looks at survey research design, including sampling. Fourth, it outlines the stages in survey construction, including types of questionnaires and designing and testing questions. Fifth, it looks at methodological innovation in relation to the use of new technologies in the social survey. Sixth, it considers the analysis of survey data, and finally, it considers the survey in critical perspective.

The image of a person standing in a crowded shopping centre with a clipboard, stopping people, asking them questions and then ticking boxes, is a common one. While this is often market research, the use of surveys is also a central part of social research as they provide a rapid and relatively inexpensive way of discovering the characteristics and beliefs of the population at large. Survey method is frequently employed in social research and is used by government, academic researchers in universities and campaigning organizations alike. Nearly all surveys are character- ized by the collection of data from large, or even very large, numbers of people. They can range from relatively small local surveys of just a couple of hundred people to large-scale national surveys of several thousand. The planning of a social survey requires attention to both the research design and the method of data collection. Virtually all surveys aim to describe or explain the characteristics or opinions of a population through the use of a representative sample. A population can be anything from all of the inhabitants of a country such as France or the United States, to the users of a local train service.

Large-scale government surveys, such as the British General Household Survey, collect a wide range of socio-economic data, on a regular basis. This allows a description not just of the changing characteristics of 'households', but of British social life in general. Local government and health authorities use surveys to gather data that is used to benchmark their surveys, for example, the UK Place Survey and Patient Survey. Campaigning organizations often use surveys to measure support for their cause, while academic researchers often use surveys to test aspects of sociological, psychological or political theory.

TYPES OF SURVEYS

Surveys have been characterized under four headings: factual, attitudinal, social psychological and explanatory (Ackroyd and Hughes 1983). First, factual surveys are one of the earliest types to be used systematically in Britain. They aim to gain information from individuals concerning their material situation rather than attitudes or opinions as such. The cost of these surveys is an important consideration: to interview everyone in a population would be prohibitively expensive. For this reason, the Census takes place only once every ten years and is not a sample, but a total *enumeration* of the population. Other surveys of samples are run annu- ally gathering in-depth data on different topics. These include the Labour Force Survey and General Lifestyle Survey.

The second type of survey moves away from an interest in the material conditions of the population, towards the use of surveys for gaining data on attitudes: for example, what people think about life in general and events in particular. This constitutes a shift away from the so-called 'hard data' basis of factual surveys. The idea of public opinion is perhaps the key to this type of survey. For countries with democratic aspirations, it is important that they gauge the beliefs of their citizens. Often a policy is justified by 'what the public demands'. However, how do we know what the public demands? Attitude surveys can fulfil the function of providing this information. The Northern Ireland Life and Times (NILT) survey collects data on a wide range of topics including opinions on policy outcomes relating to the Good Friday Agreement (see www.ark.ac.uk/nilt).

Political opinion polls also fall into this category. These attempt to predict how people will vote. Therefore, there is an assumed correspondence between what people say they will do and what they will actually do (will someone who says they are going to vote Liberal Democrat in the UK actually do so on the day?). On average, the polls are said to be fairly accurate. This does not suggest that one individual poll is correct, but that if you calculate the average results of all the polls, they will predict the outcome. Occasionally this fails when, for example in 1992, opinion polls failed to predict the result of the British general election. Conversely, in 1997, opinion pollsters accurately predicted the scale of the Labour victory, and in 2010 pollsters accurately predicted the hung parliament with a resulting coalition between two of the main political parties. One reason for the improved poll accuracy was that analysis of the 1992 poll predictions showed that Conservative voters were more likely either to refuse to answer opinion poll questions, or to give answers inconsistent with the way they actually voted. Once this bias was known, pollsters could 'weight' their polls accordingly. Nevertheless, attempts at accurate measurement of opinions do not address the argument that the polls themselves do not simply reflect, but also structure public opinion (C. Marsh 1979).

The results of using attitude surveys developed other interests among researchers, in particular, the relationship between attitudes and behaviour. In this sense, both the social psychological and explanatory surveys are more theoretically oriented. The measurement of attitudes has become the subject of many an academic paper. The question is exactly how do you measure attitudes? Attention is also focused on the relationship between attitudes and behaviour: quite simply, does the possession of a certain attitude necessarily mean a person will then behave in a particular way? However, this change in focus was not so much an interest in attitudes themselves, but in attitudes as one characteristic of the 'personality' of an individual. By building up a profile of personality types – using attitude questions among other techniques – it is believed possible to explain a person's behaviour. These developments within social psychology led to a movement away from an interest in general statistical profiles of the population – as in factual and attitude surveys – to a concern with small group behaviour.

To some extent all surveys are explanatory. They ask questions about, say, voting behaviour and seek to explain how people's attitudes or intentions are linked to their background or other *explanatory variable*. However, explanatory surveys are specifically designed to test hypotheses which are derived from theories: for example, Durkheim's (1952) idea that suicide is inversely related to social integration.

THE LOGIC OF SURVEY METHOD

Surveys have their origin in the positivistic tradition (described in Chapter 1), but to describe contemporary surveys as simply 'positivist' is not accurate. Surveys do employ a methodology that has similarities to those used in the physical sciences (see M. Williams 2000: Chapter 3). While some surveys explicitly set out to test theories and some aim to construct theories, all begin with at least some theoretical assumptions.

Good survey research follows a common process in the testing and development of a theory (even though in the latter case, because theory is being developed, the researcher may begin only with a 'hunch') whereby a hypothesis or hypotheses will be formed. A *hypothesis* is conjecture which is deduced from a theory, which if found to be true would support the theory. Conversely, if it is found to be false, all or part of the theory is rejected. The question of confirmation and falsification of theories is complex and controversial (see M. Williams and May 1996: Chapter 2), but usually researchers seek statistical evidence for a theory rather than 'proof'. It is often said that surveys aim to show causal relationships: for example, what 'causes' people to migrate from one part of a country to another? Might it be low wages, unemployment, or the desire for career advancement? For the most part, however, surveys can show only the strength of statistical association between *variables* – literally any attribute or characteristic that can vary. For instance, if we were interested in the relationship between the variables of migration and unemployment, we might hypothesize that it is more *probable* that an unemployed person will migrate than an employed person.

Because surveys measure facts, attitudes or behaviour through questions, it is important that hypotheses can be *operationalized* into *measures*. This means that they must be turned into questions that respondents (the people who answer the questions) can understand and are able to answer. The answers must then be capable of categorization and quantification. Having collected and analysed the data, the researcher is then in a position to decide whether the hypotheses have been confirmed or falsified and what this means for the theory. While it is possible that a single survey will wholly 'confirm' or 'falsify' a theory, this is unlikely and the usual outcome is the amendment of the theory in light of the new findings. This, in turn, generates the material for new hypotheses and new surveys.

Survey research aims to remove as much bias from the research process as possible and produce results that are replicable by following the same methods, the first of which is *standardization*. This refers to the conditions under which a survey is conducted, but specifically how a questionnaire is designed, administered and analysed:

> The crucial assumption here is that of 'equivalence of stimulus'; that is, we have to rely on the interviewer's skill to approach as nearly as possible the notion that every respondent has been asked the same questions, with the same meaning, in the same words, same intonation, same sequence, in the same setting and so on.
>
> (Oppenheim 1992: 67)

The assumption is that if the above is the case and if a difference in opinion is expressed in reply to those questions, the resulting variations can be attributed to a 'true' difference of opinion, rather than as a result of how the question was asked or the context of the interview. Thus questionnaires concentrate upon the replies of respondents within a *structured* interviewing situation (see Chapter 6). Their responses and characteristics are then quantified and aggregated with others in the survey sample, in order to examine patterns or relationships between them by employing the techniques of statistical analysis.

Second, there is *replicability*. It should be possible for other researchers to replicate the survey using the same type of sampling, questionnaire and process. A replication of a survey producing the same results with different groups at different times will increase confidence in the first findings. This also relates to *reliability* and *validity*. A survey should aim to be both reliable, whereby we obtain the same result from the same measurement on different occasions and valid, whereby it measures what it is intended to measure:

> In fact, it is not the measure that is valid or invalid but the use to which the measure is put. We might use educational level to measure social status. The issue is not whether we have measured education properly but whether this is a suitable measure of social status.
>
> (de Vaus 2002a: 53)

Reliability can be assessed using the test-retest method, where respondents are asked the same questions twice and the correlation measured. Alternatively, a split-half method may be deployed where items are divided into two matched halves (Moser and Kalton 1971: 353–5). While these measures exist, reliability is best addressed through the construction and piloting of survey questions. While reliability and validity are inter-twined, a reliable measure may not be a valid measure for it may measure something different from its original intention.

Finally, there is *representativeness*. As it is the intention to make gener-alizing claims about a population, it is important not only that the sample is representative of the population, but also that the findings are statisti-cally significant, that is, whether they are larger or smaller than would be expected by chance alone. Now let us turn to the important topic of research design and sampling.

SURVEY RESEARCH DESIGN

The research design provides the framework for the collection and analysis of data from a population. The population may be characterized into different social groupings selected according to the research topic: for example, age, gender, class and income. These background data are used as the control for exploring differences and similarities in the generated data. Using a cross-sectional design, this captures data at one point in time and selects sufficient cases according to those background charac-teristics that are then used to detect relationships and associations. In the case of political polls, different voting patterns will then be examined for associations by gender, class and age. Repeated cross-sectional designs capture data at two or more time points, with either a new set of respondents or follow up on the initial respondents as part of a longitu-dinal design.

Sampling

Surveys, through the use of questionnaires, measure some characteristic or opinion of its respondents. Depending upon its aims, the procedures it adopts and the number of people who are interviewed, generalization can then take place from the sample of people interviewed to the population as a whole:

> A sample is a portion or a subset of a larger group called a popula-tion. The population is the universe to be sampled. Sample popula-tions might include all Americans, residents of California during the 1994 earthquake, and all people over 85 years of age ... A good sample is a miniature version of the population – just like it, only smaller.
>
> (Fink 1995: 1)

It is important that the sample characteristics will be the same as those of the population. For this reason, sampling is central to survey design.

There are many types of samples but all samples are either probability samples (often called random samples) or non-probability samples. Strictly speaking only probability (or random) samples allow a statistical generalization from sample to population. However, for reasons described below, it is not always possible to use such a sample.

Probability samples

Probability samples are so called because it is possible to express the mathematical probability of sample characteristics being reproduced in the population. An important principle is that each person in the population of interest has an equal chance of being part of the sample. The population can be anything from the population of a country, or a town, to a doctor's list of patients. The Postcode Address Finder (PAF) for Great Britain is often used to locate households for some large UK government surveys. However, what is vital for a probability sample is that a complete (or as complete as possible) list of the population exists. This 'list' is called a *sampling frame* and from this a sample is randomly selected. Hence the other name for this type of sampling is *random*. Random in this case does not refer to a haphazard selection of names, or addresses, but instead means mathematically random whereby each person or address in the sampling frame is given a unique number starting at one and a mathematically random selection of the sample is then made. Usually this is done with the aid of a computer or specially produced random number tables (de Vaus 2002a: 72).

The most basic 'simple random sampling' technique is where the sample is randomly selected from the entire sampling frame: for example 500 people from 5000. However, it can be a problematic technique to adopt for a variety of reasons that include availability of resources and sample accuracy (de Vaus 2002a: 71). This leads us to modify the 'simple' design.

Suppose our sampling frame was a list of all voters in a particular county or state – say 300,000 people – we would need to find a method that would obviate the need to select randomly from all of these people. In this case we might use *multistage cluster sampling* whereby our initial sampling frame might be a district, or electoral wards within the county or state. The sampling may be in several stages, but in each the random procedure remains the same. In a two-stage procedure we may select 20 out of 200 electoral wards and, having obtained those, select voters from within those wards.

Sometimes the researchers' concern is that the group they are interested in is fully represented in the sample. In this case a *stratified random sample* may be used whereby a stratification according to characteristics such as age group, gender, type of housing, and so on is first made and then a random sample drawn from each of the stratified lists. This allows

researchers to weight the sample – in other words over-represent a particular characteristic. In both these modifications of probability sampling,
some care is required to ensure accurate representation (Moser and
Kalton 1971: 111–16).

Finally, there is *systematic random sampling*. Here the researcher
begins by selecting a random number as a start and then systematically
samples every *n*th person, household and so on. The issue here is that
the systematic nature of the sampling can build in bias through a
common characteristic. The best way to illustrate this is through a survey
of residents in high-rise flats in London that asked them about the quality
of their housing. Results showed that a frequent complaint was noisy
lifts. However, every fourth flat has been selected and because of a
common building design, it was always the one closest to a lift! While
it was a legitimate concern, the results were not representative of all
the flats.

Non-probability samples

Probability sampling requires the existence of some sort of sampling
frame and importantly the size of *n* must be known. This is not always
the case or perhaps no sampling frame is available. In these cases the
researcher must use a non-probability sample. In the case of theory-
building, generalization from a sample to population may not be so
important, while in other cases, such as market research, statistical
accuracy may be less of a concern than being 'fit for purpose'. The manu-
facturer of chocolate bars is interested only in finding out how many
chocolate bars might be sold and to whom. If a cheaper sampling method
is taken to deliver the results then that is likely to be considered 'good
enough'.

Market research has used quota sampling. Here the general characteristics of a population are often known from other data; for example, the
Census. Here the proportion of people in particular groups or classes is
known beforehand. This method is often used for street interviewing and
while arguably representative if people are properly selected, it often
suffers from bias due to the selection process. A researcher who is required
to interview 20 people between the ages of 25 and 45, may pick those
people who are more obviously in that age group thereby omitting people
at the extremes of the age distribution.

Purposive sampling occurs where a selection is made according to a
known characteristic, such as being a politician or trade union leader and
is often used in political polling. Numbers may be small and once again,
the 'fit for purpose' defence may be deployed. Similarly, newspapers,
radio stations and websites often use availability samples asking people
to phone in their views on topical matters or complete online surveys, the
representativeness of which should be treated with considerable caution.

Organizations, such as pressure groups or charities, also obtain information through leaving questionnaires in particular places for members of the public to complete (van Zijl 1993).

When a population is widely distributed or elusive, such as homeless people or intravenous drug users, snowball sampling may be the only way of obtaining survey data. In this approach initial contact may be made with a member of the population who will lead the researcher to other members of the same population (also see Chapter 7). Here generalization is not really legitimate, mainly because we have no idea of the size of the population. At the same time, this method has proved valuable as a means of learning about a population prior to using techniques designed to estimate the size of a given population (Sudman et al. 1988).

Sample size

How large should a sample, *n*, be? There is no simple or straightforward answer. There are many factors that should be considered and the goal for most researchers is to gather enough data to undertake meaningful analyses. As we have seen from the discussion above, if we have sufficient information about the population then we should consider drawing a probability based sample. Where population characteristics are known and a sufficient sampling frame exists, then we can draw a representative sample using one of the random sampling techniques.

A researcher will wish to draw a sufficient size of sample in order to be able to measure differences or *variability* in the sample and to use these findings as estimates of the population. Sample size will depend on the size of the population, the amount of *variability* in the measure and the size of the *effect* to be captured. In general terms it is worth noting that a large population may not necessarily require a larger sample size and the greater the variability in the variable, or what is being measured, the larger the required sample size. In cases of research where only small *effects* are expected in the population, such as exploratory medical research, a larger sample may be required. Here power analyses are a useful tool to determine sample size requirements (see Gravetter and Wallnau 2005).

With a probability sample the researcher on average aims to collect data that has a similar distribution to the population value. The aim is to minimize the difference between the true population value, known as the parameter and the value collected in the sample, known as the sample statistic. This difference is known as the *sampling error*. Thus, if the population average weekly income, measured by the mean, is $4000 and the average weekly income of the sample is $5000, there is a sampling error of $1000. While larger sample sizes are generally better, doubling the sample size does not halve the sampling error. There is a sample size (~1200 cases) after which there is only a small reduction in the margin of error (~3 per cent). A rule of thumb is that the smaller the population, the bigger the ratio of sample to population has to be (de Vaus 2002a: 80–2).

There are online sample size calculators available to calculate sample sizes for different size populations (for an example, see the Survey System Sample Size calculator at www.surveysystem.com/sscalc.htm). At a practical level sampling decisions are made in the context of resources available with financial costs and time key factors. A researcher will often take calculated decisions on what is realistic and achievable within the funding allocation and time frame for a project. One further consideration here is estimates of non-response and the impact of the characteristics of the non-respondents on the representativeness of the final data collected. Where non-probability sampling techniques are used, the size of sample is less precise with the principle that the sample size should be large enough to gather the data that you require. Such instances will require the researcher to take into account the representativeness of different groups or subgroups within the target population.

SURVEY CONSTRUCTION

Moving away from the place of questionnaires in social research, research design and methods of sampling, this section looks at some of the key issues in the construction of surveys.

Preliminary work

Having identified the underlying theory or theories informing the potential research, there is a great deal of preliminary work to do before designing the questionnaire. First, it is crucial to have spent time reading around the topic of interest to see what theories other researchers have held and what research has already been conducted. From a solid base of familiarity with the topic, it is possible to develop testable hypotheses, but a crucial question is whether or not a survey is the best way to approach the research. In some cases, research questions may require a *multi-method* approach.

Having decided that a survey is appropriate to the research question, decisions must be made about who the population is, how they will be sampled and what type of questionnaire should be used. If you were interested in educational achievement and/or opportunity, the population may not necessarily be those still in education, but instead those who have left. While the research question may be about the views held by, say, the US population as a whole, it may be more meaningful to think in terms of different populations. Those who had left education would be in a position to take an overall and retrospective view of their experience, while still in education would offer insights on their day-to-day experiences. The current or past experience of education is what defines them as different populations.

Sampling decisions are bound up closely with the survey's target population. Furthermore, the unit of analysis – that is the person or thing being studied – may not be an individual, but may be a household, political party, school or college etc. In the case of households, although individuals may respond to the questionnaire, the analyses produced will be the characteristics of the household, rather than the specific individuals who answer the questions.

Types of questionnaires

The type of population, the nature of the research question and the resources available will determine the type of questionnaire to be used. Traditionally data collection in surveys is conducted mainly through three types of questionnaires: the mail or *self-completion* questionnaire, the *telephone* survey and the *face-to-face* interview schedule (Aldridge and Levine 2001). More recent developments have seen an increase in the use of internet based surveys, which are covered in a later section.

Mail or self-completion questionnaire

The mail or self-completion questionnaire offers a relatively cheap method of data collection over the personal interview. As its name implies, it is intended for the respondent to fill out themselves. As a result, once the questionnaire is sent out after the pilot work, the researcher has little control over the completion of the survey. A covering letter explaining the purpose of the questionnaire and stressing the need for cooperation and the anonymity of replies is therefore required. At the same time the questionnaire provides people with a medium for the anonymous expression of beliefs: for example, in researching an organization in times of rapid change where feelings ran high, this method provided an outlet for the anonymous expression of strongly held views which were further examined through other methods (May 1991). That said, unless people have an incentive, either through an interest in the subject which the survey is covering or some other basis, then response rates are likely to be low and the figure of 40 per cent, or four out of every ten people sent a questionnaire, is not uncommon. Interest in the survey will affect the response rate and this will depend on the target population. The return rates of a random sample of the general population might well be lower than a specific targeting of people with similar interests.

Once the questionnaire is sent to people's addresses or distributed for self-completion, the researcher then has no understanding of the considerations which people make in answering a question. The layout, instructions and questions must therefore be simple, clear and unambiguous. That said, mail questionnaires are cheap to administer, but you usually need to send reminders to people in order to raise response rates. Stamped addressed envelopes are required and reminders may be sent two and four weeks after posting the initial questionnaire:

> A rule of thumb is that 300 to 400 envelopes and stamps and 160 questionnaires may be needed for every 100 people in the sample (200 envelopes – outward and return – being used in the first mail-out).
>
> (Hoinville and Jowell 1987: 138)

We can now summarize the main strengths and weaknesses of mail questionnaires. First, they have a lower cost than face-to-face interviews. Second, if dealing with ethically or politically sensitive issues, their anonymity may be advantageous. Third, people can take their own time to fill in the questionnaire and consider their responses. Fourth, as interviews are not used, this could lead to less bias resulting from the way in which different interviewers ask the questions. Finally, it is possible to cover a wider geographical area at a lower cost. There are some disadvantages, however. First, it is necessary to keep questions relatively simple and straightforward as the researcher has no control over how people are interpreting the question once it has been mailed. Second, there is no possibility of probing beyond the answer that people give. Third, there is no control over who answers the questionnaire; you may wish to target women in the household, but men might fill it in instead. Fourth, the response rate may well be low and it is possible that you cannot check on the bias of the final sample.

Telephone survey
Telephone surveys are a growing part of the researcher's methodological armoury. By the mid-1980s in the United States:

> telephone surveying had become commonplace, and in many instances it is the most preferred approach to surveying. It is a methodology that has achieved a respected status as a valid means of gathering information to aid effective decision making in both the public and private sectors. In fact, much more money is spent on telephone surveys by market researchers than by public opinion pollsters and academic researchers combined.
>
> (Lavrakas 1987: 10)

At one time, this method was considered to be highly problematic due to its inbuilt bias. If you used a telephone directory (your sampling frame) several problems arise. First people will, for various reasons, opt to be ex-directory. Second, in phoning someone you may get the wrong person, or the right person at the wrong time, thus causing problems in response. Careful administrative procedures are required to arrange a suitable call-back time. Third, in many countries there is an inbuilt class and gender bias in telephone directories. It is likely that it will be the males in the household whose names will be in the phone book. Market research often uses Random Digit Dialling (RDD) to generate land line telephone numbers which in more recent years has been extended to mobile phone numbers (see www.sampleanswers.com).

The advantages of telephone surveys, as with postal surveys, are that they are convenient and relatively cheap:

> Postal surveys and telephone interview surveys can both cost roughly half as much as surveys using personal interviews, but telephone surveys have the additional advantage of greater speed.
>
> (Hakim 1987: 59)

Further, response rates may be higher as people might be less concerned about talking to someone on the phone, rather than opening a door to a caller. In addition, the monitoring of the work of telephone interviewers can be done from a central office where the dialling takes place. However, people may 'break-off' an interview more frequently than in a face-to-face situation, and the information may not be so detailed, for instance, the interviewer's ability to describe the environment of the interviewee in terms of their housing, area, lifestyle and so on.

Face-to-face interview schedule

Whether the researcher administers the questionnaire, or whether a team of researchers do, the theory is still one of standardization. However, in the face-to-face interview schedule the interviewer is also able, if required, to record the context of the interview and the non-verbal gestures of the respondent. As a result, unlike the other methods, there is a visual interactional component between interviewer and interviewee. This has both advantages and disadvantages. As Fowler (1988) notes:

> Because of the central role they play in data collection, interviewers have a great deal of potential for influencing the quality of data they collect. The management of interviewers is a difficult task, particularly in personal interviewer studies. Furthermore, the role of the interviewer is a somewhat neglected topic in many survey texts.
>
> (Fowler 1988: 107)

From this Fowler considers three roles which the interviewer has to perform in the collection of data. First, to locate and then secure the cooperation of the respondents. Second, to motivate and then guide the respondent through the questionnaire. Third, to ask questions in a clear, standardized and concise way, to record the answers carefully in accordance with the survey instructions and maintain a rapport with the respondent (Fowler 1988: 107).

In comparison with the other two methods, this method yields a high response rate, at a high cost (depending on how many interviewers are used), with a higher control of the interview situation, but at a slower speed. The actual mechanics of this process will be elaborated upon in the next section noting that the design of the questionnaire will depend upon its aims, the audience to which it is directed and the amount of resources available for conducting the research.

Designing and testing questions

The most important part of the design of questions is to construct them unambiguously and to be clear in your own mind what the question is for, who it is to be answered by and how you intend them to interpret it. You might think that the meaning of a question is clear enough, but it does not follow that the people answering the question will agree with your interpretation, thus affecting reliability and validity. This is why it is useful to conduct some initial fieldwork based either on interviews and/ or observation work with the sample. This assists the researcher in understanding the concerns of the people who are being questioned and how they might interpret particular questions.

This is the point where the *operationalization* of the hypotheses begins so it is important to establish clear definitions. Operationalization means to define a concept or variable so that it can be identified or measured (de Vaus 2002a: 47–9). If you are interested in the issue of homelessness, you must be clear and consistent about what you mean by the term (Avramov 1999). However, it is important that the definition not only of concepts in the hypotheses is clear, but also of other concepts to be used in the construction of the questionnaire. A study on homelessness may require information from respondents on their housing prior to being homeless, whether they work, the state of their health and so on. These concepts need to be turned into clear indicators so that both researcher and respondent are clear about the meanings they have. The process of clarification and question construction is aided by drawing up a list of topics that can be clarified and then turned into questions.

A useful framework for working through this process is the *descending ladder of abstraction* (de Vaus 2002a). Starting with the broad concept under study, it should be clearly defined from existing literature and/or fieldwork. The next step down is to consider the different dimensions of a concept; for example, the concept of fear of crime has dimensions according to different types of crime including a fear of crime against property and personal safety. Within each of these dimensions further subdimensions may be identified: fear of crime involving personal safety can have further subdimensions that include physical confrontations, verbal abuse and racially motivated attack. From each of these dimensions or subdimensions operational definitions can be developed from which indicators and survey questions can be devised.

The good news is that there are plenty of existing concepts with definitions and indicators, mainly relating to demographic and attitudinal measures, from a wide range of disciplines that are available to the researcher. Many of these have been developed from research work undertaken as part of government sponsored survey programmes and have been subjected to reliability and validity checks. The UK Office for National Statistics has produced a set of harmonized or standardized concepts and question sets that are used across surveys (see www.ons.gov.uk/about-statistics/harmonisation/index.html). The concepts and questions are varied including income, sexuality, educational attainment, social capital, general health, crime and fear of crime. Any use of the questions sets need careful consideration of how both the concept(s) are defined and the indicator(s) are developed before being applied to a new study. These questions can be adapted to reflect the context of new research (see www.surveynet.ac.uk).

Even if initial fieldwork is possible or standardized questions are adopted, the questionnaire still needs to be piloted on a subsample before it reaches the full sample. This pre-testing phase enables you to assess both individual questions and how the measurement tool functions as a coherent whole in the field. During this stage, after people have answered the questions, if possible it is worth having a chat with them concerning their opinions on the order of the questions, the types of questions themselves and any difficulties they experienced in answering them. Following this, it is then possible to revise the layout, question wording and design to take account of any criticisms and problems. Therefore, piloting aims to see if the questionnaire works and whether changes need to be made.

Questions also need to be asked which the target population will not only understand, but also possess the knowledge to answer (Oppenheim 1992: Chapter 8). Asking students, for example, about their experience of drug taking during the Second World War is not likely to elicit a uniform response, for this question assumes that they would have lived during this period in history. However, even if you interviewed those who lived through and remembered this period, you would also be presupposing that the sample either was aware of drug taking or engaged in it themselves. While this appears to be an extreme example, it is still possible to build in presuppositions in the design of questions which are less apparent, but which still have a direct effect upon the answer.

Types of questions

Classification questions

Classification questions are the 'personal' section of the questionnaire and are often referred to as demographic or face sheet information such as age, income, housing, and so on. For examples, see Figure 1, Questions A, B and C. The problem is that if you ask these questions at the beginning of the questionnaire, it may put people off. If you ask at the end after eliciting the person's opinions and they then refuse to answer, this may jeopardize your chances of analysing the answers according to what are known as these *explanatory variables*: for example, age being associated with certain views held by people. Quota samples mostly use these questions at the beginning of the questionnaire, otherwise it may be a waste of time if the person is not in the quota group the interviewer wishes to target.

Figure 1   Examples of questions with response categories and pre-codes included

ID			

A   Are you ...

Male   ☐ (1)

Female   ☐ (2)

B   In which way do you occupy your current accommodation?
        Please tick one category only

Own outright   ☐ (1)

Buying it with a mortgage   ☐ (2)

Part buying and part renting   ☐ (3)

Renting – social housing / local authority   ☐ (4)

Renting – private landlord   ☐ (5)

Living here rent free   ☐ (6)

Squatting   ☐ (7)

Other   ☐ (8)

Please specify _____

C Which of the following daily newspapers have you read in the last week? Please tick ALL relevant categories.

Telegraph   ☐ (1)

Independent   ☐ (1)

The Times   ☐ (1)

Financial Times   ☐ (1)

Guardian   ☐ (1)

Daily Mail   ☐ (1)

Mirror   ☐ (1)

Sun   ☐ (1)

Our local daily newspaper   ☐ (1)

Other   ☐ (1)

Please specify _____

D How worried are you about any of the following incidents occurring to you when you are on the university campus during daylight hours

	Very worried	Worried	Not worried	Not at all worried
	(4)	(3)	(2)	(1)
(a) Being mugged or robbed	☐	☐	☐	☐
(b) Being verbally insulted or pestered	☐	☐	☐	☐
(c) Being physically attacked	☐	☐	☐	☐
(d) Being sexually assaulted	☐	☐	☐	☐

The use of classification questions requires a word of explanation to the respondents, otherwise they may fail to see the need of them. You might have to stress how opinions need to be related to the kinds of people answering the questionnaire. For instance, you might be interviewing a student population and ask which course they are registered for. A general word of explanation for such questions not only adds to the chances of a good response, but also assists with the important aim of communicating the need for research and enhancing its participatory rather than parasitic nature.

Factual questions

Most surveys concern themselves with either facts or opinions. With *factual questions*, as opposed to opinions, more latitude can be given to the interviewer to probe, explain and possibly even vary the question wording in a way which would bias an opinion question. For example:

> In a housing survey it was found that many respondents reported fewer bedrooms than their houses actually contained. They simply did not think of a study, a playroom, a sewing room or a guest room as 'bedrooms' in the sense intended by the survey.
>
> (Oppenheim 1992: 125)

Probing can yield factual information that would not be readily given by a respondent in answer to the initial question. Factual questions can also included questions that aim to gather questions on an individual's *behaviour* or *knowledge*. For example, they may seek to gather information on patterns of public transport usage or information on eating or alcohol consumption patterns. The difficulty with this type of question is that the respondent may try to give the socially desirable response. In the case of alcohol consumption, answers may vary considerably depending on the nature of the survey, a market research conducted on behalf of a beer producer may illicit a higher number of beers drunk than if the same questions was asked by a doctor as a part of a health check. Furthermore, these questions lead to problems of the typicality of that behaviour and a problem of sampling periodic behaviour (Oppenheim 1992: 130–3).

Opinion questions

With *opinion questions*, wording alterations can easily elicit different answers. According to the principle of standardization, each respondent must reply as a result of unambiguous questions and not as the result of poor question wording, the way in which the question is asked, or as a result of the context of an interview. On this latter point, administering a face-to-face questionnaire to a person in front of a group of friends may well elicit a different answer from when the person is interviewed alone. Unlike questions of fact, the interviewer can only repeat the question and not elaborate upon it as this would bias the answer.

Open and closed questions

There is also the decision of where and when to use *open* or *closed questions*. Open questions give respondents a greater freedom to answer the question because they answer in a way that suits their interpretation. The interviewer then records as much as possible of the answer, which is analysed after the interview. With closed questions there is a list of categories to select from that limits the number of possible answers to be given and makes the analysis quicker and cheaper. Many questionnaires will use at least some open questions, but if it is found that many, if not most, of the questions are of this type it may be worth rethinking about whether a survey, as opposed to in-depth or semi-structured approaches, is the best way to approach the research question. Sometimes open questions will be used in the pilot or pre-test phase and the answers collected used to generate the discrete categories for a closed question.

In summary, the advantages of closed questions are that they are cheaper to use and analyse relative to open questions and they also permit comparability between people's answers. However, they also compartmentalize people into fixed replies (often considered an advantage) and they are problematic if people have not thought about the question which is asked. One report, comparing the two, suggests that open questions are a useful follow-up to closed questions (for example, 'You answered X earlier – could you tell me why you thought that?'):

> When situations are changing very quickly . . . open questions may prove the better form. Finally, as survey responses are increasingly used as a basis for historical research, open responses have the value of enabling researchers to explore raw data and to devise new coding categories.
>
> (Social and Community Planning Research 1981: 7)

Attitude scales

Within question design, attitude scales play an important role. They consist of a set of statements which the researcher has designed and the respondent is then asked to agree or disagree with the pre-coded answers. It is then possible to test a series of attitudes around a particular topic and not to rely upon one question as an indicator of a possibly complex set of attitudes (Oppenheim 1992: Chapter 10). Question D in Figure 1 is an example of what is known as a *Likert* scale, which places people's answers on an attitude continuum. Statements are devised to measure a particular aspect in which the researcher is interested; the respondent is normally invited to agree strongly, agree, neither agree nor disagree, disagree or disagree strongly with these statements.

Other scaling methods include the Osgood Semantic Differential scale, Guttman scale, Thurstone scale and Factorial scales (see Henerson et al. 1987; Fowler 1995). The Semantic Differential scale was developed as a quantitative measure of meaning on subjective dimensions. In this

Figure 2   Semantic differential scale

Good							Bad
Slow							Fast
Hot							Cool

technique, people are asked to tick a box between pairs of opposite adjectives, normally on a seven-point or ten-point scale (see Figure 2). This yields rating scales, for example, between good/bad, fast/slow, mild/strong, cool/hot, and so on. Of course, their use will depend upon the aims of the research. However, this is said not only to provide matters of opinion, but also to rate the images which people have of particular topics or items; one example would be to evaluate people's images of a product in market research. Here, projective and enabling techniques can also be used to gather data on attitudes, emotions, feelings, using a variety of methods that include word association, sentence completion, visualization and choice ordering (McGivern 2006: 201–2). Their use is advocated as an approach to overcome barriers relating to respondent awareness, irrationality, inadmissibility and politeness (Oppenheim 1992: 211).

Specific issues that also arise when using attitudinal statements include respondent avoidance of using the extreme ends of the scales known as the 'error of central tendency' and the 'halo' effect of one attitude response impacting on the next responses. In this instance, respondents may give a logical sequence by attempting to be consistent in their responses to similar attributes (McGivern 2006: 324). As discussed later, the use of new technologies can help minimize this issue.

Question wording

Having decided upon the nature and types of questions to be used, the process of actual question wording is of central importance:

> In reality, questioning people is more like trying to catch a particularly elusive fish, by hopefully casting different kinds of bait at different depths, without knowing what goes on beneath the surface!
> (Oppenheim 1992: 120–1)

Eleven points are listed below which you should consider when writing your questions. These points are not intended to be exhaustive and you are recommended to consult some more specific texts before proceeding (see Fowler and Mangione 1990; Oppenheim 1992; Schuman and Presser 1996; de Vaus 2002a).

1 Ensure that questions are not too general or insufficiently specific. 'What do you think of the Prime Minister?' is vague. Instead it would be better to break the question down (perhaps) to create attitude scales on various aspects of the Prime Minister's performance or personality.
2 Use the simplest language possible to convey the meaning of the question, bearing in mind the intended audience.
3 Avoid using prejudicial language. Apparently straightforward questions can be, unwittingly, sexist or racist in their assumptions. This is illustrated by Margrit Eichler (1988), who takes the following two questions from an interview schedule in which a person is asked to either agree or disagree:

> It is generally better to have a man at the head of a department composed of both men and women employees.

> It is acceptable for women to hold important political offices in state and national governments.

Both of these questions assume a male norm against which women are measured. Indeed, it is not possible to express a preference for a female head of department – just to agree or disagree with the statement. On the other hand, the questions could be phrased as:

> What do you think is generally better: to have a woman or a man at the head of a department that is composed of both men and women employees?

> What do you think is generally better: to have women or men hold important elected political offices in state and national government?

> (Eichler 1988: 43–4)

Answers might then range around the preference which the person answering the question has for women and men in such posts.
4 Avoid ambiguity, that is, using words with several different meanings, double negatives, or 'two questions in one', for example, 'How long have you been unemployed and in receipt of benefit?'
5 Eliminate vague words as they encourage vague answers.
6 Avoid leading questions such as 'You don't think that . . . do you?' People replying will either react negatively to your presumption or answer in accordance with what they believe to be your wishes when the aim is to discover their opinions.
7 Ensure that respondents have the necessary knowledge to answer the question.

8 Do not presume that respondents follow the patterns of behaviour you wish to know about. If you are interested in how many cigarettes people smoke a day, don't ask this straight away. You could begin with a *filter* question (no pun intended!) 'Do you smoke cigarettes?' If the answer is 'Yes', you could then ask 'And how many cigarettes do you smoke per day?'

9 Avoid hypothetical questions, which elicit hypothetical answers. People may simply shrug their shoulders and say 'Who knows?'

10 Exercise some caution in the use of personal questions for both ethical and practical reasons. Insensitive use can lead to a termination of the interview or a refusal to answer the rest of the questionnaire.

11 Recognize the problem of recall. An element of caution is required in the use of memory questions. Quite simply, people may not remember the information which is required, or it may not have had the significance in their lives which you presuppose. If the research topic involves life history consider using prompt techniques from biographical research (see B. Roberts 2002).

Finally, the order of your questions needs to be well planned and the questionnaire well laid out and word-processed; instructions on its completion to either the respondent (mail questionnaire) or interviewer (face-to-face) should be clear, unambiguous and easy to follow. Pilot work can avoid arising problems. The purpose of the questionnaire should normally be explained at the outset so that people feel involved with what you are doing. The opening question should also put people at their ease. Beginning a questionnaire with personal information concerning a person's sexual orientation is not a good start. This may seem like an obvious point, but prejudice and insensitivity can operate in less obvious ways. The questions themselves should be interesting and not simply personal; they should also relate to each other. One method is to start with broader questions and then move to more specific ones. Therefore, the order of the questionnaire is not the best *logical* sequence, but the best *social-psychological* sequence.

Categories and coding

The majority of questionnaires will have closed questions and the responses can be pre-coded to allow for the classification of responses into analysable and meaningful categories. Category answers should fulfil two criteria: they should be not only *mutually exclusive* but also *exhaustive*. In other words, it should not be possible for someone's answer to fall into two of the categories used (exclusive) and all possible answers should be encompassed by the categories chosen (exhaustive). If you are asking people about the type of housing they live in (for example, Question B in

Figure 1), the categories used should cover all possible replies from the sample and no reply should be able to be categorized by more than one answer. Including an 'Other' category with 'please specify' is used to catch any answer that is not covered by the preceding categories.

Data from each question are stored as a variable, a discrete piece of information for analysis. Recording categories as category names limits the type of analysis that can be undertaken to simple counting, where data recorded as numeric and entered into software packages for statistical analysis can be subjected to a greater range of statistical analysis tools. Coding is

> the way in which we allocate a numeric code to each category of a variable. This coding process is the first step in preparing data for computer analysis. It constitutes the first step in mapping our observations into data.
>
> (D. Rose and Sullivan 1996: 38)

There are a number of different formats for closed question response categories. Examples are shown in Figure 1. Question A has only two response categories with each category assigned a numeric value, typically 1 and 2. This type of question is most often used to gather factual information and often used as a funnelling question to direct respondents to answer only specific sections of the questionnaire. Questions B and C have a list of responses, with B requiring respondents to tick only one response category and C requiring respondents to tick all applicable. The pre-coding for B would be to assign a numeric value starting at 1, adding 1 to the value for each subsequent category. The pre-coding for C is slightly different as there are multiple responses and each category is coded 0 'Not ticked' and 1 'Yes'. Question D has an ordinal format where the categories can be placed in a rank order. Here the pre-codes are assigned in order from lowest to highest.

These types of questions and response categories are typical of attitudinal scales and a number of different coding strategies can be adopted: for example, coding may be reversed for negative statement, 4 to 1, or where a scale has a neutral category, such as a five-point (strongly agree, agree, neither, disagree, strongly disagree) the pre-coding may be from +2 through to −2 with neither being a 0 value. Questions that ask for a numeric value, for example, age in years or income in pounds, are scales and do not require coding.

Handling missing data due to non-response or not applicable responses can also be considered at the pre-code stage. Typically, missing values are coded as −9, with other types of missing responses for example, not applicable, coded as −8. It is also good practice to include a variable that records the number of the questionnaire. This will enable any potential data entry errors or inconsistencies in subsequent analysis findings to be checked against the original paperwork. A box in the top left or top right corner normally suffices for this purpose (see Figure 1).

Managing coding processes: coding frames and codebooks

The overall project management of the survey will need to consider how to record the coding process of the survey responses. The approach in Figure 1 archives the coding onto the survey. However, it does not include other valuable coding information that is used in setting up the data file for analysis. This typically will include variable names, variable and value labels, missing data codes, and data type. It is common practice to include a code book or coding frame (David and Sutton 2011: Chapter 16). Figure 3 shows an example of a separate coding frame.

In summarizing this section, Table 4 is designed to assist you in considering and remembering the procedures in questionnaire construction.

In this process we move from the conceptual aims and hypotheses informing the survey through to its operationalization in a questionnaire, to the results. These can then be analysed to see whether the original

Figure 3   Example coding frame

Variable	Question number/ description	Codes	Non-response missing values	Data type
ID case	Questionnaire number	Enter actual number	–	–
Gender	Gender of respondent	1 = Male 2 = Female	–9 = Did not respond	Nominal
Accom.	Type of accommodation respondent living in	1 = Own outright 2 = Buying it with a mortgage 3 = Part buying and part renting 4 = Renting – social housing / local authority 5 = Renting – private landlord 6 = Living here rent free	–9 = Did not respond	Nominal

Table 4   Stages in questionnaire construction

What is the theoretical starting-point of the research? What is known already? What research has been done? What can your proposed research contribute and therefore what are its aims?

↓

What information is required to fulfil these aims?

↓

Undertake exploratory initial fieldwork

↓

What type of questionnaire will be used and how will the sample be derived?

↓

Consider the most appropriate questions to ask, which will depend upon the aims of the research, the research design, the target population and the time and resources at your disposal

↓

Construct a first draft taking into account that pre-coded questions are easier to analyse and the order of questions is the best social-psychological sequence

↓

Pilot the questionnaire and elicit the opinions of a subsample. Gain critical but supportive comments from those familiar with the design and analysis of questionnaires

↓

Edit the questionnaire to check on form, content and sequence of questions. Make sure the questionnaire is neatly typed and all instructions and coding are clear and filter questions, if any, are understandable

↓

Administer the questionnaire noting the dynamics of the interviews and comments of the interviewers (if used)

↓

Analyse the questionnaire drawing upon statistical techniques

theoretical propositions require modifying or new information has come to light. Thus, to return to the discussion in Chapter 2, this process is a combination of both inductive and deductive techniques of social research.

METHODOLOGICAL INNOVATION, TECHNOLOGY AND THE INTERNET IN SURVEY RESEARCH

Technological developments have enabled social researchers to conduct survey research in different formats, engaging with participants through a range of different environments that reflect the broader changes in communication methods in social life. These developments relate to both the data collection and analysis stages of the research.

The survey has progressed from being paper or telephone based to a wide range of tools that are known under the umbrella term 'Computer-Assisted Survey Information Collection' or CASIC (Vehovar and Manfreda 2008). Sophisticated data and statistical analysis techniques have also been developed as a result of software availability and advanced quantitative data analysis research initiatives (for example, see www.ncrm.ac.uk). This section outlines developments in data collection specifically focusing on the use of computer technology and the internet (Hewson et al. 2003).

Development

The initial use of computer technology supported data collection where the interviewer administered the questionnaire survey tool stored as a computer-based version: for example, face-to-face or telephone-based completion Computer Assisted Personal Interviewing (CAPI) involves the researcher visiting the participant in person and using a laptop that displays questions. The interviewer then asks the questions and records the answers given. A variation of this is Computer Assisted Self Interviewing (CASI) where the interviewer is still present and the laptop is passed to the participant, who completes the questions by themselves.

Computer Assisted Telephone Interviewing (CATI) is similar to CAPI, although it can involve more complex computer networks with multi-interviewer users, with the survey tool being administered by the interviewer via the telephone. These tools enable more efficient data collection as coded data are automatically stored into a data file that can be analysed accordingly. It represents considerable resource saving, both in terms of data entry and in minimizing data errors and subsequent data cleaning. Flags and alerts can be included in computer-based questionnaires to minimize non-response to questions, speed up routing and question 'skips'. CASI can also provide a convenient approach for the asking of sensitive or personal questions.

The most significant development has been in the area of online or internet surveys. Here the researcher is absent and the respondent is able to complete the survey questions at a time and place that is convenient to them. With modern communication technologies and increasing proportions of households having access to the World Wide Web, the use of internet surveys has been increasing, with developments occurring within the market research sector.

Online surveys represent considerable resource savings to the researcher and are seen as minimizing the intrusion of the researcher in the respondent's everyday life. In the early years of their development, internet-based surveys were most often sent via email to the respondent, who completed and returned by email to the researcher. Nowadays most internet surveys are hosted on a web server that is completed by the respondent online, with respondents being invited to complete the survey. The UK 2011 Census includes an option for households either to submit a paper-based questionnaire or to complete an online version. Online surveys do require consideration of how the end-user, or research participant, is supported. Typically, as with paper-based surveys, online surveys will include telephone and/or email support lines:

> Internet surveys are positioned at the intercept of computerization and absence of an interviewer. The computer technology enables significant improvements over traditional paper and pencil modes. Answers collected from respondents are immediately stored in a computer database and ready for processing ... Furthermore, computerized questionnaires using the graphical interface of the World Wide Web (WWW) offer advanced design features, like question skips and filters, randomization of answers, control of answer validity, inclusion of multimedia elements.
>
> (Vehovar and Manfreda 2008: 178–9)

Software tools support the design, data collection and analysis phases of the research (Kaczmirek 2008), enabling increasingly sophisticated survey designs. Web surveys offer flexibility in the format and design style of questions with the use of visually attractive response formats. Typically these include the use of drop-down or pull-down menus, radio buttons for single response questions, multiple check boxes for 'tick all that apply' questions and the use of check boxes or radio buttons in matrix style questions (Couper 2008). Conditions and alert flags can be placed on responses to minimize incorrect or non-response.

The use of screening and filter questions allows for subsequent questions to be tailored accordingly without the respondent necessarily being aware of the underlying process. To overcome some of the potential bias with question and category sequencing, software tools often include options to randomize the sequencing of questions, the organization of attitude statements and the order of categories for matrix or list questions. The development of internet questionnaires has enabled researchers to make claims on the assessment of measurement quality through the investigation of response effects of different survey formats and designs. These have included the use of techniques such as eye-ball tracking (Galesic et al. 2008) and the analysis of paradata that is produced as a by-product of the survey process (Couper 2008; Kreuter and Casas-Cordero 2010).

Web surveys also differentiate between paradata that include characteristics of a respondent browser captured from server logs (server-side
paradata) and respondent behaviour captured by embedding JavaScript
code into the instrument (client-side paradata). Response times and
key stroke measures have been used to study aspects of the response
process . . . to guide interventions in web surveys.

(Kreuter and Casas-Cordero 2010: 5–6)

There has been considerable research undertaken to assess the relative
response rates of internet and postal surveys. Dolnicar et al. (2009)
consider the format effects of a tourism survey that was administered
using a mixed method of online and postal. Respondent and responses
analysis suggested that online respondents had a lower dropout rate and
produced less incomplete data. Response times were quicker for the
online survey over the completion and mail back of a paper postal survey.
However, as internet surveys have become more commonplace, there is
evidence to suggest that responses rates to online surveys are now
declining and the proportion of non-deliverable emails increasing
(Sheehan 2001; McDonald and Adam 2003). Utilizing a mixed mode
approach with paper and online surveys may yield a higher response rate
and allow the researcher to balance maximizing the response rate against
survey costs (Greenlaw and Brown-Welty 2009).

Sampling and internet surveys

The population, as with any research, needs to be defined and, where probability sampling techniques are to be used, an adequate sampling frame
needs to be available. The issue with the internet is that there is no one
source of all email addresses. Instead, identifying an adequate sampling
frame will be dependent on lists compiled of other smaller populations.
These are likely to be existing email distribution lists that an organization
holds, although it is possible to compile a list based on other contact information from which first contact is made. However, such an approach tends
to counteract the resource savings of internet survey adoption.

The coverage of an email list in relation to the research topic and population will require careful consideration. Although internet broadband
access is rising at a fast rate, it should be remembered that there are
significant groups and numbers in the population who may have no, or
only limited, access. For these reasons the coverage of internet samples
and the generalizability of subsequent research findings to the wider
population are frequently challenged. Solutions to this under-coverage
have been offered involving a statistical correction or weighting based on
data collected from a smaller reference survey (Bethlehem 2009).

In cases where a sampling frame does exist, a probability-based technique can be adopted. However, this will often be a simple random sample unless more detailed respondent information (age, gender, etc.) is attached to each email address. Used extensively in customer satisfaction research and depending on the research topic, one alternative approach is to make use of website visitors as the sampling frame. A systematic sampling technique can then be deployed to use an intercept survey inviting participation in the main survey to every nth visitor.

Where no suitable email list exists, it is possible to derive sampling lists based on the 'harvesting' of email addresses from existing databases. There are a number of commercial companies that offer this service in relation to business directories. It is possible for researchers to devise their own harvesting of databases using appropriate organization databases. A survey of volunteers in the third sector, for instance, could involve gathering volunteer databases from a variety of organizations to construct a sampling frame.

Other approaches adopt an entirely different approach. Online consumer panels are regularly used by social and market researchers, particularly where the survey needs to include a wide geographical coverage. Commercial companies compile panels or lists of subscribers to participate in online fieldwork (for example, see www.researchnow.com, www.today.yougov.co.uk and www.tnsglobal.com). While probability-based sampling techniques may be used to draw the sample from the panel list, it should be remembered that these panels are voluntary in nature with members opting into the panel often receiving rewards for participation. While these organizations stress the representativeness of their respective panels, they are technically for research purposes no different to convenience samples often based on quotas established from population profile statistics – a point often overlooked at the reporting stage.

QUESTIONNAIRE ANALYSIS

Having obtained data from completed questionnaires it is necessary to analyse them. This section provides an overview of the process of data analysis. There are texts on data analysis (J. Fielding and Gilbert 2006; Field 2009), how to present data (Sprent 1988; Fink 2003), as well as how not to (Huff 1993; Goldacre 2008). Analysis of survey data tends to be through the use of a computer, utilizing a number of statistical analysis software packages (SPSS, MINITAB, STATA and SAS), and non-commercial ones are also available to social science researchers (see www.cran.r-project.org/index.html and www.cmm.bristol.ac.uk).

Levels of measurement

The methods of analysis depend upon the data produced. In order to use some statistical methods legitimately, it is necessary that data are of a certain type. There are three levels of measurement applicable to the social sciences: *nominal, ordinal* and *scale* (also referred to as *interval/ratio*).

Nominal variables are simply those that collect data based on discrete categories such as 'religious affiliation'. Ordinal variables *rank* the differences in replies, for example, answers on the agree–disagree continuum of the Likert scale. Ordinal scales, however, cannot specify that the differences between each of the scores will be identical (for example, the difference between agree and agree strongly is not the same as between disagree and disagree strongly). For this purpose, measurement at a scale (interval/ratio) is required. Examples of true interval scales would be number of children in a family or age in years. In the social sciences most variables are of a nominal or ordinal form and for those reasons statistical techniques which require an interval level of measurement are frequently invalid (Blalock 1984: 20). In order to overcome these limitations, researchers have devised sophisticated statistical techniques for social science research.

Data analysis strategies

Data will need to be entered into a computer-based data file. There are a variety of data file formats, of which nearly all can be used in the wide range of analysis software packages available. Typically the data file structure is one where variables or fields, pieces of data collected from each question, are stored in columns and cases or records, individual sets of responses are recorded in rows. Data are entered as numeric codes with corresponding labels for variable description and category labels attached.

The analysis of survey data can be structured into three distinctive phases. The initial phase will involve describing the sample survey data using tables, graphs and descriptive statistics. Data will be described both as individual variables and through the exploration of relationships between variables. From these observed differences, the second phase is to use statistical techniques based on probability theory to estimate population parameters, assess the differences between groups, measure associations and assess statistical significance (J. Fielding and Gilbert 2006; Field 2009). The final phase is to use more sophisticated statistical modelling techniques to extend multivariate analysis and enable, where appropriate, prediction (Tarling 2009).

Describing data

Using descriptive statistical techniques allows the researcher to understand, explore and perform validity checks on the sample. The first stage of description is to analyse responses to survey questions. Key sample statistics, such as age, class and gender, can be matched to known population parameters to assess for under- or overrepresentation and non-response. For category responses, nominal and ordinal, a frequency table is commonly produced that gives a breakdown of the number and percentage of respondents answering each category. Where data are scale appropriate measures include the mean (average), minimum and maximum values and standard deviation (the average amount of spread around the mean; see Figure 4: Table A and Table B).

The process of specifying the exact relationship between variables is achieved by *elaboration* (see Rosenberg 1968, 1984; Moser and Kalton 1983). The aim is to examine patterns among replies to questions and explore the relationships between variables that the questions represent. This takes the form of seeing to what extent one variable is influenced by another. Variables are described as *dependent* or *independent*. A dependent variable is 'explained' by reference to the influence of the independent variable. This analysis requires you to consider the time order; independent variables should occur before dependent variables.

Figure 4   Describing data

Table A Gender of respondents (%)	
Male	46.7
Female	53.3
Total % (n)	100 (1200)

Table B Age characteristics of respondents (years)	
Minimum age	16
Maximum age	98
Mean (std deviation)	45.2 (18.7)

Table C Voting preference by age (%)		
	'Younger' 39 years and under (%)	'Older' 40 years and older (%)
Conservative	35	40
Labour	38	35
Liberal Democrat	25	24
Other	2	1
Total	100 (n = 1200)	100 (n = 1200)

Where observable changes in the independent variable are accompanied by a change in the dependent variable then there is said to be an association between the two variables. Where both variables are categorical, a cross-tabulation or contingency table can be used (see Figure 4: Table C). In the example given, the dependent variable would be voting preference including a conservative category. The extent to which a person is 'conservative' might be explained by the person's age – the independent variable, here classified into two age groups. Alternatively a conservative outlook might be explained or associated with a different independent variable such as social class; it is possible that people of different socio-economic groups have a different outlook on life. There could be a relationship between class and voting behaviour, *independent* of age. A younger person who is a member of a profession may be more conservative than an older person who is a manual worker. In this instance it may not be age, but social class, which influences a particular outlook on life. It is then the task of the researcher to discover exactly what variables are influential and in what manner.

Statistical inference

There are many different data analysis techniques based on probability theory. These techniques can be applied to data collected from probability samples, although they are sometimes applied to non-probability samples where the claim is that there is adequate representation. In survey research they are used in hypothesis testing and can be classified as *tests of significance* (to see to what extent it is legitimate to generalize from the sample to the population) and *measures of association* (which tells you how strongly the sample variables are related). Together, they allow you to infer that one variable is related to another.

The logic of hypothesis testing requires the researcher to establish the null hypothesis of no association or significance and the alternative hypothesis of association or significance. If the appropriate statistical test is significant, the null hypothesis can be rejected thus accepting the alternative hypothesis. The level of statistical significance is normally set at 95 per cent, meaning that there is a 1 in 20 statistical chance of reaching the wrong conclusion. In most statistical packages the significance is estimated; a level of significance below 0.05 means that the null hypothesis is rejected. Errors in hypothesis testing are classified as type I, the incorrect rejection of the null hypothesis, and type II, the incorrect acceptance of the null hypothesis.

Tests involving scale data are known as parametric tests, whereas those tests involving nominal and ordinal data are non-parametric. There are different techniques for analysing interval level data compared to ordinal data. Each statistical test has a different statistical power and assumptions regarding the distribution of values; 'the data must consist of randomly selected, independently measured cases' (Erickson and Nosanchuk 1992: 251) and for tests such as chi-square a minimum expected cell count of 5 is required (Field 2009: 691–2). Common tests of significance used by social researchers include the chi-square test of independence; Mann Whitney U test; Kolmogorov Smirnov z; Kruskall Wallis; Independent Samples T-Test; ANOVA and F Test. Measures of association include Pearson's r; Spearman's *rho*, Phi; and Cramer's V (de Vaus 2002b).

Modelling and multivariate analysis

Data models in empirical social science research enable researchers to consider the complex relationships between different social data. Models are used in many other academic and professional disciplines: for instance, architects and town planners routinely build scale models of buildings and landscaped areas to help understand build requirements and consider how individuals interact with their surroundings. In the natural sciences, climate and environmental data are used to understand and predict future climate change that contributes to global warming.

Social researchers use modelling to improve the understanding of causality through the testing of competing theories. Models are said to enable prediction, are useful for risk assessment in policy-related areas and allow assessment of different characteristics where there are multiple independent variables and interactions. As with all data analysis models, these require careful interpretation and a narrative of explanation and are dependent on the level of measurement. They are theory driven rather than data driven, with variables selected according to the theoretical model rather than just randomly selecting from a list of variables. Modelling techniques include the following: simple and multiple regression; logistic regression; log-linear analysis and multilevel modelling (Gilbert 1981, 1993; Agresti 1996; Tacq 1997; Agresti and Finlay 2009; Field 2009; Tarling 2009). Techniques of factor analysis and cluster analysis are also widely used in market research (see Mazzocchi 2008).

SURVEYS IN CRITICAL PERSPECTIVE

In this chapter we have moved from a conceptual consideration of surveys to a hands-on approach to the design and analysis of questionnaires. It remains to consider the criticisms of the survey method. The survey method and particularly the statistical representation of the social world are not without problems or critics. Statistics are only a tool and when it comes to a critique of survey research, its opponents are not impressed by numbers, whether they are percentages, means, statistical tests or multilevel models.

Let us recap on some of the characteristics of questionnaires: the idea of causality; the concern with measurement versus understanding; the concept of standardization and the testing of hypotheses. Each of these has been addressed, albeit indirectly, in the earlier chapters. A common criticism of survey method is that it attempts to show causal relations between variables, a strategy which is simply not applicable to the realm of human action which is rule-following, not 'caused'. Age or occupation, for example, does not simply *cause* opinions. Two variables may be associated, but this *correlation* does not mean that one variable causes a change in another. To say that there is a correlation between age and conservatism does not mean that age *causes* conservatism. While causality (that is the claim that A occurs only when B does) is attributed to phenomena only after 'looking at variation in that variable across cases and looking for other characteristics which are systematically linked with it' (de Vaus 2002a: 5). In most cases researchers do no more than show the strength of association between different variables. In any case, causal claims would not be legitimate in considering only two variables in isolation, but this does not rule out the possibility of measuring association.

An associated criticism is that the survey method rules out the possibility of understanding the process by which people come to adopt particular values or behaviours. This criticism seems entirely legitimate if survey research is conducted without a thorough grounding in theory. Yet surveys are often used as part of a multi-method or mixed method approach wherein qualitative methods precede and/or follow a survey, thus permitting the development of an understanding of agents' perspectives, social process and context (see Plano Clark and Creswell 2008). Adopting a position of methodological pluralism using a triangulation of well-designed methods can provide breadth and depth. However, there is a danger and it is often seen in commercial commissioned research reports, as favoured by government departments, that data collected is not blended together, but instead presented separately.

A further criticism is that researchers have presuppositions, such as the relationship between age and voting behaviour that leads them to ask particular questions. Because these restrict the way in which people can answer, it becomes inevitable that the theories are 'proven'. By the very design of questionnaires, it has already been decided what are the important questions to ask. It is then said that this deductive method fails precisely because the theorists' presuppositions have guided the research. The survey researcher might reply that it is also inductive because the results of the answers generate relationships between variables which either lead to new ideas, as in the use of bivariate analysis, or refute the theories themselves. How can this be so? By using the concept of standardization, people do not have the opportunity to challenge ideas on their own terms. Furthermore, the myriad of differences in people's attitudes and the *meanings* which they confer on events can hardly be accommodated by compartmentalizing them into fixed categories (closed questions) at one point in time (the actual completion of the questionnaire).

Differences are accommodated in questionnaires by the 'fixing' of complex answers within a series of simple categories. Yet not only is this a simplification of a complex social world, but also it takes no account of change in opinions across time. To correct for this, some surveys are *longitudinal*. Of these, a *panel study* takes a group or cohort of people and interviews them across time: for example, groups of children born at a particular time are then interviewed at five-yearly points in their life cycles to see how their attitudes, opinions, values and so on change over time (de Vaus 2002a: 33–5). Yet these are expensive and thus not a common form of research, while it still remains the case that if the researcher is relying on only a questionnaire method of research, people's opinions are represented by a fixed number of categories.

The above problems are thought to be overcome by an attention to design, measurement and good pilot work. However, this can simply become an empiricist concern with measurement. The central issue in social research for the critics of questionnaires is a hermeneutic one: how can researchers legitimately understand the ways in which people interpret the world around them and act within their social universe? How can survey researchers guarantee that their questions will be interpreted by the respondent in the manner in which they intended when there is no opportunity for a participatory dialogue in order to reach understanding? As noted:

A bland choice of 'level of satisfaction', where 1 = very dissatisfied and 5 = very satisfied, leaves the interpretation of 'satisfied' open to the respondent. The irony here is an assumed congruence of meaning between what the designer intended and the ways in which it is interpreted by the respondents. From this point of view, one could say that all quantitative research assumes an ethnographic dimension to its design where the latter is characterized as being concerned with meaning construction in everyday life.

(M. Williams and May 1996: 140–1)

A response to this issue, as we have seen, is to argue for meaning equivalence between design intent and interviewee interpretation. Even if meaning equivalence can be upheld, as some research suggests it can, by deriving the categories used in the questions from prior fieldwork (Social and Community Planning Research 1981), this still leaves survey research with another problem: attitudes and actions are two different things, or what people say they do is very different from what they actually do. This is an issue equally of relevance to interviewing although with greater potential opportunity to probe and explore attitudes.

The problematic relationship between attitudes and actions was considered by Richard Lapiere as long ago as 1934 and remains relevant today. Having surveyed hotel proprietors with the aim of obtaining 'comparative data on the degree of French and English antipathy towards dark-skinned peoples' (Lapiere 1934: 230), he found a widespread prejudice against letting rooms to those who fell into this category. However, he then had the opportunity to travel with a 'young Chinese student and his wife' (Lapiere 1934: 231). In a hotel with a reputation for its prejudiced attitude, he noted the receptionist's 'raised eyebrow', but they were admitted without hesitation:

Two months later I passed that way again, phoned the hotel and asked if they would accommodate 'an important Chinese gentleman'. The answer was an unequivocal 'No'.

(Lapiere 1934: 231–2)

From this point on, despite the widespread prejudice uncovered by the questionnaire, there was only a single incident in a total of 251 in which they were refused accommodation. As he concludes:

If social attitudes are to be conceptualized as partially integrated habit sets which will become operative under specific circumstances and lead to a particular pattern of adjustment they must, in the main, be derived from a study of human beings in actual social situations.

(Lapiere 1934: 237)

Lapiere neatly encapsulates the difference between attitudes and actions and the problem of tapping what people 'mean' when answering questionnaires. However, his concluding comments also appear to be a recommendation for good pilot work. For this reason, there are those who would argue that questionnaires can tap meanings if adequately designed and piloted and that the divide which is often thought to exist between quantitative and qualitative research actually 'impoverishes' the aim of understanding and explaining human relations (McLaughlin 1991).

Catherine Marsh (1982) argued that questionnaires can adequately deal with meaning. While she acknowledged that ambiguous questions must be avoided, people will answer in a different way depending upon the meanings they attribute to a question. Other questions built into the questionnaire can enable the researcher to capture the reasons for this variation, as she noted in discussing the work of Brown and Harris (1978). Broadly speaking, Brown and Harris (1978) studied a series of life events, to which women reacted, which then produced such feelings of hopelessness they induced clinical depression. The dimensions of this study thus included both the understanding of these reactions and these events as 'causal' factors leading to depression. As Marsh then noted:

> The first involves asking the actor for her reasons directly, or to supply information about the central values in her life around which we may assume she is orientating her life. The second involves collecting a sufficiently complete picture of the context in which an actor finds herself that a team of outsiders may read off the meaningful dimension . . . the mistake is to think that it is only action that is human and understandable – reactions are too.
>
> (C. Marsh 1982: 124)

Brown (1984) was also to show how it was possible to capture both the meanings which actors attributed to an event and explain those in causal terms. As quantitative researchers have argued (Husbands 1981; C. Marsh 1984), the use of questionnaires in these various ways distances them from a positivist legacy upon which critics tend to focus.

In the quest to compartmentalize surveys within a positivist orientation and to produce a dichotomy between qualitative and quantitative methods of social research, their broad appeal can be easily overlooked. For instance, Ken Young (1981) argues that the outcome of policy is governed by two issues: first, the degree of control an organization exercises over its discretionary officials, and second, the extent to which the officials and policy-makers' definitions of the situation inhabit common ground (K. Young 1981: 45). By the study of what he calls 'assumptive worlds', or 'definitions of the life situation' (K. Young 1977: 4), it is possible to begin to understand the 'subjective factors' and 'situational determinants' that different actors, at different levels of an organization, have and experience. These 'assumptive worlds' can be tapped through the use of questionnaires.

SUMMARY

In this chapter we considered the logic of survey method, issues of design, sampling and analysis. Despite the broad appeal of survey method, a debate still remains over the place and applicability of questionnaires in social research. There are those researchers who would not, under any circumstances, countenance their use. Others would slavishly apply these methods without due regard to their weaknesses, and then hide behind a mask of elaborate statistical analysis. Somewhat ironically, the development of new technologies allows for ever more sophisticated analysis, but it also has the potential to provide statistical and technological camouflage; the issues of attitudes, actions and meanings remain.

There are also those who know of the weaknesses of particular methods of research and make a judgement of which method to use based upon this information and the aims of their research. They may even decide to use multi-method approaches in their research, combining quantitative and qualitative approaches, to resolve some of the above difficulties. An important skill in becoming a researcher, as noted, is the ability to weigh up the practical value and methodological limitations of particular methods of social research.

Questions for your reflection

1 List the stages that should be considered in designing a survey. What are the problems which you envisage at each stage and what should the researcher be aware of during these?

2 What type of research problem is particularly suited to an internet survey?

3 'Questionnaires measure only attitudes; they tell us nothing about the way that people behave.' Is this a valid criticism of surveys as a method of research?

4 If you were asked to devise a questionnaire that examined the relationship between race and crime, what ethical, political and theoretical questions might this raise for you as a social researcher?

SUGGESTED FURTHER READING

Couper, M. P. (2008) *Designing Effective Web Surveys*. Cambridge: Cambridge University Press.

de Vaus, D. (2002) *Surveys in Social Research*, 5th edn. London: Routledge.

Fielding, J. and Gilbert, N. (2006) *Understanding Social Statistics*, 2nd edn. London: Sage.

Marsh, C. (1982) *The Survey Method*. London: George Allen & Unwin.

6   Interviewing: methods and process

The aim of this chapter is to provide an understanding of the place of interviewing in social research. For this purpose I have divided it into four sections. First, an examination of the various types of interviewing that are used in social research. Second, accounts of the ways in which interviews are conducted along with the issues that inform this process. Third, an overview of the ways in which interview data can be analysed, and finally, critiques of the place of interviewing in social research.

INTERVIEWS IN SOCIAL RESEARCH

The methods of maintaining and generating conversations with people on a specific topic or range of topics and the interpretations which social researchers make of the resultant data constitute the fundamentals of interviews and interviewing. Interviews yield rich insights into people's biographies, experiences, opinions, values, aspirations, attitudes and feelings. In order to achieve such an outcome social researchers need to understand the dynamics of interviewing, including contexts and dispositions, sharpen their own use of the method and understand the different methods of conducting interviews and analysing the data, together with an awareness of their strengths and limitations.

Broadly speaking, there are four types of interviews used in social research. While these characterizations appear to demarcate strictly one method from another, a research project may not simply be one of the following, but a mixture of two or more types, as well as methods. They are the structured interview, the semi-structured interview, the unstructured or focused interview, and the group interview and focus group.

In moving from the structured interview to the unstructured interview, researchers shift from a situation in which they attempt to control the interview through predetermining questions and thus 'teach' the respondent to reply in accordance with the interview schedule (standardization), to one in which the respondent is encouraged to answer a question from their own point of view. With this in mind, we can characterize interviews along a quantitative–qualitative dimension, varying from the formal standardized example (surveys), to an unstructured situation of qualitative depth which allows the respondent to answer without feeling constrained by pre-formulated questions with a limited range of answers.

In evaluating these different methods we should attend, as is a main contention of this book, not so much to matters relating to a quantitative–qualitative divide in social research as if one automatically produces a better 'truth' than another, but to their strengths and weaknesses for producing social knowledge. Qualitative research deploys numbers and quantitative researchers cannot help but attend to issues of meaning; it is thus unhelpful to practice and its understanding to perpetuate simple divisions. To understand such issues requires an overview of the aims and practice of different forms of interviewing and so I shall expand on each of these types in turn.

Structured interview

The use of structured interviews is associated with survey research. This is a technique that many people may find familiar although the idea of the 'focus group', at least in terms of being deployed for political purposes to test policies among populations as well as market research, has gained greater public recognition. While the other techniques, particularly focused interviews, may directly involve the researcher as a subject and co-participant in the data production process, this method relies upon the use of a questionnaire as the data collection instrument.

The theory behind this method is that each person is asked the same question in the same way so that any differences between answers are held to be real ones as a result of the deployment of a method and not the result of the interview context itself. Validity may then be checked by asking the respondent about the same issue, but employing a different form of question wording and then comparing the answers. In this context, the role of the interviewer is to direct the respondent according to the sequence of questions on the interview schedule and if clarification is sought, then little or no variability in any elaborations should be apparent in order not to influence the answers. The neutrality of the interviewer's role is emphasized in this manner. The rules for conducting such interviews are standardization of explanations, leaving little room for deviation from the schedule; eliciting only the responses of the person with whom the interview is being conducted; not prompting or providing a personal view; not interpreting meanings and simply repeating the questions, and finally, not improvising (adapted from Fontana and Frey 1994).

The method is said to permit *comparability* between responses. Its deployment may often be associated with particular forms of expertise where, for example, a diagnosis of a particular medical or psychological condition may be sought. In such instances situational prompts may be introduced that are then controlled for in terms of subsequent analysis. What is being sought, therefore, is a uniform *structure*. In addition, as noted in Chapter 5, a calculated number of people may be interviewed so that they are held to be a statistically representative sample of the population for the purposes of undertaking generalization. Resultant data are then aggregated and examined for patterns of responses among the target population via statistical analysis. For instance, an interest in the relationship between class and educational attainment would necessitate the eliciting of data on both class position and educational qualifications. Its success is dependent upon good pilot work and the training of interviewers in order that a range of possible responses are covered by the interview schedule and the replies result from questions which are asked in a uniform and non-directive manner.

Despite these issues, as one comprehensive report on survey research notes in relation to language, even 'with the most carefully designed and tested questions, [it] is too imprecise to allow exactly uniform communications' (Ornstein 1998: 63). As a result we find responses to these issues being introduced in order to balance situational variations against overall validity and reliability of the technique. These include concerns with the interviewer being similar to the target group, who, in turn, need to share a similar culture in order that the interpretation of the questions and the dynamics of the interview do not vary to any significant degree or, if there is variance, it can be accounted for during analysis. Given this, in instances where languages are diverse and there is little commonality in terms of values and where people may fear talking to strangers, this method of interviewing may not be applicable. Nevertheless, the relative strengths and weaknesses may then be overcome through using a multi-method approach: for example, in investigating issues associated with reflexivity and social mobility (Archer 2007) and the use of archive, survey, local history, secondary data and family interviews to understanding patterns of lifelong learning to enable an iterative research design also based upon textual and numeric data (see Gorard 2004: Chapter 5).

The above considerations noted, in cases where complex questionnaires are used, training and particular prompts may be deployed to address these issues. For instance, in the collection of life-history data both quantitative and qualitative methods have been employed. In the German Life History Study, which dealt with quantitative data in order to collect information concerning the characteristics of activities and timing of events, interviewers were selected according to their levels of education and previous experience in conducting complex interviews. They were then trained through the provision of written instructions, but high degrees of interviewer error were detected. Day seminars were then held for small groups of interviewers that incorporated practice interviews. Anonymous surveys of the interviewers then found higher degrees of confidence and commitment, along with a better understanding of the history and aims of the project (Brückner and Mayer 1998).

This method of interviewing is popular in telephone interviews for marketing purposes. Here a supervisor can walk around a room of interviewers listening to conversations and checking the extent to which those charged with its administration adhere to the schedule. Indeed, there is a growing popularity of such methods as they permit economies of scale along with the surveillance of performance. Here, issues of the politics of research relate not only to the researcher–respondent relationship, but also to the organization of the data production process in terms of the conditions of service in which such employees might find themselves, as well as the use to which the subsequent information is then put.

Semi-structured interview

In between the focused and structured methods sits one that utilizes techniques from both. Questions are normally specified, but the interviewer is freer to probe beyond the answers in a manner which would appear prejudicial to the aims of standardization and comparability. Information about age, sex, occupation, type of household and so on, can be asked in a standardized format. The interviewer, who can seek both *clarification* and *elaboration* on the answers given, can then record qualitative information about the topic. This enables the interviewer to have more latitude to *probe* beyond the answers and thus enter into a dialogue with the interviewee.

A semi-structured interview represents an opening up of the interview method to an understanding of how interviewees generate and deploy meaning in social life:

> The idea that interviewees may be 'answering' questions other than those we are asking them, and making sense of the social world in ways we had not thought of, lies behind many qualitative interview strategies. The logic that we should be receptive to what interviewees say, and to *their* ways of understanding, underpins much of the 'qualitative' critique of structured survey interview methods.
>
> (Mason 2002: 231, original emphasis)

Semi-structured interviews were deployed in one study as part of a range of methods to evaluate community health projects designed to meet the needs of remote and rural populations. Here, the need for evaluation met with the wish to involve participants in the 'monitoring, reflection and resultant change processes' (McKie 2002: 270). In another study of police socialization, the interviews were accompanied 'by a thematic guide with probes and invitations to expand on issues raised' (N. Fielding 1988b: 212). In this case the meaning of the statements contained within the interview data were analysed in terms of the cultural resources available to police recruits. The data then enabled an understanding of 'the conventions and devices recruits use when asked to offer accounts of action and belief' (N. Fielding 1988b: 212).

These types of interviews are said to allow people to answer more on their own terms than the standardized interview permits, but still provide a greater structure for comparability over that of the focused or unstructured interview. If a researcher has a specific focus for their interviews within a range of other methods employed in their study, the semi-structured interview may be useful (for example, see Newton 1996; May and Marvin 2009). As with all of the interviewing methods, the interviewer should not only be aware of the content of the interview, but also be able to record the nature of the interview and the way in which they asked the questions. However, in comparison with the structured method, the context of the interview is an important aspect of the process. In its literal sense, the standardized method assumes to elicit information untainted by the contextual conditions of the interview which are thereby 'controlled' in order to obtain validity.

Given the greater degree of latitude offered to the interviewer in the semi-structured method and a need to understand the context and content of the interview, although trained interviewers may be used, researchers may well conduct interviews of this type themselves. The use of this method then enables comparison as there will be a variation in the quality of information that is generated in each interview:

Inevitably, some interviews will provide more useful information than others. No single interview, however revealing, can offer more than limited insights into general social forces and processes. Only by comparing a series of interviews can the significance of any one of them be fully understood. And, in the long run, each interview will add to the final story.

(Gerson and Horowitz 2002: 211)

Unstructured or focused interview

The central difference of this form of interviewing from both the structured and semi-structured interview is its open-ended character. This is said not only to provide it with an ability to challenge the preconceptions that the researcher may bring to the interaction, but also to enable the interviewee to answer questions within their own frame of reference. Some might regard this as a licence for the interviewee simply to talk about an issue in any way they choose. Nevertheless, this apparent disadvantage is turned into an advantage because there is a concern for the perspective of the person being interviewed and those things, such as apparently diverging from the specific topic, can actually reveal something about their forms of understanding (Bryman 1988a).

It was noted earlier that in life-history interviews, collecting information on events and characterizations may be achieved via quantitative techniques. Some researchers have argued that while such methods produce statements regarding those things that have already occurred, they are less useful when it comes to reflections on ongoing processes of social transformation. In this sense, they can reveal the subjective basis for lasting social change in the patterns of perception and behaviour of particular social groups (Segert and Zierke 2000: 230).

Sometimes called the 'informal', 'unstandardized' or 'unstructured' interview, this method is said to achieve a different focus for the following reasons. First, it provides qualitative depth by allowing interviewees to talk about the subject within their own frames of reference. By this I mean drawing upon ideas and meanings with which they are familiar. This allows the meanings that individuals attribute to events and relationships to be understood on their own terms. Second, it thereby provides a greater understanding of the subject's point of view.

This technique includes what are known as life-history (although, as noted, these also include quantitative techniques), biographical and oral history interviews. Biographical research is said to have the 'merit of aiding the task of understanding major social shifts, by including how new experiences are interpreted by individuals within families, small groups and institutions' (B. Roberts 2002: 5). In relation to life-history interviews, writers have noted the importance of preserving a 'feel' of the exchange between interviewer and interviewee in their resultant transcripts (Simeoni and Diani 1995).

In asking women about their experiences, as opposed to assuming that they are already known, this approach is said to challenge the 'truths' of official ways of seeing and reveal 'how women felt about what they did and can interpret the personal meaning and value of particular activities' (K. Anderson et al. 1990: 95). In terms of how relationships change with the transformation of socio-economic conditions and its effects upon a community, what emerged from one study was how men and women experience a loss of a way of life based upon 'a sense of friendship and relation, of basic dignity and respect' (Charlesworth 2000: 10).

We are now at the qualitative end of the research spectrum. Structured interviews are thought to allow very little room for people to express their own opinions in a manner of their choosing. They must fit into boxes or categories which the researcher has predetermined.

The focused interview obviously involves the researcher having an aim in mind when conducting the interview, but the person being interviewed is freer to talk about the topic. Thus *flexibility* and the discovery of *meaning*, rather than standardization, or a concern to compare through constraining replies by a set interview schedule, characterize this method. With flexibility in mind, Ray Pahl (1995) preferred the term 'restructured interviews' in his study on anxiety and stress among the 'rich and successful'. Not only were transcripts sent to interviewees for their comments and amendments after the interviews, but also the purpose for which the data were collected was altered both during and after the interviews were conducted (Pahl 1995: 197–201). While in her study of contacts, encounters, negotiations and space in cities, Sophie Watson (2006) undertook in-depth interviews with market traders, children and older people, supplemented not only by visual methods, but also by focus groups.

Group interview and focus group

Group interviews constitute a valuable tool of investigation, allowing researchers to explore group norms and dynamics around issues and topics which they wish to investigate. The extent of control exercised over the group discussion will determine the nature of the data produced by this method. One method within this broad category of interview techniques has become more widely known in the recent past as the *focus group*. The main difference between the group and focus format is that in the latter participants are more explicitly encouraged to talk to one another, as opposed to answering questions of each person in turn (Kitzinger and Barbour 1999). That noted, this can equally apply to group interviews when participants comment and discuss their opinions and answers without waiting for guidance from the group interviewer, or are explicitly encouraged to do so in order to elicit elaboration and/or clarification.

A typical group interview involves between eight and twelve people who, guided by a group interviewer, discuss the topic(s) under consideration for anything between an hour and a half and two and a half hours (Stewart and Shamdasani 1990: 10). A balance needs to be struck between the group being too small for interactive study or too large thus preventing all group members from participating in the discussion. However, as with all research guidelines, this will depend on what is possible in circumstances over which the researcher may have little or no control, as well as the aims of the investigation and the resources available.

Group interviews have been used in a variety of contexts, including in market research and therapeutic practice, over a long period of time. Robert Merton, with two collaborators, wrote an influential book on the subject after his work during the Second World War on radio broadcasts (see Merton and Kendal 1946; Merton et al. 1990). There is a rich history in their use: for example, in studies of steel workers who experienced changes in working practices (Banks 1957); the effects of long-term imprisonment (S. Cohen and Taylor 1972); conflicts within organizations (Steyaert and Bouwen 1994); women's experiences of mental health (A. Butler 1994); community views on risk and nuclear safety (Waterton and Wynne 1999); and innovation processes in city regions (May and Perry 2010).

In Banks's (1957) study, steel workers were interviewed both individually and as a group. While a degree of consistency was found between the data yielded by both methods, the group responses tended to take account of the situations of others present and there was a greater tendency to express grievances with the management. Waterton and Wynne (1999) found that opinion polls had constructed a simplistic view of communities' feelings about the local nuclear industry that were challenged by the complex ways in which people spoke about risks during their group interviews, while May and Perry (2010) deployed the method in order to enable a more collective view to emerge over key strategic priorities and the means for understanding the success of interventions to catalyse innovative activities.

It appears to be possible to gain different results from using group and individual interviews (whether focused or via opinion polls). However, it does not follow that one result should be regarded as simply 'true' and another 'false'. Of course, poorly designed opinion poll research can produce a distorted and even false picture of attitudes. Nevertheless, we should also be sensitive to group and individual interviews producing *different* perspectives on the *same* issues. This comparison demonstrates, for example, that interaction within groups (such as on the factory floor) affects us all in terms of our actions and opinions.

As most of our lives are spent interacting with others, it comes as no surprise that they are modified according to the social situation in which we find ourselves. For this reason, group interviews can provide a valuable insight into both social relations in general and the examination of processes and social dynamics in particular. At the same time, caution should be exercised in attributing the opinions of such a group to whole populations. This is particularly important given the current trend for using this method among market researchers and political parties. When matters of cost and the demand for ever-faster means of gathering data only to prove already existing prejudices abound, issues of selectivity, representation, validity and reliability do not disappear as a result!

CONDUCTING INTERVIEWS IN SOCIAL RESEARCH

The first section of this chapter covered types of interviewing which have different ideas and methods underlying their practice. For this reason and by way of an introduction to the process of conducting interviews, I concentrate in this section on the main points which you might consider if adopting one or more of these techniques. However, the actual use of these pointers will clearly depend upon the interview method being employed. This section is also demarcated as texts on social research tend to adopt a particular perspective when it comes to the interviewing process. First, it considers common prescriptions for interviewing which are mainly, but not exclusively, applicable to structured and semi-structured forms. Second, it moves on to consider the process of conducting focused or unstructured interviews. As will become evident, those inspired by critical, humanist, feminist and narrative inspired approaches have, in particular, criticized certain accounts of the interviewing process as both impractical and undesirable. Given this, the third subsection will outline the main issues to consider when conducting interviews, having taken onboard these criticisms.

Prescriptions for interviewing practice

Commonly, a tension is thought to exist between subjectivity and objectivity in the interviewing process with resolutions to such issues being sought through the deployment of particular methods. As one text puts it in relation to field research, the researcher should seek to maintain as much control as if they were conducting an experiment in a laboratory and when it comes to obtaining participants, researchers 'are at the mercy of whoever happens to be at home on any given day. Thus, with field research, you have less control over participants than in the laboratory' (Bordens and Abbott 2008: 164).

On the one hand, interviews are constructed to elicit knowledge free of prejudice or bias on the part of interviewers; on the other, a self-conscious awareness on the part of the interviewer is needed to let the interview 'flow'. As Jody Miller and Barry Glassner, in their reflections on the 'inside' and 'outside' in interviews, write:

> Those of us who aim to understand and document others' understandings choose qualitative interviewing because it provides us with a means for exploring the points of view of our research subjects, while granting these points of view the culturally honoured status of reality.
>
> (J. Miller and Glassner 1997: 100)

For this purpose the interviewer and interviewee need to establish an intersubjective understanding in terms of the aims of the work, expectations of the participants and also what they may obtain as a result of the work being undertaken. At the same time, the pursuit of objectivity requires a 'distance' in order to socially situate the responses. We seem to have two polar opposites – full engagement to detached analysis. The result is that a sustained relationship appears to produce a successful interview from a qualitative point of view, while a more detached and standardized form is assumed to produce more reliable data (Cicourel 1964). A 'balance' seems to be required between these two, apparently contradictory, criteria.

In examining these issues, texts on interviewing highlight a number of points that need to be considered by the researcher. First, there is the question of the interviewer's role: what effect is the interviewer having on the interviewee and hence the type of material collected? Is the interviewer's role during the interview one of impartial scientist or friend and how does this affect the interview? Related to this are discussions on the characteristics of interviewers: what are their ages, sex, race and accent? This is an important issue which directly affects the type of information elicited. For instance, a study was conducted in Tennessee among black respondents using white interviewers. The idea was to consider the attitudes of black people and the extent to which they were satisfied with their social, political and economic lives. When interviewed by white interviewers, the people's attitudes were classified as expressing a 'high' level of satisfaction. However, when interviewed by black interviewers, attitudes changed and a more radical opinion was expressed.

Before conducting interviews it is important to consider a match of characteristics, on the basis of not only race, but also such factors as age, sex and accent. This helps to guard against the substitution of the interviewer's words for the respondents. Thus, texts speak of 'blending-in'. Quite simply, it may not be appropriate for a grey-suited person who appears more familiar with the financial world to interview Hell's Angels about their beliefs and actions. Nevertheless, this observation should be tempered by reference to the purpose, expectations, content and context of the research process itself. Three necessary conditions have been suggested for the successful completion of interviews (Moser and Kalton 1983). Although specifically discussing survey interviews, these authors raise issues which are worthy of more general consideration.

First, there is the issue of *accessibility*. This refers to whether or not the person answering the questions has access to the information which the interviewer's seeks. This may seem a simple point yet, as noted when discussing questionnaires in particular, a gap may exist between the interviewer's and interviewee's modes of understanding. Of course, depending upon the interviewing method used, the interviewer may possess the flexibility to clarify the questions. Such a lack of information may result for several reasons. For instance, the person once knew the answer, but has now forgotten; for the person to disclose certain types of information involves undue emotional stress; a certain type of answer or method of answering is expected which the person is not familiar with (the frames of reference are discrepant) or, quite simply, people may refuse to answer for personal, political or ethical reasons, or a combination of any of these. In such situations the interviewer must make a judgement whether or not to continue the line of questioning, or even the interview itself.

The second necessary condition is *cognition*, or an understanding by the person being interviewed of what is required of them in the role of interviewee. Interviews are social encounters and not simply passive means of gaining information. As with all social encounters they are guided by implicit understandings and the parties bring with them expectations of their content and the role they may adopt as a result. It is important, therefore, that interviewees not only know the information that is required, but also understand what is expected of them. Without this, the person being interviewed may feel uncomfortable and this affects the resultant data. For these reasons, clarification is not only a practical, but also an ethical and theoretical consideration. Once again, this will depend on the type of interview being used. In a structured situation, the nature of the answer is guided by the interview schedule. On the other hand, the focused interview rests its strength upon eliciting answers which are, as far as possible, in the person's own words and frame of reference in particular contexts that the interviewer is seeking to understand. Thus in relation to online interviewing:

> People who are actively involved in virtual communities, social media, or immersive environments have online identities, friends, and

colleagues. Online interviews allow researchers to better understand the participant's cyber experience.

(Salmons 2010: 9)

Third and related to the above, there is the issue of *motivation*. The interviewer must make the subjects feel that their participation and answers are valued, for their cooperation is fundamental to the conduct of the research. This means maintaining interest during the interview (Moser and Kalton 1983: 271–2). Once these matters are considered and acted upon, during the course of the interview there are certain techniques for asking questions. First, a distinction is made between 'directive' questions, which require a Yes or No answer, and 'non-directive' questions, which allow more latitude for the response. Thus, an interviewer may ask for a reply to be framed in a particular way, or the interviewer may be rather less directive and ask, for example, 'Could you tell me a little more about that?' Another recommended method is to repeat what the person has said, but with a rising inflexion in the voice. For instance, if the answer is, 'I enjoyed meeting them', the interviewer then responds, 'You say you enjoyed meeting them . . .?' This is said to gain important elaborations of a person's statement.

In everyday life we sometimes find ourselves in conversations where a person is either hostile to the line of questioning or becomes embarrassed for one reason or another. The interview is no exception to this. Of course it may be wrong to pursue the line of questioning, but one method of preventing embarrassment or hostility is to ask by way of generalization. Instead of posing a direct question, 'What do you think about *X*?', you might ask, 'Many people consider that . . . do you have an opinion on this?' This use of probes is widely recommended. Probing is defined as 'encouraging the respondent to give an answer, or to clarify or amplify an answer' (Hoinville and Jowell 1987: 101). These vary from so-called neutral probes in standardized situations, to more open types in unstructured interviews.

An ability to probe is reduced as the interview becomes more structured, for any variations in probing will reduce comparability and from this methodological viewpoint, validity. However, a change in the emphasis of a question, or a similar question posed in a different way, not only can provoke further thought on the subject, but also offers a catalyst enabling the interviewee to make links to other answers already given. This allows elaboration by a method of using information subsequently gained during the interview and applying it to a later stage in the conversation. There are some parallels here with the idea of 'retrospective–prospective interpretation' (Garfinkel 1967; J. Scott and Alwin 1998).

Along these lines, it is also possible to ask people about *future* possibilities in relation to *past* experiences. This enables the interviewer to gain an idea of how people think about issues or come to terms with events in their lives, allowing them to build up a picture of the event or issue so that it is not 'compartmentalized', but related to other factors that are considered important. Another technique commonly urged is probing for comparable and codeable answers. This falls more in to the structured and semi-structured methods. In interviewing people they may make similar responses to those previously interviewed. As a result of this knowledge, you may decide to pursue the line of questioning in order to understand the extent to which the answers are similar and may therefore be coded in the same way.

Without due consideration to interviewees as persons in their own right, they can easily be left with the impression that the researcher is doing them a favour – a bizarre twist of circumstances! Practically speaking, if people feel valued then their participation is likely to be enhanced – as well as their attitudes towards future involvement in social research. One idea which can help researchers is to imagine themselves in the same position in similar circumstances. Would they be prepared to cooperate and answer their own questions? In order to assist this process, attention is given to the issue of *rapport*. This refers to the development of a mutual trust between the parties that enables an interview to flow more freely. This issue brings us round to a discussion of focused interviews and the establishment of rapport utilizing this method.

The practice of focused interviews

The establishment of rapport in focused interviews is of paramount importance given that the method itself is designed to elicit understanding of the interviewee's perspectives. Initial contacts with, for example, managers, may elicit official responses reflecting how the organization ought to appear in terms of the rhetoric of its own image. We need to remember, therefore, that language is more than an act of speaking; it is also an act of representation of a position and identity. In this case, if researchers wish to move beyond official representation, to find out how things actually are, then they will have to seek the trust of the individuals being interviewed – assuming their willingness to enter into such a dialogue.

Building up and establishing contact is a central part of the process. As Whyte (1984) puts it in considering the build-up of first contacts:

> The interviewer deliberately keeps the conversation away from evaluative topics and tries to get the informants to make descriptive statements. We may begin asking informants just what their jobs entail, what they do at what time, and how their jobs fit into the whole production process.
>
> (Whyte 1984: 104)

The establishment of rapport has been described as a four-stage process (Spradley 1979). First, there is an initial apprehension that both the interviewer and interviewee have of the process. This is perfectly understandable if the parties are strangers and the interviewer should not feel that it is a personal weakness on their part. To overcome this, both parties should begin to talk to each other using *descriptive questions*. These include, for instance, the amount of time that a person takes to perform a task in which the interviewer is interested, or their formal role in an organization. These could take the form of 'grand tour' questions such as asking someone to give an account of an average day at work, whether in the home or elsewhere. This could be reduced to 'mini-tour' questions by asking someone what tasks are actually involved in the performance of a given role.

It is also possible to ask people about particular things that have happened to them. While undertaking one of our projects in SURF we were researching the relationship between science and governance in the UK, France, Germany and Spain (Perry and May 2007). One of many interviews we conducted was with a leading chemist. Prior to the interview we had written to him and asked to speak about the relationship between science and regional investments. He agreed to the interview. When he entered the large office that he occupied at the top of a building which was funded by the regional authority, he threw his papers onto the desk from several feet away before sitting down and announcing that he had 'no interest' in the region and how it related to his scientific activity and had only ten minutes for the interview! Clearly this was not a good start! So, rather than start the interview according to the areas of interest that we wished to explore, I asked how he ended up working in the area and about his career. One hour later we were having an interesting and productive discussion about the role of regions in scientific work.

More generally, you could ask people what experiences they particularly remember surrounding the topic in which you are interested or, finally, asking people what terms they use for particular places or things. The use of such questions also helps in the second stage of establishing rapport: *exploration*. Here each party to the interview begins to discover what each is like and how the interview will proceed and for what reason. Again, this is assisted by asking descriptive questions which leads to the third stage of *cooperation* where each party to the interview 'knows what to expect of one another' (Spradley 1979: 82). The final stage could take many weeks to arrive at and will depend upon the time at the disposal of the researcher and respondent. This is called *participation*.

Participation is a core part of an action approach to research in which there is a movement from the traditional view of the researcher as spectator of practices to one in which the participants in the research collaborate in co-generating relevant knowledge, engage in mutual learning, interpret the research findings and take actions as a result (Greenwood and Levin 1998). In this approach the researchers:

> Encourage the practitioner researchers we support to examine, clarify and articulate their own values as their living standards of judgement, which means that they also have to examine, clarify and articulate their logics.
>
> (Whitehead and McNiff 2006: 88)

Here we see action research in general, like the focused interview in particular, necessitating a process of building up trust and cooperation. It utilizes not only descriptive questions, but also what Spradley (1979: 120) calls *structural questions*. These enable the interviewer to explore areas of a person's life and experiences in greater depth; they can also be used to explore and disconfirm particular ideas the researcher has. These 'verification' questions might take the form of asking what types of people the interviewee tends to socialize with. However, there is a need to be aware of the sensitivity of some issues and how to phrase such enquiries.

As with all research, interviews do not simply begin when the first question is asked. Preparation by reading and initial exploratory work, understanding the situation into which you are going, clarifying any ambiguities which people might have of the research and eliciting their cooperation and being sensitive to ethical, political and theoretical considerations in the process, form a central part of its practice. It may be the case that the people whom the researcher wishes to interview are not amenable to direct approaches or are difficult to trace. In terms of the former, two researchers on biker gangs noted how 'Bikers would not humor many questions and they did not condone uninvited comments' (Hopper and Moore 1990: 369).

In these circumstances the technique of *snowball sampling* may be employed. Here small groups of people who are the initial interviewees are asked to nominate their friends, who are then interviewed by the research. This process continues until the researcher is satisfied that their data are sufficient for the purposes of the study, or time, possible interviewees and/or resources run out! This form of non-probability sampling is very useful in gaining access to certain groups, including through the use of telephone numbers and email contacts. However, whatever the means deployed, researchers have to be aware that they inherit the decisions of each individual as to who is suitable for interviewing. This may not present a problem, but it may lead the researcher to collect data which reflect particular perspectives and thereby omit the voices and opinions of others who are not part of a network of friends and acquaintances. To this extent it is necessary to guard against the tendency to succumb to 'Methods Are Resembling Saloon Bar Sociology (MARSBARS)' (Pahl 1995: 198)!

Another method of assisting in the process of rapport and recall is called *sequential interviewing*. This may be applicable to all methods of interviewing, but is of particular interest to those which permit a greater flexibility for the person to answer in his or her own terms; it involves interviewing people about events in the way they might, or have, unfolded. By using this chronological format it enables people to reflect on or project their experiences in terms of the event(s) which are of interest. For example, in interviewing people about housing problems, Pierre Bourdieu asked respondents to talk about their previous places of residence, how they had ended up living there and their conditions of access 'giving rise to some accounts of an unhoped-for frankness' (Bourdieu et al. 1999: 618), as was apparent in a further study on housing markets (Bourdieu 2005).

If an unstructured format is used, its flexibility allows people to return to a point previously made and elaborate upon it. Further, as the account of the event unfolds, it also enables the interviewer to ask about a previously stated belief in terms of the information gained. This method of 'reflecting back' allows interviewers to confirm their interpretations and to seek elaborations upon the person's account. It also allows interviewees not only to elaborate, but also to correct and/or modify their accounts. This method is particularly valuable in terms of linking historical changes with alterations in people's life courses (see Giele and Elder 1998).

The chronological method of interviewing is associated with the idea of a person's 'career'. Originating in the work of the Chicago School of social research (see Bulmer 1984a; Kurtz 1984), this does not mean changes in a person's occupational status, but the transformations people undergo in adopting particular roles as the result of new experiences. Erving Goffman spoke of the value of this idea in terms of its 'two-sidedness':

> One side is linked to internal matters held dearly and closely, such as image of self and felt identity; the other side concerns official position, jural relations, and style of life, and is part of a publicly accessible institutional complex.
>
> (Goffman 1968: 119)

While a point is being made here regarding the use of observation of people's actions to check their accounts of those actions through interviews, Howard Becker (1963) employed this method in his classic study of marijuana users.

In this study, 50 interviews were conducted on the process through which people learn to become marijuana users and build up an identity as a user of the drug. The simple fact of smoking, in itself, was not enough. People developed the habits, techniques and patterns of other users before they were able fully to enjoy its effects. The novice was

> curious about the experience, ignorant of what it may turn out to be, and afraid it may be more than he [sic] has bargained for. The steps outlined below, if he undergoes them all and maintains the attitudes developed in them, leave him willing and able to use the drug for pleasure when the opportunity presents itself.
>
> (Becker 1963: 46)

The stages through which people had to pass were then mapped in Becker's account by using extracts from the interview data collected. These illustrated how each stage was an important part of learning to become a marijuana user. They were 'learning the technique', 'learning to perceive the effects' and 'learning to enjoy the effects'. Through this method Becker was able to chart a person's socialization into a subculture from an initial willingness to try a drug, to a first experience of it, to learning techniques to obtain a 'high' and finally, learning to enjoy what was likely, at first, to be an unpleasant experience (dizziness, thirst, tingling of the scalp and misjudgement of time and distance). By adopting the concept of a career in the interviewing process, we end up with a fascinating insight into what is often regarded as deviant behaviour.

At this end of the interviewing spectrum life-history and biographical interviews may be found. Both types seek qualitative depth. Typically, they are detailed conversations which attempt to gain a fuller insight into a person's biography. Clifford Shaw's (1930) work uses a life-history method which relates the story of a teenage boy who was in prison for Jack Rolling (a similar type of offence to the mugging of drunks). Shaw focuses on the early childhood of Stanley (the Jack Roller) and the death of his mother. After this period, he ran away from home and spent time in various institutions, before finally living on the streets and becoming a Jack Roller. The data upon which his life story was based took six years to collect. The flexibility of this method enabled Shaw to return to Stanley from time to time when he was asked to expand on his accounts. Shaw was then able to build up a picture of his life and the circumstances which led to his actions.

Interviews: encounters in understanding

Ann Oakley (1979) interviewed women about their experiences of the transition into motherhood. The research involved 233 interviews that generated 545 hours and 26 minutes of tape-recorded data (Oakley 1979:

309). The women whom she interviewed were at a critical stage in their lives and wished to know the answers to questions, or simply be comforted in the ordeal ahead of them. As a result, she was asked a total of 878 questions, 76 per cent of which were requests for information on medical procedures, physiology, baby care and so on. The remainder of the questions she was asked were divided into 'personal' and 'advice', as well as those concerning the research process itself. Personal questions included her being asked about her own experiences of motherhood and childbirth (Oakley 1984).

In the face of these requests, how is an interview expected to be a one-way process of information extraction in which answers are obtained by the interviewer, but questions that are asked of them are ignored? Ideas of disengagement are not a realistic possibility, but a process that is constructed after the event. As a result the experiential aspects of the interviewing process are subsumed by theoretical categories which are used, retrospectively, to interpret the data. This is not to suggest that theoretical preparation and background work for conducting interviews is not important, or that reconstruction after the interview is not inevitable, but that the experiential need not be bracketed in seeking scientific rigour.

Three reasons have been suggested for why disengagement in the interview process is not possible. First, to seek such an interaction may lead to exploitative relationships with research participants: for example, a feminist faced with questions such as 'Does an epidural ever paralyse women?' is not likely to answer 'That's a hard one, I have never thought of that' (Oakley 1990: 48). That might be in line with certain textbook prescriptions, but it is hardly satisfactory. Second, what is the aim of the research itself? As noted earlier, action research approaches these issues through collaborative endeavour so it is not an option, while feminist research aims to counter a public–private divide by giving a voice to women's issues and experiences. Therefore, Ann Oakley regarded her work as a way of 'giving the subjective position of women not only greater visibility in sociology, but, more importantly, in society, than it has traditionally had' (Oakley 1990: 48).

Third, the idea of not answering questions posed by the interviewee is not conducive to establishing rapport as a precondition for a successful interview. A refusal to answer, or an evasive answer, is not a reciprocal gesture. To expect someone to reveal important and personal information without entering into a dialogue is untenable. For these reasons, *engagement*, not disengagement, is a valued aspect of dynamic interviewing inspired by action research, feminist and critical approaches to the research process.

These critiques have come from different traditions. For feminist inspired work, disengagement is seen to reflect a 'masculine paradigm' of research (Oakley 1990) whose implications require researchers to examine their own assumptions and perspectives according to a reflexive methodology (Alvesson and Sköldberg 2009). The idea of 'controlling' the social distance or familiarity between interviewer and interviewee, or controlling for the dangers of 'over-rapport' as some texts put it, is a contradiction in terms 'between what the textbooks say interviewing is all about and how a feminist feels she should treat other women' (Ann Oakley, quoted in Mullan 1987: 194). Establishing 'rapport', being 'disengaged' and conducting the interview in a hierarchical relationship between the parties are all rejected in both theory and practice. As one conclusion of a review of the literature on approaches to interviewing puts it:

> the literature cited in this chapter emphasizes the need for awareness of ways in which the relationship between the interviewer and interviewee affects how the research topics and questions are approached, negotiated, and responded to – indeed, how the co-construction of meaning takes place.
>
> (Heyl 2001: 379)

In contrast to the apparent need to establish rapport, one researcher was 'startled by the readiness with which women talked to me' (Finch 1984: 72). This was not simply the result of using an in-depth interviewing technique, but that a woman interviewing other women is 'conducive to the easy flow of information' (Finch 1984: 74). This was attributed to three factors. First, women are more used to intrusions into their private lives through visits from doctors, social workers, health visitors and others, and are therefore less likely than men to find questions about their lives unusual. Second, in the setting of their own homes, the interviewer becomes more like a 'friendly guest' than an 'official inquisitor'. Third, the structural position of women in society and their 'consignment to the privatised, domestic sphere . . . makes it particularly likely that they will welcome the opportunity to talk to a sympathetic listener' (Finch 1984: 74).

Other considerations in feminist-based interviewing are interactions between men and women and the ways in which everyday conversations are structured, thus affecting any dialogue involving the two sexes. Are everyday conversations between men and women a genuine and mutual exchange of views without social power operating in such a way as to bias the exchange in the male's favour? According to the results of one study, men tend to dominate conversations and differ in the way they maintain interactions (Fishman 1990), while in another study, based on group discussions, the language that men deploy to describe emotions are drawn from particular means of expressions in which the intensity and relevance of the emotional subject position is downplayed, so that the individual does not appear *too* emotional. The occupation of such a position would implicitly conflict with a masculine subject position and the discourses upon which that position is based.

(Walton et al. 2003: 56 original emphasis)

In other words, if we take for granted the 'normal' manner of conversation in our work, the chances are that it will exclude from consideration how language constrains as well as enables what we can say and how. Once again, a reflexive examination of research practices becomes a fundamental part of the interviewing process and will be informed by the orientations that the researcher brings to the encounter. We should also be aware of how our positions, not just theoretical influences, inform what is obtained and constructed from an interview. The differences this can make are evident from the experiences of a male and female researcher who were studying the sensitive topics of abortion and sexual violence. The nature of the elaborations varied according to the experiences of the interviewee and the gender of the interviewer (Padfield and Procter 1996).

THE ANALYSIS OF INTERVIEWS

In this section I outline the ways in which interview data can be analysed, as opposed to the actual mechanics of analysis. However, these are only some of the ways analysis may be performed. During the course of the discussion I shall therefore refer to works on data analysis in order that you are aware of alternative sources should you wish to pursue this topic further and draw your attention to issues raised in Chapter 1. As the use of analysis for questions using structured interviewing has already been covered in Chapter 5, I concentrate here on other methods.

It is helpful to start with two conventions that characterize interviews: *equality* and *comparability* (Benney and Hughes 1984). The former operates to the advantage of the respondent in so far as it aims at a participatory dialogue in the interviewee's own terms – as some exponents of the focused techniques would advocate and the above section illustrated. Yet we also find a lack of structure in these interviews. This makes the task of comparison more difficult because the responses to particular questions, except as we might move to more semi-structured forms, will not be uniform. Therefore, for researchers the structured and to some extent also the semi-structured format are preferred because of the issue of meaningful comparison. However, as noted, interviews have different *aims* and the convenience of analysis should not be a reason for choosing one method rather than another. It is the issues in which we are interested and our research questions, along with an assessment of the applicability of methods towards those ends that should drive our considerations and judgements.

Videos may be deployed with interviews. Researchers deploying such techniques have noted the ethical and practical considerations concerning visual methods, as well as their advantages and disadvantages in social inquiry (Hindmarsh 2008). Yet there is no substitute, in terms of preparation and the understanding that derives from fieldwork in terms of obtaining familiarity with a social setting that then informs such analysis:

> Even in settings that seem utterly familiar – schools, homes, museums and the like – it can also encourage reflection on the activities that arise, the participants involved and the various material, and increasingly digital, resources on which people rely.
>
> (Heath et al. 2010: 50)

The same may be said of whether tape recording is practical and ethical, as well as the need for familiarity within settings in which the interview is conducted and/or concerned. In terms of practicality, we interviewed over a hundred people using unstructured and semi-structured interviews across different countries. In these instances matters of language and understanding became important, as do such matters as knowing in advance where an interview may take place and whether background noise will prevent the interview taking place.

In terms of ethics and the use of tape recorders, this may again be illustrated through an example. During research to generate learning among stakeholders on implementation of an initiative, one interviewee on a particularly sensitive topic actually preferred a busy and noisy reception area for the interview so we could not be overheard. Given the context it was not possible to use the tape recorder and the interviewee's preference had to be respected. The result was a thorough interview, most of which could not be documented due to the speed of my handwriting and the need to maintain an insightful interaction through eye contact.

Another issue also arose. We have a commitment to confidentiality in the interviewing process. Unless the person actually gave their permission to be identified, if we judged their response to be prejudicial to their position, we would not use the data. In addition, we provided the interviewees with our report prior to more general circulation in order to ensure these standards were being met. Despite these conditions, the interviews enabled the generation of insights that we tested and elaborated upon in our interviews and observations in the subsequent stages of the research.

We can see how recording has both advantages and disadvantages. These fall under three headings: interaction, transcription and interpretation. At an interactional level, some people may find the tape recorder inhibiting and not wish their conversations to be recorded. Transcription itself is also a long process – a one-hour tape can take eight or nine hours to transcribe fully, depending upon typing ability. Tape recording can assist interpretation as it allows the interviewer to concentrate on the conversation and record the non-verbal gestures of the interviewee during the interview, rather than spending time looking down at their notes and writing what is said. Further, once the conversation is started, many people can forget the tape is on (including the interviewer when the tape shuts off noisily in the middle because the recording time was not long enough!).

Such an outcome has, fortunately, become less of a concern with advances in digital recording and automatic tape continuation. However, it is still necessary to be aware of such limitations. Then, editing the tapes, according to categories in which the analyst is interested, assists in the comparative analysis of interview responses. Finally, tape recording guards against interviewers substituting their own words for those of the person being interviewed, but it can also make the analyst complacent as it is frequently believed that once the data are collected, most of the work has been achieved, as if analysis and translation were not of central importance.

Following the interview, the work is only just starting. Not only does the writing up of notes or transcription of tapes have to take place, but also so does the analysis. Here we find an expectation that certain concepts will somehow be evident within the data, as if studies of workplace behaviour might automatically reflect states of alienation or anomie. To this issue we can add the effort needed in explaining the texts we have transcribed:

> it is clear that some texts receive a great deal more interpretative work that others; some texts are very transparent, others more of less opaque to particular interpreters; interpretation is sometimes unproblematic and effectively automatic, but sometimes highly reflexive, involving a great deal of conscious thought about what is meant, or why something has been said or written as it has.
>
> (Fairclough 2003: 11)

It then becomes necessary to employ techniques which can make some analytic sense of the raw data. Conventional methods of achieving this involve the *coding* of open-ended replies in order to permit comparison. Coding has been defined as

> the general term for conceptualizing data; thus, coding includes raising questions and giving provisional answers (hypotheses) about categories and about their relations. A code is the term for any product of this analysis (whether a category or a relation among two or more categories).
>
> (Strauss 1988: 20–1)

Strauss's prescriptions in his detailed monograph on qualitative analysis follow the methodology of grounded theory (Glaser and Strauss 1967; Strauss and Corbin 1990) which, as Clive Seale puts it in his survey of this body of work, requires of the researcher 'a rigorous spirit of self-awareness and self-criticism, as well as an openness to new ideas that is often the hallmark of research studies of good quality' (Seale 1999: 104). Using categories in grounded theory not only enables comparisons, but also presents issues in analysis (Dey 2010). Yet even if analysts are not a follower of this method, the ways in which they begin to categorize data will still depend upon the aims of their research and theoretical interests. These, in turn, should be open to modification and challenge by the interview data analysed. It could be, for example, that a researcher is interested in the ways in which people negotiate their roles, performances or senses of space in particular contexts (Strauss 1978; S. Watson 2006). The researcher would then focus upon the data in order to understand how people go about their daily lives and compare each interview in this way to see if there are similarities. If replies are similar, they can be categorized under particular headings such as 'methods of negotiation', which allows the analyst to index the data under topics and headings.

Whyte (1981) used two methods to index interview materials in his study of the social organization of 'street corner society'. First, in terms of the respondents and their relationships to each other, and second, their references to events in terms of what actually happened and how important it was to the person being interviewed (Whyte 1984: 118). By focusing upon the ways in which people spoke of one another and made sense of the events which they experienced, this enabled him to build up a picture of the meaning of relationships to people and type of language used to describe each other and the events which took place. This is a form of *ethnographic* analysis achieved through becoming familiar with the interview data in order to understand the culture that people inhabit and their relationships to each other (Gerson and Horowitz 2002).

Writing up notes or transcribing tapes and simply listening to the conversations assists the important analytic stage of becoming familiar with the data. This is further assisted if the technique of 'developmental interviewing' has been employed. By moving, chronologically, through a person's account of an event and their experiences of it, a picture is constructed. Focusing on the ways in which different people relate their experiences, according to the circumstances they found themselves in, enhances a comparison of accounts. If a tape recorder was used, this can be achieved by editing each tape according to various topic headings which the analyst chooses. Each tape would then comprise a part of the interview that is relevant to these categories. These, together with notes on the course of the interview and any significant non-verbal gestures employed, assist the researcher in becoming familiar with the data and the particular nuances of each interview. On the other hand, if written notes were used, once they are fully written up, they simply have to be ordered in the same way to permit comparison in responses.

There are computer packages for the analysis of qualitative data which search for key phrases and the frequency with which people use certain words and in what context (N. Fielding and Lee 1991; Kelle 1995; N. Fielding 2002; Salmons 2010). Qualitative data analysis software programs facilitate the process of comparing categories, as well as enabling exploration of the data enabling links and patterns to be discerned and stored in new files, building up understandings. Here we should note that while of considerable use, the process of analysis should not come to over-ride the need to be familiar with the data produced. Furthermore, while directly inputting data on to a computer has been used in telephone surveys, it is increasingly being used in face-to-face interviews. However, once again, we encounter issues over the maintenance of rapport as well as the source of our ideas:

> Those who use qualitative software testify both that they get ideas from working with the software and that they get ideas in the traditional ways, in the bath, in the middle of a conversation, while landing at night. Using software won't prevent the 'eureka' effect but it won't guarantee it either.
>
> (N. Fielding 2002: 176)

As technological innovations continue at such a pace, different opportunities are being opened up for other forms of data collection that complements interviewing: for example, video conferencing and real-time interviewing on the World Wide Web. In relation to the latter, time, transcription, expenses and access may be advantages. At the same time, the development of appropriate expertise and access to equipment that introduces biases into the sample become disadvantages (Chen and Hinton 1999) and issues also arise in such forms of research (Salmons 2010). Here, as always, a researcher has to exercise a critical scrutiny, rather than enthusiastic embrace of the latest technique without an adequate conceptualization of the issues that surround and inform its practice.

In all of this, we should not forget that talk has to be situated. Analysts need to ascertain what C. W. Mills (1940) termed 'vocabularies of motive'. These may be given during the interview as reasons why people performed various actions within particular situations in which they found themselves. Pierre Bourdieu (1992, 1999) argues that the analysis of talk requires more than linguistic analysis, as if speech were constructed in a hermetically sealed universe. What is also required is an explanation of the position of the speaker in terms, for example, of their class, race, gender, occupational position and so on. This 'positioning' will be missed if concentrating upon the form of speech alone. Erving Goffman made a similar point:

> linguists have reason to broaden their net, reason to bring in uttering that is not talking, reason to deal with social situations, nor merely with jointly sustained talk ... For it seems that talk itself is intimately regulated and closely geared to its context through non-vocal gestures which are very differently distributed from the particular language and sub codes employed by any set of participants.
>
> (Goffman 1981: 122)

Other researchers have argued that accounts people give of their actions are either 'justifications' or 'excuses'. These, in turn, may be viewed as indicative of how people identify themselves and routinely negotiate their social identities (M. Scott and Lyman 1968). An account given during an interview is 'the presentation not only of reasons but of oneself' (Harré 1988: 167) within a social context. It is characterized, therefore, by a duality: 'as an index of location in a material world, and an index of moral position in a world of discursive values' (Harré 1998: 135). This has led to the development of a particular approach to positioning theory in social inquiry (Harré and Moghaddam 2003).

The analysis of interviews focuses not only on motivations and reasons, but also on social identities and how these are constructed within the social settings in which people live and work. In this context, Dorothy Smith and her research collaborator Alison Griffith, influenced by feminist standpoint epistemology, examined the relationship between mothering and schooling. They focused on

> the social relations in which the work that mothers do in relation to their children's schooling is embedded. Their ongoing practical knowledge of the concerting of their activities with those of others is expressed in how they speak about those activities.
>
> (Smith 1988: 189)

To express it another way, how the relationship between mothering and schooling was constructed and reflected upon within the settings in which a mother entered (the school, home, workplace and so on), all of which takes place within a method of inquiry known as 'institutional ethnography' (Smith 2002, 2005).

Finally, there are also those who have moved away from the idea that interviews tell researchers the 'truth' about the actions or events which people engage in (a positivist oriented position) or that they demonstrate a relationship between position and utterances via which people routinely act and interpret events and relationships (a realist oriented position).

Simply expressed, the assumption that there exists something beyond the accounts that people give is abandoned. Instead, what are examined are regularities and features of the account. Gilbert and Mulkay (1984) employed such a method in a study of scientists' accounts that moved them towards an ethnomethodological perspective that stresses what people 'do' in performing their utterances. The emphasis is therefore upon how accounts serve as justifications, accusations and so on. What is then opened up is the field of studies known as conversation analysis (see Heritage 1997; Hutchby and Wooffitt 2008).

Although the above has been referred to as a form of 'discourse analysis' (Wetherell and Potter 1988), it does need to be separated from a number of other approaches that may be placed under this broad heading: for example, critical discourse analysis (Fairclough 1995, 2003), narrative research (Lieblich et al. 1998) and socio-psychological approaches (Willig 1999). It also needs to be distinguished from poststructuralist-inspired work where the stress is upon how discourses constitute subjects as objects. Here, the focus of analysis moves beyond the performance of the speech itself, to how such discourses order a domain of reality which has repercussions beyond those understood or intended by the speaker. The effect of such discourses may then be to 'silence' certain voices through their ability to construct channels of communication, which authorize only certain persons to speak in particular ways (see Wetherell and Potter 1988). That noted, a focus upon these 'circuits of power' (Clegg 1989; May 2006b) does not necessarily mean adopting a post-structuralist methodology, while different perspectives have the potential to be combined in imaginative ways for knowing the social world (G. Miller 1997).

I have mentioned these approaches to the analysis of interview data for the interested reader and in order to show the variety of ways in which they may be interpreted (see also Gilbert and Abell 1984; Silverman 1985, 1993, 2010). Interview analysis, whatever the focus of study, can be a long process in which perseverance, theoretical acumen and an eye for detail is paramount. It is frequently said that the hard work starts only when the data are collected and analysis begins – that is frequently the case. The success of its execution, in turn, lies in the hands of the researcher. In this section I have simply given an overview of its main elements and the different approaches employed. Yet to be faced with many hours of tapes or pages of transcripts can be a daunting prospect. However, if you choose to use interviewing yourself, do not think the hours of frustration you might experience are the result of problems peculiar to you. They are not likely to be. The process can be alleviated by experience, reading around the subject and seeking supportive individuals for their opinions on the data, the interviewing process, your coding and mode of analysis.

ISSUES IN INTERVIEWING

I have covered a range of perspectives on interviewing. In this process it has been noted how structured interviewing does not simply reflect positivism, nor does unstructured interviewing reflect a social construction approach associated with idealism. In terms of social constructionism, the section on analysis covered an ethnographic approach using cultural analysis, to a form of discourse analysis which focuses upon language use. As a result of covering such a broad spectrum I have, implicitly at least, covered many of the criticisms. However, consider the following issues.

Interviews are used as a resource for understanding how individuals make sense of their social world and act within it. However, ethnomethodological approaches are interested in interviews as topics in their own right. It is thereby assumed that the link between a person's account of an action and the action itself cannot be made: it tells the social researcher little about a reality that is 'external' to the interview. Instead, an interview is a social encounter like any other. The prescriptions of interviewing books to control the situation are just attempts to produce a false social situation which has no validity beyond the interview; they cannot be assumed to produce data which reflect a real world beyond interpretation. For this reason, interviews are a *topic* of social research, not a *resource* for social research:

> interview data report not on an *external* reality displayed in the respondent's utterances but on the *internal* reality constructed as both parties contrive to produce the appearances of a recognisable interview.
>
> (Silverman 1985: 165, original emphases)

The focus now moves to the methods that people employ in constructing the interview, not the interview data themselves; as noted above, the use of language as performance. This leads to a form of conversation analysis (see Heritage 1984, 1997; Schegloff 1988; Boden and Zimmerman 1993) which has been used to study such topics as embarrassment (Heath 1988), doctor–patient interactions (Heath 1981; Heath and Hindmarsh 2002); and telephone calls (Houtkoop-Steenstra 1993; Heritage 1997). Note, however, that we have taken a methodological route back into the discussion in Chapter 2, where so-called practical reasoning and the methods that people use to make sense of the social world around them were considered topics for social research and theorizing. The same criticisms of this perspective apply to this focus on interviewing as a topic for social research.

The issue of qualitative depth in focused interviews and quantitative patterns of relationships which emerge from structured interviewing also raise their heads. In Chapter 5 we saw how it was argued that questions of meaning could be understood using a structured format. Yet more instrumental and less theoretical considerations also place a schism between these methods. In-depth qualitative interviewing with a large number of people is both expensive and time consuming; these considerations frequently dictate the methods employed. However, this does not prevent the researcher from understanding that the aims and limitations of different methods still apply, nor from lobbying sponsors for the use of the method(s) which would best suit the aims of the research. Researchers thus have a duty to themselves and to others to reflect upon and acknowledge both the strengths and weaknesses of the different methods that they employ.

There are also the criticisms of interviews as extractions of data rather than encounters in understanding which have been briefly covered. The spurious distinctions between reason and experience and of objectivity as detachment, are just some of the underlying arguments which inform this critique. Yet, as noted in Chapter 5, feminists have also used structured interviewing and in the section above I concentrated on focused methods. Thus, while sharing the critiques of malestream research, there also exists a debate around interviewing methods among those who would regard themselves as feminist researchers. Further, some have argued that Ann Oakley's characterization of textbook prescriptions is inaccurate (Malseed 1987). In reply to this critique, Oakley (1987) argued that this did not detract from the substance of her arguments.

In a final criticism, I examined the contention that interviews rely on people's account of their actions as representing something beyond the interview situation. Several possibilities arise from this. First, accounts may simply be inaccurate for one reason or another. Second, while accounts may be a genuine reflection of a person's experiences, there might be circumstances or events which surrounded these of which the person was not aware. Third, a fuller understanding can be achieved only by witnessing the context of the event or circumstances to which people refer. The only way in which the researcher could examine these is to be there at the time. This, with an element of contrivance on my part, now brings us round to the subject of participant observation.

SUMMARY

In many walks of life interviews are used on a daily basis to understand and appraise individuals in particular and gain information in general. While the aims of such interviews are different in form from those used in social research, this common usage is a point often lost on those who concentrate solely upon their validity, instead of the way they are used as instruments for gaining information and, often, employing social power for the purposes of recruitment and assessment. Interviews in social life are not only topics, but also employed as means of appraisal which may determine life chances. At the same time, interviewing utilizes particular skills. For these reasons, researchers need to maintain an interest in their interviewing practices, as well as what is said and done as a result of the interview, for the overall purpose of improving our understanding of the social world. Simply maintaining a divide between the quantitative and qualitative may not be helpful towards this end. It has been argued, for example, that it is comparison as an important dimension to social research which is often missing in practice. As such, error can be present in both quantitative and qualitative methods as ways of knowing the social world and to maintain that they are opposed to each other may replicate the very biases that feminist researchers, for example, seek to address and overcome (Oakley 1998, 2000).

Lastly, it is worth emphasizing that the data derived from interviews are not simply 'accurate' or 'distorted' pieces of information, but provide the researcher with a means of analysing the ways in which people consider events and relationships and the reasons they offer for doing so. Yet they are mediated not only by the interviewee, but also by the interviewer. It is their presuppositions in the interpretation of the data that should also be a subject of the analysis. Quite simply, if both the strengths and weaknesses of different methods of interviewing and approaches to their analysis are understood, they can provide us with an essential way of understanding and explaining social events and relations.

Questions for your reflection

1 What are the essential attributes of a structured and focus group interview and why?

2 Do different approaches to interviewing reflect incompatible ways of viewing social reality?

3 You are asked to conduct life-history interviews with a group of inmates in a prison. What methods would you choose and what do you think would be the issues you need to consider before, during and after the interviews themselves?

4 Is an interview a topic of social research or a resource for social research? What perspectives inform this debate and what is your opinion on it?

SUGGESTED FURTHER READING

Mann, C. and Stewart, F. (2000) *Internet Communication and Qualitative Research*. London: Sage.

Roberts, B. (2002) *Biographical Research*. Buckingham: Open University Press.

Salmons, J. (2010) *Online Interviews in Real Time*. London: Sage.

Silverman, D. (2010) *Doing Qualitative Research: A Practical Handbook*, 3rd edn. London: Sage.

7   Participant observation: perspectives and practice

In the politics of persuasion and allusions to particular ideas of what constitute scientific findings, the power of numbers cannot be doubted. In scientific writings, quantification is often presented in terms of justification of hypotheses, while qualitative research is concerned with discovery. When it comes to reception, one method may be seen to prove the truth of falsity of an assertion or impression, while the other acts as an under-labourer to be subjected to the rigours of quantitative methods. Yet as I have repeatedly argued and questioned, the dichotomy produced between the two obscures more than it clarifies and it rests upon unhelpful assumptions if our overall aim is to understand the world in better ways.

As social systems become more abstract and complicated, but are implicated in power relations that have effects upon everyday life, quantitative analysis may be the only means to reveal their workings and consequences, while historical researchers have excavated the terrain of common assumptions in order to debunk the idea that epistemological allegiances actually inform the choice to adopt different research methods (Platt 1996).

However, to push this too far runs counter to the ethos of this book: that is, the reproduction of a separation between issues and methods by invoking the rational exigencies of situated decisions that appear free from assumptions and/or consequences (May 1997). An examination of the interactions between social research communities and those which they study assists in making the pre-reflexive assumptions of the social scientific community more clear in order to sharpen our practices.

Our practices are intended to capture social reality. For some, our ideas about the world are now so saturated by media images that the difference between reality and its representation has collapsed: 'our reality . . . has been swallowed up by the media' (Jean Baudrillard, quoted in Gane 1993: 160). Adverts persuade us to consume goods by employing visual media that have nothing whatsoever to do with the product in terms of the needs it might satisfy; shops might play different types of music according to their assumed ability to influence spending patterns and large shopping areas are less likely to have clocks in order, presumably, that those customers who can afford to will lose all sense of time in an orgy of consumption. Desires are created in these ways and so we have become sold on and by the images we consume.

These ideas have not met without criticism (Rojek and Turner 1993; O'Neill 1995; Smith 1999; Bourdieu 2000; Goldthorpe 2000; May and Powell 2008). In examining the work of Baudrillard, Zygmunt Bauman (1992) concludes with a recommendation: 'It becomes a philosopher and an analyst of his time to go out and use his feet now and again. Strolling still has its uses' (Bauman 1992: 155). To 'stroll' in this sense is to listen, observe and experience and to expose theories and biographies to new and unfamiliar social settings and relations, with a view to enhancing an understanding of them. This is precisely what the historian Raphael Samuel did in his rich reflections on living history. In his footnotes one gets a sense of the origin of his ideas when he refers to 'notes on a perambulation' (Samuel 1994: 117).

Understanding living history, strolling, experiencing and listening are all part of the science, art and skill of observation. The use of observation and the ideas upon which it is based are the subject of this chapter. First, it introduces the ideas and place of participant observation in social research. Second, it examines the process of conducting research using this method. Third, it considers the methods of analysing observations. Finally, it moves on to discuss the issues associated with this method of social research.

PARTICIPANT OBSERVATION AND SOCIAL RESEARCH

Participant observation has a quite distinct history from the positivist (or variable centred) approach to research. While its origins may be sought in social anthropology, it was the Chicago School of social research, particularly Robert Park, who encouraged students to study, by observation, the constantly changing social phenomena of Chicago in the 1920s and 1930s. This led to a wide body of research on areas such as crime and deviance, race relations and urbanism (see Bulmer 1984a; Kurtz 1984). It should be noted, however, that the distinctions that are now made between quantitative and qualitative research in relation to participant observation were not intrinsic to the Chicago School at this time (Platt 1996).

The Chicago School and participant observation

The aims of participant observation, as well as its history, are different from what is commonly termed positivism: for example, the design of questionnaires involves the researcher in developing ideas and testing or exploring these using questions. Critics argue that researchers employing this method assume that they already know what is important. In contrast, participant observation is said to make no firm assumptions about what is important. Instead, it encourages researchers to immerse themselves in the day-to-day activities of the people whom they are attempting to understand. In contrast to testing ideas (deductive), they may be developed from observations (inductive). That noted, there are those who combine methods in their quests for understanding and explanation. As William Foot Whyte puts it in reflecting upon his research practices:

> From 1948 on, working with students on surveys, I came to recognize that, while the method had limitations, it also had important strengths. Many years later, in the course of our research programme in Peru, I became convinced not only of the importance of integrating surveys with anthropological methods but also that the study of local history could enrich our knowledge.
>
> (Whyte 1984: 20)

In the Chicago tradition of research, we witness a merging of two intellectual traditions. First, there is the tradition of *pragmatism* from the work of American philosophers such as William James, Charles Peirce, John Dewey and George Herbert Mead (see Thayer 1981; Mounce 1997). Within this tradition it is emphasized that social life is not fixed, but dynamic and changing. In the words of Paul Rock (1979), social life is both 'incremental' and 'progressive'. Therefore, if people's social lives are constantly changing, we must become part of their lives in order to understand how it changes; we must participate in it and record our experiences of those transformations, their effects on people, as well as their interpretations. Knowledge of the social world does not come from the propositions of logic upon which the theorist then descends upon the world to test. Knowledge comes from experience and the undertaking of detailed and meticulous inquiries through which we generate our understandings.

Practitioners tend to shun what is known as the *a priori* (a proposition that can be known to be true or false without reference to experience), preferring the *a posteriori* (knowing how things are by reference to how things have been or are):

> They attempt to make their research theoretically meaningful, but they assume that they do not know enough about the organization *a priori* to identify relevant problems and hypotheses and that they must discover these in the course of the research.
>
> (Becker 1979a: 312)

This is not an assumption of interviews in so far as if someone is asked for an account, the researcher does not consider it necessary to have personally experienced the event or relationship to which it refers in order to analyse or understand it. Such an approach leads two advocates of grounded theory to say that it is 'currently the most widely used and popular qualitative research method across a wide range of disciplines and subject areas' (A. Bryant and Charmaz 2010: 1).

Researchers who employ positivist presuppositions in, for example, questionnaires are not said to be immersing themselves in the social world in which people are busy experiencing, perceiving and acting according to their interpretations of that world. Instead, it is important to participate in social relations and seek to understand actions within the context of an observed setting. Why? Because it is argued that people act and make sense of their world by taking meanings from their environment. As such, researchers must become part of that environment for only then can they understand the actions of people who occupy and produce cultures, defined as the symbolic and learned aspects of human behaviour which include customs and language. The technique, it is argued, is least likely to lead to researchers imposing their own reality on the social world they seek to understand.

The second strand informing the Chicago School tradition is known as formalism. While social relationships may differ from each other, they take forms that display similarities. In this way, we do not simply talk about one setting or group being 'unique', but ask the extent to which it displays similarities or is typical of other groups or settings. The focus of social inquiry is upon the interactions of people within social settings, not individuals as such. An advocate of this idea, Georg Simmel, argued that 'the investigator must proceed, as in all other sciences, on the basis of methodical abstraction' (Frisby 1984: 61). The content of interactions may vary, but the forms may be similar:

> social groups which are the most diverse imaginable in purpose and general significance, may nevertheless show identical forms of behaviour toward one another on the part of their individual members. We find superiority and subordination, competition, division of labor, formation of parties, representation, inner solidarity couple with exclusiveness towards the outside, and innumerable similar features in the state, in a religious community, in a band of conspirators, in an economic association, in an art school, in the family. However diverse the interests are that give rise to these sociations, the *forms* in which the interests are realized may yet be identical.
>
> (Simmel 1964: 22, original emphasis)

Formalism is also concerned with the ways in which particular social and cultural forms of life emerge. In keeping with pragmatism, they are argued to come from the practical concerns of people's everyday lives 'but that once established they take on a life of their own' (Hammersley 1990a: 37). These forms may actually conflict with each other, but the task of the researcher is to understand how they evolve. It is not surprising that Robert Park, a student of Georg Simmel, encouraged his students to 'stroll' – to stroll in order to understand the flux of social life in which the individual self is also subject to change. Anticipating what was to become an apparent insight in later accounts of flux in the individual subject, he wrote:

> the empirical self is always changing, and is never self-consistent. This means that the individual cannot be viewed as a basic unit; both from the above standpoint and in terms of the systems of relationships investigated by sociology, the individual does not constitute a permanent uniformity.
>
> (Park 1972: 29)

These strands of thought also combine with the idea of *naturalism* which 'proposes that, as far as possible, the social world should be studied in its "natural state" undisturbed by the researcher' (Hammersley and Atkinson 2007: 7). However, this does not mean that people simply react to their environments. According to this view, influenced by different theoretical and philosophical traditions, people are busy interpreting and acting within a social world infused with meaning. Thus, any concern with change and process must take this as its starting-point:

> I wish to point out that any line of social change, since it involves change in human action, is necessarily mediated by interpretation on the part of the people caught up in the change – the change appears in the form of new situations in which people have to construct new forms of action.
>
> (Blumer 1972: 191)

The process of learning behaviour is argued to be absent from other forms of research: for instance, a questionnaire asks questions at one particular time. It is a 'static-causal snapshot' of attitudes; how and why people change is not understood. In practice, observers record their own experiences in order to understand the cultural universes which people occupy. Participant observation may therefore be defined as:

> The process in which an investigator establishes a many-sided and relatively long-term relationship with a human association in its natural setting, for the purposes of developing a scientific understanding of that association.
>
> (Lofland and Lofland 1984: 12)

Ethnography, as it is often referred, leads to an empathic understanding of a social scene. It is said to exclude, over time, the preconceptions that researchers may have and exposes them to new social milieux that demand their engagement and understanding. According to one view, theory is then generated from data (Glaser and Strauss 1967). Glaser and Strauss propose two criteria for this purpose. First, it should fit the data and not be forced on to it. Second, it should be meaningfully relevant to the behaviour under study. As the researcher is exposed to each new social scene, this acts as a control on hasty theoretical conclusions (Silverman 1985; A. Bryant and Charmaz 2010). The more varied the scenes of interaction that are viewed and circumstances experienced, the more one can understand actions within social contexts.

Reflexive waters

The above tradition has had a considerable impact on the aims and methods of participant observation and for that reason I have included an overview of its history. However, the point has been made throughout this book that perspectives do not dictate but inform methods, and different perspectives frequently use the same methods or combination of methods. All too often crude representations of various methods cloud a considered judgement of their strengths and limitations. Participant observation is no different in this respect and no overview of its place in social research can fail to acknowledge this state of affairs.

We have encountered a number of dichotomies in social research which, on closer examination, have tended to be less clear cut than the doctrinaire posturing of much literature on social research would suggest. Here I am thinking, in particular, of the simple distinctions made between quantitative and qualitative social research, theory and fact and modern and postmodern ideas. In the literature these differences are frequently assumed rather than subjected to the rigours of sustained examination. While the methods that we use will influence the nature of the data we produce, it is worth noting that 'differences between the two approaches are located in the overall form, focus, and emphasis of study' (Van Maanen 1979: 520).

Qualitative researchers often resort to the language of quantification in their work and while surveys are argued by researchers to tap questions of meaning, they must first understand people's frames of reference and for this reason have a qualitative dimension to their design and interpretation. In other words, there is an ethnographic component to successful survey work, while numbers may equally appear in the representation of ethnographic studies.

Imaginatively combining work in this way can capture insights that have been derived from complexity theory and its implications for social science (see Byrne 1998). One of these is 'emergence':

> Emergence occurs when interactions among objects at one level give rise to different types of objects at another level. More precisely, a phenomenon is emergent if it requires new categories to describe it which are not required to describe the behaviour of the underlying components. For example, temperature is an emergent property of the motion of atoms. An individual atom has no temperature, but a collection of them does.
>
> (Gilbert and Troitzsch 1999: 10)

Thus we find that an abstract system of production and exchange (capitalism) can be the emergent property of routine, everyday interactions, while global forces also influence local dynamics (Burawoy et al. 2000). Participant observation may therefore be an appropriate method for capturing the dynamics of the latter, but not the former where different methods of social investigation may be required in order to understand emergent properties and their interactions with everyday life.

As discussed earlier in the book, the idea that there are facts which we can gather on the social world is highly problematic, for our factors, including theory, mediate our interpretations. For this reason it is better to say that data are produced, not collected. Yet the emphasis of the above approach to participant observation has tended to be upon induction and naturalism. Data are collected and somehow 'naturally occurring' – without being mediated by the theoretical concerns and biography of the researcher – while theory is derived from observations.

These assumptions have been subjected to scrutiny and found wanting (Hammersley 1992; Hammersley and Atkinson 2007). For these reasons researchers influenced by other perspectives have employed the method of participant observation and it would be an error to gloss over them and present the method as if its practice reflected a unified perspective. Thus, in studies of the urban lifeworld different traditions have played their part (Madsen and Plunz 2002) as is the case in research on organizations which has included critical action research addressing issues of power, knowledge and positioning (Sykes and Treleaven 2009). However, two features certainly differentiate it from positivist oriented research. First, the subject matter of the social sciences differs from the natural sciences, and second, to assist in understanding social reality, we must also directly experience that reality (Bryman 1988a: 52).

In terms of the direct experience of reality, Dorothy Smith has employed the method within what she has termed 'institutional ethnography'. This approach does not take its questions from such schools of thought as Marxism, symbolic interactionism or ethnomethodology, but this does not mean that

> it makes no use of such theories, but the central project is one of inquiry which begins with the issues and problems of people's lives and develops inquiry from the standpoint of their experience in and of the actualities of their everyday living.
>
> (Smith 2002: 18)

A commitment to learning from the actualities that the ethnographer studies is core to this approach, which is seen as a dialogue in which the researchers themselves are changed (Smith 2005: 50–1).

Paul Willis (1977) used the method of participant observation within the realist tradition. Spending time with a group of 'lads', he charted their progression from school to work. From his observations on their everyday lives, he derived a theory which argued that capitalist relations structured not only their actions, but also their expectations. However, this did not assume that the 'lads' were simply cultural puppets. On the contrary, they were active in their resistance to oppressive social structures by not only understanding, but also questioning and mocking, the authority of teachers. Such a tradition is continued in the work of those such as Simon Charlesworth's (2000) study of working-class experience in the North of England with its clear debt to the work of Pierre Bourdieu.

We have seen how both attention to subjective experiences and its links to objective conditions are evident in the tradition of critical realism. Sam Porter (1993, 2002), following Roy Bhaskar (1989), has deployed ethnography to investigate racism in doctor–nurse relations. Given an emphasis upon the generative social mechanisms which underlie these interactions, this enabled him to compare his results with other social settings of a similar type (Porter 1993: 607) thereby enabling generalizations based on an analysis of both actions and structure:

> Whilst structures provide the context for actions, that context is itself determined by the particular combination of structures pertaining and the degree to which actions reinforce or undermine the relative strengths of those structures.
>
> (Porter 2002: 70)

Aaron Cicourel (1976) worked in the ethnomethodological tradition in order to show how juvenile justice was the product of negotiation between officials, parents and juveniles. Michèle Lamont (2009) included observations in her study on peer review and academic judgement, as did Stephen Hilgartner (2006) in his work on scientific property, the law and laboratory work, while Mary Pattillo-McCoy's (1999) study on the black middle class in Chicago is an example of the rich and distinctive work that has come from a long tradition of studies. There are also those who have conducted ethnographic studies on the internet which raises particular issues about observation, access, validity and reliability within virtual environments (Lyman and Wakeford 1999; Hine 2000; Kozinets 2010). Finally, feminist researchers, of differing theoretical orientations, have used observation methods to study women quantity surveyors (Greed 1990); women and social class (S. Webb 1990; Skeggs 1997, 2004); gendered work in the tourist industry (Adkins 1995); the formation of friendships among 'girls' (Hey 1997), and single parents and schooling (Griffith 2006).

I am now in a position to summarize the positive aspects of this method. First, it is least likely to lead researchers to impose their own reality on the social world they seek to understand. Second, the process of understanding action is omitted from other forms of research and how and why people change is not understood. Third, during interviews, there may be language or cultural differences expressed. In this case, observers may record their own experiences in order to understand the cultural universe which people occupy (subjective experiences) and convey these observations to a wider audience (from field notes) within the context of explaining their data (theoretical framework). The process by which these are achieved is the subject of the following sections.

THE PRACTICE OF PARTICIPANT OBSERVATION

This method is one that those who are new to social research often believe they can undertake with ease. On first glance it appears to be just about looking, listening, generally experiencing and writing it all down. It is equally plausible to argue that participant observation is the most personally demanding and analytically difficult method of social research to undertake. Depending on the aims of the study and the previous relationship of researchers to those with whom they work, it requires them to spend a great deal of time in surroundings with which they may not be familiar; to secure and maintain relationships with people with whom they may have little personal affinity; to take copious notes on what would normally appear to be everyday, mundane happenings; to possibly incur personal risks in their fieldwork and then, if that is not enough, to spend months of analysis after the fieldwork. From this point of view, it is worth bearing in mind that when the fieldwork stops, the work itself is just starting! Nevertheless, to those who are prepared, willing and able, it is also one of the most rewarding methods that can yield fascinating insights into people's social lives and relationships and, more generally, assists in bridging the gap between people's understanding of alternative lifestyles and the prejudices which difference and diversity so often meet.

The researcher's role

Participant observers may work in teams, which assists in sharpening insights and generating ideas. Very often, however, researchers work alone. In the process they witness the 'reflexive rationalization' of conduct, that is, the continual interpretation and application of new knowledge by people (including themselves) in their social environments as an ongoing process. The ethnographer is 'the research instrument par excellence' (Hammersley and Atkinson 2007: 17). Ethnographers gather data by their active participation in the social world; they enter a social universe in which people are already busy interpreting and understanding their environments. This can involve a number of different methods:

> It can involve gathering information by moving closely among people, sometimes quite literally 'living among people', and observing their everyday lives . . . In other forms of study, in-depth interviews and life-histories which could never be obtained simply by 'hanging around' and 'watching the action'. Not uncommonly, different methods are mixed together.
>
> (Pearson 1993: ix)

In adopting this first form of study it does not follow that researchers comprehend the situation as though it were 'uncontaminated' by their social presence. For this reason, among others, naturalism, in its literal sense, is regarded as 'dishonest' by denying the effect of the researcher on the social scene. Accounts of ethnography, following this course of action, are viewed as mythologies that 'present an over-simplistic account of research' (Stanley and Wise 1993: 161). On the contrary, the aim of understanding is actually enhanced by considering how they are affected by the social scene, what goes on within it and how people, including themselves, act and interpret within their social situations – hence the term *participant* observation.

In 'doing' ethnography, engagement is used to an advantage. Furthermore, being part of the social world which we study 'is not a matter of methodological commitment, it is an existential fact' (Hammersley and Atkinson 1983: 15). In this process, ethnographers have explicitly drawn upon their own biographies in the research process: for example, having been personally and politically engaged in protest as part of a group, before deciding to turn attention to its analysis (Roseneil 1993). Our own cultural equipment is thereby used reflexively to understand social action in context (Coffey 2002).

Reflexivity is something of a contemporary 'buzzword' in social research and while important in methodological terms (Alvesson and Sköldberg 2009) it requires some clarification regarding its actual uses in understanding the social world (May 1998a, 1998b, 2011). In terms of its implications for ethnography, it

> acknowledges that the orientations of researchers will be shaped by their socio-historical locations, including the values and interests that these locations confer upon them. What this represents is a rejection of the idea that social research is, or can be, carried out in some autonomous realm that is insulated from the wider society and from the biography of the researcher.
>
> (Hammersley and Atkinson 2007: 15)

Depending upon the aim and history of the research, the particular roles which researchers adopt will vary and this, in turn, will affect the data produced. However, we may wish to adopt a particular role, but the circumstances do not permit it. As the experiences of Buchanan et al. (1988) suggest, while organizational researchers, for example, should be 'opportunistic' in their fieldwork, if the possible and desirable clash, the former will always win through! Equally, experiences of research on topics close to home raise issues concerning the need for closure (Alvesson 2009) and issues can arise in relation to power and expertise within the field (Haney 2002). The reasons why we are not able to adopt a particular role, while frustrating, might also become the topics of our research for they may tell us a great deal about the operation of social power and relations in the setting under study.

In what has now become a standard reference on fieldwork roles (originally written in 1958), Gold (1969) identifies four roles of field research which assist in the process of reflexive analysis when it comes to field notes. A central part of the analytic process is a reflexive consideration of how the researcher is positioned within field relations, what effects that may have on those relations as well as a consideration of those 'actions at a distance' (May 2003) that may not be apparent in immediately observed social contexts.

The first role that Gold identifies is the *complete participant.* The researcher employing this role attempts to engage fully in the activities of the group or organization under investigation. Their role is also covert for their intentions are not made explicit. This is the role that Humphreys (1970) adopted in his work (discussed in Chapter 3). Among its advantages, it is argued to produce more accurate information and an understanding not available by other means (for examples, see Festinger et al. 1956; Ditton 1977; Rosenhan 1982; Graham 1995), while to remind ourselves of our discussion on ethics, there are also those who argue that covert and unobtrusive methods within netnography enables research on sensitive topics (Langer and Beckman 2005).

Second, there is the *participant as observer.* This person adopts an overt role and makes their presence and intentions known to the group (for example, see A. Campbell 1984; May 1991; T. Watson 1994; May and Perry 2010). In this process they attempt 'to form a series of relationships with the subjects such that they serve as both respondents and informants' (Denzin 1978: 188). Despite traditional concerns with 'establishing rapport' or what is called 'going native' and hence not being 'objective', for many researchers who possess the capabilities to understand, listen and learn, these are not problems and reflect a particular view of scientific inquiry which has been subjected to scrutiny and found wanting.

This role often means becoming a 'fan' (Van Maanen 1978) who desires to know and understand more from people within the setting. It does not, however, mean attempting to act as one of the group studied. This is particularly the case when it comes to research on crime and deviance. Polsky (1985) puts this forcefully: 'in doing field research on criminals you damned well better *not* pretend to be "one of them", because they will test this claim out' (Polsky 1985: 117, original emphasis). At the same time, attention to the accurate recording of events is still paramount and problems with this, or the previous role, may focus on the researcher's recall. This is particularly the case in situations where note taking is not possible. In the case of researching motorcycle gangs, for example, two authors spoke of the physical threats they faced:

Even seemingly insignificant remarks sometimes caused a problem. In Biloxi on one occasion, we had an appointment to visit a biker clubhouse late on a Saturday afternoon in 1986. When we were admitted into the main room of the building, two women picked up four pistols that had been lying on a coffee table and scurried into a bedroom.

(Hopper and Moore 1990: 369)

Third, we move away from the idea of participation to build up, over time, an understanding of a social setting, to the role of *observer as participant.* Strictly speaking, this would not be regarded as participant observation:

> The observer-as-participant role is used in studies involving one visit interviews. It calls for relatively more formal observation than either informal observation or participation of any kind.
>
> (Gold 1969: 36)

There was no lasting contact with people, and so Gold (1969) notes the possibility in this role of misunderstanding due to unfamiliarity with the culture and the language employed. It is more of an encounter between strangers which does not utilize the strengths of time in the field and getting to understand the rules, roles and relationships within the settings observed.

Similarly, the *complete observer* is a non-participant role. At this end of the spectrum, the role completely removes the researcher from observed interactions and is epitomized by laboratory experiments which simply involve the mechanical recording of behaviour through, for example, one-way mirrors.

Access

If participant observation involves becoming part of a group or organization to understand it, it is obviously not simply a case of 'hanging around'. To become part of a social scene and participate in it requires that the researcher is accepted to some degree. This period of 'moving into' a setting is both analytically and personally important. Those aspects of action which are 'strange' to the observer may be 'familiar' to the people who are part of the study. However, how people manage and interpret their everyday lives is an important condition of understanding a social scene. In this sense, the experiences of the observer are central. As we experience a new scene it feels 'strange': Fineman and Gabriel (1996) utilized this by drawing upon the accounts of new recruits to a variety of organizations, as do Simon Down and Michael Hughes (2009) in a first-hand account of becoming a manager in a steel works. After a time, it becomes more familiar and it is understanding 'how' people achieve this which becomes a legitimate focus for participant observation:

We learn what we can in advance about this relatively unknown
territory, but once we are there, the first requirement is to gain some
initial familiarity with the local scene and establish a social base
from which we can continue our exploration until we are able to
study some parts of that territory systematically.

(Whyte 1984: 35)

It becomes important to regard the normal as unfamiliar. Further, in
negotiating access into an organization, for instance, the researcher
should be aware of power relations within the setting. As Severyn Bruyn
(1966) notes:

The participant observer who studies a complex social organization
must be aware of the fact that clearance at one level of the organization does not insure clearance at another level. It is very important
that the researcher takes into account the levels of power and
decision-making extant in the group.

(Bruyn 1966: 204)

If management is your level of entry into an organization, that could
mean that others in the organization may be suspicious of your intentions. After all, they may consider that you are part of a management
strategy of change. In such situations, the researcher must address these
issues. However, while initial suspicion may be experienced, it is important not to regard this as a personal weakness, for it may be an understandable reaction on the part of the people within the setting or
organization. Of course, this could block your entry, but access is not
simply a stage, as many texts suggest, through which an observer passes
before 'uncontaminated' data are supposedly derived (May 1993).

Initial reactions to your presence can cause a sense of personal discom-
fort, but tell you a great deal about relations and concerns of people and
should be recorded and not simply regarded as personal problems or
weaknesses. For instance, only two days after starting research on changes
in a public sector organization (May 1991), I was questioned by two
people who were apparently suspicious of my intentions. The questions
were forcefully put and difficult to answer at the time. Yet I learnt from
this episode. I learnt that suspicion was understandable due to the
politically charged atmosphere surrounding organizational change. I
learnt that my credibility as an impartial researcher was to be a central
issue as I moved through different levels within the organization. My
level of entry was management and not to have positively acted in
the light of this initial suspicion would have meant, by default, carrying
this suspicion with me. I also learnt that the two people who did the
questioning had a vested interest in the changes taking place within the

organization and, as such, any research associated with it. As Amanda Coffey (1999) puts it:

> The fieldnotes which we collect and *write* have always embraced the personal. Fieldnotes describe places and people and events. They are also used as textual space for the recording of our emotions and personal experiences . . . fieldnotes are the textual place where we, at least privately, acknowledge our presence and conscience. The self is part of the reality of fieldnotes.
>
> (Coffey 1999: 119–20, original emphasis)

Frequently in literature on the practice of participant observation, questions of access and the identity of the researcher as the instrument of data production are regarded as methodological and/or theoretical inconveniences to be overcome. Researchers' actual experiences of fieldwork are then reserved for separate volumes (see C. Bell and Newby 1977; C. Bell and Roberts 1984; Bryman 1988b; Van Maanen 1988; H. Roberts 1990; D. Bell et al. 1993; Hobbs and May 1993; May 2002; Ybema et al. 2009; Davies et al. 2010). On the contrary, experiences gained during negotiations for access to a group or organization, as well as the researcher's reflections on the research in general, are fundamental to the aims of enhancing understanding and explaining social relations.

Utilizing flexibility

One of the main advantages of participant observation is its flexibility:

> If you're half-way through a survey and one of the questions isn't working, you're worried, what are you going to do? You can't change it. Whereas if I learn today something useful from my field research, my observation, I can go out tomorrow and use it.
>
> (Howard Becker, quoted in Mullan 1987: 120)

Fieldwork is a continual process of reflection and alteration of the focus of observations in accordance with analytic developments. It permits researchers to witness people's actions in different settings and routinely ask themselves a myriad of questions concerning motivations, beliefs and actions. Here are just a few for your reflection which could preoccupy any fieldworker: why did that happen and to whom? What do people ordinarily do in this setting and why? What would happen if people did X? What do they think about Y? What are the usual rules of the social scene? How are the rules negotiated? What are the verbal and non-verbal gestures employed? Who said what to whom and why? What do they mean and how do they relate to particular relationships and actions? Why is X not done? What would happen if something different happened? Finally, how does physical space relate to the setting and the interactions which take place within it (adapted from Lofland and Lofland 1984)?

These are just a small number of possible questions that ethnographers would routinely ask themselves during the course of fieldwork. It is then possible to focus the next series of observations on answering these questions and thereby utilizing the flexibility of the method. In addition, participant observation often employs the unstructured interview technique as a routine part of its practice (see Gerson and Horowitz 2002). The comparison of data derived from these two methods is not assumed to be incompatible. The very opposite is the case for such comparisons illuminate the researcher's understandings and provide information which is simply not available through observation:

> Observation guides us to some of the important questions we want to ask the respondent, and interviewing helps us to interpret the significance of what we are observing. Whether through interviewing or other means of data gathering, we need to place the observed scene in context, searching for the potential positive or negative sanctions, which are not immediately observable but may be important in shaping behaviour.
>
> (Whyte 1984: 96)

The questions to which we are directed are formulated according to an exposure to the social scene over time and an observation of people's everyday actions. This, together with an explicit analytic framework and aims for the study, enables us to focus research inquiries. For this purpose Whyte uses what he calls an 'orientating theory' which 'simply tells us in the most general terms what data we are likely to need at the point of analysis' (Whyte 1984: 118). Data are collected under two headings (also mentioned in Chapter 6 under analysis): first, the identification of relationships within the social setting, and second, a description of events and situations which took place. Observation and the writing up of notes under these headings, together with any relevant interview data, provide a rich insight into social relations, events and processes. Data production and analysis and the decision as to when to withdraw from fieldwork may then take place together in what Glaser and Strauss (1967) refer to as 'theoretical sampling' and 'theoretical saturation', the latter referring to the time when observations no longer serve to question or modify the theories generated from earlier observations, thus rendering the theory 'saturated' with data through, for example, the grounding of categories (Dey 2010).

Field notes

The 'data logging process', as Lofland and Lofland (1984) call it, is often regarded as boring but 'if the researcher lacks any personal emotional attachment to the concerns of the research, project quality (even completion) may be jeopardized' (Lofland and Lofland 1984: 47). This relies not only upon commitment, but also on the quality of the researcher's observations, field notes and analytic abilities. In relation to field notes, there is a series of guidelines that can be given which I shall briefly overview in this section, but researchers do vary in their methods. Some prefer to use school exercise books with wide margins on the left-hand side. These margins enable you to highlight particular observations in which you are interested, make analytic notes, or notes to yourself to investigate an event or relationship in more depth. It may also include notes to read other literature on a topic or theme which you have observed or which has arisen from your observations.

The notes made will depend upon the focus of your inquiries. As noted, the flexibility of this method is a considerable advantage and some time will be spent in familiarizing yourself with the social setting and the people within it (and they with you). Following this initial period, to take notes on anything and everything which happens is not only impossible, but also undesirable; your theoretical interests will guide your observations and they, in turn, modify or alter those. You will also need to minimize the time from observations to full notes to maintain good recall and in the initial stages of your research, make a running description of events noting those questions for the ethnographer outlined above, and any others which may arise or you wish to pose.

While the nature of relationships are noted, the order and setting in which events unfolded are important to note, as are the rules employed and your reflections upon the events observed (the latter being for the left-hand margin). Over time, a picture is built up of the roles, rules and relationships between people. For instance, Bob Burgess (1990), in his study of a school, moved from a general description to more detailed and focused records on positions of teachers in the staff common room and from there to a wider group of people 'until I could subdivide the groups in the staff common room according to their major characteristics' (Burgess 1990: 169).

A particular notation and filing system for your notes is important: for example, key words to jog your memory; different quotation marks to indicate paraphrased and verbatim quotes; files on individuals, topics and events; theoretical 'memos' (see Strauss 1988; Lempert 2007) to yourself on the research, plus any supplementary data in the form of documents or previous literature and research on the subject. Whatever method you devise, the important issues are *consistency* and *accessibility*.

Subjective adequacy

In writing notes, the feeling often arises that the observer may have missed something or is being too selective in their observations or even too general. Severyn Bruyn (1966) assists in this concern by listing six indices of what he calls 'subjective adequacy' to enhance the understanding of the researcher and thereby the validity of the research. These are time, place, social circumstances, language, intimacy and social consensus. As authors on validity and qualitative research have noted (Kirk and Miller 1986), while this concept tends to be couched in terms of a positivist framework, Bruyn's ideas do assist in the continual process of reflexivity towards the ends of representation, responsibility and reliability (Sánchez-Jankowski 2002).

Time is the first of the indices. Quite simply, the more time that the observer spends with a group, the greater the adequacy achieved. As 'process' is a focus of inquiry,

> It is time which often tells us how deeply people feel about certain subjects. It is time that tells us how long it takes an outside influence to become a meaningful part of the lives of people in a culture. Those social meanings which really count in people's lives cannot be calculated by reference to the temporally limited, stimulus–response framework of the experimentalist. Cultural influences have an incubation period which takes time and close association to study.
>
> (Bruyn 1966: 207)

Second, there is *place*. A concentration on this dimension enables the researcher to consider the influence of physical settings upon actions. The researcher should record not only the interactions observed, but also the physical environment in which it takes place. Third, and closely related to this, are *social circumstances*. The more varied the observer's opportunities to relate to the group, in both terms of status, role and activities, the greater will be his or her understanding. In work on the probation service (May 1991, 1993), I spent time with officers in prisons, day centres and different types of courts, allowing me to observe probation work in different settings and the relationship between actions and social environments.

Fourth, there is *language*. The more familiar that researchers are with the language of a social setting, the more accurate will be their interpretations of that setting. Bruyn (1966: 212) is using the term language in its 'broadest sense' to encompass not only words and the meanings that they convey, but also non-verbal communications such as facial expressions and bodily gestures in general. As researchers become more familiar with this aspect of the social setting, they learn the language of the culture and record their impressions and any changes in their own behaviour: 'language threads through subject and object, creating, expressing, and representing the life and character of the people studied' (Bruyn 1966: 213).

Fifth, there is *intimacy*. The greater the personal involvement with the group and its members, the more the researcher is able to understand the meanings and actions they undertake. This not only links in with social circumstances, but also provides access to a more private or 'backstage' world, which underlies the comments of one of the greatest observers of human action, Erving Goffman. He speaks of the 'front' and 'backstage behaviour' of people which the observer can witness:

> there tends to be one informal or backstage language of behaviour, and another language of behaviour for occasions when a performance is being presented. The backstage language consists of reciprocal first-naming, co-operative decision-making, profanity . . . The frontstage behaviour language can be taken as the absence (and in some sense the opposite) of this.
>
> (Goffman 1984: 129)

Finally, there is *social consensus*. This is the extent to which the observer is able to indicate how the meanings within the culture are employed and shared among people. This ability is clearly assisted by being exposed, over time, to the culture and noting under what conditions and in what settings the meanings are conveyed. This links into what is known at the 'principle of verifiability', which enhances the reliability of the study. As Hughes (1976) describes it, social researchers achieve 'understanding' when they know the rules of a social scene and can communicate them to another person who could then 'become a member of the actor's group' (Hughes 1976: 134). In other words, this requires not only a degree of familiarity, but also the ability to communicate to other persons the rules operating within the setting in such a way that they could enter that setting and feel part of it. This is a regulative ideal which researchers should aim at, not something which can be easily achieved as such.

In this section I have sought to present an overview and introduction to the main issues involved in the process of undertaking participant observation: from the researcher's role, through access to a social scene, to the flexibility of the method and finally, questions of subjective adequacy. During each of these elements of the research process, the question of reflexivity has been raised. While this is applicable to all forms of research, with participant observation in particular, researchers and their experiences and observations are the means through which the data are derived. For this reason, a process of constant questioning takes place whether in the form of considering explicit theoretical formulations, or reflecting upon personal experiences which form an important component of those. Seeing these as a central part of the process greatly assists when it comes to the final analysis and writing-up of the research. Before moving on to the next section, I just wish to note a particular issue associated with reflexivity.

While it is important to locate the ethnographer at the centre of the research in terms of their interpretations, role and interactions, the current trend for reflexive accounting sometimes reads like an excuse for introspective indulgences. This can actually disempower the reader in terms of their ability to critically engage with a representation of events. What is required is an understanding of the context and nature of inter-actions observed, *along with* an understanding of the relationship between observation and interpretation. A preoccupation with the latter, while of clear methodological importance, can actually render little justice to the subject matter under investigation (May 1999b, with Perry 2011). A balance in ethnographic accounts allows connections to be made and understandings to be enhanced on the part of the reader. An active and critical engagement thereby results.

THE ANALYSIS OF OBSERVATIONS

Both the concept of reflexivity and the advantages of flexibility empha-size the process of analysis as part of fieldwork itself. At the same time, it was noted that researchers will also be constrained by the setting itself which may limit their abilities to conduct in-depth analysis at that stage. Therefore, the opportunity for reflection on experiences and a detailed analysis of the data may not come until the researcher has decided to withdraw from conducting any further fieldwork.

Howard Becker (1979a) lists four distinct stages of analysis whose overall aim is the categorization of collected data in order that the events, relationships and interactions observed may be understood or explained within the context of a developed theoretical framework. The first of the stages towards this aim is the 'selection and definition of problems, concepts and indices'. At this stage, researchers seek problems and concepts within the field setting which enable them to develop their understanding of the social setting; to determine the types of data which may be available by this method and to what extent observed social phenomena are related. Once established, observed phenomena are then placed within a theoret-ical framework for further investigation. Thus, in his research on medical students, Becker et al. (1961) observed them referring to particular patients as 'crocks'. By focusing upon the interactions between students and patients, a theory of how some groups within the hospital classified other groups, and for what reasons, was developed by further observations.

The second stage is a check on the 'frequency and distribution of phenomena'. This means focusing the inquiry in order to see what events 'are typical and widespread, and by seeing how these events are distributed among categories of people and organizational sub-units' (Becker 1979a: 317). It is at this point that the distinction between quantitative and qualitative work also breaks down (but not between good and bad research), because the researcher enters the realm of probability; in other words, how likely is it that a given phenomenon is frequent in the social setting and for what reason? It is possible to check such observations through interviewing and utilizing these forms of data, together with, say, documents on events – if available. This enables a check to be made against observations but, as Becker (1979a) notes, this may not always be possible in the field, so observers have to consider what other evidence they may need at the final stage of analysis and collect it accordingly. For example, collecting the minutes of organizational meetings and comparing these with your notes at those meetings if observing the policy process in an organization (May and Landells 1994; Gray et al. 1999; May and Marvin 2009). It is not infrequent to find yourself confronted by enormous amounts of data, much of which may not be of help in your theoretical formulations. However, it is better to have it at your disposal.

Third, Becker notes the 'construction of social system models' as the final stage of analysis 'in' the field, which 'consists of incorporating individual findings into a generalized model of the social system or organization under study or some part of that organization' (Becker 1979a: 319). This is similar in form to Glaser and Strauss's (1967) movement from substantive to formal theory and the need to make broader links in observational studies (Silverman 1993; Seale 1999). In each setting, one may derive a concept of substantive theory grounded within observations. In analysing different contexts, the researcher can then move to more formal theory composed of abstract categories. I shall give some examples.

Glaser and Strauss (1967) studied the concept of loss in the case of nurses dealing with dying patients. In each setting, nurses understandably experienced social loss which manifested itself in various ways. However, this in turn depended on the general concept of what social value was attached to individuals. So they moved from the particular (observed experiences of social loss) to the more general (how people attach social value to each other and how that affects their experiences of loss).

Becker's (1963) work on marijuana use led to an interest in the process through which people redefine experiences in order to 'neutralize' their deviant status. Yet in his eagerness to show how wrong previous literature on drug use was, he ignored a larger and more general question: that is, 'how do people learn to define their own internal experiences?' (Becker 1986: 148). This focus led to a whole series of empirical studies leading towards a general theory of self-identifying activity. As Becker notes in deploying literature on the topic to help you generate theory, the moral of this story is: 'Use the literature, don't let it use you' (Becker 1986: 149).

Finally, the importance of making broader links is clearly illustrated by Laurie Graham's (1995) study of the production line at Subaru-Isuzu. Her focus is upon new management techniques which seek to enhance quality and in so doing exercise greater control over the workforce. After providing rich and detailed accounts of work on the production line itself, she then situates these changes within a broader framework of what has been termed the 'Japanization of work' (Bratton 1992). These strategies are thus examined in terms of the differential skills that workers possess and their abilities to control certain aspects of these managerial changes whose overall aim is 'to manipulate workers' social experience within production' (Graham 1995: 152).

Aside from the use of previous literature, this method requires the constant comparison of data on the phenomena in which the researcher is interested. Thus, triangulated inquiry allows a comparison of data from interviews, observations, documents and surveys (see Jick 1979; Whyte 1984; N. Fielding and J. Fielding 1986; Gorard 2004). The important point to remember is the level of generality at which you are operating, for this obviously differs between substantive and formal theory:

> Both types of theory exist on distinguishable levels of generality which differ only in degree. Therefore in any one study each type of theory can shade at points into the other. The analyst, however, needs to focus clearly on one level or the other, or on a specific combination, because the strategies vary for arriving at each one. Thus, if the focus is on the higher level of generality, then the comparative analysis should be made among different kinds of substantive cases and their theories, which fall within the formal area.
>
> (Strauss 1988: 242)

The need to make comparisons between substantive cases to generate formal theory makes the task of using a consistent method of filing notes, theoretical ideas and secondary sources (other studies, books and documents on the topic) all the more important.

Assisting at this and the other stages of analysis is the use of 'units'. A 'unit is a tool to use in scrutinizing your data' (Lofland and Lofland 1984: 71). In their outline of qualitative analysis, John and Lyn Lofland note that they emerge as the scale of organization increases and each new one contains past ones. Thus, in this process of emerging social properties, you start with *meanings* such as cultural norms and people's definitions of the situation and the variations in the scope of rules in the social scene. You may then focus on *practices* such as recurrent categories of talk and action which you consider have analytic significance. You might then consider *episodes*, for example, the remarkable and dramatic such as crowd disorder and sudden illness and then move on to *encounters* (see Goffman 1961) where two or more people in each other's presence strive to maintain a single focus of mutual involvement. While how people 'get on' with each other appears mundane, it is also part of the social fabric which is observed and is worthy of attention in its own right.

A unit of analysis called *roles* is then of use. The focus here is directed towards the labels that people and organizations use to organize their own activities and describe those of others. How are these used? What are the issues in performing a role and what difficulties are encountered in their execution? These are just some of the questions to be asked. Then there are *relationships*. Noting Whyte's suggestion above on dividing data in terms of events and relationships, we would note how people regularly interact over time. From relationships we move to *groups* defined as those who conceive of themselves as a social entity (the 'we') having hierarchies, cliques and the means to cope with circumstances by mutual support or adaption. How and why these come about would be one focus of study of this social unit.

The units increase in abstraction with a focus upon *organizations*. The questions to ask yourself at this point and how this unit is defined are summarized by John and Lyn Lofland as:

> Consciously formed collectivities with formal goals that are pursued in a more or less planned fashion. Some major aspects of the analysis of organizations include the circumstances of their formation, how they recruit and control members, the types and causes of goal pursuit strategies they adopt, and the causes of their growth, change, or demise.
>
> (Lofland and Lofland 1984: 87–8)

Continuing with the theme of more general social units which encompass previous ones, there are *settlements*. These are beyond the grasp of the participant observer given their complex history and abstract nature. They comprise encounters, roles, groups and organizations within a defined territory which perform a range of functions. Examples of this type of settlement analysis are Whyte's *Street Corner Society* (1981, originally published 1943), Mary Pattillo-McCoy's (1999) 'Groveland' and Sophie Watson's (2006) studies of urban encounters.

A more general and abstract social unit is that of *social worlds* which manifest themselves in terms of modern transportation and communication systems providing the means for the proliferation and rise of social units. However, these are 'sprawling, shapeless entities' (Lofland and Lofland 1984: 91) which are not reducible to any one of the other units they contain. Thus, we speak of 'business worlds' or 'political worlds'. Finally, there are *lifestyles* considered as global adjustments to life by a large number of similarly like-minded and situated individuals. Here we might consider the social forces that create or channel our tastes and structure our cultural lives (for example, see R. Williams 1981; Williamson 1987; Bauman and May 2001; Žižek 2009).

Each of these different units may have different questions asked of them by the analyst. However, as we move away from what can be observed to more abstract entities, so too we move away from substantive to more formal theories. Yet this method of analysis is very useful for orientating the researcher to data which may, on first glance, appear unmanageable. This is where the development of an analytic framework during fieldwork renders the data both manageable and intelligible.

Becker (1979a) notes a final stage: the withdrawal from the field to analysis and writing-up of the results. At this stage there might be a search for data which does not appear to represent your emerging theoretical considerations. If so, it requires your consideration, understanding and explanation. At the same time, evidence is systematically collected in order to illustrate a theme which arises from the data or to illustrate the particular way in which an episode, encounter or relationship unfolded and the practices and the meanings utilized by the people concerned. This may lend itself to a *sequential* analysis whereby the chronological unfolding of a topic or event is examined. This goes back to the methods described in Chapter 6 for analysing focused interviews.

Aside from the suggestions of Glaser and Strauss (1967), Becker (1979a), Lofland and Lofland (1984) and Strauss (1988), there have been a number of interesting innovations in the analysis of qualitative data, one of which, as noted, employs computer programmes for the mechanical indexing of the data. Others have specifically explored the relationship between feminism and fieldwork (A. Williams 1990; Skeggs 2001; Smith 2005), deconstruction in postmodern research strategies (Clifford and Marcus 1986; Game 1991; Denzin 1994; Lather 2001), critical realism (Porter 2002) and semiotics (Manning 1987, 2001). This latter method focuses upon codes and signs used in social interaction whose analysis can be used for interpretative understanding of human relations and, for the purposes of policy analysis, organizational actions. Researchers may then focus upon the relationship between the use of language and human actions or study how language is employed in the social setting. Either way, what is often a difficult area of study may be utilized in interesting new directions for qualitative researchers.

No matter how well the data are analysed, the results must be presented and communicated in a way which is persuasive, well argued and accessible to the audience, although the actual witnessing and recording of actions can cause problems when it comes to publication (see Becker 1979b). The final result of your work is a text which attempts to persuade the audience of the authenticity of your descriptions and their analyses.

In this sense, writers have focused on texts not only as reporting a reality 'out there', but also in terms of their abilities to construct social reality (P. Atkinson 1990) in the sense that 'the writer's "voice" pervades and situates the analysis, and objective distancing rhetoric is renounced' (Clifford 1986: 12).

Nevertheless, to admit of the centrality of the ethnographer in the interpretative process does not imply an automatic opening for what is termed 'postmodern ethnography'. Here there is the attempt to deny any authority for the observer through, for example, allowing the narratives of the researched to 'speak for themselves' (see Fontana 1994). Such are the multiplicity of voices in this process that to speak in the name of something that apparently does not render justice to these differences is held to be an injustice. However, as Dorothy Smith (1999: 128) notes, 'it is precisely the multiplicity of experience and perspective among people that is a necessary condition of truth'.

In thinking about these issues, I would like to conclude this section with a brief look at the writing of ethnography, noting that many of these points are equally applicable to other methods.

Writing ethnography

Harry Wolcott (1990) suggests several points which need to be borne in mind when writing up fieldwork. First, maintain a focus on the topic and continually ask the question: 'What is this (really) a study of?' (Wolcott 1990: 46). However, do not let yourself suffer from writer's cramp:

> you have already made many choices when you sit down to write, but probably don't know what they were. That leads, naturally, to some confusion, to a mixed-up early draft. But a mixed-up early draft is no cause for shame. Rather, it shows you what your earlier choices were, what ideas, theoretical viewpoints, and conclusions you had already committed yourself to before you began writing. Knowing that you will write many more drafts, you know that you need not worry about this one's crudeness and lack of coherence. This one is for *discovery* not *presentation*.
>
> (Becker 1986: 17, emphases added)

Second, Wolcott (1990) suggests that data must be 'ditched' as you home in on the topic. While interesting to you, a long rambling description of an event, without analytic mileage, may not be to the audience. Third, if you do not have the evidence for some issues, do not let it grind you down. Check your materials and if it is not available, there is little you can do. Remember, researchers cannot claim to know everything! Fourth, unless otherwise prevented, write in the first person. Do not overdo it with constant use of 'I', but you were centre stage in this method of data production, and reflexivity and biography are a legitimate part of its practice. Fifth, Wolcott (1990: 47) suggests the past tense for writing to prevent the use of present and past tenses together. Sixth, to illustrate analytic points, use specific instances from field notes. This is part of Clifford Geertz's (1973) notion of 'thick description' as it aligns the analytic framework with the imagination of the reader and a description of people's relationships and the events observed. Seventh, consider the audience for whom you are writing. Wolcott's suggestion is to write for those who know little of the area of study. This is a good discipline as it enables a degree of general accessibility to areas of academic study and is particularly important when considering action or evaluation research on behalf of an organization to whom you have to report.

Finally, there is the brevity of your writing. While it is important to get it first written and not just 'right', the craft of writing remains of central importance. Corrections, additions, revising and editing of the text are all part of the writing process through which everyone has to travel (Becker 1986). Again, a supportive and knowledgeable friend or supervisor can always be asked for their opinions in cases of doubt.

There has also been a great deal written about the role of the author in the writing process. As I have noted elsewhere (May with Perry 2011), while the reflexivity of the author is an important dimension to the research process, it cannot serve as a justification for introspective indulgence. We can admit that the ethnographer is implicated in this process as Amanda Coffey (1999, 2002) makes clear in her discussions on the 'ethnographic self' but, at the same time, one is reminded of the long-standing tale of a conversation between a fieldworker and a respondent. Clearly exasperated because of continual references by the fieldworker to their own biography, the respondent eventually blurted out: 'Could we talk less about you and more about us!' After all, the worth of social research is judged in terms of 'what it tells us about those under study, not just what it reveals about the social scientist' (Fay 1996: 217).

ISSUES IN PARTICIPANT OBSERVATION

I have characterized the method of participant observation as not being the preserve of one school of thought and in so doing have again pre-empted some of the criticisms which are made by one perspective on the practice and theory of another. Those researchers inclined towards inter-actionism, for example, might focus upon the operation of rules in social interaction, but not upon how these rules are formulated by people in context and so are criticized for presupposing their existence. Yet I have noted that how rules are formulated, negotiated and employed within interaction is a legitimate area of inquiry for observation. That point made, the ideas which inform 'naturalism' are worthy of further consideration for they are often apparent, in various guises, in the process and production of ethnographic research. Martyn Hammersley (1990a, 1990b, 1992), in particular, has turned his attention to the problems of naturalism and those of ethnography in general.

As noted in relation to interviewing, the idea of disengagement to produce 'untainted data' is something of a myth and is based upon a particular view of 'scientific procedure' challenged by feminists, postmodernists and those who generally emphasize the importance of reflexivity in the research process. Naturalism, although different in history and aim, often becomes translated as positivism by concentrating upon the production of data about the social world whose validity is based upon it being 'untainted' by the medium of its collection. Hence a lot of material on observation is devoted to 'reactivity', 'going native' and so on. On the other hand, naturalism focuses upon social life as a process in direct contrast to the positivist viewpoint. Given this state of 'flux', the positivist criteria of being able to replicate a study in order to justify its scientific status is rendered problematic (see Marshall and Rossman 1989).

While data production, in general, is mediated by the researcher, in participant observation there is a different form of reliance upon perceptions and abilities to discern the nuances of interaction. It is possible that researchers will omit a whole range of data in order to confirm their own pre-established beliefs, leaving the method open to the charge of bias. Further, the observation of small-scale settings leaves it open to the charge that its findings are local, specific and not generalizable: it lacks *external validity*. This may be challenged by arguing that the observed social scene is 'typical', by adopting the perspective of realism and examining the generative mechanisms of human interaction (Porter 1993, 2002), or through using a variety of data sources. However, on the latter point, Denzin's (1978) original prescriptions for methodological, data, investigator and theoretical triangulation often read like a positivist desire to mediate between sources of data in the search for some 'truth' about the social world *independent* of people's interpretations and creations of it:

> Underlying this suggestion is, ironically, once more, elements of a positivist frame of reference which assumes a single (undefined) reality and treats accounts as multiple mappings of this reality.
>
> (Silverman 1985: 105)

Norman Denzin (1988, 1994) would no longer subscribe to these views, while this interpretation does not render justice to the spirit of his original text. Yet this does not detract from the issue that the strict separation between fact and value that is found in versions of naturalism is highly problematic. In actual practice (as noted in Chapter 1), researchers have argued that a strict representation of social reality through straightforward ethnographic methods is not adhered to by many (Hammersley and Atkinson 2007), while practitioners of ethnography have noted how it often 'embodies implicitly masculine perspectives' (P. Atkinson 1990: 148).

Realists, while utilizing this method, have also criticized the idea that we can observe events or relationships free from theories or concepts. Thus, any distinction between theory on the one hand, and empirical data through neutral observation on the other, must be challenged for we mediate our observations through concepts acquired in everyday life (Sayer 1992, 2000). The difference between 'natural' and 'artificial' settings as presupposed by naturalism must therefore be highly questionable. Reflexivity, biography and theory lie at the heart of research practice in general and ethnography in particular. This emphasis recognizes that we are part of the world we study, that we bring to any setting our own experiences, that there is a constant interaction between theory and data, and that these issues cannot be separated from each other.

Aside from the assumptions of naturalism, the problems of external validity and a masculine bias in its practice, participant observation has, for want of a better phrase, practical limitations. It demands that researchers spend time with relatively small groups of people in order to understand fully the social milieu which they inhabit. Hammersley and Atkinson (2007), while advocates of this method, note that:

> in relation to empirical generalization from a sample to an extant population, it is not usually able to employ statistical sampling theory, which can allow survey researchers to produce findings that have a high, and specifiable, probability of being representative of that population.
>
> (Hammersley and Atkinson 2007: 234)

Once again we are left with not one single method as being the answer to all the methodological problems of social research. The use of a method or combination of methods will depend upon the aim of our research, the practical difficulties which are faced in the field and the time and money available to conduct the research in the first place. Its successful execution depends upon the skills of the researchers and their understanding of the issues which inform research practice. In this there is not an either/or choice between seeing ethnography as a neutral and accurate reflection of a social milieu on the one hand and a work of fiction on the other. Instead, the reflexive ethnographer considers the methods through which their interpretations are constructed and will use the cultural resources at their disposal. After all:

There is little point in the academic agonizing over epistemology and methodology, or suffering the slings and arrows of data collection, only to have no disciplined awareness of the means available to report those efforts.

(Hammersley and Atkinson 1995: 243)

SUMMARY

Participant observation is about engaging in a social scene, experiencing it and seeking to understand and explain it. The researcher is the medium through which this takes place. By listening and experiencing, impressions are formed and theories considered, reflected upon, developed and modified. It examines process of change and the ways in which people act in and make sense of their environments and how those, in turn, inform and influence their actions. Combined with an engaged and fluid writing style, much insight can be gained from the reading of a rich ethnography.

Participant observation is not an easy method to perform or to analyse, but despite the arguments of its critics, it is a systematic and disciplined study which, if performed well, greatly assists in understanding human actions and brings with it new ways of viewing the social world. As is the case with all research methods, anyone looking for the means to secure the Truth through its successful operation will inevitably be disappointed. What they will find, however, is yet another means through which we can gain better understandings of ourselves and the environments we inhabit. With that end in mind, I now turn to documentary methods of social research.

Questions for your reflection

1 What are the strengths and weaknesses of participant observation compared to other methods of social research?

2 'Fiction or social fact?' What do you think is the status of ethnographic investigation?

3 Do the different roles performed in conducting observation produce different accounts of social life and does that matter?

4 How might you combine surveys with observational methods and what would be the advantages and disadvantages of doing so?

SUGGESTED FURTHER READING

Brewer, J. D. (2000) *Ethnography*. Buckingham: Open University Press.

Hammersley, M. and Atkinson, P. (2007) *Ethnography: Principles in Practice*, 3rd edn. London: Routledge.

Kozinets, R. V. (2010) *Netnography: Doing Ethnographic Research Online*. London: Sage.

May, T. (ed.) (2002) *Qualitative Research in Action*. London: Sage.

8

Documentary research: excavations and evidence

I mentioned the use of documents, alongside observational data, in Chapter 7. At one level this was introduced as a means of enhancing understanding through the ability to situate contemporary accounts within an historical context. It could also allow comparisons to be made between the observer's interpretations of events and those recorded in documents relating to those events. These sources may also be utilized in their own right. They can tell us a great deal about the way in which events are constructed, the reasons employed, as well as providing materials upon which to base further research investigations. Therefore, the broad heading of documentary research is deserving of our attention and it covers a wide variety of sources, including statistics, photographs, texts and visual data, in general. The cautionary comments made in Chapter 4 on using secondary sources for research should thus be read alongside the following accounts.

THE PLACE OF DOCUMENTS IN SOCIAL RESEARCH

There are a wide variety of documentary sources at our disposal for social research. Documents, read as the sedimentations of social practices, have the potential to inform and structure the decisions which people make on a daily and longer-term basis; they also constitute particular readings of social events. They tell us about the aspirations and intentions of the periods to which they refer and describe places and social relationships at a time when we may not have been born, or were simply not present. Nevertheless, despite their importance for research purposes and in permitting a range of research designs (Hakim 1987; Bechhofer and Paterson 2000), relative to the other methods we have come across, the volume of writings devoted to this topic does not appear so great. Why should this be so?

Ken Plummer (1990) offers an answer to this question that is worthy of consideration. While we apparently live in the age of post-positivism, there is no shortage of places where this insight has apparently bypassed the actual practices of social research. The twin influences of positivistic methodologists and abstract theories on social research may lead documents to being dismissed as 'impressionistic', or to the use of any type of data being regarded as nothing more than crude empiricism (thus conflating the terms empiricism and empirical). Therefore, despite the richness of insights that are available from documents, research reports based upon these sources may find themselves subject to misunderstanding. In contrast to these tendencies, it is clear that social research has much to learn from such sources.

A further reason focuses upon the use of documents for historical research. History is often thought to sit uneasily alongside social science disciplines (Goldthorpe 1984). There is also a difference of emphasis between disciplines to the extent that sociologists, for example, 'do not seek to tie their arguments to specific time and space co-ordinates so much as to test the extent of their generality' (Goldthorpe 2000: 31). Another possibility focuses upon the method itself. Documentary research is, in comparison to the other methods we have covered so far,

> not a clear cut and well-recognized category, like survey research or participant observation . . . It can hardly be regarded as constituting a method, since to say that one will use documents is to say nothing about *how* one will use them.
>
> (Platt 1981a: 31, original emphasis)

Let us take each of these points in turn. Positivism has been criticized as being based upon a limited concept of science which, upon examination, cannot live up to its own canons of scientific inquiry, while its methods reproduce and reflect biases already contained within society. As for the debates on the relationship between history and social research, space precludes a detailed discussion. However, history as a discipline in its own right provides us with a sense of our 'past' and with that, the ways in which our 'present' came about. The nature of past social, political and economic relations are there for us to see through acts of historical research that enable us to reflect on contemporary issues. For instance, Geoff Pearson (1983) examines the view that hooliganism is symptomatic of a contemporary moral decline following a 'permissive age'. By employing a range of documentary sources going back to Victorian times, he examines what are often thought to be these 'golden ages', only to find identical fears being expressed in each period considered. This study demonstrates that this phenomenon is not peculiar to contemporary times, as is widely believed by those predisposed to ahistorical views.

We can also see how new questions, arising from contemporary concerns, may turn us back towards an interrogation of history to uncover those aspects of the past that had, until that time, remained hidden from view. As Sheila Rowbotham (1999) puts it in relation to history and the women's movement and the consciousness it raised, there was a widespread belief that women had achieved little and yet, 'the more I read, the more I discovered how much women had in fact done' (Rowbotham 1999: 20). Clearly, the types of questions we ask of history and how our contemporary existence informs this process, have a bearing on what we discover and importantly, what is ignored as a result.

The ways in which documents are used is clearly a methodological and theoretical question, as well as a matter for the technicalities that surround method. Take, for example, the idea that a document is a monument to the past. We can say, from this point of view,

> that history, in its traditional form, undertook to 'memorize' the *monuments* of the past, transform them into *documents*, and lend speech to those traces which, in themselves, are often not verbal, or which say in silence something other than what they actually say; in our time, history is that which transforms *documents* into *monuments*.
>
> (Foucault 1989a: 7, original emphases)

In order to achieve this mode of analysis, matters of relevance, scope and relations between events need to be established. The means for doing so is to utilize the idea of a constant that may, for example, be invoked to demonstrate the gradual unfolding of history in terms of progress. Indeed, much of the history we read about is exactly of this type. What if, however, an event is analysed without invoking its relation to other events as part of, say, the forward march of rationalization towards a supposed better world? To question necessity in this way would require us to see events and thus documents of those events, not as self-evident, but as part of the ways in which truth is produced. This investigation of the mode of ordering of the social world is precisely what

Foucault used in his studies of medicine, mental illness, sexuality and criminality:

> If I have studied 'practices' like those of the sequestration of the insane, or clinical medicine, or the organization of the empirical sciences, or legal punishment, it was in order to study this interplay between a 'code' which rules ways of doing things (how people are to be graded and examined, things and signs classified, individuals trained, etc.) and a production of true discourses which serve to found, justify and provide reasons and principles for these ways of doing things.
>
> (Foucault 1991a: 79)

Such an approach is taken to enable us to see ourselves differently and as a product of history and so amenable to the changes that have taken place throughout the past (May and Powell 2007). These different approaches to documents are fundamental to how we see our surroundings and ourselves. Yet on a more instrumental level, the ambiguities and tensions surrounding documentary research are changing as more researchers use documents due to the increasing availability of data in modern societies – particularly via the internet. Researchers thus need to be aware of the documentary sources that may be used for research, as well as the ways in which they are used in understanding and configuring practices. The next section considers various documentary sources for social research and the second part of the chapter examines the perspectives and processes which inform their use and collection.

SOURCES OF DOCUMENTARY RESEARCH

Sources include historical documents, such as laws, declarations, statutes, statistics and people's accounts of incidents or periods in which they were actually involved. Although many definitions of documents are narrow in scope, the following broad definition is useful for research purposes:

> a document in its most general sense is a written text . . . Writing is the making of symbols representing words, and involves the use of a pen, pencil, printing machine or other tool for inscribing the message on paper, parchment or some other material medium . . . Similarly, the invention of magnetic and electronic means of storing and displaying text should encourage us to regard 'files' and 'documents' contained in computers and word processors as true documents. From this point of view, therefore, documents may be

regarded as physically embodied texts, where the containment of the text is the primary purpose of the physical medium.

(J. Scott 1990: 12–13)

A report based on official statistics would be covered by this definition. To these we could add other government records: for example, Hansard, ministerial records, debates, political speeches, administrative and government committee records and reports. In addition, under the broad heading of 'documents' we also find the content of the mass media, novels, plays, maps, drawings, books, the internet and personal documents such as biographies, autobiographies, diaries and oral histories, some of which may be used in work and life-history analyses (Samuel 1982; K. Anderson et al. 1990; Plummer 1990; Dex 1991; Giele and Elder 1998; B. Roberts 2002; Alaszewski 2006). We can call biographies and diaries 'lifecourse documents' which, as Rom Harré puts it,

> are generated after the events they describe, but they are written on the basis of those events. The diary is a contemporaneous record of the psychological life-course, whereas the biography must be constructed from a past which must be revived before it can be described. In consequence, biography and autobiography are epistemologically distinct from diary.
>
> (Harré 1993: 220)

To this list we can add photographs which, although existing on the borderline between the 'aesthetic' and 'documentary' (J. Scott 1990: 13), may be records of events, as well as the use of visual materials (Emmison and Smith 2000; G. Rose 2001). For that reason researchers have also deployed photographs in their investigations with interesting results (Sontag 1978; Bourdieu et al. 1990; Farran 1990; Spence and Holland 1991; Ball and Smith 1992; A. Young 1996; Emmison and Smith 2000; Stanley and Wise 2006; Franklin 2010; Vázquez 2010). It is not surprising, given such a catalogue of sources that Scott's book aims 'to recognise this diversity in documentary sources as a valuable feature of social research' (J. Scott 1990: 13). Let us examine both the physical and documentary sources available to researchers.

According to E. Webb et al. (2000) researchers may use 'physical traces' as part of what they call 'unobtrusive measures' of social research, much as Sherlock Holmes used 'physical' evidence in his deductions. These authors define this as

> those pieces of data not specifically produced for the purpose of comparison and inference, but available to be exploited opportunistically by the alert investigator. *It should be emphasized*

that physical evidence has greatest utility in consort with other methodological approaches.

(E. Webb et al. 2000: 36, emphasis added)

Into this category would fall evidence left at the scene of a crime such as hair, or a piece of fabric from clothing. These are further subdivided into 'erosion' and 'accretion' measures. *Erosion measures* are defined as those 'where the degree of selective wear on some material yields the measure' (E. Webb et al. 2000: 36). One example might be the degree of wear on a carpet to determine the frequency of its use, or the wear on library books for a similar purpose. Indeed, the wear on vinyl tiles surrounding an exhibit in a museum in Chicago provided an approximate indicator of its popularity with visitors (E. Webb et al. 2000: 37). In terms of the popularity of library books, this could be ascertained by using library records whether in manual or computer format. Indeed, it might even be possible to determine when people attend their places of work by whether they have collected their mail and, if using a computer, how often they log in and at what times.

Accretion measures are 'where the research evidence is some deposit of materials' (E. Webb et al. 2000: 36). One such example, to continue with the detective analogy, is the deposit of mud on shoes. The mud can be analysed and its likely location established, telling detectives where the suspect or victim may have come from. In a similar way, archaeologists estimate the populations of ancient sites by the size of the floor area of excavated buildings and the origin of buried persons through dietary effects on remaining teeth and the use of geographic information systems (see Renfrew and Bahn 2008).

Literature on the classification of documents (Denzin 1978; Burgess 1990; J. Scott 1990; Calvert 1991; Forster 1994; R. Lee 2000; E. Webb et al. 2000; Prior 2003) tends to fall into three main groups: first, primary, secondary and tertiary documents; second, public and private documents; and third, unsolicited and solicited sources. Primary sources refer to those materials which are written or collected by those who actually witnessed the events which they describe. In Bertrand Russell's (1912) terms they represent knowledge by *acquaintance*. It is therefore assumed that they are more likely to be an accurate representation of occurrences in terms of both the memory of the author (time) and their proximity to the event (space). However, these sources must also be seen in social context and for this purpose, the researcher might employ secondary sources (Burgess 1990). These are written after an event which the author had not personally witnessed and the researcher has to be aware of potential problems in the production of this data. Tertiary sources enable us to locate other references. They are 'indexes, abstracts and other bibliographies ... There are even bibliographies to help us find bibliographies' (Calvert 1991: 120). Libraries often possess collections of abstracts and reference manuals which assist in this process. To these we can add search engines and subject gateways on the internet (see Stein 1999; Mann and Stewart 2000; Kozinets 2010), but is important to distinguish between what Stuart Peters (1998) called 'online junk' and 'valuable information':

> As a researcher, once you have discovered how to locate information rapidly, you may even begin to depend on the Web, saving yourself time that might otherwise have been spent trawling through more traditional sources.
>
> (Peters 1998: 1)

The distinction between public and private documents is an important one. The fact that materials may exist tells us little about whether the researcher may gain access to them. For this reason, John Scott (1990) divides documents into four categories according to the degree of their accessibility. They are closed, restricted, open-archival and open-published.

In terms of public documents, the largest category are those produced by national and local governments and would include, for example, registrations of births, marriages and deaths and also police, taxation and housing records. Some of these documents may be protected by the Official Secrets Act (1989) and are therefore closed. Few official records, as Scott (1990) notes, fall into the restricted category; one example is the British royal papers, to which access may be granted only by the monarch (J. Scott 1990: 17). Open-archived records are stored in the Public Records Office (PRO) in London and the National Archives' collection has over 11 million historical and public records (www.nationalarchives.gov.uk). In the case of the United States, the Library of Congress holds 'millions of books, recordings, photographs, maps and manuscripts in its collections' (www.loc.gov/index.html). Open-published documents include many of those covered in Chapter 4, plus Acts of Parliament and Hansard records of parliamentary debates.

Finally, we come to the third group: solicited and unsolicited documents. This distinction is introduced on the grounds that some documents would have been produced with the aim of research in mind, whereas others would have been produced for personal use. Diaries, for example, may be used in social research by asking participants to record particular events and/or express their opinions upon them, with their development informed by technical, social and religious changes (Alaszewski 2006). However, even if they are for personal consumption and are accessible to a researcher, they are still 'addressed to an audience'

(Thompson 1982: 152), or what has been called a 'model reader' (Eco 1979) as expressions of a 'narrative identity' (Ricoeur 1984). It is this sense of social context and to whom a document or text may be addressed and what it expresses, that brings us round to a discussion of the perspectives in and processes of documentary research.

THE PROCESS OF DOCUMENTARY RESEARCH

There are several ways in which researchers might conceptualize a document and frame their research questions accordingly. In one guise or another, we have encountered most of them in our discussions of other methods. For some researchers a document represents a reflection of reality. It becomes a medium through which the researcher searches for a correspondence between its description and the events to which it refers. Yet if we can read off the accounts of a document, separate from the methods we employ to achieve this, are we not suggesting, once again, that there are social facts which exist independently of interpretation? We have already encountered the problems of this approach to social research.

In contrast, other approaches consider documents as representative of the practical requirements for which they were constructed. In this focus we would examine what Cicourel (1964) called the 'unstated meaning structures' of documents. The document itself is taken to stand for some underlying social pattern or use value. Thus, in his study on juvenile justice (Cicourel 1976), he examined the translation of oral conversations between juveniles and police and probation officers into written reports. These reports attempted to justify the procedures adopted for this purpose, but were also open-ended in their translation. This provided for 'various constructions of "what happened"' (Cicourel 1976: 17) and were seen to be based upon a form of 'practical reasoning' that rendered the social order of juvenile justice accountable and comprehensible and yet also open to negotiation and manipulation by interested parties. There are parallels here with the discussion on official statistics as 'accomplishments' and interviews as topics and not resources in the sense of 'how' texts and visual data seek to make sense of reality (R. Watson 1997; Heath et al. 2010).

A further example of this form of research is on caseworkers' use of documents in a welfare agency that places them within a framework orientated towards 'practical organizational purposes' (Zimmerman 1974). On most occasions, information contained within them is accepted without question as 'fact'. If it is questioned by, for example, a welfare claimant, the document then stands as the arbitrator of these 'facts'. Indeed, agency staff regarded the suggestion that the document may be false as 'incredible':

> For them, the possibilities opened up by such a doubt, including the possibility of a conspiracy between the applicant and the document producing organization, were not matters for idle speculation. The possibility of error was admitted, but only as a departure from ordinarily accurate reportage.
>
> (Zimmerman 1974: 133)

Moving away from the idea that a document independently reports social reality, or its production is yet another method by which people accomplish social order, we now utilize our own cultural understandings in order to 'engage' with 'meanings' which are embedded in the document itself. Researchers do not then apologize for being part of the social world which they study but, on the contrary, utilize that very fact. A document cannot be read in a 'detached' manner. Instead, we must approach documents in an engaged, not detached, fashion. This emphasis on *hermeneutics* (discussed in Chapter 1 and elsewhere) submits the analyst to consider the differences between their own frames of meanings and those found in the text. A researcher might then begin with an analysis of the common-sense procedures which came to formulate the document in the first instance, but their analysis need not end there. The document may be located within a wider social and political context. Researchers next examine the factors surrounding the *process* of its production, as well as the social *context*. It then becomes 'necessary to rise above, not only the particularity of texts, but also the particularity of the rules and recipes into which the art of understanding is dispersed' (Ricoeur 1982: 45).

What people decide to record is itself informed by decisions which, in turn, relate to the social, political and economic environments of which they are a part: 'both learned and imaginative writings are never free, but are limited in their imagery, assumptions, and intentions' (Edward Said, quoted in Easthope and McGowan 1992: 59). Documents may then be interesting for what they leave out, as well as what they contain. They do not simply reflect, but also construct social reality and versions of events. For some, therefore, the element of suspicion would be paramount in assessing what is recorded:

> You should always assume that officials representing a position, administrators, people who have authority and power over others, et cetera, are all involved in keeping their places and their authority intact. It is therefore the role of the intellectual, at least as I see it, to keep challenging them, to name names and cite facts.
>
> (Said 2004: 420–1)

The search for the documents' 'meaning' continues, but it is not assumed that documents are neutral artefacts which independently report social reality, or that analysis must be rooted in that rather nebulous concept, common-sense reasoning.

Documents are now viewed as media through which social power is expressed. They are approached in terms of the cultural context in which they were written and may be viewed 'as attempts at persuasion' (Sparks 1992). Approaching a document in this way 'tells us a great deal about the societies in which writers write and readers read' (Agger 1991: 7). It might, for example, reflect the marginalization of particular groups of people and the social characterization of others. Thus, in her study of the way in which the media represented the Greenham women who protested against nuclear weapons, Alison Young (1990) did not take their reports at face value, but instead examined the modes through which the media 'continually foster the desire for consensual world views, unifying and objective underlying orders, monolithic structures and the obscuring of differences' (A. Young 1990: 164–5).

Within this approach, the very act of reading a text may become the revision of its premises. Thus, for Adrienne Rich, a feminist reading of a text is also an act of refusal. The researcher concentrates on the way in which it constructed the contribution of women to an event, but the strategy of refusal enables women to see their contemporary social and political situation in a new light because 'Until we can understand the assumptions in which we are drenched we cannot know ourselves' (Adrienne Rich, in Humm 1992: 369).

Critical approaches to documentary sources are far from being unified bodies of thought. As noted, Michel Foucault's work, for instance, is a critical project which is not so concerned with the relationship between the author and the document, but the ways in which the use of a document is linked to the present as acts of historical writings are linked to current uses (Dean 1994, 2007; N. Rose and Miller 2008).

The poststructuralist work of Michel Foucault and Jacques Derrida, in their different ways (see Game 1991; Kamuf 1991; Kendall and Wickham 1999), are influenced by a 'semiotic' approach to textual analysis (mentioned in Chapter 7). This is particularly evident in the work of Roland Barthes (1967). What we see here in approaching documents is the work of 'problematization' which

> doesn't mean the representation of a pre-existent object, nor the creation through discourse of an object that doesn't exist. It's the set of discursive or non-discursive practices that makes something enter into the play of the true and false, and constitutes it as an object for thought (whether under the form of moral reflection, scientific knowledge, political analysis, etc.).
>
> (Foucault 1989b: 456–7)

In contrast, there are those who are critical of this approach as it appears to suggest that a text does not refer to anything beyond itself nor to the intentions of the author. We return, once again, to the issue of whether a text (which would include an interview transcript or observation field notes) corresponds to the events which it describes: is it a topic *of* social research or a resource *for* social research? It is argued that a text must be approached in terms of the intentions of its author and the social context in which it was produced.

Following the work of Anthony Giddens (1979, 1984), John Scott (1990) suggests that a researcher should approach a document in terms of three levels of meaning interpretation. First, the meanings that the author *intended* to produce, second, the *received* meanings as constructed by the audience in differing social situations, and third, the *internal* meanings that semioticians exclusively concentrate upon. However, they cannot 'know' these 'independently of its reception by an audience' (J. Scott 1990: 34).

We can say that texts are important as a means for mediating and coordinating between the local and the general in social relations and activities. However, as texts organize, they are also organized by local activities and whether they appear in an electronic or printed form, it has been argued that they possess the property of 'indefinite replicability'. They may be activated by reading in local contexts as an active process of interpretation, but also bear within them non-local relations and so organize practices and create 'something like an escape hatch out of the actual' that regulates and coordinates 'beyond the local setting of their reading and writing' (Smith 1999: 79–80). Noting that when it comes to digital technology it creates, modifies, destroys and replaces information with little effort and so raises questions concerning traditional notions of validity and reliability (Kotamraju 1999), interacting with a computer may still be said to share 'with other text-mediated forms modes of being and action "lifted out" of the local time and place of the bodily being of the reader/writer' (Smith 1999: 80).

These are just some of the new directions in which documentary research has moved away from the positivist emphasis that Plummer (1990) identified as one impediment to their use in social research. Collectively, they represent various approaches to analysis and combine elements of realism, critical theory, feminism, postmodernism and post-structuralism. These are not easy ideas to grasp, particularly as positivism has held such a grip on social research for so long. However, to present the 'how' which Platt (1981a) referred to as being one perspective on documentary research would be an inaccurate representation of their contemporary use (as well as being counter to the philosophy underlying this book).

Using documents

The above perspectives outlined, I now wish to move on to the collection of documents. For this purpose I shall consider several examples – in the process of which it will become evident that the methods used depend not only upon the researcher's perspectives, but also on the time and resources available, the aims of the research, accessibility and issues encountered in the collection of data.

There exist a number of accounts of the process of conducting documentary research. As noted before, this often takes place alongside other methods, while the process of understanding the place and role of documents in the production and reproduction of social life relates, but is not necessarily determined by, the perspectives of the researcher. I say this because there are often practical impediments to the realization of research aims and the data may simply not be available or gatekeepers do not grant access to it. In addition, the researcher may judge that the publication of materials may be detrimental to the memory of an author or group of people, or anticipate that such publication would lead to a public outcry that would not advance understanding of a process or event.

Issues concerning the practical problems encountered in the research process may be seen in an account of the relationship between a naval dockyard and the local community (Dunkerley 1988). It demonstrates that researchers are subject to issues associated with time and money and the availability and accessibility of documentary evidence.

The aim of the study was to examine the origins of the labour force employed in the dockyard and the 'extent of intergenerational job transmission, internal work structure, job security and political attitudes, and the effect of mobility opportunities' (Dunkerley 1988: 85). Three methods of documentary inquiry were chosen for this purpose. First, a sample of population censuses dated since 1851, which are kept at the PRO. The aim was to gain information on levels of employment, birthplaces and so on, across time. Second, the use of local histories, as well as Admiralty and Treasury Papers (also at the PRO). These sources would specifically relate to dockyard labour relations, employment opportunities and skills to be found within the locality. Third, the use of oral histories based on interviews with three generations of dockyard workers.

Three immediate issues arose in what the author notes was an ambitious exercise given the constraints of time and resources (Dunkerley 1988: 86). First, it was assumed that the historical records would be available. As it transpired, local information either was not available or no longer existed (due to bombing raids during the Second World War). In addition, what there was turned out to be catalogued in the PRO under obscure headings. Second, the type of material collected by the

Census changed over the years, either making its collection a non-starter, or rendering the ability to compare changes, across time, untenable. Third, when it came to more recent and detailed information, it was 'subject to closure and simply not available to the bona fide researcher' (Dunkerley 1988: 86). What information there was also proved to take considerable time to extract and compile. As a result of these problems and the distance that the researcher had to travel to get to the research site, the aims of the study were altered. In the end, it concentrated upon 'technological and historical development covering a period spanning the last century' (Dunkerley 1988: 87).

Imagination, along with an understanding of the issues and methods of social research, is often required in practice. Consider, for example, what sources one might employ for cross-national urban historical research on municipal policies. Here we find a dearth of such work in the past and this necessitates some thought as to how such a study might proceed. In examining the data sources for such work, as well as reflecting upon the reasons for this deficiency, Elfi Bendikat (1996) identifies some possibilities. Noting that urban research has concentrated on selected areas – administration, technical infrastructure, socio-political processes and economic and political factors – Bendikat attributes this to the existence of documentary sources. These comprise the following: administrative correspondences; publications; memoirs; biographies; organizational surveys; municipal records; periodicals; newspapers; diaries; election reports; minutes of meetings; pleas, petitions and complaints to municipal bodies; oral histories and audio-visual materials, including documentary films. Taking these together and considering them in relation to their strengths and limitations for the purpose of producing data in relation to municipal policies, enables the experienced researcher to design a study that is potentially rich in the insights and understandings that it offers. Such work can then

> open up a space within which debates about alternative futures can be launched or engaged in, even if at one time that space appears to be dominated by the latest policy fashion apparently delivered from on high.
>
> (Cochrane 2007: 145)

While archival work can open up the present to future possibilities, researchers do have to be aware of the possibility that the information they seek is 'closed'. In researching people over the age of 90, for example, researchers have been prevented from obtaining sample names from records (Bury and Holme 1990). Furthermore, even if documents are available, if they are handwritten the researcher may have problems in reading them, or they may have been damaged over time. Diaries and other personal documents, in particular, use abbreviations and coded references to individuals or events which may be difficult to interpret. One of the most famous diarists, Samuel Pepys (1633–1703), often used codes in his diary entries (J. Scott 1990: 179). Finally, in terms of the use of documents generally, as well as specifically in relation to organizational research, it is worth remembering: 'They should never be taken at face-value. In other words, they *must* be regarded as information which is context-specific' (Forster 1994: 149, original emphasis).

Another example is based upon a field of study which examined the relationship between the media and their depictions of criminal or deviant activity (also see Caputi 1987; Sparks 1992; A. Young 1996; I. Marsh and Melville 2009). While they differ in their methodological and theoretical approaches, they all employ documentary sources in one form or another. In order to consider this process, I shall concentrate on the work of Richard Ericson and his colleagues which raises some core issues and remains a series of insightful studies.

Richard Ericson, Patricia Baranek and Janet Chan (1991) examined the content of news sources on crime, law and justice. Following their previous work (Ericson et al. 1987, 1989) their perspective viewed news as not only reflecting, but also actively constructing, our sense of the social reality to which it refers. Journalists themselves are implicated within societal apparatuses of social control by constructing news which visualizes and symbolizes crime and attempts to convince the audience of the authority of its descriptions. After all, most people learn of crime, law and order via the media:

> Through dramatized descriptions, metaphoric language, and pictures, news depicts events that are called up in the mind (visualized) even while they remain invisible to the eye. News representations are symbolic in the sense they embody, stand for, or correspond to persons, events, processes, or states of affairs being reported. News representation involves authorization of who can be a representative or spokesperson of a source organization, of what sources are 'authorized knowers'.
>
> (Ericson et al. 1991: 5)

The aim of the study was to examine the ways in which different media sources operated according to the markets they were located within. For this purpose the authors took a sample of radio, television and newspaper outlets, covering issues of crime, legal control, deviance and justice in the Toronto region of Canada. This provided a comparison of the different ways in which news was depicted. These sources were also grouped into 'quality' and 'popular' so the variations between markets could be examined. However, this was a study of news 'content'. Yet it has been emphasized that social 'context' is fundamental to under-standing the meanings contained within documents. The authors were only too aware of this point:

> News, like law and science, is a socially constructed product that is highly self-referential in nature. That is, news content is used by journalists and sources to construct meanings and expectations about their organizations. This means that the analyst of news *content* must examine the meaning used by news producers in the *construction* of their product.
>
> (Ericson et al. 1991: 49, emphases added)

In order to locate the study of patterns of meanings in media texts by the use of *content analysis*, they drew upon their previous ethnographic work on journalists and the construction of news sources (Ericson et al. 1987, 1989). The texts themselves were sampled over a period of 33 days to study them across time. The aim was to compare quality and popular newspapers, with an evening broadcast on quality and popular television and an evening quality and popular radio broadcast. The newspapers were sampled by pages, the television broadcasts were videotaped and the radio broadcasts audio taped. The radio and television reports were transcribed – verbatim – along with notes on the use of 'visuals' and the use of sounds other than words. The result was a vast number of data which were analysed in considerable detail and located within their previous studies on news construction.

I have chosen my final example because it relates to a particular source that is often believed to be 'neutral' in its reflection of reality: maps. There are many enthusiasts of maps and their accessibility as applications on mobile phones, the internet and so on has made them even more popular than before. At the beginning of his study on the cultural boundaries of science, Thomas Gieryn (1999) writes:

> I have always been fond of maps. My mother insists that I learned how to read from a street map of Rochester, New York, where I grew up. From an early age, I spent hours drawing maps of imagined cities, crude ones at first in thick black lines, then more sophisticated efforts in colored pencil, water colors, rapidograph pens, transfer letters – and most recently, with graphics software on my Mac.
>
> (Gieryn 1999: vii)

Maps can also represent a fantasy – a belief in the final conquest of space that lies at the heart of the geographical enterprise. Crime and public health are among those things in which the combination of maps and knowledges are part of art of government: 'the sciences of man were born at the moment when the procedures of surveillance and record-taking of individuals were established' (Foucault 2007: 180). Inquiry then came to serve as an administrative and fiscal model and so in geography we can find 'a good example of a discipline which systematically uses measure, inquiry and examination' (Foucault 2007: 180).

With this in mind Jeremy Crampton (2007) examines the work of the American Geographical Society. What was called the 'Inquiry' was a secret research group, set up under President Woodrow Wilson, as part of American preparations for peace and was designed to inform American policy after the First World War. The deliberations that took place oscillated between colonial-based perspectives and those based on the attributes and qualities of populations, as well as those advocating that the only way to peaceful coexistence would be through national self-determination through the exercise of the 'will' of the people. This, however, would require the identification of particular populations within defined territories. When it came to the Balkans, the Inquiry found little space which was not the subject of dispute, leading to 'neutral' European maps being 'contrasted with the "propaganda" of the Serbs, Bulgarians, Greeks and Albanians, allowing the latter to be easily dismissed' (Crampton 2007: 228).

While reports, fieldwork, statistics and documents were compiled, along with hundreds of maps, no simple assumption was made between identity and space. Nevertheless, the relationship between 'territory and its rightful populations could be discerned if you looked hard enough and assembled the right data' (Crampton 2007: 240). Equally, there were those who worked with the Inquiry who believed in eugenic principles leading to a mass of index cards and a focus upon 'problematic populations'. Yet this cannot simply be reduced to the work of a few racist men, but part of an exercise in mapping based on sets of assumptions. The idea of an unambiguous spatiality would later haunt Europe and, as Julian Crampton (2007) notes, these imaginaries that deploy particular forms of data continue into the present day, particularly around issues of immigration.

Approaching a document

Having discussed these examples, it remains to consider in this section with what questions a researcher should approach a document. This is not an exhaustive list, but points to the main themes raised in the process of documentary research. John Scott (1990) proposes four criteria for assessing the quality of the evidence available from documentary sources. They are authenticity, credibility, representativeness and meaning.

The issue of a document's *authenticity* is essential to the conduct of this form of research: 'Judgement of authenticity from the internal evidence of the text comes only when one is satisfied that it is technically possible that the document is genuine' (Calvert 1991: 121). Even an inauthentic document, however, could be of interest because 'it cannot be fully and correctly understood unless one knows that it is not authentic' (Platt 1981a: 33). Platt therefore provides several guidelines for assessing their authenticity.

First, the document may contain obvious errors or is not consistent in its representation. Second, different versions of the same document exist. Third, there are internal inconsistencies in terms of style, content, hand-writing, and so on. Fourth, the document has passed through the hands of several copyists. Fifth, the document has been in the hands of a person or persons with a vested interest in a particular reading of its contents. Sixth, the version derives from a suspect secondary source. Seventh, it is inconsistent in relation to other similar documents. Finally, it is 'too neat' in terms of being representative of a certain group of documents (Platt 1981a: 34). Forster (1994), in his suggestions for analysing company documentation, sums up these checks on authenticity by suggesting that the researcher ask the following questions:

> Are the data genuine? Are they from a primary or secondary source? Are they actually what they appear to be? Are they authentic copies of originals? Have they been tampered with or corrupted? Can authorship be validated? Are the documents dated and placed? Are they accurate records of the events or processes described? Are the authors of documents believable?
>
> (Forster 1994: 155)

In her own study of the history of research methods in the United States, for example, Jennifer Platt (1996) examined writings on method using articles in leading journals and textbooks of the period in question (1920–60). While not assuming that they were representative of commit-ments to particular methods, this allowed her to consider to what extent reports of practice conformed to particular theoretical commitments at the time. By using various sources, including interviews, she was able to build up a picture of the relationship between theory and method and argued that the former could not explain the adoption or genesis of the latter (May 1997).

Following the questioning of a document's authenticity, there is its *credibility*. This 'refers to the extent to which the evidence is undistorted and sincere, free from error and evasion' (J. Scott 1990: 7). Questions to ask at this point include the following: are the people who record the information reliable in their translations of the information that they receive? How accurate were their observations and records? To achieve this, we may employ other sources on the life and political sympathies of the author. This will enable the researcher to establish the social and political context in which the document was produced.

Representativeness has been referred to as a question of 'typicality' in Chapter 7. The issue of whether a document is typical depends on the aim of the research. 'Untypical' documents may be of interest, so we should not become too obsessed with this issue as it is driven as much by the aims of the study. Nevertheless, if we are concerned with drawing conclusions which are intended to argue that there is a 'typical document' or a 'typical method' of representing a topic in which we are interested, then this is an important consideration in order to demonstrate how one interpretation of an event predominates to the exclusion of others. For instance, Calvert (1991) notes how some documents are deliberately destroyed and there are protests in the United States over the 'systematic bias' of a series entitled *Foreign Relations of the United States*.

Finally, there is the question of a document's *meaning*. This refers to the clarity and comprehensibility of a document to the analyst. Two questions are of concern: 'what is it, and what does it tell us?' (J. Scott 1990: 8). However, these are far from easy questions to answer. Going back to the example of the media research of Ericson and his colleagues, meanings were set within a social context derived from previous studies. Thus, while meanings change and the use of words varies, an idea of social context enables understanding.

The method of documentary research, like all of those we covered so far, requires not only some practice, but also a reflexivity on the part of the researcher. For instance, it has been noted that using documents on the internet may raise particular issues in relation to validity and reliability (Kotamraju 1999; Lee 2000). That said, documents provide an important source of data for understanding events, processes and transformations in social relations. The idea of systematic reviewing is a method designed to capture large amounts of evidence that is of good enough quality concerning a specific topic which is then condensed into transparent and rigorous forms. Reliability and strength of data are considered to be paramount in this process (Prior 2003: 154). Documents, in their broadest sense, are core to such an understanding. It now remains for me to consider the analysis of documents and issues in their use.

THE ANALYSIS OF DOCUMENTS

We have considered a document in terms of its authenticity, representativeness, credibility and meaning; John Scott (1990) divides the latter into intended, received and content meaning. Building on these themes, this section will follow the same pattern as in Chapters 5–7 in presenting an overview of approaches in order that you may pursue particular areas of interest. This is particularly pertinent given that a number of theoretical issues have been raised, from mainstream positivism, through the interpretation of documents in terms of common-sense reasoning, to semiotic, hermeneutic, feminist and critical approaches. Differences of emphasis clearly exist in terms of how a document is approached. In terms of life histories, Plummer's (1990) approach considers the intentions and purposes of the author. Yet to those influenced by Barthes (1967), the text takes on a life of its own, separate from the author. Given these differing perspectives, it is not surprising to find documents analysed in both quantitative and qualitative ways.

Quantitative and qualitative approaches

Documents do not stand on their own, but need to be situated within the contexts in which they are produced in order that its content is rendered intelligible and a theoretical frame of reference so it is amenable to analysis. For this purpose we can use *content* analysis. Content analysis can take both quantitative and qualitative forms and comprises three stages: stating the research problem, retrieving the text and employing sampling methods and interpretation and analysis. The focus considers the frequency with which certain words or particular phrases occur in the text as a means of identifying its characteristics. To that extent those using content analysis share a point of view with those researchers undertaking statistical analysis of surveys. One can start with a clear idea of what is being looked for and break the text into its component parts. Alternatively, the grounded theory method of constant comparison can generate theory and shares its logic of comparison with other methods such as experimental design. Overall, quantitative content analysis

> seeks to show patterns of regularities in content through repetition, and qualitative content analysis . . . emphasizes the fluidity of the text and content in the interpretive understanding of culture.
>
> (Ericson et al. 1991: 50)

As with interviewing and observation, the use of computer packages in the analysis of texts is helpful towards these ends. These assist in searching for individual words and phrases and their frequency or context in the text; they can also help in analysing connections between codes or categories of behaviour that the production of the document might represent (see N. Fielding and Lee 1991; N. Fielding 2002; Kozinets 2010). Content analysis is employed on a commercial basis by those interested in the computing, communications and media sectors and it is possible to retrieve newspaper text on either CD-ROM or commercial online databases, bearing in mind the cost differential:

> Having the text on CD-ROM offers advantages in terms of unlimited use (once the disc has been purchased), unlike the use of on-line data-bases where usage is restricted by the cost of on-line time and the cost of lines of text read.
>
> (Hansen 1995: 150–1)

As with the discussion on standardization in Chapter 5, the quantitative analyst would seek to derive categories from the data in order that it can be compared. Words or phrases in the document are transformed into numbers. The number of times in which a word occurs in the text is taken as an indicator of its significance, a strategy assumed to enhance both the reliability and validity of the classified data. Therefore, it is taken for granted 'that there exists a defensible correspondence between the transformed account and the way the information was meant in its original form' (Garfinkel 1967: 190–1).

In considering the problems of a quantitative count, the issues covered in previous chapters are again raised. First, this method considers product and says little of process. In the context of this discussion, it deals only with what has been produced, not the decisions which informed its production which tell us so much about its received and intended meanings. Second, an empiricist problem is raised for it deals only with information which can be measured and standardized and for this reason considers only data which can be simplified into categories. Third, in this preoccupation, it reproduces the meanings used by authors in the first instance, as opposed to subjecting them to critical analysis in terms of the political, social and economic context of their production. Fourth, from an ethnomethodological perspective, it fails to understand the common-sense context of their production and interpretation as part of the methods by which people make sense of their social world (Benson and Hughes 1991; Heath and Hindmarsh 2002; Heath et al. 2010). Fifth, it assumes that the audiences who receive the message must translate it as the analyst does. By default, it thereby negates the idea that a text is open to a number of possible readings by its audience (would all people read the same meanings into a diary account or newspaper report? If not, why?). To return to the discussion in Chapter 1, this can so easily become a crude stimulus–response model of human behaviour: that is, what people read is what they think. Analysts have only to read the text to know what the audience is automatically thinking.

The frequency with which words or phrases occur in a text (a quantitative emphasis) may therefore say nothing about its 'significance within the document' (a qualitative emphasis):

> It may be that a single striking word or phrase conveys a meaning out of all proportion to its frequency; and a non-quantitative approach

may be better able to grasp the significance of such isolated references. The content analyst must engage in an act of qualitative synthesis when attempting to summarize the overall meaning of the text and its impact on the reader.

(J. Scott 1990: 32)

Thus, to return to the points made earlier, the text (be it a document, diary and so on), the audience of the text and its author become three essential components in a process of John Scott's meaning construction (intended, received and content meaning). According to him, for researchers to grasp its significance, they should concentrate upon what the author intended when they produced the document; the meaning given to it by the potential audience (including the analyst who, by an act of reading, is part of that audience and thus needs to act reflexively) and finally, between these two, the text itself which the content analysts and semioticians concentrate upon. These components add up to a simple observation: 'A document's meaning cannot be understood unless one knows what genre it belongs to, and what this implies for its interpretation' (Platt 1981b: 53).

Qualitative content analysis, on the other hand, starts with the idea of process, or social context, and views the author as a self-conscious actor addressing an audience under particular circumstances. The task of the analyst becomes a 'reading' of the text in terms of its symbols. With this in mind, the text is approached through understanding the context of its production by the analysts themselves. This may be derived either through the use of secondary sources or, as in the above example, other methods such as observational studies:

In the process, the analyst picks out what is relevant for analysis and pieces it together to create tendencies, sequences, patterns and orders. The process of deconstruction, interpretation, and reconstruction breaks down many of the assumptions dear to quantitative analysts.

(Ericson et al. 1991: 55)

The flexibility of this method, as with participant observation, is regarded as a prime advantage. It enables the researcher to consider not only the ways in which meaning is constructed, but also the ways in which new meanings are developed and employed.

From the above we can say that although it is important to link the text to its author (the writer's intended meanings, as a diarist, journalist or the writer of an autobiography), texts are also used in ways which depend on the social situation of the audience (the reader's received meaning). As with interviews and observational data, analysis using computing programs may assist in this process (N. Fielding and Lee 1991; R. Lee 1995; N. Fielding 2002; Silverman 2010).

Aside from an emphasis on intended and received meaning, there is also content meaning upon which content analysts and semioticians focus their attention. Semiotics is a complicated area of study in which interpretations of documents are placed within systems of cultural representations. We can take Umberto Eco's idea of a 'specific semiotics' to illustrate this:

> A specific semiotics is, or aims at being, the 'grammar' of a particular sign system, and proves to be successful insofar as it describes a given field of communicative phenomena as ruled by a system of signification. Thus there are 'grammars' of the American Sign Language, of traffic signals, of a playing-card 'matrix' for different games or a particular game (for instance, poker).
>
> (Eco 1984: 5)

From a methodological point of view we can say that semiotics is concerned with examining the relationship between a signifier and a signified (the idea or concept to which the signifier refers). The latter may not refer to a material object, but the way in which a system of language, through its signs, organizes the world. A semiotician thus approaches a document in order to explain its principles of signification; the overall aim being, as Peter Manning (1988) puts it,

> to explain how the meanings of objects, behaviours, or talk is produced, transformed and reproduced ... The interpretant connects an *expression* or signifier (a word, a picture, a sound) with a *content* or signified (another word, image or depiction).
>
> (Manning 1988: 82, original emphases)

For this focus to be meaningful, in the senses employed thus far, the text must be located and analysed alongside intended and received meanings. In other words, the writer will assume a competence on the part of the audience and it is these assumptions which the analyst needs to engage with by employing, reflexively, their own cultural understandings alongside an understanding of the context in which the document was produced.

In practical terms, the questions asked of a document at the level of content meaning focus upon relationships *within* the text and its relationships to *other* texts:

> What is the relationship of a text's parts to each other? What is the relationship of the text to other texts? What is the relationship of the text to those who participated in constructing it? What is the

relationship of the text to realities conceived of as lying outside of it? What empirical patterns are evident in these intra and intertextual relations and what do these indicate about the meaning?

(Ericson et al. 1991: 48)

A critical-analytic stance would consider how the document represents the events which it describes and closes off potential contrary interpretations and possibilities through a particular construction of reality as self-evident. We would now consider the ways in which texts seek to assert power over the social world it describes. In so doing, the social world might be characterized by the exclusion of valuable information and the characterization of events and people in particular ways according to discrete interests. Here, description, interpretation and explanation are brought together:

A special feature of this approach is that the link between socio-cultural practice and text is mediated by discourse practice; how a text is produced or interpreted, in the sense of what discursive practices and conventions are drawn from what order(s) of discourse and how they are articulated together.

(Fairclough 1995: 97)

In a practical example of this approach, the language of politics and the content of policies formed the basis of a study (Fairclough 2000), while in elaborating on this approach in terms of the analysis of texts, discourses are seen in terms of both their forms of representation and relationship to 'other social elements' (Fairclough 2003: 129).

Characterizations of the analysis of documentary research can assume a simple dichotomy between quantitative and qualitative approaches. While there are clear differences of emphasis, throughout this book questions have continually been raised regarding this dualism. It is not surprising, therefore, to find researchers from different theoretical vantage points utilizing both methods with interesting results. However, they do not necessarily share the underlying assumptions of much content analysis as outlined above. Indeed, Catherine Marsh, whose comments on meaning and quantitative analysis were noted in Chapter 5, has employed computer packages to examine work history data (C. Marsh and Gershuny 1991) in a volume which attempts to challenge the quantitative–qualitative divide (Dex 1991). Silverman (1985) and Billig (1988), from different theoretical vantage points, have employed simple counting methods to analyse the speeches of a trade union leader and politician. Platt (1996) employs a similar method in her study of the history of American research methods, as do Stanley and Wise (2006) in their study on children in concentration camps during the South African War.

Computer programs for the analysis of documents have been regarded as useful if they follow criteria of meaning interpretation (J. Scott 1990) and have clear applications in relation to the analysis of diaries (Alaszewski 2006). Nevertheless, the use of quantitative analysis does not sidestep the need for researchers to account for the interpretations they have employed in analysing the document(s).

A note on presenting findings

In the second of two articles on documentary research, Jennifer Platt (1981b) notes the connection between the justification of the interpretative procedure used in the analysis of documents and how the research results are presented in an authoritative manner. As with research in general, the art of communication is fundamental to the research process. As she notes (Platt 1981b: 60), this differs when it comes to the presentation of a small number of cases or instances of a social phenomenon. The author then attempts to appeal to the authority of their interpretations in particular ways. One method is to resort to presenting all the data which substantiate a point that you wish to make. Another is to make liberal use of footnotes in order to elaborate upon the text. This is not an easy problem to solve. However, there are ways in which to steer a course between total data display and appeals to interpretative authority. Before moving on to issues in documentary research, I shall summarize these below for consideration in the presentation of your findings.

The first strategy is to provide an account of the method utilized at the outset. This removes the obligation to elaborate on the procedure when you wish to make a particular point in the interpretation of the document(s). However, the problem with this strategy is that the method is not demonstrated at each point in the analysis, but asserted at the beginning. As a result, it requires a high level of trust in the author (Platt 1981b). The researcher could then use a second strategy and give an account of the method as each conclusion unfolds – a method similar to the historian's use of footnotes. Each positive and negative instance in relation to the results would be reported in order to substantiate the inferences. However, 'the danger here is that it could become as cumbrous as giving all the data' (Platt 1981b: 61).

Finally, the researcher might employ an 'illustrative style' as a strategy. Data are then selected in relation to the ability to illustrate general themes which emerge and which can be supported by the use of specific examples. Again, however, the reader must trust the authority of the interpretations. Not surprisingly, therefore, given the advantages and disadvantages of each strategy, Platt (1981b) advocates the use of all three depending upon the nature of the data used and the types of conclusions reached. For large amounts of data, a sampling and coding procedure would need to be explained. In terms of small-scale data, the sources and methods of inferences would need to be described. If examples are used to illustrate points and if others are available, how were they chosen? Finally, there is the possible use of a general account of the process of analysis and checks on the interpretative procedures employed:

> This amounts to saying that where a systematic procedure has been used it should be described, and the results reported will then carry the conviction which the procedure deserves. The issue thus comes back to that of devising satisfactory systematic procedures of analysis and interpretation.
>
> (Platt 1981b: 62)

ISSUES IN DOCUMENTARY RESEARCH

Criticisms of documentary research tend to stem from how documents are used, as opposed to their use in the first place. Both implicitly and explicitly, many of these have been covered. Here, I consider the bias of documents and selectivity in their analysis as key issues in the process of deploying these methods.

The importance of seeing a document in terms of its potential bias has been emphasized. History itself and our understanding of it can be informed by a selective reading of documents or those documents themselves may also be selective. Thus, what people decide to record, to leave in or take out, is itself informed by decisions which relate to the social, political and economic environment of which they are a part. History, like all social and natural sciences, is amenable to manipulation and selective influence. In undertaking documentary research, we should be aware of these influences and not assume that documents are simply neutral artefacts from the past.

Clearly, how far in the past we are dealing with, differences in cultural production and reception and the practical availability of documents for evidence, are all important issues for reflexive consideration. The availability to both store and communicate documentation on the internet and World Wide Web, for example, provides a rich basis for research. Yet it can also prompt an uncritical adoption of yet another means of marginalizing people along, for example, race, class, ethnic, gender and cultural lines. Such issues lead one author to emphasize less the actual content of documents, but the context:

> if we are to get to grips with the nature of documents then we have to move away from a consideration of them as stable, static and pre-defined artifacts. Instead we must consider them in terms of fields, frames and networks of action. In fact, the status of things as

'documents' depends precisely on the ways in which such objects are integrated into fields of action, and documents can only be defined in terms of such fields.

(Prior 2003: 2)

In an age in which new technologies have speeded up communications, we are offered both possibilities and potential problems for the purposes of undertaking research. While this raises particular issues to do with reliability and validity, researchers have to exercise a critical reflexivity if they confront the belief that somehow the internet is democratic in its mode of operation, as well as in relation to the storing and distribution of information. Large corporations spend enormous sums of money ensuring that their images reach the public domain in particular ways, or when they do not, they can be rapidly countered by the production of more favourable representations. Equally, while digital technology provides opportunities for new forms of research, it should be borne in mind that it also: 'lends itself to the creation, modification, destruction, and replacement of information with very little effort and very little cost' (Kotamraju 1999: 467).

Texts and technologies have the capacity to shape understandings. Here the role of 'boundary objects' becomes of interest and these may draw from scientific, technical, ethical and experiential sources. Take the example of maps. These might show, for instance, regional economic disparity in the UK through the use of gross value added (GVA) data which, as noted in Chapter 4, frames issues in ways that exclude important considerations about quality of life. Different groups will have different interpretations of such data and will selectively use what are the same maps for different interests. The overall result may be that interpretative frames remain unchanged. Therefore, while they do not have any transformative effect upon perceptions of reality, they could perform a coordination role that prevents alternative representations and reinforces the status quo.

The above returns us to a general issue for social research practitioners: using documents without due regard to the process and social context of their construction. Semioticians examine a text in terms of meaning 'content', without a consideration of 'intended' and 'received' components of meanings. The tradition of social thought that underlies such approaches stands in contrast to those that regard the intention and purpose of the author as an important part of analysis. Authors of this perspective would not approach a document as simply reflecting the social 'reality' to which it refers, as those with simplistic empiricist approaches would assume.

SUMMARY

The title 'documentary research' reflects a very broad spectrum of perspectives and research sources. Documents may well be part of the practical contingencies of organizational life, but (as we have also seen) they are viewed as part of a wider social context. They have been considered in terms of the centrality of their authorship, while others do not consider the author as being of such significance. These latter influences have seen a move towards more literary styles of analysis that sit uneasily alongside the positivist legacy which may be detected in social research. In considering this issue we might bear in mind the philosophy that underpinned Raphael Samuel's approach to historical writing as one applicable to the social sciences as a whole when he writes that history is

a social form of knowledge; the work, in any given instance, of a thousand different hands. If this is true, the point of address in any discussion of historiography should not be the work of the individual scholar, nor yet rival schools of interpretation, but rather the ensemble of activities and practices in which ideas of history are embedded or a dialectic of past–present relations is rehearsed.

(Samuel 1994: 10)

With an increase in information available through the means discussed here, documentary research, concerning different times in history, will become more popular and relevant. It will be used alongside other methods, yield valuable insights into societies and the dynamics of social life and be subject to different forms of analysis.

Questions for your reflection

1 What documentary sources would you use in studying policy implementation in an organization?

2 What issues should be considered in examining 'meaning' in the production of documents?

3 In approaching a document for analysis, what questions would preoccupy you as a researcher?

4 You are asked to devise a study which employs 'unobtrusive measures' of police performance. Clearly, you would first have to define the idea of 'performance'. However, holding that aside, what sources would you use? To get you started, is the level of graffiti in public places an indicator? Or the number of pairs of boots an officer goes through in a year of beat patrols?

SUGGESTED FURTHER READING

Emmison, M. and Smith, P. (2000) *Researching the Visual: Images, Objects, Contexts and Interactions in Social and Cultural Inquiry*. London: Sage.

Lee, R. M. (2000) *Unobtrusive Methods in Social Research*. Buckingham: Open University Press.

Prior, L. (2003) *Using Documents in Social Research*. London: Sage.

Scott, J. (1990) *A Matter of Record: Documentary Sources in Social Research*. Cambridge: Polity.

9   Case study research
With Beth Perry

Writings on the status, validity and applicability of case studies as tools to better understand the social world take their inspiration from different philosophical traditions. We see how critiques of case studies stemming from positivistic traditions have been refuted, absorbed or transcended by researchers through alternatively appropriating the language of scientific legitimacy, or through developing new ways of social scientific justification for their use. It still remains possible to detect within this broad method of social research controversies between positivist and humanist approaches (D. Harvey 2009).

Case study research is prevalent across a range of academic disciplines. Yet even among experienced researchers there is a tendency to leave to one side the specific meanings, interpretations and insights that are implied in its adoption. An expansion in the use of case studies has been accompanied by an underwhelming degree of reflection on its status, role and value. If anything can be a case study, then what is its distinctiveness, the circumstances in which it might usefully be deployed and its relevance for social practice, theory and thought?

In this chapter we consider these issues. We first examine the place and status of the case study, before moving on to consider the process of case study research. We emphasize the specific choices or techniques that a case study may entail, rather than those methods that may comprise elements of the case study process (such as interviews, documentary analysis, participant observation) but which are not exclusive to its production. Finally, we discuss issues relating to the analysis and representation of case studies.

Critiques and defences of case studies relate to bias, subjectivity, reliability and validity, for instance. Few are unique to the process of case study research and have been discussed elsewhere. A distinctive view – and contribution to this book – is formed by considering case studies through the lens of 'generalization' and the value and usefulness of a focus on the 'specific One' (Stake 2005: 444). As with all chapters, we wish to bring to critical awareness the issues, choices and implications of case study research in the context of wider debates.

THE PLACE OF THE CASE STUDY IN SOCIAL RESEARCH

In considering the 'place of the method' there are those that have developed a specifically historical perspective. Jennifer Platt charts the development of the case study through the rise and fall of the Chicago School of social research, set against the broader pre- and post-war political economy of research and the increasing use of statistical methods (Platt 1992a). Hamel and colleagues (1993) delve back further and situate the case study within both sociological and anthropological traditions through the work of Bronislaw Malinowski (1884–1942) and Frédéric Le Play (1806–82), which made it the approach of choice for early studies in the United States and informed the development of different traditions within the Chicago School itself (Hamel 1993: 13). Others have made contributions to the debates on case studies through the following: a defence and justification of the role and place of the case study by refuting a set of common misunderstandings (Flyvbjerg 2006), proactive positioning of the case study approach based on philosophical orientations (Stake 1978, 2005) and presentation of a systematic process for doing case study research, as one method among many at the disposal of the social scientist depending on the kinds of research questions being posed (Yin 1981, 2009).

Across different writings we see how the case study has been interpreted as a method, technique, strategy, approach, design, methodology or heuristic (Hartley 2004; Tight 2010). Even the most fervent advocates acknowledge that the term has entered into understandings with little specification or discussion of purpose and process. One of the reasons for the plethora of critiques and defences of the case study lies in the relationship between its purpose and use in social research and the three broad schools of thoughts outlined in Chapter 1 (positivist, idealist and bridge-building). The case study belongs to and has been reinterpreted by different traditions, with none having a monopoly on its place or status.

Critique, defence and appropriation

For those who hold that there is a world out there that is knowable to us as social scientists, the question is then how and with what methods this becomes possible? Acknowledging the impossibility of studying society as a whole, the case study has been seen as one answer to this question, offering a vantage point from which to draw broader conclusions about societal trends and developments. It is this view that underpinned the development of case study methods in the work of Malinowski and Le Play, the former selecting the 'village' as a focal point on society and the latter the family unit. Drawing on these traditions, later scholars in the Chicago School selected the 'city' as 'providing a miniature replica of problems frequently encountered within the society' (Hamel 1993: 15). The vantage point changes, but informing these approaches is the search for some replicable reality in a single case that is seen to offer an accurate reflection of a knowable social world. In Hamel's terms, it is the singularity of the case study that offers 'a concentration of the global in the local' (Hamel 1993: 38). Early studies were often based on the assumption that societies could be delimited and had sufficient homogeneity that the right unit of analysis, or case, could provide a mirror on a broader social system.

Key protagonists in the history of the case study build on alternative philosophical positions. If the world we live in is one that can only be understood intersubjectively, through understanding the world as it is constructed through the meanings and interpretations given to it by different actors in the lifeworld, then it becomes a method through which to describe and understand the rich, complex sets of interrelationships between different social interests. Case study research thus finds a resonance with participant observation and the ethnographic traditions exemplified in early anthropological studies in which the importance of a single case is stressed. The emphasis is on personal experience and since individuals may attach different meanings to events or act differently at one time from another, proponents of this view would hold that generalizations about the social world are not possible.

What links these different perspectives is the idea that the case study is a single, bounded unit. Where they differ is in their purpose and the extent to which they indicate *generalizing* or *particularizing* modes of interests (D. Harvey 2009), linked to their potential for theoretical development. In the first instance, the purpose of case studies, regardless of methodological approach, is to contribute to the sum of total knowledge through theorization. Alternatively, it is held that such a totalizing view is neither possible nor desirable given the complexities of the social world and its composition of autonomous, irrational human actors. Research may add to human knowledge, experience and thus contribute to learning, but not be driven by the need for explicit theorization. Critiques and defences of case studies reflect these different approaches, while much contemporary writing seeks to overcome such narrow dichotomies and their conflation with positivistic/quantitative or interpretative/qualitative studies.

In the pre-war era, the case study was a method of choice in its own right, yet subsequent developments eroded its boundaries and undermined its distinctiveness (Platt 1992a; Hamel 1993; D. Harvey 2009). Its popularity declined in the 1950s and 1960s as naturalistic methods gained dominance, particularly under the influence of statistical methods and the increasing use of computers and information technology to generate testable models and carry out large-scale analyses. This related not only to quantitative but also qualitative approaches as social scientists were increasingly ascribed roles in predicting and controlling awkward social problems, such as immigration (D. Harvey 2009). Case studies were discredited for the degrees of bias and subjectivity introduced (often closely associated with the use of participant observation and immersion in the field); for producing common-sense as contrasted with scientific knowledge and for their increasing inability to offer valid vantage points in the context of multicultural, heterogeneous, complex societies. Under such pressures, its practices did not vanish, but disappeared from methodological discussions (Platt 1992a: 34).

When the case study re-emerged in methodological writings in the 1980s, it tended to do so with a positivistic bias. The emphasis was on studies that were more like experiments than inductive techniques leading to better understanding. No longer seen as having intrinsic value, the case study became a step in theory-testing or refinement, reflecting techniques popular in the experimental sciences. Case studies were seen to share a similar epistemological logic with statistical methods, through the development of logically consistent models or theories from which specific observations could be derived and tested in order to further develop or revise existing theory (George and Bennett 2004: 6).

An essentially positivist approach to social inquiry can be seen in a systematic, clear process that develops testable propositions to guide data collection and analysis and that relates the case study explicitly to previous theory. In this view, case studies reflect a research strategy that is like an experiment, but without the control (Yin 1981). This appears as a logical choice, rather than one grounded in a philosophical tradition:

a case study is an empirical enquiry that investigates a contemporary phenomena within its real life context, especially when the boundaries between phenomena and context are not clearly evident.

(Yin 1994: 13)

In such an approach, statistical generalization such as we see in relation to surveys and large-scale sampling is not the goal. Generalization is not based on notions of selecting a 'representative sample' in which the results reflect a wider population, but on 'analytic generality' (Yin 1981, 2009) or 'logical inference' (Mitchell 1983). It is theoretical reasoning that matters in producing generalizable conclusions. Thus, in one definition of case studies, they are 'best defined as an intensive study of a single unit with an aim to generalise across a larger set of units' (Gerring 2004: 341), while another sees the case study as a 'detailed examination of an event (or series of events) which the analyst believes exhibits (or exhibit) the operation of some identified general principle' (Mitchell 1983: 27).

For proponents of this view, the case study becomes a 'receptacle for putting theory to work' (Eckstein 1975, quoted in Mitchell 1983). Alongside theory-testing there are those that have emphasized theory-building through an inductive approach to case studies, but one which nonetheless retains the emphasis on generalization. Building on grounded theory, Eisenhardt (1989: 533) has developed a 'near complete roadmap' of how to build theory from case study research through the development of testable hypotheses which are generalizable across settings (also see Eisenhardt and Graebner 2007). Here the use of qualitative and quantitative techniques, along with the desire to build bridges between inductive and deductive approaches and an emphasis on the rich, real-world context of research, seemingly transcends traditional dichotomies. Yet a particular emphasis remains in 'keeping researchers from being carried away from vivid, but false, impressions in qualitative data' (Eisenhardt 1989: 538, 546).

As we noted in Chapter 2, we see not only induction and deduction, but also falsification in efforts to link research with theory in our accounts of scientific progress. Popperian wisdom is particularly well suited to case studies, in so far as the emphasis on a single case may be sufficient to disprove an accepted theory. One case of a talking pig would be all that is needed to unsettle existing certainties about the speechlessness of swine! (Siggelkow 2007). Here we find that 'the exception is taken as seriously as the rule' (Simons 2009: 125). Those within the Chicago School raised similar points with the need to pay special attention to negative and marginal cases as a precursor for theory development (Platt 1992a).

Positivist approaches to case study design have been critiqued not for seeking generalization per se, but for the prescriptive and philosophically narrow methods through which it is sought. Yin, in particular, is seen to offer

> a logic of design not an ideological commitment . . . it could provide the basis for legitimation and reconciliation with what has been seen as the enemy, but at the cost of giving up some of the traditional claims and strengths.
>
> (Platt 1992a: 46)

These discussions of case studies seek to defend through appropriating the language of the natural sciences, to refute through absorption. The emphasis has been on rigour, objectivity, theoretical legitimacy and an emphasis on the explanatory value of case studies, through building on the 'standard philosophy of social science' (Mjoset 2009). Underpinning such defences is a 'totalizing' view based on the assumption that we can know the social world through case studies which mirror the procedures and assumptions of those that study the physical world.

Description, narrative and bridge-building

Where the outcome of the above approaches may be better theories of the social world, for others the singularity of the case itself remains the focus of study. Here we find a set of arguments that seek to refute the critiques of bias and a lack of validity, reliability and generalization through rejection of the very basis on which those critiques have been made. An emphasis on description and understanding replaces one on explanation, as scholars have emphasized how the case study remains a valuable and valid tool for social research precisely because 'the aim is particularisation – to present a rich portrayal of a single setting to inform practice, establish the value of the case and/or add to knowledge of a specific topic' (Simons 2009: 24).

Robert Stake is a well-known defender of the case study in these terms. Following an interpretivist perspective, singularity is seen as a strength that enables a focus on the particularity and complexity of a single case and coming to understand its activity within important circumstances (Stake 1978, 2000, 2005). A suspicion of attributing causality to complex social situations is manifest as explanations are more often multiply sequenced, contextual and coincidental. Instead the emphasis is upon researchers being 'ever-reflective' in their search for the sequence and course of events which are interrelated and contextually bound (Stake 2005: 449).

Reflexivity and context are consistent themes. Intersubjectivity is not only legitimate but also inevitable and turns to bias only if researchers do not remain sensitive to their membership of and participation in the social world they study. It is precisely a viewpoint from within that provides for the intimate knowledge through which definitions are established or meanings understood. Expertise is then seen to be constituted through tacit skills in which 'virtuosity' and 'true expertise' are reached only via experiences (Flyvbjerg 2006: 223).

An emphasis upon expertise may be problematic given an emphasis on the importance of incorporating everyday worlds into the social sciences. Such an approach has 'commonly resulted in smaller-scale research projects and more interactive kinds of research methods and methodologies' (Nast 1994). In place of expertise, the case study is particularly well suited in highlighting the contestability of different knowledge claims through explicit acknowledgement of different perspectives on a single event. Engagement and the realignment of the power base between researcher and researched become important here, with the role of the researcher to 'co-construct perceived reality through the relationships and joint understandings we create in the field' (Simons 2009: 23).

The use of case studies also reflects the tradition of humanism, represented in Wilhelm Dilthey's plea to pay attention to humanistic values, life, expression and understanding (Stake 1978). From this point of view collective knowledge accumulation may be achieved without formal generalization (Flyvbjerg 2006: 227). The power of cases as stories is one such mechanism towards collective learning. Here the case study becomes an 'authenticated anecdote' (Simons 2009: 4): 'the way of the artist, who achieves greatness [and who] through the portrayal of a single instance locked in time and circumstance . . . communicates enduring truths about the human condition' (MacDonald and Walker 1975, cited in Simons 2009: 3).

Within these perspectives the case study is not only pre-experimental but also valuable in its own right. Theoretical development is not the primary aim, but generalization remains possible, albeit in a different guise. Stake (1978) saw description-rich, singular case studies as being a natural basis for generalization given their epistemological resonance with the reader's experience and researchers have emphasized that the issue of generalization cannot be ignored (Gomm et al. 2000). Others have valued case studies for their emphasis on learning, construction, discovery and problem-solving and as 'quintessential social science' (Van Wynsberghe and Khan 2007: 2). This view is particularly prominent among those that use case studies in policy research or for evaluation where a greater concern is with the practical application of findings (Ruddin 2006; Ragin 2009).

A case study is now opposed to the idea of an experiment as outcomes and processes cannot be replicated. A contextualist position then develops which

implies scepticism towards generalising statements on fundamental
features [and] is committed to the analysis of a totality, but *the
totality of a case*, thus not sharing the social philosophical focus on
the totality of driving forces or cognitive deep structures.

(Mjoset 2009: 49, emphasis added)

Here we see an attempt to forge a middle ground between generalization
and particularization. This is a common trend in contemporary discussions of case studies as we see an increasing emphasis on the role of
case studies in developing middle range theories. Others follow a
similar path, proposing such outcomes as 'fuzzy generalisations' (Bassey
2001; Hammersley 2001) or 'moderatum generalisations' (Payne and
Williams 2005).

The goal for many proponents of case studies – and social research
methodologists in general – is to overcome dichotomies between generalizing and particularizing, quantitative and qualitative, deductive and
inductive techniques. Arguments related to the complexity of the social
world, the need for longitudinal studies and the nature of causality have
further been mobilized in defence of case studies. In response to those
that argue that the growing complexity of the social world makes it
increasingly difficult to know, some have tackled this challenge head-on.
Thus, while positivist accounts emphasize extracting research from its
context and decomposing this into variables to produce general, predic-
tive laws, Ragin (2000) has sought to transcend the boundaries between
quantitative and qualitative research through a process of qualitative
comparative analysis (QCA) (Ragin 2000; B. Cooper 2005). His case-
oriented approach takes context and complexity into account to produce
holistic causal explanations (Piekkari et al. 2009).

Complexity justifies an understanding of how processes play out over
time, which in turn requires rich longitudinal data (Siggelkow 2007).
Criticisms of the case study for being bounded by time and space and
thus unable to generate broader understandings are refuted through an
emphasis on 'extended cases' to connect the past, future and uncertainty
together (Evens and Handelman 2006: 46). Looking to the future, we
also see the emergence of prospective approaches that seek to demonstrate the applicability of the case study beyond a particular moment in
time (Bitektine 2008). It is the notion of causality itself that is problematic for others as different mechanisms may produce the same outcome
(Hammersley 2008; Byrne 2009). Again, however, this is an argument for
and not against the case study, given its role in revealing the complexities
in context of phenomena and accounting for alternative interpretations.

Across these past and contemporary writings it is difficult to ascribe
indelible labels to different scholars in terms of their attitudes to
case study research. Positivist and interpretivist camps can be loosely

identified but the varied aims of generalization and particularization cut across both; few accounts reflect a simple philosophical or epistemological position. In Bent Flyvbjerg's refutation of five misunderstandings about case study research, we find appeals to the case study as a critical element in falsification; a defence of the case study's role in understanding and learning and the Kuhnian observation that a scientific discipline cannot proceed without systematic production of exemplars (Flyvbjerg 2006). Another turn can be seen in an emphasis on case studies as narratives that fulfil a social rather than theoretical purpose. Across various accounts, however, we can detect an appropriation and use of the language of the natural sciences (D. Harvey 2009; Mjoset 2009; Piekkari et al. 2009).

There are definitions that have accommodated both positivistic and alternative conceptualizations of case study research. The case study has therefore been defined as 'a strategy that examines, through the use of a variety of data sources, a phenomenon in its naturalistic context, with the propose of "confronting" theory with the empirical world' (Piekkari et al. 2009: 569).

Such definitions have led some to argue that the distinctiveness of the case study within social research has been eroded. Its overuse and overextension has stripped it of any integrity and value, limiting its usefulness and applicability (Tight 2010). That gives rise to a paradox in which our understandings of the social world are drawn from case study research that survives within a 'curious methodological limbo' (Gerring 2004: 341). The debate will continue. What matters is that the researcher is clear on the relative strengths and weaknesses of the approach, how they understand the place and value of case study research and with what consequences for practice. With that in mind, let us now turn to the process of doing case study research.

THE PROCESS OF CASE STUDIES

The above discussion has illustrated differences on the relative status of the case study as an approach, design, strategy or method. From this we can draw three distinct implications for the process of doing case study research. First, the distinctiveness of the case study lies in its bounding, while the methods (interviewing, participant observation, documentary analysis etc.) are generic across the social sciences. Second, there is an emphasis upon choices being made relating to number (small n versus large N) and relative depth, resulting in efforts to tailor advice on good practice in qualitative research to the production of case studies. Third, distinctiveness may be seen only in the analysis and specific relationship between generalization and particularization, linked to theory development. There are differences between those that have sought to identify particular techniques for analysing data and those that substitute analysis with representation, in line with an emphasis on the singularity and richness of 'the One'. We pick up on these latter perspectives in the next section. Here we examine the process of casing and the other choices that may be made in case study design.

To case or not to case?

Across discussions of case studies and their application within multiple disciplines there remains a point of agreement: the distinctiveness of the case study lies in the question, what is a case? This is not seen to be a methodological choice, although as we shall discuss below, extensive attention has been given to the process through which data should be collected and analysed. Rather, a case needs to be defined in terms of its theoretical orientation (Hartley 2004: 324). Rationales for choosing case study research may vary, from theory-building, testing and refining; policy evaluation or illuminating complexity and human experience as a precursor for better understanding, leading to a differential emphasis on description, explanation, evaluation or prescription (Dopson 2003).

The defining choices in case study research are whether, when and how to bound the case? For many this first step is essential in ensuring the quality and rigour of case study research:

> representativeness is therefore ensured by the 'sociological imagination' displayed in the methodological tactics and selections employed in determining which case should be used, or more accurately, which subject should be investigated.
>
> (Hamel 2003: 36)

The selection of the case may be a conscious and deliberate decision or a self-evident choice. If a case study is 'instrumental' in theory development (Stake 2005), then cases must be selected with this specific aim in mind. We saw above how theoretical reasoning as the basis for generalization requires theoretical and not statistical sampling. Cases are chosen for the extent to which they illuminate and extend understanding of relationships between constructs: 'the extrapolation is in fact based on the validity of the analyses rather than the representativeness of the events' (Mitchell 1983: 26).

We may see the selection of a typical case as one having similar characteristics to other cases of the same type. A case may be chosen because its analysis will reveal conclusions that can be taken as representative of a wider class of cases. If, therefore, we are interested in understanding whether the creation of new regional institutions in the English regions has challenged the traditionally centralized model of governance in

England, we may select any region as a 'case', or vantage point, through which to examine the reconstitution of power relations between the centre and the regions. Yet representativeness in this example can be assumed only on the basis of identifying fixed characteristics that are invariable across regions, as well as accounting for similarities in how power is exercised by and through different actors irrespective of regional context, personal biographies and so on. The notion of typicality thus assumes a homogeneity and basis for extrapolation from one region to the next.

Issues are now raised over whether cases can be typical if we see the social world as composed by social actors that are shaped by and shape the structures and institutions of society. The reverse position would be to select 'atypical' or 'extreme' cases which may play a greater role in learning, understanding and illumination, 'where the concatenation of events is so idiosyncratic as to throw into sharp relief the principles underlying them' (Mitchell 1983: 37). For Stake, the potential for learning is a superior criterion to representativeness in terms of generating understanding (Stake 2005: 451). An emphasis upon 'intrinsic' case studies which aim to develop the case's own issues, contexts and interpretations is evident in this approach.

While instrumental case studies depend on knowing the critical issues in advance, case studies that involve intrinsic interest have no such aim. Following the example above, we may select a region to generate understanding about central-local power relations precisely because it has exercised its roles and responsibilities in a particularly unusual or innovative manner to produce different outcomes. Overall, this would emphasize 'how' things are done in order to better understand 'what' has been achieved. Alternatively, we might emphasize a unique instance of a given phenomena, linking the notions of atypicality and criticality. The creation of the first regional science and industry council in the North West of England could then be seen as a critical case for questioning whether a 'regionalization' of English science policy was taking place (Perry 2007).

If we follow the logic of falsification, we might see cases as critical or crucial. A single case can hold the possibility of disproving existing theories and paradigms. Cases would be selected according to whether they are least likely or most likely to falsify a theory. Along with such possibilities, the language of instrumental, intrinsic, typical, atypical and critical cases has entered into common usage. We have also seen a differentiation between 'apt illustrations', 'social situations' and the 'extended case' study (Gluckman 1961, cited in Evens and Handelman 2006). They may be 'configurative ideographic', 'disciplined configurative' or 'heuristic', where the core differences lie in the relationship between the case study and theoretical development (Eckstein 1975, cited in Mitchell 1983).

In certain accounts we see a clear process for determining cases according to the questions being asked, the control an investigator has over events and the focus on contemporary as opposed to historical issues (Yin 2009). In contrast, it is the relevance of context that occupies others, requiring the researcher to either reconstruct events (reconstruction) or intervene in existing processes in time (intervention) (Mjoset 2009). Following Ragin, cases may be 'found', may be seen as 'objects', can be 'made' or are 'conventions'. A distinction is also evident here between realist perspectives that see cases as either given or empirically discoverable and a nominalist view that sees cases as the consequence of theories or of conventions (Ragin 1992: 8).

Issues are now raised in terms of case selection over the epistemological and ontological bases of the approach. David Harvey characterizes cases as complex entities in their own right with autonomous claims of their own, requiring an emphasis on the transformational dynamics of case-objects as evolving socio-historical entities. Through typological simplification, 'systematic glosses lead to a premature closure of self-critical possibilities' (D. Harvey 2009: 22). This gives rise to four criteria for case-study work: case objects must support a self-standing narrative and provide 'meaningful analytic closure' and a 'well informed explanatory narrative'; a case object must be a minimally integrated social system; case objects are open historically evolving systems and they are dialectically reproduced by human intentionality and by institutional stasis (D. Harvey 2009: 22).

In these different accounts we see a preoccupation with bounding and definitions. Intentional design logic then becomes evident whereby the nature of the case and the object of study needs to be known in advance. An alternative approach is to see an 'emergent logic' (Piekkari et al. 2009) where the 'case' is defined throughout the work and may not even emerge until the end of the research process. An inductive approach is clear here and one in which the intuition of the researcher and their intimate knowledge and depth of understanding of the case is legitimately seen to enter the research process. Again, links with grounded theory are apparent, with one study perhaps having multiple cases. For Ragin (2009: 532), 'it is only by casing social phenomena that social scientists perceive the homogeneity that allows analysis to proceed'.

Flexibility in the social research process is a prerequisite and advantage of such an approach. A clear theoretical framework at the outset or clear propositions to test may not be evident. What a study is a 'case of' then emerges over time. Such flexibility, however, 'is not a licence to be unsystematic, [it is] controlled opportunism in which researchers take advantage of the uniqueness of a specific case and the emergence of new themes' (Eisenhardt 1989: 539).

Design and emergence, deduction and induction need not be incompatible. You may start with a specific theoretical proposition to test, but long-term immersion within and engagement with different perspectives, viewpoints and possibilities may enable alternative propositions to emerge, enabling different answers to the question of 'What is this a case of?' In Figure 5 we see a movement within and between a case study orientation that is both instrumental and intrinsic at different points in time and illustrates a sensitivity to the depth and breadth of field materials and their subsequent treatment in analysis.

Figure 5 What is this a case of?

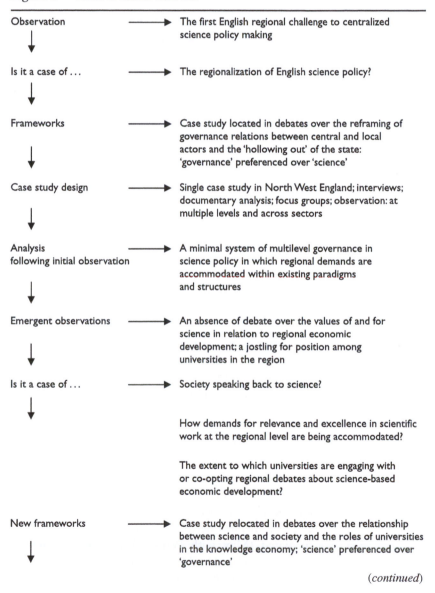

Observation ⟶ The first English regional challenge to centralized science policy making

Is it a case of ... ⟶ The regionalization of English science policy?

Frameworks ⟶ Case study located in debates over the reframing of governance relations between central and local actors and the 'hollowing out' of the state: 'governance' preferenced over 'science'

Case study design ⟶ Single case study in North West England; interviews; documentary analysis; focus groups; observation: at multiple levels and across sectors

Analysis following initial observation ⟶ A minimal system of multilevel governance in science policy in which regional demands are accommodated within existing paradigms and structures

Emergent observations ⟶ An absence of debate over the values of and for science in relation to regional economic development; a jostling for position among universities in the region

Is it a case of ... ⟶ Society speaking back to science?

How demands for relevance and excellence in scientific work at the regional level are being accommodated?

The extent to which universities are engaging with or co-opting regional debates about science-based economic development?

New frameworks ⟶ Case study relocated in debates over the relationship between science and society and the roles of universities in the knowledge economy; 'science' preferenced over 'governance'

(*continued*)

Figure 5   Continued

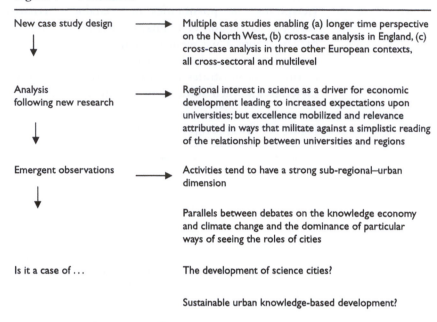

New case study design ——▶ Multiple case studies enabling (a) longer time perspective on the North West, (b) cross-case analysis in England, (c) cross-case analysis in three other European contexts, all cross-sectoral and multilevel

Analysis following new research ——▶ Regional interest in science as a driver for economic development leading to increased expectations upon universities; but excellence mobilized and relevance attributed in ways that militate against a simplistic reading of the relationship between universities and regions

Emergent observations ——▶ Activities tend to have a strong sub-regional–urban dimension

Parallels between debates on the knowledge economy and climate change and the dominance of particular ways of seeing the roles of cities

Is it a case of ...   The development of science cities?

Sustainable urban knowledge-based development?

A simplified example, building on research funded by multiple academic (research council), government and industry sources between 2002 and 2008.

In a further example, we can see movement between stand-alone policy evaluations, concept development and hypothesis elaboration. In our own work we built on a policy think-piece on the roles of universities in the urban knowledge economy in Manchester to pose, through comparative work in cities across England, a question around the different capacities and capabilities of universities to engage with cities in the context of a so-called post-industrial economy. Through interviews with those within different institutions (universities, government and industry) and at multiple scales we developed a series of initial typologies and concepts to differentiate between responses. For instance, we characterized different kinds of urban response according to whether they were representative, additive or transformative (May and Perry 2003); strategies according to their emphasis on processes, products or acquisitions (Perry 2008); distinguished between ways of conceptualizing the relationship between excellence and relevance (Perry and May 2006) and developed concepts such as 'active intermediation' to explain how the relationships between universities and 'their' localities may be better mediated (May with Perry 2011). Taken together, a hypothesis then developed related to the dominance of a technocratic, neoliberal economic policy agenda that crowds out more socially just alternatives to the knowledge-based society, all of which can be taken into comparative case study contexts for further analysis.

It is also worth noting at this point that the practicalities of doing case study research, in terms, for instance, of sources of research funding, levels of staffing or the time-span of the project, shape the choice of case study and the subsequent approach to a greater degree that is often publicly acknowledged. Practical choices are inevitable in terms of location, travel requirements and time allocation. Access is a particular consideration, comprising not only physical location but also social location in terms of networks and processes (Dopson 2003; Payne and Williams 2005). For a longitudinal and cross-comparative study, particularly one that may involve a small number of in-depth cases in different contexts, knitting different funding sources together is a prerequisite.

Case study design and methods

While many remain critical of the case study as a method, others have sought to illuminate the choices that doing case study research entails. One set of choices relates to how many cases to select and whether comparison is necessary. Instrumental studies related to theory development tend to involve multiple cases favoured by those who seek analytic generalization with an optimum number of cases for theory development lying in the range between 4 and 10 (Eisenhardt 1989; Eisenhardt and Graebner 2007). By extension, comparison, which will be examined in Chapter 10 in more detail, becomes essential. For many this is the only basis on which case studies can be seen as a valid, reliable and rigorous research tool and this reflects what is taken to be 'a growing consensus that the strongest means of drawing inferences from case studies is the use of a combination of within-case analysis and cross-case comparisons' (George and Bennett 2004). Qualitative research involving a small number (n) of cases is often at the forefront of theoretical development, while large numbers (N) are seen to offer little flexibility or sensitivity to the diversity and potential heterogeneity of the cases (Ragin 1987, 1991; Becker 1992).

Intrinsic case studies, on the other hand, are often characterized by $n=1$. If a single case study is chosen because it is revelatory or unusual, then it is depth not breadth that counts. This is not a necessary trade-off if longitudinal studies of small numbers of cases can be carried out, but it is inevitable that the depth and understanding inherent in the analysis of a single, as compared with multiple, cases will differ significantly. The danger is that comparison becomes the focus, rather than the case itself, undermining the original aims of the study and generating 'less trust-worthy' conclusions (Stake 2005). Comparison may be useful, but only to illuminate difference and not to ensure representativeness. An intrinsic case study may also lend itself to inductive and participative techniques, while deductive theory-testing enables a clear delineation at the outset of the research about what may be included or excluded from the focus.

This brings the question of data sources and collection to the fore. In the link between case study research and participant observation, an ethnographic tradition can be identified. In Malinowski's research on village life in Melanesia in the Trobiand Islands, complete immersion in the field, a cataloguing of data, observation and interviews with those directly involved and other social interests, comprised the study (Hamel 1993). Since then the range of techniques or methods have broadened across the qualitative and quantitative spectrum, including observation, interviews, focus groups, documentary analysis, surveys, modelling etc. It is this lack of specificity that has led some to criticize textbooks and 'how to' guides for their repackaging of standard good practice in social research as somehow specific to the case study process: 'most of the guidance given is fairly generic in nature, and could readily be applied to other qualitative, and even some quantitative, forms of research' (Tight 2010: 5).

Two points stand out within discussions of the case study process. First, there is some agreement that multiple methods are essential to case study research. Even where theory development is not the aim, rich descriptions are obtained by maximum confrontation through various mechanisms between the researcher and the field of study. Second, a strong emphasis is placed on iteration between data and analysis in several accounts. In the development of grounded theory, the joint collection of, coding and analysis of data is explicitly prescribed, necessitating continuous comparison between data and theory (Eisenhardt 1989: 533–4). Similarly, it has been argued that 'fieldwork materials and conceptualisation shape and use one another, producing recurrent epistemological surprise and, correlatively, inventing an anthropology not only of but also as practice' (Evens and Handelman 2006: 47). Even those of a greater positivistic slant have acknowledged the lack of fit between a linear process from question specification, to data collection and analysis and the conduct of case study research.

Misgivings over the distinctiveness of the process of case study research have not prevented the search for its essential ingredients. That is apparent among those who have responded to critiques of case studies by demonstrating that their methods are equally as rigorous as those in the natural sciences. Yin (2009) identifies five components of a case study: its questions; its propositions which reflect on a theoretical issue; its units of analysis; the logic linking the data to the propositions, and the criteria for interpreting the findings. That, in turn, leads to an emphasis on multiple sources of evidence; establishing a chain of evidence; getting feedback on reports; doing pattern matching; building explanations; using time series analysis; using replication logic in multiple case studies; developing and using a research protocol and developing a case study database. Following on from a differentiation between *types of cases*, we can identify different *case study designs* (Yin 2009). Thus we see that designs may be single or multiple, as noted above, but also vary according to whether they are holistic or embedded.

Terminological distinctiveness is further sought in processes such as triangulation, a phrase used by different schools of thought to represent how to handle multiple sources of data. This process entails making sure that evidence from different sources can corroborate the same fact or finding and is closely linked to recommendations of setting up a database and establishing the chain of evidence which 'consists of the explicit citation of particular pieces of evidence, as one shifts from data collection to within-case analysis to cross-case analysis and to overall findings and conclusions' (Yin 1981: 63). Triangulation can also be seen in interpretivist approaches, despite an emphasis on the meanings attached to events by participants rather than the chain of evidence per se. Stake (2005) identifies five key requirements for the case study, including issue choice, triangulation, experiential knowledge, contexts and activities. The purpose of corroboration here, however, is not to arrive at a single explanation but to uncover the diverse 'emic meanings' of people within the case (Stake 2000: 441).

Others have their own approaches. In a roadmap for building theory from cases, Eisenhardt (1989) outlines eight key steps: getting started; selecting cases; crafting instruments and protocols; entering the field; analysing data; shaping hypotheses; enfolding literature and reaching closure. In prospective case study design, pattern-matching techniques are employed to compare testable predictions against the subsequent development of events (Bitektine 2008). Qualitative comparative analysis is said to constitute a distinctive contribution to the debate (Ragin 2000). An example of this can be found in Barry Cooper's (2005) study of the relations between social class origin, sex, ability and subsequent educational achievement. Others have developed good practice guides that seek to synthesize across these different accounts (Rowley 2002; Dopson 2003).

Whatever choices are made will inform and be informed by questions of values and ethics. Commonly case study research is seen to entail a greater degree of subjectivity both in the initial bounding and orientation of cases as well as in their conduct. As noted above, one approach is to seek to manage out the presumed bias of the researcher through closely defining methods and process. Hence we see systematic, step-by-step processes of theory-testing in which data are collected and analysed away from the research site and those that comprise it. That raises ethical issues of its own in terms of the assumption of a privileged vantage point on behalf of the researcher, as well as an extractive approach leaving matters of communication, commitment and engagement to one side. Alternatively we might see that 'a constant juxtaposition of conflicting realities tends to "unfreeze" thinking and so the process has the potential to generate theory with less researcher bias than theory built from incremental studies or armchair, axiomatic deduction' (Eisenhardt 1989: 547).

In search of mutual knowledge between the observer/participant and the social world, we cannot deny our being part of that world but must instead acknowledge and incorporate that fact as a precondition of doing research. Even with an inductive approach to case studies, 'an open mind is a good one; an empty mind is not' (Siggelkow 2007: 21). Researchers need to be aware of but not constrained by initial hunches and frames of reference and importantly retain an emphasis on both 'sending' and 'receiving' sites (Payne and Williams 2005). In the contextualist perspective, the scientific community is considered as a society embedded in society at large, necessitating consideration of both 'internal' and 'external' perspectives (Mjoset 2009). It is to these issues and their relationship to questions of analysis and representation that we now turn.

ANALYSIS OF CASE STUDIES

Building on the above it could be argued that it is in the analysis of field materials, rather than techniques for collecting them, that the distinctiveness of the case study lies. Where theory development is the aim – whether through inductive or deductive techniques – the analysis of field materials is critical. Analysis may involve the development of constructs, typologies or categories for tabulating and coding the data. In the movement from 'within case' to 'cross-case analysis' categories and typologies play a role in the process of pattern-searching. Different approaches may lend themselves to this process through comparing within-group and inter-group similarities and differences; selecting pairs of cases or seeking to divide the data according to source to get unique insights from different sources (Eisenhardt 1989).

A cross-case approach involves constructing an explanation for each case singly and knowing the acceptable levels of modification in the original explanation as new cases are identified. The emphasis on comparison with other cases in order to 'improve the basis for generalisation' (Dopson 2003: 224) is often the singular difference between advice on case study analysis as opposed to generic good practice guides. This may involve not only your own research but also comparison with cases carried out by others. The evidence used to support conclusions may be second- or even third-hand which 'underscores the communal nature of case use in social science' (Platt 1992b).

Many accounts have the emphasis on triangulation, looking for confirming and non-confirming data and considering alternative explanations. This implies not only a need for analysis but also synthesis and integration of data: specific insights may be gleaned not only from analysing by data source, but also by looking across to identify complex interdependencies and causal processes. 'Process-tracing' then becomes a specific technique, linking possible causes and observed outcomes (George and Bennett 2004). Here the emphasis is on developing conceptual validity, driving new hypotheses, exploring causal mechanisms or modelling and assessing complex causal relationships.

Yin (2009) is one of those who offer concrete ideas on how to analyse case studies. He suggests a three-step process involving, first, following the theoretical propositions that led to the case study in order to focus attention on certain data, second, considering rival explanations, and third, developing a descriptive framework for organizing the case study. Here analysis takes place against the backdrop of the conceptual framework and theoretical propositions already known at the outset of the study. An inductive approach, on the other hand, relies more heavily on defining categories, properties and subcategories following data collection, with a greater number of distinctions allowing for historical context and enabling the movement from 'crisp' to 'fuzzy' sets (Ragin 2000; Mjoset 2009: 58).

Take one example. We may think of the distinction between urban and rural areas as a first level identification of different types of national space. Through numerous case studies the 'urban' has been subdivided according to size (world cities; metropolitan cities; medium-sized cities); according to location (port cities; peripheral cities); according to industrial base and specialization (old industrial; financial centres); according to population and flows (large net importer; exporter of population) and so on. With each step, levels of sensitivity to historical trajectory and context are increased leading to an emphasis on the 'exemplar' rather than any 'representative' typical case to account for both similarities and differences between categories.

A different analytic approach is implied in case studies dependent on whether the case is defined at the beginning or at the end of the research process. Irrespective of this distinction, however, is the need to give explicit attention to generalization. For Payne and Williams (2005) moderate generalizations can be achieved through five steps: considering to which/ how many other settings might the findings of a study apply; acknowledging the limits of time frames; considering how accurately the research has characterized the study topic; limiting claims to basic patterns or tendencies so that others can find something similar and establishing the ontological status of the phenomena in question. In this latter point, we see that stronger claims can be made about some things rather than others, for instance, we can have greater certainty about the fixed properties of physical objects than we might about group relationships or psychological dispositions or behaviour (Payne and Williams 2005: 307).

Where case studies are not aimed at theoretical development or generalization, analysis takes a different meaning. The aim with intrinsic case studies is to capture the wholeness of the case, to provide a detailed write-up of the case as a stand-alone entity: 'the purpose of a case report is not to represent the world but to represent the case' (Stake 2005: 460). The organization of the data becomes essential in preserving the unitary character of the social object being studied (Goode and Hatt 1952, cited in Mitchell 1983: 27). With an emphasis on natural generalization, it is not incumbent on the researcher to connect findings to a broader theoretical or social universe, reflecting an empiricist slant in which the materials will speak for themselves. This reflects an emphasis on narrative and representation, but we should be careful not to falsely juxtapose this as excluding analysis. Indeed, multiple case narratives that are preceded by analytic reasoning also have their advocates in the case study literature (Abbott 1992).

The relative status of field materials and their representation in research reports varies according to the aim of the case study. On the one hand, theory may be abstracted from data and case materials excluded from being published. Here participants may be represented as statistics behind the conclusions ('we interviewed 25 people within these kinds of organizations') but their accounts not directly reported in the text. On the other hand, it is the description of the case through the collected data that matters. In this we see a differing emphasis on case study field materials as the means or the ends in themselves. The case study is not only a strategy or design but also the outcome of the research process.

This raises the question of who and what the case study is for? Academic audiences are often assumed to be more interested in theory development than in detailed case studies (Siggelkow 2007). Intrinsic case studies are commonly associated with policy evaluation and aimed at different 'lay' audiences. What arises at this point is the question of language. It might be argued that the development and use of a social research language is a necessary differentiator between lay and expert knowledge as protection against relativist perspectives and simple appropriation into existing states of affairs. Hamel (1993) recommend an analytic process in which field materials are deconstructed so that the researcher's object may be produced and constructed in a social scientific form. This language 'should be free of any stylistic features eliciting other forms of knowledge such as literature, should be concise and avoid ambiguities and should display an irreducibility of language' (Hamel 1993: 48). Specific advice then follows on how to construct an explanation that is demonstrable through the description and that does not draw on 'any intuitive, tacit and imitative fields of knowledge' (Hamel 1993: 48).

Where natural generalization is the aim, a prerequisite of research is the mirroring of everyday language that resonates with the reader. This allows the audiences of case study reports to vicariously experience what was observed and utilize their tacit knowledge in understanding its significance (Simons 2009). The 'irreducible quality of good case narratives' leads to a defence of minutiae so as not to lose the complexity and inter-penetrating nature of social forces (Flyvbjerg 2006). However, choices must be made, even with intrinsic case studies, in the representation of data about what to leave out or to preference, which stories and whose stories to tell. The treatment of context is one such example and the extent to which this features explicitly in causal accounts differs (Mitchell 1983; Hartley 2004; Simons 2009). A different choice relates to the extent that methodological statements reflect research experiences or an assumed template of good research practice because 'mistakes, surprises and changes of plan tend more often to be concealed or reserved for the appendix' (Platt 1992b: 47).

What is at stake is the relationship between the production of a case study and its reception, mediated by different techniques of analysis and interpretation. These issues are often reduced to simplistic equations between theorization for academic audiences written in technical discourses and policy-oriented case studies written in non-technical languages. Cutting across this is a form of deployment of case studies that may be either indicative or illustrative depending upon the audience one is seeking to reach and the overall aim of the work. In relation to the indicative as representative of general global trends, Pam Odih's (2007) aim in using the case of the international clothing company Burberry is to

> reveal how the globalization of markets has intensified competitive pressures to produce clothing at lower costs, with contracted lead times and increasing differentiated product lines . . . This has precip-itated a new wave of outsourcing, enabled by technological advances, directed towards making the labour process more versatile.
>
> (Odih 2007: 176)

For the purposes of using a case to demonstrate what can be achieved in business that is socially responsible and environmentally sustainable, Sushil Bhatia (2010) deploys the DeCopier as an illustrative green inno-vation. This takes a used piece of paper and produces it as reusable:

> Looking at the development of the DeCopier, one can learn that it is possible to develop green, sustainable, and commercially feasible products. This case also illustrates that it is possible to develop prod-ucts which can meet multiple market needs and applications.

DeCopier not only reduces the paper waste but also helps save confidential information, offering a dual advantage to the end user.

(Bhatia 2010: 156)

In research practice, as many contemporary social theorists and methodologists emphasize in overcoming narrow dichotomies between research methods and philosophical audiences, case study research may serve multiple purposes outside that originally intended at the outset. Aims may change over time, particularly with commissioned policy evaluations, where the initial emphasis may be on understanding dynamics and context-specificity (internal 'intrinsic') while a subsequent priority may emerge in relation to transferable lessons (external 'instrumental'). Regardless, the separation of policy relevance and generalization through theory development is a false divide if we remain conscious of the ways in which our research may impact on, with and through the social world we study:

by starting with more reflection on the end point of the research process, researchers should be better placed to adapt their research design, so avoiding excessive generalising claims and engaging actively with expressing their more modest claims in clearer terms.

(Payne and Williams 2005: 311)

Notwithstanding these points, there is a clear question about how far to go in anticipating the reception of work without undermining the distinctiveness of the research itself (May with Perry 2011).

None of these issues is unique to case studies but they are set in sharp relief, given the status of the case study as output as well as method and that it is designed to be *read*. Reflexivity around, rather than capitulation to, contexts of knowledge reception as well as production is necessary (May et al. 2009). No simple 'analysis-versus-narrative' exists (Abbott 1992: 53). Rather, a single study may be analysed in different ways, for different audiences and with multiple outcomes. In our previous example, our study of the development of Manchester in its efforts to become a self-proclaimed 'knowledge capital' not only has value as a stand-alone case to understand the dynamics, perspectives and insights of different actors and so to improve local effectiveness, but also contributes to theoretical development in a relatively new field of study and has provided transferable and comparative lessons for national policy development. A single case study may provide the basis for an academic article or policy piece, while a series of case studies over time can form the basis for a more systematic treatment of a particular thesis (Hodson and Marvin 2009, 2010).

It is appropriate that we end with a consideration of closure. This is implied in many discussions both in relation to the collection of field

Figure 6   Closing the loop

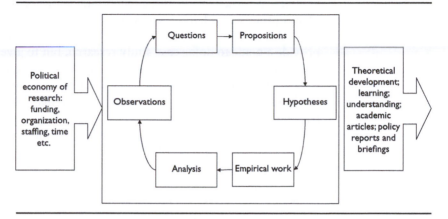

materials and their analysis, illustrated in David Harvey's (2009) four criteria for case studies noted above. The bounding of a case study in time indicates a finishing point whereby, to use a detective analogy, the case may be closed. An alternative route may nonetheless be identified: 'the opposite of closing down and summing up is to keep it open' (Flyvbjerg 2006: 238). Such an outcome is inevitable as the case study 'proliferates rather than narrows', leaving further avenues of inquiry to the researcher (Stake 1978: 7). By closing the loop between inductive and deductive techniques, for instance, and knitting together the insights from different studies over time within a coherent framework of analysis, it may be desirable, feasible and even necessary to keep both case study objects and findings open to continuous re-evaluation and reassessment (see Figure 6). Replacing the need for resolution with that of constant reinterpretation and revision is the hallmark of a mature social research practice.

SUMMARY

In this chapter we have discussed the place, process and analysis of the case study in social research. Ontological and epistemological issues remain, with varying interpretations on what a case may be and how it contributes to knowledge. Core to this debate is the question over the distinctiveness of case studies: their prevalence within social research has been widely debated but on what basis is their propagation founded? We have suggested that this is a question of bounding the case and in the analysis and representation of field materials, rather than in the methods deployed themselves.

   A central thread through the chapter has been to consider the relationship between generalization and particularization, moving from the content of debates through to their practical implications for process and analysis. We see, as with all the techniques explored in this book, particular approaches with a contemporary emphasis on a middle way and the need to transcend traditional dichotomies. Our aim has not been to provide a guide to doing case study research, but to give a sense of orientation to a wide set of literatures that cut across disciplinary boundaries. As with all chapters, we find a series of choices and reflections that assist in deciding whether and how case studies may be relevant to your research.

In the relationship between generalization and particularization, we have seen how comparison has been attributed a central role. The single case has value in its own right. Yet when placed against the rich insights from multiple cases, a route from particularization to generalization can be traced, leading to both theory development and comparative learning. It is with that in mind that we turn in the next chapter to the issue of comparison.

Questions for your reflection

1 Is there anything distinctive about case study research?

2 What is the relationship between case study research and theory development?

3 What can we learn from a single case and how?

4 What and who are case studies for?

SUGGESTED FURTHER READING

Byrne, D. and Ragin, C. C. (eds) (2009) *The Sage Handbook of Case-Based Methods*. London: Sage.

Hamel, J. with Dufour, S. and Fortin, D. (1993) *Case Study Methods*, English translation. London: Sage.

Ragin, C. C. and Becker, H. S. (eds) (1992) *What is a Case? Exploring the Foundations of Social Inquiry*. Cambridge: Cambridge University Press.

Yin, R. (2009) *Case Study Research: Design and Methods*, 4th edn. Thousand Oaks, CA: Sage.

Comparative research: potential and problems
With Beth Perry

Globalization, cosmopolitanism and comparative research
  The place of comparison in social research
Processes of comparative research
Issues in comparative research
Summary
Suggested further reading

The idea of comparison has a long and rich history. Writers on the subject invariably start their accounts by noting how people compare as easily as they breathe, making continuous value judgements over which product to buy, which clothes to wear, which foods to eat, or which course of action to choose (Caramani 2009). For some, social research is, by definition, comparative research that involves understanding and explaining variations 'which cannot be accomplished without previous reflections on similarities and dissimilarities underlying the variation' (Øyen 1990b: 4).

Comparative research is characterized by a pluralist approach, centred not only on comparing countries, but also on subsystems, cultures, groups, policies and people. While all research involves comparison of some type, the terms 'cross-national' and 'cross-cultural' have been frequently employed to emphasize the importance of comparisons between countries and cultures. This has been a central foundation in the development of the comparative method and cross-cultural research in general (Lijphart 1971; Ember and Ember 2009; Pennings et al. 2009). As one contribution to a reader on comparative policy research begins: 'States, kingdoms and principalities have been compared for approximately 2,500 years' (Deutsch 1987: 5). International organizations and institutions such as the European Union or Organization for Economic

Cooperation and Development, fund increasing amounts of work in the area of cross-national studies. The results of these studies can be found in books and journals in many subject areas including economics, politics, human geography, urban studies, sociology, history, social policy, anthropology and business studies.

As the world we live in becomes more complex and interrelated and boundaries between nations, societies and cultures become more porous, debates on the place and process of comparative research have multiplied. For some the pluralistic approach to comparison is clearly positive, with others concerned about a lack of specificity that renders engagement with issues and processes rather problematic. Attention is therefore increasingly turned to the methodological sphere. Do the concepts of the 'nation-state' or 'society' still continue to have relevance in our globalized, cosmopolitan world? If not, what should we compare? Does comparative research require alternative methodologies? What is the balance between the breadth and depth of knowledge for comparison and how well suited are qualitative and quantitative techniques to addressing differences in aim and orientation? The following observation remains of relevance to this discussion when we find a situation characterized by

> methodological pluralism, with many open-minded initiatives and a corresponding diversity of priorities concerning research goals and techniques of analysis. But this state of affairs is not an end in itself. Pluralism is good but it does leave us with some peculiar questions. To what extent is open-endedness a snare for the unsuspecting?
>
> (Apter 1971: 3)

To assist in a general understanding of this topic, this chapter begins with a discussion of the relationship between globalization, cosmopolitanism and the rising importance of comparison in social research. The second section then considers the process of cross-national research and the varied positions that researchers take towards its utility and purpose. These issues inform the final section, which considers the problems associated with cross-national and cross-cultural research. The intention of this chapter, therefore, is to offer an overview of the potential and problems of comparative research, as opposed to wholesale and uncritical adoption or rejection.

GLOBALIZATION, COSMOPOLITANISM AND COMPARATIVE RESEARCH

As nation-states developed, so too did the opportunities for cross-national research. In contemporary times, with increases in communications and technological advances, the world is 'getting smaller'. The invention of the wireless, for example, created what Barbara Adam has termed a 'global present' in collective grief when news of the sinking of the *Titanic* was announced (Adam 1995: 111). Such occurrences find their parallels in contemporary national-global events in relation to acts of terrorism, or increased vulnerability to natural ecological disasters (Žižek 2010a). News programmes keep us up-to-date on events on the other side of the globe and telephones, mobiles, texts and emails enable those who can afford it to converse with friends, relatives or business people in other countries – almost in an instant. Documents and video conferencing link us across national boundaries and oceans. 'Real-time' interactions via mobiles and social networking communities such as Twitter or Facebook add a dynamic to this hypermobile interactivity that appears to reduce the relevance of national boundaries to lived experiences of everyday people. The problem, as Øyen (2004) reminds us, is that comparative methodology has not developed at the same speed as these information communication technologies (ICTs).

Globalization and the spread of ICTs have a clear impact on the organization of societies and cultures. For some opportunities are created with consequences that are not immediately visible, while for others, intensified globalization leads to retreat and the desire to form communities that are presupposed to be characterized by a homogeneous culture (Bauman and May 2001). Under these circumstances it has become less possible to speak of a 'society'. Modern industrial societies are not hermetically sealed off from the world, with the social bonds of old often seen to be giving way to a process of 'detraditionalization' marked by chaos and uncertainty (see Heelas et al. 1996). Globalization may be defined as an 'intensification of worldwide social relations which link distant localities in such a way that local happenings are shaped by events occurring many miles away and vice versa' (Giddens 1990: 64).

For many this implies a convergence between nation-states, a blurring of cultural identities and the diminishing relevance of distinct development trajectories. Hence it is argued that 'there are shared, universally identifiable, pressures and trends working across all industrialized societies' (O'Reilly 1996: 41).

A desire to seek general explanations across different contexts via an examination of possible processes of convergence is counterbalanced by the increased complexities of social, economic and political life that have accompanied globalization: differences and diversities exist not only within, but also between nations. Increasing divergence then questions the goals of cross-national empirical generalizations and the possibility of what have been termed 'metanarratives' of theoretical explanation (Lyotard 1984). Contingency is celebrated over generalization. Add to this arguments that signs no longer indicate a reality beyond them

(Baudrillard 1983a, 1983b) and any attempt at seeking a basis for cross-national research appears futile and without foundation.

Uncertainties as to the future, particularly given a resurgence of nationalism and the 'breaking-up' of previous nation-states, open up the possibilities of fatalism and pessimism. Yet in the face of this ambivalence, comparative research becomes of greater importance. While we cannot assume similarity between and homogeneity within societies, an opportunity presents itself in terms of contributing 'more effectively to the shaping of social futures' (Smart 1992: 221). This requires a practical intervention enabled by research that is sensitive to differences *and* similarities in terms of the interactions between the global and local:

> The tensions between the views of those in different but inter-dependent positions have to be confronted and negotiated. There are invariably local views within, and of, large, grand structures, but we need to discover what links up those local views, not eagerly fragment them into separate, non-communicating discourses or local knowledges.
>
> (Sayer 2000: 75)

As the local and global interact, what is then required in research terms are accounts that recognize 'both the structured character of global communication and the contextualized, hermeneutical character of the production/reception process' (Slevin 2000: 206). Cross-national research has a clear role here through providing a perspective on both the peculiarities of local experiences and the forms and consequences of general processes (Heynen et al. 2006). After all, insights into forms of life are enhanced by studying the ways in which different cultures and societies organize their social and political affairs.

What is raised at this point is not whether but what to compare? With the boundaries of nation-states encroached upon 'from above' by internationalization or supra-national organizations (such as those of the European Union) and 'from below' by increasingly politically mobilized and economically powerful cities and regions, new forms of governance between levels of action have arisen (Jessop 2004). At the same time scholars have questioned what we mean when we talk of the 'state' in the context of redefined roles and responsibilities between public and private actors, privatization, deregulation and new mechanisms of control and surveillance (Brenner 2004; Crow 2004; Søderbaum 2009). For Levi-Faur (2006) *sectors* should now form the key unit for comparative analysis rather than nation-states, while elsewhere we see an emphasis on trans-national 'scapes' (for example, mediascapes and technoscapes) and on flows and networks (Appadurai 1996).

To simply employ the idea of society can ignore or stifle the differences. Thus, a sensitivity to comparison *within* (intra-societal comparison), as well as *between* (inter-societal comparison), societies is required. The former method might examine differences between how groups of people are processed through the criminal justice system (as per the example in Chapter 4), or the industrial geography of the UK (Massey 1995). The latter method might compare societies which display both similarities and differences, for example, in relation to their provision of welfare (Esping-Andersen 1990) and issues relating to social exclusion (Byrne 2005).

The appropriateness of different units of analysis for comparison is raised via Beck and Sznaider's (2006) plea for a cosmopolitan social science which

> entails the breaking up of the process through which the national perspectives of politics and society, as well as the methodological nationalism of political science, sociology, history and law confirm and strengthen each other in their definitions of reality.
>
> (Beck and Sznaider 2006: 5)

Their answer is to call for a 'methodological cosmopolitanism' that transcends the traditional dualisms between global and local, national and international, and us and them through new forms of conceptual and empirical analysis. The decisive point here is that 'national organization as a structuring principle of societal and political action can no longer serve as the orienting reference point for the social scientific observer' (Beck and Sznaider 2006: 4). This also points to Beck's earlier work on the risk society (Beck 1992, 2009) and the ways in which this has informed more recent critiques, such as those of Slavoj Žižek (2010b). Researchers must reflect not only on how the world has changed, but also on how our perspectives and tools of analysis must also alter to recognize and make visible the 'background assumptions' (Gouldner 1971) we hold and their epistemological foundations (Walker and Wong 2004).

The place of comparison in social research

In the above we see reflected the philosophical traditions that have informed the practice of social research. Comparative research has been embraced as a quintessential ingredient of social science and rejected by others as impractical, unfeasible and even undesirable. It draws on the foundations of the natural sciences, in terms of an emphasis on experimentation as well as reflecting the more interpretative traditions of the case study.

The central methodological question which faces comparative research is: does it require a different practice and set of procedures from other forms of research? Within the literature, there appear to be several responses to this question. First, there are those who consider that comparative work is no different from any other. The units of analysis, whether political parties or welfare systems, need no special theoretical accounts or methodological discussions. This group Øyen (1990a) calls the 'purists', adding the caveat that this is a tendency to which many researchers succumb. Second, there are those who are ethnocentric in their approach – the primary, though not exclusive, targets of Beck and Sznaider's critique of 'methodological nationalism' above. Researchers of this type are not sensitive to social context and historical and cultural differences and simply 'add on' their findings to existing ways of under-standing and explaining – the consequence being that cross-national data are not assumed to add to the complexity of social science research (Øyen calls this group the 'ignorants'). Third, there are those whom Øyen refers to as the 'totalists'. This group appears to be aware of the issues involved in cross-national research and its methodological and theoretical pitfalls. At the same time, 'They consciously ignore the many stumbling blocks of the nonequivalence of concepts, a multitude of unknown variables interacting in an unknown context and influencing the research question in unknown ways' (Øyen 1990a: 5). Finally, there are the 'comparativists'. This group recognizes the arguments of the purists and totalists, but believes that cross-national research is a distinc-tive topic. As a result, they undertake their work in a different manner and frame their research questions accordingly. Clearly, these four groups are ideal types: that is, they are devices that enable us to think through and engage with issues, as opposed to being assumed to reflect an unproblematic reality.

Many researchers now compete for the position of comparative expert. This may have desirable consequences depending on the values, positions and dispositions of researchers. Take, for example, different orientations to research along the global–local excellence–relevance continuum discussed in Chapter 3. The search for international excel-lence in academic work may give rise to the desire for recognition or for the development of theoretical models that can be transplanted (and sometimes commodified) to make scientific reputations across academic and policy worlds. Conversely, good work may be done by those who systematically seek to conduct research which is excellent *and* relevant and which links in-depth understanding with detailed 'modest' general-izations developed over time (Payne and Williams 2005). Simply tacking on preconceived ideas and even prejudices on the operation of societies does little to advance our understanding and counters the idea of a reflexive basis to research practice.

Between rejection – in which comparison is impossible due to the fundamental incompatibilities of concepts, cultures and units of analysis – and full-scale embrace without due consideration of context, lie a number of different approaches to undertaking comparative research. We shall characterize these in the following ways: the *import-mirror* view, the *difference* view, the *theory development* view and the *foresight* view. These are not distinct, but interrelated themes which enable an interrogation of the literature written by those who see comparative research as having the potential to enhance our understanding and explanation of human relations.

The import-mirror view suggests that the project of comparative analysis is worthwhile because in producing findings on the practices of other countries, we are better able to see the basis of our own practices. On an instrumental level, this means the borrowing of ideas from other countries in the spirit of learning from one context to transplant into another: 'the goal is lessons rather than creating or testing theory. Countries that are similar are more likely to borrow from one another' (Teune 1990: 58). According to this view, the results generated by comparative study may permit the importation of different methods of organizing a society's affairs to improve their efficiency. On a less instrumental dimension, this also allows us to reflect upon our own social systems and cultural ways of behaving. It thereby possesses the potential to challenge our background assumptions by producing findings on different social contexts and cultural practices.

Such a strategy allows those who are studying other countries to have a particular insight into their practices. While it is advantageous to be an 'insider', 'outsiders' (as researchers) can raise questions which may not have been thought of by those who take their own practices for granted. Of course, we do not necessarily require cross-national research for this purpose as there may be sufficient diversity within our own societies. However, societies and the systems they devise reveal variable historical conditions leading to current practices and policies. Thus, and this brings us round to the second advantage, comparative analysis is undertaken to explain and understand differences and similarities.

By examining different societies, we can ask why some have developed in similar ways and others in diverse ways. This adds to an understanding and explanation of the complicated relationships between economic, social and political systems without, by theoretical fiat, opting for the convergence or contingent perspective (beyond which generalization is not possible). For instance, Esping-Andersen's (1990) study is centred on the belief 'that only comparative empirical research will adequately disclose the fundamental properties that unite or divide modern welfare states' (Esping-Andersen 1990: 3). Further, the contributors to the volume by Ian Taylor (1990) examine the 'cultural specificities' which any adoption of free-market policies has to take account of, thereby blending the contingent with the convergent models. Through comparative accounts of five western-style societies, the limits to market-based policies are illuminated. Differences within and between these societies expose the problem of adopting a philosophy of 'free markets' given the profound social costs which this ideology entails.

Comparisons which reveal difference and diversity or, in the above example, cultural impediments to the implementation of policy enable us to consider the macro factors which influence social and political change and the micro factors peculiar to each social setting. This relates to a third advantage, which sees an improvement in theoretical development resulting from the growth of comparative research. For those who consider that the goal of social research is the discovery of general theories which explain the way societies are organized: 'comparative studies are absolutely essential' (Robert Holt, quoted in Grimshaw 1973: 19). It is through comparison, moreover, as we saw in Chapter 9, that the possibility of generalizing and theorizing on the basis of case studies becomes possible. From this point of view comparison must entail not only description – or the setting side-by-side of multiple country or case narratives – but also explanation (Ember and Ember 2009). An emphasis on why and how, as well as what, is implied here necessitating a concern with causal interpretations and process-tracing.

With an emphasis on explanation, a close relationship between comparison for theory development and comparison for policy learning can be seen, depending on how research is conducted and the ways in which results are handled. On the one hand, cross-national studies can have the effect of altering the focus of research efforts with considerable implications for policy initiatives. Consider, for example, the drift from measurements of poverty to those associated with 'social exclusion'. In an insightful discussion of this issue in relation to Europe, Jos Berghman (1995) notes how the European Observatory on Policies to Combat Social Exclusion, along with the European Community Programme to Foster Economic and Social Integration of the Least Privileged Groups, acted as catalysts for an analytic shift with practical consequences.

On the other hand, theories generated on the basis of comparison may be stated at such a level of abstraction they are not useful for the interpretation of data or the application to particular policy environments. Furthermore, such abstraction may ignore important differences between countries through, for example, a preoccupation with structure over culture. A clear example can be seen here in the development of models of innovation ecosystems both at the national and regional levels that tend to be reduced to checklists of 'ingredients' for success without any understanding of what and how models may be relevant, if at all, to different national and subnational contexts (Perry 2008). As Hurrell (2005: 39) asserts, 'the study of comparative regionalism has been hindered by so-called theories of regionalism which turn out to be little more than the translation of a particular set of European experiences into a more abstract theoretical language'.

Given these issues, there are those who would steer a middle course between universalistic theories which are assumed to be generally relevant to societies across time and space and particularistic theories which are applicable only to particular social settings and thus not generalizable. This is said to take account of differences within societies, as well as similarities between them:

> Anyone who engages in comparative research immediately notices differences between countries. Yet anyone who persists in wide-ranging comparative analysis also recognizes boundaries to these differences: for example, among two dozen countries, the variations in methods of electing a Parliament are limited. Since the time of Aristotle, the first task of comparison is to observe the extent to which countries differ or are similar. The second task is to ask why. Under what circumstances do differences occur?
>
> (R. Rose 1991: 447)

To allow for the possibility of diversity and similarity, comparative analysis considers both *endogenous* and *exogenous* factors. The former are those which are peculiar to the country which is being studied, while the latter are those elements, such as international capital, gender and race relations, which while influencing that country's social and political relations, are not simply peculiar to it. However, as the discussion on Ian Taylor's (1990) work indicated, comparative researchers need to be sensitive to the 'cultural specificities' which affect *how* exogenous factors influence each country. In our own work on building science regions and cities, we employ the concept of *mediation* to explore how assumed global pressures and drivers are mediated, transformed, translated or transcended by different national and regional systems or institutions to produce differences in subnational responses (May with Perry 2011). At the same time, what is required is an understanding of whether, if any, these forms of mediation result in significantly different outcomes (and if so for whom?).

Esping-Andersen's (1990) comparative study could be summarized as an example of a middle-course genre. Alongside empirical comparison his work was informed by the need for theoretical generation:

> Existing theoretical models of the welfare state are inadequate. The ambition is to offer a reconceptualization and re-theorization on the basis of what we consider important about the welfare state. The

existence of a social program and the amount of money spent on it may be less important than what it does. We shall devote many pages to arguing that issues of decommodification, social stratification, and employment are keys to a welfare state's identity.

(Esping-Andersen 1990: 2)

The latter part of this quote refers to the concepts which Esping-Andersen employed to understand and compare the identity of welfare states. This is a central point in theory development. The use of such concepts, it is argued, enables the researcher to have a common point of reference in order to group empirical data which are differentiated along both linguistic and geographical dimensions (Ferrari 1990; R. Rose 1991). By approaching the comparison of welfare states in this way, Esping-Andersen (1990) was able to show, using a considerable amount of data and 'ideal-type' welfare regimes (liberal, conservative and social democratic), how countries' welfare states evolved as a result of different historical forces. Thus, he compares, but in so doing does not ignore, differences between countries. The result is a novel theoretical analysis of contemporary changes in welfare states (although it has been criticized for the absence of gender as a significant social category in comparative welfare-state analysis, as well as for the form of comparative analysis employed: see Langan and Ostner 1991; Shalev 2007).

Finally, we come to the fourth view: the enhancement of foresight through comparative work. According to this view, not only can the potential for the success of particular policies, systems or practices in a given society be understood, but also their outcomes can be acted upon, once their effects in other societies and social and cultural contexts are examined. Accordingly, organizations or governments may embark upon particular courses of action knowing their probable consequences.

One must exercise caution here, lest the ability to generate knowledge to enable a greater understanding of the likely consequences of actions in the future be confused with a notion of prediction that assumes we can know a certain future. There may be degrees of predictability that can be attributed to aggregated social phenomena, but it does not follow that the intentions of policy are thereby aligned with outcomes. Quite simply, there are unintended consequences to social actions, at whatever level they may arise. Thus, in her comparison of women's employment in Britain and France, Veronica Beechey (1989: 377) notes the similarity of developments in these countries in terms of economic restructuring, but a clear variation in their form. The same observation may be made in relation to comparisons between countries in relation to cities, social locations, gender, class and ethnicity (Byrne 2005).

These motivations for comparative research are interrelated particularly in the context of the contemporary *knowledge-based* era. Writers have emphasized how we now live in a post-Fordist, post-industrial age in which knowledge has supplanted land, labour or capital as the dominant factor of production (Bryson et al. 2000); how the speed and prevalence of knowledge production – through universities, but also private research industries and consultancies – has intensified (Stehr 2004) and how knowledge has assumed a central position in relation to all domains of political, economic, environmental and cultural decision-making (Turner 2003). Accordingly the knowledge-based era has taken on a particular resonance in the policy world with increasing demands for evidence-based policy that is founded on 'what works'. The 'what works' mantra is then linked, through discourses on globalization, connectivity and economic competition, to the ubiquitous assumption that such evidence must, by definition, be comparative: 'the choice *not* to conduct a piece of research cross-nationally requires as much justification as the choice to conduct cross-national research' (Livingstone 2003: 478, original emphasis).

What then results is a collapse between different motivations for carrying out research, accompanied by a range of dubious cross-national information-gathering techniques, referred to as 'research', which amass data on different countries or units of analysis – often for the purpose of ranking and measurement rather than learning or policy effectiveness (Dogan 2004). The import-mirror view merges with the foresight view such that it is 'translation' of models across contexts that takes place and wholesale borrowing, rather than considering issues of context, consequence or applicability. At the same time, reflected in the rise of the evidence-based agenda is a very particular view of what evidence is and how it should be produced. One particular manifestation of this is in relation to the spread of business incubator models, science parks and innovation processes from one context to another based on often narrowly and quickly defined evaluation methods (May and Perry 2006; Yu and Nijkamp 2009). That points to the need to consider how comparative knowledge is produced and what is assumed to constitute a solid evidence base for this purpose.

PROCESSES OF COMPARATIVE RESEARCH

Debates on the place of comparison have focused upon these key themes of convergence and divergence, difference and similarity, the global and the local. Questions have been raised over the balance between within-country and cross-country analysis and even what the appropriate units of analysis should be. Both quantitative and qualitative techniques are implied – with explicit hierarchies often invoked – in the comparative analysis between units of analysis across or within countries. We may compare different units of analysis at the same time period ('synchronic') or a single unit of analysis at two distinct time periods ('diachronic'); make world-wide or regional comparisons and build on secondary or primary data (Ember and Ember 2009). Not discounting those who see a role for multiple interpretative studies set side by side as a basis for natural generalization (see Chapter 9), what links many accounts of comparative methodologies is an emphasis on explanation and by extension, generalization (Caramani 2009). The purpose of comparing is not only to describe differences or similarities, but also to explain how and why these differences occur.

The evidence base for comparison is linked to a search for causal analysis. Here we see a clear lineage between comparison and the experimental method, seen by many as the epitome of science. Broadly speaking, the experimental method randomly allocates people to particular groups and subjects them to controlled stimuli. Behavioural or physiological changes can then be measured as the scientist monitors the effect of these controls. A sequence of cause and effect is established in the observed pattern of events. Thus, in medical trials, one group may be given a test drug and another group is given either no drug or a placebo (a drug without effect in order to act as a control on the group). Differences between the two groups are measured and any 'real' physiological or biological effects of the new drug established. The three key principles of experimentation are seen to be manipulation, control and random assignment. A further mark of a 'good' experiment is that it could be repeated ad infinitum and would produce the same results.

In pursuing a belief in the parallels between the natural and human sciences, there are those who seek to emulate its techniques. According to the above principles, however, the experimental method has a number of methodological and theoretical flaws when applied to the social world. For instance, in order to observe the relation between cause and effect a number of 'standing conditions' must be specified in order to allow for genuine comparison. This means introducing a constancy into experimental situations that presupposes they are closed systems. Social life is, on the other hand, an open system and so not amenable to such attempts at artificial control. This raises particular problems, for instance, when it comes to the replication of experiments as time, place, context and character cannot be reproduced exactly in different social settings.

Given that social life is more complicated than closed systems can allow for and subject to numerous forces at any one moment, social researchers frequently resort to what are known as 'quasi-experiments' (D. Campbell and Stanley 1963). This refers to a

> study that takes place in a field setting and involves a change in a key independent variable of interest but relaxes one or both of the defining criteria of laboratory and field experiments: random

assignment to treatment conditions and controlled manipulation of the independent variable.

(Grant and Wall 2009: 655)

This is said to enable recognition of the fact that social systems are open, not closed. We should note, therefore, that the desire for control is tempered by the realities of social life, while control also operates at the levels of research design and analysis in order to raise the probability of producing better knowledge. Furthermore, to impose an artificial and inapplicable method upon a phenomenon is actually to undermine this goal. In these instances, the researcher has less control over *exogenous* variables which could influence *endogenous* behaviour (see Kidder 1981; Moser and Kalton 1983; Shipman 1988; Bechhofer and Paterson 2000).

Comparison in social science can be seen as a natural form of quasi-experimentation. As one of the founding fathers of the Chicago School, Albion Small (1854–1926), put it:

All the laboratories in the world could not carry on enough experiments to measure a thimbleful compared with the world of experimentation open to the observation of social science. The radical difference is that the laboratory scientists can arrange their own experiments, while we social scientists for the most part have our experiments arranged for us.

(Small 1921: 188, cited in Gross and Krohn 2005)

To establish causal relationships that have internal and external validity, a control group is needed. In the case of comparative social research, we can seek to identify what happened before or after particular significant events or, for instance, what happened in one region as a result of the introduction of a policy intervention, technology or practice, but did not happen in another region with comparable characteristics. This method was adopted in a study to apply a quasi-experimental regional analysis to an energy boomtown in the United States (Isserman and Merrifield 1987).

These methods are still practised, such as the randomized control trial (RCT) which enjoys a particular status as observed changes may be subject to statistical tests to see if they are due to chance. We can see this in research which seeks to evaluate whether a particular programme of activity is achieving its stated ends in, for example, the field of education (Gorard 2004). As one of a series of texts on evaluation research puts it: 'Without any *comparison* group, it is hard to know how good the results are, whether the results would have been as good with some other program, and even whether the program has any effect on the results at all' (Fitz-Gibbon and Lyons Morris 1987: 26, original emphasis). In this quote we see evaluation linked with a post-hoc assessment of what *has* worked. Increasingly this is being replaced by the 'pilot' as a means to establish what *will* or might work. Here we see an effort to carry out social experiments with the intention of testing the efficacy of a policy intervention in a particular time and place, with a view to later upscaling or rolling out to different contexts. A move towards the greater use of pilots and experiments can be traced, particularly in the United States, but also in the UK (Howe 2004; Government Social Research Unit 2007; Stoker 2010). Examples abound as places then proffer themselves to be the sites of such experiments and to share their learning with others; in the English context we can point to the trial referendum in the North East of England on elected regional assemblies (Sandford 2009); the designation of Manchester and Leeds city-regions in England as two pilot statutory city-regions; or the setting up of test 'low carbon economic areas' in selected major cities. Practical applications may include the use of new ICTs on voter turnout or the relationship between new user IT interfaces and sustainable behaviours, such as in relation to car sharing.

It is not only policy-makers but also researchers who are restating the value of experimentation. Ann Oakley seeks to rescue experimental social research from the 'irrational disapprobation' that is exhibited towards it (Oakley 2000: 259). Gross and Krohn re-present the discourses of the knowledge society in the context of the traditions of the Chicago School to argue for a 'society of self-experimentation [which] builds its existence on certain kinds of experiments, practiced outside the domain of science' (Gross and Krohn 2005: 77). Among the new wave of advocates we also find those such as McDermott (2002) and Stoker (2010), who are paving the way for experimentation to take its place, in a modest way, as one method available to us. This requires abandoning 'purist ideas of a hierarchy of methods with experiments at the top' (Stoker 2010: 305) and replacing this with a more nuanced claim about their potential in knowledge production.

The role of the social researcher is of central importance here. In many accounts, there is only a thin line between the understanding of experiment and processes of action research, while others argue that new forms of social experimentation places the 'experimenter right in the middle of experimental practices' (Gross and Krohn 2005: 79). This implies a constructive engagement with ideas of comparison in experiment and design and evaluation research and a shift to a more inclusive idea of research with which social researchers constantly engage. As Stoker (2010) notes, we cannot rely on classic scientific norms as

> the doing of field experiments, especially if they are to connect to the world of policy, requires a capacity in terms of sensitivity to context,

contingency and the subjects of the research that might ordinarily be associated with more qualitatively oriented research styles.

(Stoker 2010: 309)

What is implied here is a different method of experimentalism from the neo-classical norm and a reordering of quantitative-experimental and qualitative-interpretivist methods (Howe 2004: 42). For those involved in the implementation of programmes that are subject to such methods of evaluation, it should be borne in mind that 'replication is not foremost in their minds' (Pawson 2006: 46).

Experimentation is one method open to the comparative researcher to establish causal chains and the relationships between different variables. Another method is that of case studies, as we discussed in Chapter 9. We see a circular referentiality here: the use of case studies to establish causality is advocated by comparative methodologists, while comparative analysis is suggested as a means for case study methodologists to make generalizations on the basis of a small number of cases (cf. Ragin and Becker 1992; Rueschemeyer 2003; Hawkins 2009). Case studies have also been described as 'quasi-experiments' (D. Campbell and Stanley 1963).

Case studies are particularly favoured by those who advocate comparative historical analysis. In contrast to the social or political experiment which emphasizes the present, the field of comparative historical analysis emphasizes the past in the search for causal explanations through an emphasis on processes over time and the use of systematized and contextualized comparison. A wide range of research methods are suggested for this purpose (Mahoney and Rueschemeyer 2003) combining not only quantitative methods but also qualitative ones, for instance, through the search for within-case causal sequences and cross-case identification of likely causal factors (Mahoney 2003).

What makes an experiment or a case study comparative is the notion that there is more than one unit of analysis being examined. This might be, as we have suggested, comparing two or more time periods, two or more units within a case or two or more cases. For Lijphart (1971),

the comparative method should be resorted to when the number of cases available for analysis is so small that cross-tabulating them further in order to establish credible controls is not feasible . . . there is consequently no clear dividing line between the statistical and comparative method, the difference depends entirely on the number of cases.

(Lijphart 1971: 684)

At the same time, he notes that the statistical method is not only an approximation of the experimental method but also superior to both case studies and comparison (Lijphart 1971: 685). Hence while this appears to advocate a distinct comparative method, it is far from emphatic on the merits of its own approach. What is reflected here is a preference for statistical analyses wherever possible. It is not only that large N studies tend to be equated with statistical quantifiable variables, while small n studies are more commonly associated with qualitative case studies, but that a hierarchy is presumed to exist between the two.

This dichotomy has particular resonance when it comes to comparative studies. Critiques of cross-country comparisons on the basis of large-scale quantitative techniques are widespread in the literature, though this has not prevented their increasing role in informing global and national policy interventions. The tensions are neatly encapsulated by Livingstone (2003), who notes, in relation to media research, that

> on the one hand, research is gripped by the ethnographic turn, emphasizing contextualized interpretation, insider accounts and critical or social theoretical work (e.g. work on globalizing forces, hybridizing identities, subcultural resistance, etc.). On the other hand, media and communications research is attracted to and funded to conduct multinational comparisons involving large-scale standardized data collection in order to advance administrative or policy goals (e.g. work on diffusion of innovation, the digital divide, information flows).
>
> (Livingstone 2003: 494)

What constitutes evidence to inform policy is largely quantitative: 'often the comparative method is nothing other than the statistical method applied to designs involving cross-country analyses' (Caramani 2009: 4). The quantitative, cross-country comparative approach has been characterized as 'one of those enormous bubbles, which afflicts social science research areas from time to time' (Kittel 2006: 647), despite the fact there have been diminishing returns on large-scale cross-national studies (Molina and Rhodes 2002). Through such techniques, data are often generated that are unproblematically taken as fact rather than critically examined. Statistical indicators tend to be national, while comparisons on the basis of large-scale databases, such as the OECD's Social Expenditure database, have such severe measurement problems to render conclusions invalid (Kittel 2006). They are seen as top-down and offer a highly aggregated view of differences and similarities by reducing units of analysis to the function of relationships between variables. A linear notion of causality is then often implied which makes cases invisible, with ambiguous results that cannot distinguish between additive effects, conditional relationships and multiple causal pathways (Shalev 2007; Swank 2007).

At the same time, the use of rankings as proxies for statistics also leads to an emphasis on 'one-size-fits-all' solutions:

> the rising tendency to transfer policy concepts which contribute to regional economic development across regions and nations is misleading, without reflecting that regional and national differences exist . . . the approach to look at prosperous regions (instead of non-prosperous ones) in order to assess causal conditions of economic growth should be seriously re-considered.
>
> (Grimm 2006: 142)

To these critiques, the following problems of large-scale quantitative comparisons have been added: the significance of the national average; the potentials and limits of survey research; the worldwide statistical analysis; the gross national product as a fallacious indicator; the scoring and scaling as a substitute for formal statistics; the need to replace isolated indicators with composite indices; the temporal lag between cause and effect and the problem of the shadow economy in comparative research (Dogan 2004). The above makes for a telling list and reflects many of the issues that have been examined throughout this book.

The alternatives to demand-driven and static tools types of approach are seen to lie in the new forms of social experimentation, quasi-experimentation and case studies that prioritize meaning and under-standing (Isserman and Merrifield 1987; Mangen 2004). Approaches that are bottom-up, open-ended, flexible and exploratory and that are based on a few cases are seen to offer routes forward. Novel methods are being proposed that combine qualitative and quantitative approaches to comparative studies and are reflected in texts on the subject (Kennett 2004; Rihoux and Grimm 2006; Hantrais and Mangen 2007; Caporaso 2009; Grant and Wall 2009). Many of the pages in these readers are covered by discussion of specific bridging methods in comparative studies, such as configurational comparative methods – which combine variable and case-oriented approaches (Rihoux and Ragin 2008; Rohwer 2010) or congruence analysis (Haverland 2010). At the same time, some inter-national organizations, such as the OECD, have recently exhibited a greater understanding of the limitations of surveys and questionnaires and developed supplementary methods of data-gathering and analysis, such as peer assessment and review (OECD 2007) as a basis for comparative understanding.

ISSUES IN COMPARATIVE RESEARCH

We have already touched upon many issues and problems that may arise in the process of comparative research. In this final section we offer some further elaborations from the literature, focusing particularly on cross-cultural issues.

One of the primary problems with comparative analysis is not only the ability of researchers to understand adequately cultures and societies which are different from their own, but also, more specifically, to generalize and explain social relations across societies and social contexts. Following the work of Winch (1990; Hutchinson et al. 2008), it has been argued that in order to understand a culture, we have to know the rules which are employed in that culture; only then can we understand the ways in which the culture views the social world. So far, so good. However, and this is the important point, there is nothing 'beyond' this understanding: for example, establishing whether a culture or society beliefs are valid through a comparison with other societies. As three sympathizers of this view express it, Winch (1990) sees the creation of a comparative social research programme as requiring

> the comparison of like with like . . . In order to decide which institutions of one society – our own in many cases – to compare with those of another we shall need to be able to match those institutions, to say what kind of part they play in their respective societies . . . However, if we are in a position to say what part each institution plays in the life of its society then we have already achieved a very good understanding of it.
>
> (R. Anderson et al. 1986: 184)

In other words, this understanding is the aim of comparison and its finishing point. We cannot explain a culture's history and development in terms of social forces which are external to it. This renders the ability to generate particular forms of cross-cultural and societal explanations untenable. Indeed, it is argued that 'even the best translation is never more than a forced alignment of discrepant accounts of social reality' (Tarafodi 2010: 227).

The potential of comparative research in allowing the outsider to 'look in' and see things in a different way which is theoretically useful appears untenable, at least, according to this view. Researchers can understand only from the 'inside' – from the social context which is peculiar and relative to that time and place. We have actually returned to the discussion in Chapter 1. Social research should look for and seek to understand the meanings within a social context where people act according to the rules of the social setting. This excludes, by definition, the search for causal explanations which may provide for generalizations across societies. Instead, the 'stranger' must be prepared to grasp what Winch (1990) calls 'forms of life' which are fundamentally different from their own, but which can be evaluated only in terms of the indigenous culture. Beyond this, there is no way of establishing a general explanation of beliefs beyond their social context. As Ernest Gellner (1974), a critic of Winch's views, succinctly summarizes this position in terms of people speaking: 'their own lives and pursue their manifold interests in the context of "forms of life", cultural/linguistic traditions, and the concepts they employ derive their validity from, and *only* from, possessing a place in these forms of life' (Gellner 1974: 143, emphasis added).

Winch's arguments can be further located and based in relation to those arguments in Chapter 2 on common sense. The researcher cannot legitimately consider, in theoretical or empirical terms, anything other than the practical use of language in everyday life or the methods which people use in interpreting the social world in their particular contexts. This position has actually been raised in previous chapters in one form or another, for it occurs throughout discussions on social research (on the meaning-equivalence of attitude scales in questionnaires, interviews as topics and not resources and documents analysed in terms of practical reasoning). We have, however, encountered limits to this perspective and here we have two other issues, in particular, to consider. First, those who have sought the rule following basis of language often demonstrate an absence of sensitivity to cultural differences in their desire to find universal explanations. Second, conflict around the exercise of power, within the same societies, questions the idea that there are beliefs which are beyond question in their own terms, let alone those of the outsider. To regard a culture as somehow hermetically sealed off from outside influence is, to say the least, highly problematic.

The question to be formulated in facing these conflicts and the relations between so-called endogenous and exogenous influences is 'why' does this occur? These are questions to which those such as Esping-Andersen (1990), R. Rose (1991), Hirst and Thompson (1999), Byrne (2005), Odih (2007) and Hodson and Marvin (2010) address themselves. The influence of global capital on a culture, or the development of whole societies, affects that culture as an exogenous factor, particularly in terms of the relationships between western societies and the majority world (often referred to as 'developing'). Large multinational and transnational companies, assisted by state power, are unlikely to regard such arguments as impediments to the realization of their global goals.

For these reasons, among others, Winch's arguments have been characterized as contradictory (Lukes 1994). The implications of Winch's arguments are reflected in the literature on comparative work. Both Esping-Andersen (1990) and R. Rose (1991) not only are aware of the importance of being sensitive to social context, but also note the similarities which are found between societies. Comparative researchers are also conscious of the issue of comparing like with like (see R. Marsh 1967; Armer 1973; Teune 1990; Byrne 2005; M. Mills et al. 2006). We all carry 'cultural baggage' (Hantrais 2004: 268), but this should not deter us from seeking understanding and insight from comparative research.

These issues find their outlet in discussions on *appropriateness* and *equivalence* in comparative research. Appropriateness refers to the methods employed and the conceptualization of issues when undertaking comparative research. Researchers cannot assume that what is appropriate for their culture will necessarily be appropriate for another. A sensitivity and understanding of cultural context are thereby required. Armer (1973) expressed this succinctly as long ago as the early 1970s: 'Appropriateness requires feasibility, significance, and acceptability in each foreign culture as a necessary (but not sufficient) condition for insuring validity and successful completion of comparative studies' (Armer 1973: 50–1).

Equivalence is a related issue. Of course meanings may vary between cultures. This raises a particular problem in the use of surveys in cross-national research where meaning-equivalence is an important component of a questionnaire's validity (see Verba 1971; Scheuch 1990). Others note, for instance, how we might characterize national benefits systems, but would need fine-grained qualitative understanding of how concepts are defined and employed and with what effects to effectively influence societal outcomes (Hantrais 2004).

In terms of the process of study, unless researchers have an understanding of the social context with which they are dealing, two samples, although random, may actually sample different age ranges or population characteristics that are not comparable. This often results from indigenous factors which the researcher either has overlooked, or is simply not sensitive to accounting for. Thus, in comparisons of international migration, different countries may classify migrants according to qualifying periods that vary from three months to a year (Singleton 1999). Alternatively, the ways in which homelessness is defined influences data collection and the concepts and categories then developed (Kennett 2004) with very real effects on how the problem is perceived or who may benefit from interventions. For this reason, as the objects we study are socially constructed, 'concepts need to be located and understood within the national regional, local and disciplinary contexts that produce them' (Hantrais 2004: 261).

A more general problem relates to appropriateness and equivalence. As Robert Marsh comments: 'the task of linguistic translation falls heavily upon the shoulders of the comparativist' (R. Marsh 1967: 272). Language differences, even if researchers have a proficient understanding of a language, require a cultural understanding of words to allow for the equivalence of meaning. That is particularly important when dealing with dialects where the meanings of words vary, or entirely different words may be employed in referring to the same phenomenon. From a methodological vantage point, it has therefore been argued that sensitivity to the context in which beliefs are generated needs to be accompanied by the employment of 'complementary methodologies to investigate the language, vocabulary and structure of people's attitudes and beliefs . . . This means a far greater use of qualitative techniques, ethnographic research, and discourse and rhetorical analysis' (Golding 1995: 231).

When it comes to examining available data on countries, it is worth bearing in mind that if not conversant with the language, the use of English translations can lead to issues of selectivity and thus bias. Issues of language, together with a drive to increase comparative work and the high costs of comparative survey and observational research, can lead many researchers to rely on official publications (Manis 1976). Any analysis based upon such documents may then produce partial and incomplete accounts.

As has been noted (Lawrence 1988), the language issue may be becoming less problematic as English comes to dominate as a world language. However, issues of meaning equivalence still remain, to say nothing of the desirability for non-English speakers of this state of affairs. For instance, dialogues between the researcher and interviewees, as well as the translation of documents and a reliance on official publications, are still matters of interpretation. Lawrence (1988) refers to this in his account of studying comparative management. Here he considers not only a delicate balancing act between inferring actions from observations in social settings by utilizing nationalist stereotypes, but also the possible misapprehensions which occur in interview situations:

> One is never quite sure that they have understood the question, or at least its nuances or comparative thrust; one worries that interviewees are responding to the question they think you asked (but you think you asked something different). The problem is compounded by the admirable vagueness of English: there is no other language more suited to the framing of open-ended questions or projective try-ons.
> (Lawrence 1988: 102)

While we are said to live in the age of the death of the author, it might equally be said that we live in the age of the translator. Translation is now a business that can make careers, money and reputations accordingly. In addition, it is not something that may be simply separated from the application and development of a theoretical perspective. Temple and Edwards (2002) argue not that researchers should cease to use translators, nor that those who cannot speak a particular language ought not to conduct research on those who do, but that there should be a dialogue between researcher and translator as it is not simply words that are conveyed, but also perspectives. In view of the latter, the researcher should be sensitive to such issues for, while all research is inevitably an act of translating experiences, it is how this takes place that is of importance. Thus, the focus is not upon what is right and wrong in an act of translation, but of a dialogic understanding that can sharpen insights into differences and similarities: 'to assume that there is no problem in interpreting concepts across languages is to assume that there is only one baseline, and that is the researcher's own' (Temple and Edwards 2002: 9). Non-verbal language and communication also play a role as we interpret not only words, but also body language, phrasing and social situations as part of the research experience (Tarafodi 2010).

We return again here to the issues of methodological nationalism and the relationship between culture, language and interpretation in the service of comparison. For some, an absence of reflexivity on the critical issues of context-sensitivity, generating comparable data and appropriating equivalence has given rise to 'asymmetries of power [which] impact the discourse and rhetoric of comparison, making them reciprocal or unilateral, dialogic or monologic . . . an invidious kind of comparison that takes the form of civilizational ranking' (Stam and Shohat 2009: 473).

How then might this be avoided? It requires not only seeing cultural comparison as a form of hermeneutics, as Tarafodi (2010: 236) has argued, but also new ways of approaching and organizing comparative work. Here we can turn globalization to our advantage through collaborations between researchers in different countries. In making the connections between the global and local, the theoretical and particular, quantitative and qualitative or large N and small n studies, collaboration is not only a practical response but also one inscribed in the research strategies of both national and international organizations. Hence we see, for instance, in the Framework programmes of the European Union, an emphasis not only on comparison, but also on collaboration between researchers, particularly those in the newer accession states in Eastern Europe. The scale and scope of research is enlarging with an emphasis on bringing scholars together to work on global problems irrespective of national boundaries.

A clustering and concentration of expertise not only poses challenges and raises new inequalities, but also provides the opportunity for new ways of working or 'modes of knowledge production' (Gibbons et al. 1994). These are heterogeneous and networked and enable both context-specificity and the potential for theoretical generalization. From an ecological perspective, collaboration is also a pragmatic response, if it can reduce rather than increase the need for international travel through drawing on the local skills and expertise of those in different places. The irony of climate change researchers flying round the world to carry out work in different contexts is noted by many, but acted upon by few. Add to this that such collaborations are more often than not multi-method and multidisciplinary (Livingstone 2003) and we have a petri dish in which knowledge, culture, society, politics and culture mix together requiring innovative, reflexive and realistic research designs for comparative work (see box).

The MISTRA Centre for Urban Futures: an emerging comparative case study design

MISTRA is a Swedish foundation that supports research of strategic importance for a good living environment. Starting in 2010 it is funding a unique multiannual programme into sustainable urban futures through transdisciplinary research that brings researchers and practitioners together in new modes of knowledge production. Running for 12 years this programme is one of the largest comparative urban research programmes in sustainability of its kind. With a core scientific programme in Gothenberg, a distinctive element of research design is the development of four 'international interaction platforms', in Greater Manchester (UK), Shanghai (China), Kisumu (Kenya) and Cape Town (South Africa).

The challenge is to develop a robust and realistic methodology for research within and comparison between these contexts. Central principles include: the establishment of distinct research teams within each research site with an understanding of local conditions, contexts and cultures; regular bilateral and multilateral research pairings or visits to develop greater reciprocal understandings and an extended start-up scoping phase in which the 'case' or 'cases' within each site are elaborated and developed. At the same time an interaction coordination function has been designed to enable comparisons to be made between the platforms with the potential for theoretical development and greater policy relevance. Hence, the unique length of the programme – which goes beyond that available publicly – enables a movement from inductive, interpretivist accounts of individual cases to hypothesis generation and subsequently theory development, allowing a potential synthesis between the global and local, the general and particular and theory and practice.

This approach is important not only to guard against the critique of 'methodological nationalism' but also to allow research concepts and cultures to define and redefine each other iteratively through the work. The intended result is not only a better understanding of particular places and the dynamics of city responses to climate change, but also a comparative framework of understanding that enhances academic work and influences practices. Such starting considerations are important, but they do not eliminate issues relating to concept equivalence, data availability or methodological pluralism. There is only so far that one can go in establishing a solid practical starting-point for a complex, comparative case study approach of this kind. Continuous reflexivity, flexibility and com-mitment in the face of unintended consequences are equally important ingredients in effective research design.

SUMMARY

Comparative research is a two-edged sword having both potential and problems. Nevertheless, this does not constitute a reason for its abandonment. If that were the case, all forms of research, both in the social and natural sciences, would cease overnight. On the contrary, increasing complexity still requires understanding and explanation in order to inform engagement. Such ambivalence requires an awareness of both strengths and limitations for practice. This means an understanding of different social contexts and cultures and the various issues which form part of the actual process of comparative research: for example, those of the relationship between theory and data and the power relations which exist within and between societies that affect the design, production, interpretation and dissemination of research results. Clearly, there are important differences between the practice of cross-national and cross-cultural research and the other methods of social inquiry that this book has covered. Yet, as has been argued throughout this book, issues and methods are not mutually exclusive topics. To that extent, it is no different and researchers thus need to act reflexively in their practice not for the purposes of introspection, but for refining their understandings in order to inform an improved engagement with social issues.

Comparative researchers cannot assume that their own countries, or those of others, are characterized on the basis of a single culture or shared value-consensus. That allows for a continuum between difference and similarity which is open to comparative empirical examination. A note of caution should be added here lest people think that the process of globalization automatically combats such thinking; it can result in more global forms of ethnocentrism. The world may move beyond the researcher's shores, only to finish at the frontiers of the west. Disputes over the exploitation of majority world countries by western societies are routinely raised and these changes will not necessarily alleviate this situation. In the face of these issues, comparative research has the potential to check against narrow thinking by its production of studies on alternative cultures and societies. A contribution to the possibility of a greater understanding and explanation of social, political and economic forces and their relationship to specific policies and human relations and cultures in general is then enabled.

Questions for your reflection

1 Why should we undertake comparative research and what should we compare?

2 Can a researcher from one culture explain the beliefs and practices of another?

3 What are the main differences and similarities between experimental, statistical, case study and comparative methods and when might they be used?

4 What are the potentials and pitfalls of collaborating between researchers in different countries to produce comparative work?

SUGGESTED FURTHER READING

Beck, U. and Sznaider, N. (2006) Unpacking cosmopolitanism for the social sciences: A research agenda. *British Journal of Sociology*, 57(1): 1–23.

Hantrais, L. and Mangen, S. (eds) (2007) *Cross-national Research Methodology and Practice*. London: Routledge.

Kennett, P. (ed.) (2004) *A Handbook of Comparative Social Policy*. Cheltenham: Edward Elgar.

Landmann, T. and Robinson, N. (2009) *The Sage Handbook of Comparative Politics*. London: Sage.

Part III Research in practice

11 Reflections on research in practice

The ebbs and flows of social research
Research, knowledge and consequence
The labour of social research: potential, limits and modesty

Over the course of its history, this book has been reviewed many times. One person, in particular, wrote with much insight concerning its content, ethos and how particular additions to the text would be valuable for readers in general. Those suggestions and other changes have been incorporated into this new edition, with just one remaining: a final set of reflections upon experiences of research in practice. Therefore, this chapter is devoted to reflections on issues in the process of social research.

THE EBBS AND FLOWS OF SOCIAL RESEARCH

Those reviews raised the issue of comparison which, as we have seen, is not only central to social research, but also part of social life in general. Their remit was driven by a specific question: 'How does this book compare to other research methods texts?' Comparison is meaningful if we compare like with like through, for example, a study of intent, process, strategy, content, conditions and anticipated consequences.

Comparisons were made with manuals that tell you about methods, but have little, if anything, to say about issues. Such books may be useful for those who happen to believe that research can be practised or taught according to a narrow understanding of its process and place in society. Nevertheless, practitioners who actually interact with co-participants in the process of research can then be left totally unprepared, while the imagination that is so important to the scientific enterprise cannot be taught through the contents of any one book.

In covering issues, methods and process, no book can claim to be exhaustive. A great deal has been covered in these pages, but no amount of words will make up for the need to practically engage in systematic research and understanding to produce good work, or reading across and within different disciplines. Learning through doing is fundamental, but so too is learning for orientation in practice: that is, considering issues that both inform and surround practice and how and in what ways they influence the process and product of research. Being sensitive to these issues and taking those into practice produces a reflexive awareness that improves the quality of what is produced and how it is achieved.

As we have seen, the social research field is broad and its subject matter often complex. Recognizing complexity does not relieve us of the need to work at understanding. For this reason we deploy lenses through which we not only gaze upon social reality, but also seek to provide understandings and explanations of its causes, reasons, dynamics and consequences. Perspectives are thus fundamental because they provide the framing that underpins our work. In so doing they build upon sets of assumptions about how social reality is constituted which, in turn, can inform what methods of study can be deployed to produce the subsequent data. Some approaches, as noted, take an absence of assumptions to embody the idea of 'science'. We then end up in a terminal point exemplified by definitional operationalism: the idea that what something is can be defined by how it is measured. What is intelligence? It is what intelligence tests measure. The path of understanding hits a wall if we take these directions.

Assumptions are an inevitable part of practice and it is only by working through these do we make progress in our understandings. For those who prefer certainty to recognition of ambivalence, solace is obtained through adopting such points of view. Identities may be more secure in the belief that what one has to say is beyond doubt and one is surrounded by those who either have similar beliefs or who do not challenge them, or one is simply misunderstood by others by virtue of their ignorance. For social researchers the outlook needs to be different. The world is richer than we can know at any one time and we should not conflate our ways of knowing with what can be open to possibility, imagination and change.

Working through such issues arises in a dynamic encounter between theory and research. Theory assists us in ordering our thinking and interpreting the findings of research and provides a means of reflecting upon and challenging our own practices and experiences, as well as those we come across in our studies. Theory, in turn, is modified, challenged and discarded according to these experiences. In this way it provides conceptualizing, orientating and sensitizing elements to research practice, but slavish application, unquestioned adherence and passive regurgitation should be avoided. There are those who believe that theories can be tested against a pre-existing empirical reality, or who believe 'facts' can be collected independent of its existence. Both of these views are found wanting. Theories are modified in a relationship with the collection of systematic empirical data. They are also influenced by extra-theoretical factors such as the biography of the researcher; the context in which they work; experiences in data collection; who has paid for the research and an anticipation of the acceptability of findings among different audiences.

Tensions between the need for theoretical orientation and the collection of valid and reliable data are part of the vibrancy of the research enterprise. Questions of whether theory is driving the data to the extent it becomes saturated by its presuppositions and devoid of content, measured against data overwhelming theory and providing little in the way of understanding, are issues that matter for the purpose of generating better insights into social life. To approach theory as a tool with which to manipulate data forgets that a tool is designed for a particular task. The vibrancy of social research is enabled by tackling and not ignoring these issues.

Mechanistic metaphors abound in our lives. In many domains of activity there are those who believe, consciously or by default, that it is simply a matter of applying a solution to a problem to achieve resolution. We deal with problems of the world, which should not be confused with our words about the world, for this relieves people of the need for active interpretation and how research may, or may not, have consequences for subsequent actions. Yet there are those who adhere to particular schools of thought as if their words provided a total explanation of the world around them. Taking facets of social and environmental dynamics to submit to analysis according to the lenses of particular orientations has undoubtedly enriched our understandings, but they should not be assumed to be exhaustive. Equally, the world does not wait for the results of research to change, nor do policy-makers base their understandings solely upon evidence, as if other factors were not also involved in their deliberations and decisions.

I have come across all sorts of practices and attitudes among policy-makers, academics and consultants that have left me thinking just how unrealistic expectations of knowledge, somehow separate from actions and interpretative efforts, have become. Allusion to the self-evidence of knowledge to relieve oneself of any interpretative responsibility towards others who are placed in differing positions is a not an uncommon reaction. An interpretative gap between what is known and what is to be done is often filled by technology and models claiming to be solutions to common problems. The important work of making sense of knowledge in context is then left to one side and becomes a problem of execution in practice, rather than the original conception of the issue, as if the two could be so easily separated.

Here we find a tendency, despite a propensity to challenge and exercise scepticism among different groups, classes and communities, to wait for the expert to pronounce upon reality as if efforts of interpretation and possible consequence were somehow secondary considerations. Although many claim to be seeking clarity, its arrival can be treated as a rude interruption to established ways of behaving, especially among the powerful as a means of relieving themselves of being held to account for their actions. Consultants may fill that gap in an uncritical orientation to research. The results of such work can then be deployed to justify changes, rather than the authors of the original brief to which they worked and the decisions that were taken before and after it took place!

We should remember that critique is more than pronouncements from the pages of reports, articles and books. Such endeavours are clearly important, but we should not confuse clarification through writing with resolution in practice. The latter comes only in active engagement with the difficulties and intransigences of the world. That requires an effort which, if individualized by a researcher who confuses what they do with what should be done, easily translates into disappointment and withdrawal. There is no substitute for active interpretation and action, should the will and position to do so be in place and whether that happens or not, is not within the domain of social research practice to determine.

RESEARCH, KNOWLEDGE AND CONSEQUENCE

Against this background varying forms of knowledge have differing degrees of attributed value placed upon them allowing, in some cases, the mode of research production to continue unaffected by wider social influences (May with Perry 2011). More public discussions, where expertise is demarcated due to different social interests being vocalized that have legitimate points of view, are not so apparent and this allows the mode of justification to be separated from application and considerations of possible consequence.

Despite this separation, we appear saturated by 'learning', 'innovation' and 'knowledge'. Who would wish to admit they do not want to learn, even if their practice remains unchanged? Who does not want to think of themselves as innovative, even if that means history is conveniently forgotten in the name of a supposedly open future for all? Who would wish to admit that their actions were not based upon knowledge? It was once put to us by a client that if they wanted to think differently about an issue then they would ask a research centre like SURF, rather than a consultant. While our experiences would indicate that this is an undoubted tendency, there are variations between and within research and consultancy practices. To make an engaged, but productive, space between the credibility and applicability of research is not easy to produce and requires supportive cultures of inquiry in the face of some of the expectations that are often placed upon its process and assumed outcomes.

To this end, research not only orders our understandings of empirical reality, but also may be deployed as a legitimizing device to justify particular courses of action despite the best intentions of its practitioners. Science can then spill over into being used to justify decisions as if technocratic solutions were a remedy to political matters. Some things are contestable for good reasons and no single reason can overcome that reality. Routes such as these have led to disastrous consequences in our history as the unscrupulous have deployed science in the name of immoral ends.

Poor consequences in the absence of participative decision-making are all too frequent. It also prevents an understanding of the limits of expectations for how particular forms of knowledge can directly inform our actions and quality of lives. In anticipation of this domain of knowledge reception, dissemination of research work is so important. Social researchers can write with the needs of different audiences in mind, but this is a skill that varies between practitioners. To expect people to wade through long reports is unrealistic and often leads to the need for 'executive summaries'. There is nothing wrong with concise overviews in these instances, along with accessible writing styles. However, I have also sat in meetings with people who feel able to say that they are 'disincentivized' when they have to read more than two pages in a process where they have committed themselves to learning!

All too often the word 'academic' is used in a perjorative sense to relieve an intended audience of the effort of interpretative dialogue. Here we may find denial running in equal measure to interpretative embrace. Sometimes things are difficult not because of how they are written, but because they challenge carefully preserved prejudices, established ways of seeing and ways of being. When questioned or placed under analysis, these raise uncertainties, with an accompanying tendency towards anxiety, and also questions power structures.

When faced with such experiences it is not easy for social researchers to find solace, unless they can retreat to a realm of an unquestioning superiority of insight or insularity from such effects. Alongside a surplus of mutual expectations, it is within interactions between research and audiences that critical insights can be afforded. The type and style of the written word then becomes important. Journal articles may afford clarification, but few judge them for inclusion and not many will read them, relative to other forms of outlet. That is not to diminish their significance in any way, but we do need to find ways of reaching different audiences. All too often the incentives to do so are not considered within research cultures, the ways in which they are funded and held to account, as well as the narrow ways in which the media select and construct issues.

The effort necessary to achieve understanding through the research process, particularly when it comes to the actions of the powerful and the considerable inequalities that exist within societies are very high. Such a situation is beyond the scope and mandate of any one researcher, team of researchers, or research as a whole, to change. A willingness to listen and learn is also variable, as is having the time to be able to consider such matters, as well as the evident powers of denial and mobilization of prejudices. We have enormous amounts of information, ably assisted by electronic means of communication, to which groups, classes, countries and entire continents possess highly differential access. The generation of intelligence is another matter.

Psychoanalysts might suggest that expecting research to produce simple answers is an example of projection: that is, taking an internal issue concerning desire or thought and displacing that into an external object. Such over-extension is apparent in the process of misrecognition between, say, how one thinks or reflects upon an issue and how one is then positioned to take those deliberations forward into actions that have actual consequences for oneself or others. To more fully understand how these interpretative spheres work, however, our level of analysis would move away from individual or group characteristics, to the socio-structural. Here is where ideology plays its part. Let me take one example to illustrate this in action.

At a socio-structural level of analysis it might be argued that certain forms of market activity have a propensity to exhibit self-organizing properties. As an explanation that is said to provide for their ability to run at optimal economic levels and perpetuate themselves over time. If this is an accurate characterization and commonly accepted, we would expect research on these systems which does not see them in this way to be rejected by those who enjoy the rewarding nature of its powers of insight. Yet what of political and social factors, as well as the environmental consequences of such systems?

These characterizations of market systems have had serious consequences for societies as the many now have to pay a considerable sum for the actions of a few within the financial sector. To take such explanations at face value says absolutely nothing about the larger political and economic systems in which they operate, nor does it make any contribution to the choices about how people might want to live in different ways, or about their consequences for such matters as social justice, income and wealth distribution and effects on natural resource depletion and climate change. It appears that we have privatized profit and socialized loss, while lessons seem to have been lost through a governmental myopia.

I deliberately used the above example, as the apparently unlimited speculations of a few within the cultures and structures of the financial sector have led to enormous and lasting consequences for levels of debt and thus how much can be spent on the social infrastructures upon which all our activities rely in our daily lives. In terms of the content of these characterizations they come from the 'endogenous constructions' of a given set of activities – that is, those that emerge within the cultures of inquiry of disciplines themselves. These two things – the content of explanation for market systems within economic research and an evaluation of the consequence of actions – can blur because they are supported by prevailing ideologies about the alleged superiority of particular forms of financial activity. They do not derive from the validity of research, but an affinity between facets of its practices and powerful ideologies.

When this happens we can say that nothing is occurring to enable a more critical and detached form of analysis to emerge that has the potential to contribute to learning and positive social, political, environmental and economic change for a greater good. Here, however, we have moved into a normative terrain in which the contestability and acceptability of research findings is informed by values. We are now concerned not just with consequences, but how we see and recognize persons, places and things.

The interpretation of research carries with it different forms of recognition for what is described and understood. These forms of recognition have both expressive and consequential elements and are influenced by values. For example, in the realms of criminology, psychology, anthropology, history, sociology, human geography or political studies, researchers may study what are seen as extreme forms of behaviour. Reactions to the results of these studies are often based on the belief that they are sympathetic to the actions of those they are researching. Acts of understanding are thereby assumed to condone the investigated behaviours.

When it comes to contestability of findings, ethics are fundamental for maintaining the integrity of research as a whole, as well as respect for co-participants and practically speaking, as a condition of research access. If research findings accord with the views of the powerful, they are more likely to be seen as legitimate by such persons. However, it does not follow that they are valid. We can say that modern societies emerged when collective actions were mobilized in response to general social problems. Their understandings and actions have led to particular forms of government, institutions and organization as a result which has been noted throughout the book.

Our impulse to question is, at root, not to take things at face value and to search for answers to what are both general and specific issues. Explanations for poverty may focus on the psychological characteristics of those who are categorized as poor and find within large parts of the population individual characteristics that explain their position in the social structure. Others might start from a socio-structural basis and note how poverty is necessary in order for the rich to exploit the labour of the poor for the purposes of extracting profit without due regard for societal consequence. Assumptions of the moral laxity of individuals thereby mix with explanations that may have particular implications for the actions of elected governments. Explanations and consequences for subsequent actions then blur with a possible favouring of those that root problems in the miraculous coincidence of psychologically like-minded people who make up a particular social category.

Against predispositions towards certain explanations, we live in an age in which scepticism exists alongside the desire for certainty and control. They do not sit easily together. Disappointment can result in the quest for an external certainty, while anxieties are heightened in the face of uncertain conditions. In this climate we find science being characterized as both the disinterested pursuit of knowledge and nothing more than an institutionalized assertion of faith with no greater claim to validity than mythology and folklore. Debates formulated in these terms generate more heat than light.

In terms of the reception of social scientific research, justification for why and how it has been conducted cannot be forced into automatic application as is so often assumed by those who look to its process and outcomes to enter into states of complicity with pre-existing worldviews. Nor can practitioners assume the results of research have automatic implications for how people should act, as if there were a simple connection between results and consequence. To slip from rendering an existing state of affairs intelligible from a social scientific viewpoint to the purpose of orientating actions according to its findings begs questions concerning 'who' judges the authenticity of findings and according to what interests and under what sort of conditions.

We should be aware of those who regard knowledge as useful according to its ability to control actions. Control is not the same as understanding and understanding does not generate automatic transformation of an existing state of affairs. In the former we see that knowledge is seen as useful only for control and it conspires with the idea that the world as it is presented to us is not one of a series of possibilities, but a natural one that reflects something inherent in our collective conditions. We see here the idea that what is written and then read is taken as being like a hypodermic upon subsequent actions without due regard to the importance of interpretation and the existence of differences.

In the realms of research process, dissemination, interpretation and consideration of consequence, expertise and democracy do not sit easily together. After all, if someone is an 'expert', why would they grant a 'lay' person equal understanding if they had spent years studying a given phenomenon? Such a gap is usually dealt with by a difference between the content of the work and its consequences. People might be granted expertise over what it is that they do, but any consequences it may have for the quality of our lives should be a matter for more general deliberation among different groups. Nevertheless, that separates 'how' from 'what' which I have already suggested can create issues in the ownership and possible deployment of knowledge.

Where exactly are these places and spaces of public deliberation in which these considerations might occur? Insightful research reports may not see the light of day at the behest of their pay masters who come from public, private and voluntary sectors of society. To counter this is not within the remit of research practice, but its future will be more vibrant were they to exist more generically and become places in which its findings are introduced, discussed, debated and if deemed appropriate, acted upon. More sustainable solutions to our common problems may then be possible. Elected representatives are expected to take up the responsibility of this task, but that varies between and within societies. Large-scale multinational corporations, able to move their money about the globe, as well as governments, have vested interests in the production of particular forms of knowledge for different reasons. Against this tendency, we need new forms of knowledge exchange to meet current and future challenges through 'active intermediaries' (May et al. 2009).

Official statistics, as we have seen, might vary from year to year, which prevents meaningful comparison over time, while longitudinal research is a relatively expensive endeavour that it is difficult to obtain funding for, particularly in times of considerable economic constraint. Private corporations may be interested only in work that can produce a product, or inform the increasing effectiveness of a particular process, rather than be driven by curiosity for its own sake, or according to other equally legitimate interests. As a result the type of funding available is likely to inform what is researched, by whom, how and why?

We see particular forms of knowledge coming to our attention via a process of media selection that leaves much in its wake. We gain particular information through descriptions and they have varying effects upon our perceptions of what is regarded as important and that, in turn, influences political processes through pronouncements of 'what the public demands' concerning particular processes, events and behaviours. While media research may approach the relationship between what is read and how it influences behaviour in different ways, overall results can contribute to the promotion of more democratic forms of representation and accountability; in other words, its content and consequences for subsequent actions.

Our predisposition to challenge forms of knowledge depends not only upon a confidence to do so, but also a competence in terms of what we think we know and what is known. Such a propensity is informed by how we are positioned in society and the extent to which research findings are seen to have implications for how actions are portrayed in the past, as well as their consequences for the present and future. There are those who enjoy positions in organizations whose confidence far outweighs their competence and those around them are only too willing to make up for such a lack through a fear of consequence.

Such a form of attributed value sets up a dynamics between 'what' is known and 'who' is known, leaving questions of deliberation and 'how' to proceed in its wake. I have seen this happen many times where those who have little confidence preface their public utterances with 'this may seem like an obvious question, but . . .' before moving on to make a highly cogent observation that exposes the unfeasible assumptions of the assembled company.

THE LABOUR OF SOCIAL RESEARCH: POTENTIAL, LIMITS AND MODESTY

The promise of scientific knowledge, in terms of its implications for how we live our lives, in all of its guises, may have been exaggerated. To place the reason for this state of affairs solely at the doors of its practice is not reasonable for it relates to matters of power and politics. While there are no ready-made solutions to our common problems, that does not mean that social research does not have a highly valuable role in informing our understandings and practices.

With the above issues in mind, we need them to inform our research practices; practices that do require a high level of technical competence. While such competence is undoubtedly a prerequisite for conducting good research, methods can be chosen without due consideration to appropriateness for the issues and questions being researched. Quantitative approaches may be avoided due to narrow ideas of their place in research, or adopted by reproducing assumptions that the generation of numbers apparently produces more value-free forms of social inquiry. Qualitative methods may be deployed because numbers are assumed to a violation of valid representation, or in-depth ethnography has been undertaken after a few people are interviewed for 45 minutes.

We should equally be wary of those who advocate mixed methods. To adopt this as a panacea for issues without due consideration to matters of integration or appropriateness for constructing and then addressing research questions, is no solution. There is simply no way round an understanding of defensible methodological procedures for conducting research as a fundamental part of its intellectual integrity and the maintenance and defence of its legitimacy among the public as a whole.

For the purpose of conducting research with the issues we have covered in mind, it is productive to think of making contributions to the possibility of better understandings, conditions for actions and quality of lives. That, in no way, means abandoning the need for validity and reliability in our work, but it does imply a certain modesty and recognition that the factors we have discussed influence how people see, act and judge the world. Research still retains a highly important role, despite the persistence of narrowly constituted attacks upon its place and role within society. Therefore, while it may not be the province of the researcher to say what our futures will be, they are, given their understandings and equal positions as citizens, entitled to engage in debates concerning challenges and prospects.

In order to remain relevant, social research will take on topics that reflect the changing form of these public debates and so will be implicated in them as a condition of their vibrancy. In so doing social research is a field of activity that provides a basis upon which we gaze in order to understand not only what we have been and what we are now, but also what we might become. It is not simply about understanding the reasons people give for their actions in terms of the contexts in which they act, as well as analysing the relations of cause and effect, but about the hopes, wishes and aspirations that people, in different cultural ways, both express and lead in their lives.

In any society that claims to have democratic aspirations beyond simply passing responsibilities over to political and policy elites, these hopes and wishes are not for social research to prescribe. For this to happen would mean that human actions were totally uniform across time and space and thus predictable. The physical sciences do not live up to such stringent criteria, while the conditions in societies that provided for this outcome would be intolerable. Why? Because a necessary condition of human freedom is the ability to have acted otherwise and to imagine and practice different ways of organizing societies and living together.

The disciplines that have informed the writing of this book – including geography, social psychology, political and urban studies, sociology, social policy, history, criminology, planning, philosophy, science and technology studies, anthropology, macro economics, and management and organization studies – may vary within and between themselves about how to pursue their disciplinary goals, but overall they contribute to a greater understanding of the workings of societies and dynamics of our lives. In terms of maintaining their public legitimacy, they are often not given due credit for this role because much of their work becomes absorbed into everyday understandings and so remains hidden from its origins. That constitutes both the relevance of their work, but often a lack of recognition for how they inform our thinking and actions.

It is this vibrancy and undoubted relevance, without resorting to simple solutions or avoiding difficult issues, which I have sought to convey in this book with my collaborators. The places where we practice our craft are so important for how we do that and what advantages it affords us. Finding others who are experiencing similar issues in conducting their research and speaking about those and realizing that they are not peculiar to you, is often the single thing that postgraduate students regard as the best thing about the conferences they attend. The processes of individualization that are studied in society as a whole by research are also reflected in its practices. We need more support and honesty about the realities of our craft to enhance our understandings, but also to deploy a positive modesty about what research can actually achieve.

Despite the reality of our experiences in SURF of seeking to puncture the hyperbole surrounding the supposed relations between such things as knowledge, innovation and sustainability and then suggest effective alternatives for deliberation, we have never given up on the value of knowledge for illuminating and informing activities. What we have produced has been highly valued, but we cannot collapse credibility and applicability if our purpose is to produce better knowledge. We have never given up on our role in learning through utilizing skills that are not taught, nor could ever be, in any module or course. Therefore, I hope that you find the places in which to practice good social research which is a vibrant and important field of activity. I hope you find the supportive places for that and celebrate it, while also knowing the limits of what can be achieved without succumbing to retreat or cynicism. Enjoy your craft, be reflexive in your practices, disseminate to different audiences and take pride in your achievements.

Bibliography

Abbott, A. (1992) What do cases do? Some notes on activity in sociological analysis, in C. C. Ragin and H. S. Becker (eds) *What is a Case? Exploring the Foundations of Social Inquiry*. Cambridge: Cambridge University Press.

Acker, J., Barry, K. and Esseveld, J. (1991) Objectivity and truth: Problems in doing feminist research, in M. M. Fonow and J. A. Cook (eds) *Beyond Methodology: Feminist Scholarship as Hired Research*. Bloomington, IN: Indiana University Press.

Ackers, L. (1993) Race and sexuality in the ethnographic process, in D. Hobbs and T. May (eds) *Interpreting the Field: Accounts of Ethnography*. Oxford: Oxford University Press.

Ackroyd, S. and Hughes, J. (1983) *Data Collection in Context*. London: Longman.

Adam, B. (1995) *Timewatch: The Social Analysis of Time*. Cambridge: Polity.

Adam, B., Beck, U. and van Loon, J. (eds) (2000) *The Risk Society and Beyond*. London: Sage.

Adkins, L. (1995) *Gendered Work: Sexuality, Family and the Labour Market*. Buckingham: Open University Press.

Agger, B. (1991) *A Critical Theory of Public Life: Knowledge, Discourse and Politics in an Age of Decline*. London: Falmer.

Agger, B. (1998) *Critical Social Theories: An Introduction*. Oxford: Westview.

Agresti, A. (1996) *An Introduction to Categorical Data Analysis*. New York: Wiley.

Agresti, A. and Finlay, B. (2009) *Statistical Methods for the Social Sciences*, 4th edn. Upper Saddle River, NJ: Pearson Prentice Hall.

Akhter, T. (2008) *The Role of Social Forestry in Power Alleviation of Rural Women*. Dhaka, Bangladesh: Academic Press.

Alaszewski, A. (2006) *Using Diaries for Social Research*. London: Sage.

Alderson, P. (1999) Disturbed young people: Research for what, research for whom?, in S. Hood, B. Mayall and S. Oliver (eds) *Critical Issues in Social Research: Power and Prejudice*. Buckingham: Open University Press.

Aldridge, A. and Levine, K. (2001) *Surveying the Social World*. Buckingham: Open University Press.

Allen, C. and Imrie, R. (eds) (2010) *The Knowledge Business: The Commodification of Urban and Housing Research*. Farnham: Ashgate.

Alvesson, M. (2009) At home ethnography: Struggling with closeness and closure, in S. Ybema, D. Yanow, H. Wels and F. Kamsteeg (eds) *Organizational Ethnography: Studying the Complexities of Everyday Life*. London: Sage.

Alvesson, M. and Sköldberg, K. (2009) *Reflexive Methodology: New Vistas for Qualitative Research*. 2nd edn. London: Sage.

Anderson, K., Armitage, S., Jack, D. and Wittner, J. (1990) Beginning where we are: Feminist methodology in oral history, in J. McCarl Nielsen (ed.) *Feminist Research Methods: Exemplary Readings in the Social Sciences*. London: Westview.

Anderson, R. and Heath, A. (2000) *Social Class and Voting: A Multi-Level Analysis of Individual and Constituency Differences*. Working Paper 83, Centre for Research into Elections and Social Trends, University of Oxford. Available at www.crest.ox.ac.uk/papers/p83.pdf

Anderson, R., Hughes, J. and Sharrock, W. (1986) *Philosophy and the Human Sciences*. London: Routledge.

Appadurai, A. (1996) *Modernity at Large: Cultural Dimensions of Globalisation*. Minneapolis, MN: University of Minnesota Press.

Apter, D. (1971) Comparative studies: A review with some projections, in I. Vallier (ed.) *Comparative Methods in Sociology: Essays on Trends and Applications*. Los Angeles, CA: University of California Press.

Archer, M. S. (1998) Social theory and the analysis of society, in T. May and M. Williams (eds) *Knowing the Social World*. Buckingham: Open University Press.

Archer, M. S. (2003) *Structure, Agency and the Internal Conversation*. Cambridge: Cambridge University Press.

Archer, M. S. (2007) *Making our Way through the World: Human Reflexivity and Social Mobility*. Cambridge: Cambridge University Press.

Archer, M. S., Bhaskar, R., Collier, A., Lawson, T. and Norrie, A. (eds) (1998) *Critical Realism: Essential Readings*. London: Routledge.

Armer, M. (1973) Methodological problems and possibilities in comparative research, in M. Armer and A. Grimshaw (eds) *Comparative Social Research: Methodological Problems and Strategies*. London: Wiley.

Ashman, K. and Baringer, P. (eds) (2001) *After the Science Wars*. London: Routledge.

Ashworth, A. and Redmayne, M. (2010) *The Criminal Process*, 4th edn. Oxford: Oxford University Press.

Assadourian, E. (2010) The rise and fall of consumer cultures, in Worldwatch Institute, *State of the World: Transforming Cultures from Consumerism to Sustainability*. New York: Norton.

Atkinson, J. M. (1978) *Discovering Suicide: Studies in the Social Organisation of Sudden Death*. London: Macmillan.

Atkinson, P. (1990) *The Ethnographic Imagination: Textual Constructions of Reality*. London: Routledge.

Avramov, D. (ed.) (1999) *Coping with Homelessness*. Aldershot: Ashgate.

Baldamus, W. (1984) The category of pragmatic knowledge in sociological analysis, in M. Bulmer (ed.) *Sociological Research Methods*, 2nd edn. London: Macmillan.

Ball, M. S. and Smith, G. W. H. (1992) *Analyzing Visual Data*. London: Sage.

Banks, J. A. (1957) The group discussion as an interview technique. *Sociological Review*, 5 (1): 75–84.

Barnes, B. (1991) Thomas Kuhn, in Q. Skinner (ed.) *The Return of Grand Theory in the Human Sciences*. Cambridge: Cambridge University Press.

Barnes, J. A. (1979) *Who Should Know What?* Harmondsworth: Penguin.

Barthes, R. (1967) *Elements of Semiology*. London: Jonathan Cape.

Bassey, M. (2001) A solution to the problem of generalisation in educational research: Empirical findings and fuzzy predictions. *Oxford Review of Education*, 27 (1): 5–22.

Baudrillard, J. (1983a) *Simulations*. New York: Semiotext(e).

Baudrillard, J. (1983b) *In the Shadow of the Silent Majorities*. New York: Semiotext(e).

Bauman, Z. (1992) *Intimations of Postmodernity*. London: Routledge.

Bauman, Z. (1997) *Postmodernity and its Discontents*. Cambridge: Polity.

Bauman, Z. (2000) *Liquid Modernity*. Cambridge: Polity.

Bauman, Z. (2008) *Art of Life*. Cambridge: Polity.

Bauman, Z. and May, T. (2001) *Thinking Sociologically*, 2nd edn. Oxford: Wiley-Blackwell.

Bechhofer, F. and Paterson, L. (2000) *Principles of Research Design in the Social Sciences*. London: Routledge.

Beck, U. (1992) *Risk Society: Towards a New Modernity*. New Delhi: Sage.

Beck, U. (2009) *World at Risk*. Cambridge: Polity.

Beck, U. and Sznaider, N. (2006) Unpacking cosmopolitanism for the social sciences: A research agenda. *British Journal of Sociology*, 57 (1): 1–23.

Becker, H. (1963) *Outsiders: Studies in the Sociology of Deviance*. New York: Free Press.

Becker, H. (1967) Whose side are we on? *Social Problems*, 14: 239–47.

Becker, H. (1979a) Problems of inference and proof in participant observation, in J. Bynner and K. Stribley (eds) *Social Research: Principles and Procedures*. London: Longman.

Becker, H. (1979b) Problems in the publication of field studies, in J. Bynner and K. Stribley (eds) *Social Research: Principles and Procedures*. London: Longman.

Becker, H. (1986) *Writing for Social Scientists: How to Start and Finish your Thesis, Book, or Article*. Chicago, IL: University of Chicago Press.

Becker, H. (1992) 'Casing' and the process of social inquiry, in C. C. Ragin and H. Becker, *What is a Case? Exploring the Foundations of Social Inquiry*. Cambridge: Cambridge University Press.

Becker, H., Geer, B., Hughes, E. and Strauss, A. (1961) *Boys in White: Student Culture in a Medical School*. Chicago, IL: University of Chicago Press.

Beechey, V. (1989) Women's employment in France and Britain: Some problems of comparison. *Work, Employment and Society*, 3 (3): 369–78.

Bell, C. and Newby, H. (eds) (1977) *Doing Sociological Research*. London: George Allen & Unwin.

Bell, C. and Roberts, H. (eds) (1984) *Social Researching: Politics, Problems and Practice*. London: Routledge & Kegan Paul.

Bell, D., Caplan, P. and Karim, W. J. (eds) (1993) *Gendered Fields: Women, Men and Ethnography*. London: Routledge.

Bendikat, E. (1996) Qualitative historical research on municipal policies, in L. Hantrais and S. Mangen (eds) *Cross-National Research Methods in the Social Sciences*. London: Pinter.

Benhabib, S. (1992) *Situating the Self: Gender, Community and Postmodernism in Contemporary Ethics*. Cambridge: Polity.

Benney, M. and Hughes, E. (1984) Of sociology and the interview, in M. Bulmer (ed.) *Sociological Research Methods*, 2nd edn. London: Macmillan.

Benson, D. and Hughes, J. (1991) Method: Evidence and inference – evidence and inference for ethnomethodology, in G. Button (ed.) *Ethnomethodology and the Human Sciences*. Cambridge: Cambridge University Press.

Berghman, J. (1995) Social exclusion in Europe: Policy context and analytical framework, in R. Room (ed.) *Beyond the Threshold: The Measurement and Analysis of Social Exclusion*. Bristol: Policy Press.

Bernstein, R. (1983) *Beyond Objectivism and Relativism: Science, Hermeneutics and Praxis*. Oxford: Blackwell.

Berridge, V. and Thom, B. (1996) Research and policy: What determines the relationship? *Policy Studies*, 17 (1): 23–34.

Bethlehem, J. (2009) *Applied Survey Methods: A Statistical Perspective*. Hoboken, NJ: Wiley.

Bhaskar, R. (1975) *A Realist Theory of Science*. Leeds: Leeds Books.

Bhaskar, R. (1989) *Reclaiming Reality: A Critical Introduction to Contemporary Philosophy*. London: Verso.

Bhaskar, R. (1993) *Dialectic: The Pulse of Freedom*. London: Verso.

Bhaskar, R. (1998) *The Possibility of Naturalism: A Philosophical Critique of the Contemporary Human Sciences*, 3rd edn. London: Routledge.

Bhat, A., Carr-Hill, R. and Ohri, S. (eds) (1988) *Britain's Black Population: A New Perspective*. Aldershot: Gower.

Bhatia, S. (2010) Developing green innovation: DeCopier paper cleaning products, in P. Banerjee and V. Shastri (eds) *Social Responsibility and Environmental Sustainability in Business*. New Delhi: Response.

Billig, M. (1988) Methodology and scholarship in understanding ideological explanation, in C. Antaki (ed.) *Analysing Everyday Explanation: A Casebook of Methods*. London: Sage.

Bitektine, A. (2008) Prospective case study design: Qualitative method for deductive theory testing. *Organisational Research Methods*, 11 (1), 160–80.

Blalock, H. (1984) *Social Statistics*, 2nd edn. London: McGraw-Hill.

Blumer, H. (1972) Society as symbolic interaction, in A. Rose (ed.) *Human Behaviour and Social Processes: An Interactionist Approach*. London: Routledge & Kegan Paul.

Boden, D. and Zimmerman, D. H. (eds) (1993) *Talk and Social Structure: Studies in Ethnomethodology and Conversation Analysis*. Cambridge: Polity.

Bordens, K. and Abbott, B. (2008) *Research Design and Methods: A Process Approach*, 7th edn. New York: McGraw-Hill.

Bourdieu, P. (1992) *Language and Symbolic Power*. Edited and introduced by J. Thompson. Translated by G. Raymond and M. Adamson. Cambridge: Polity.

Bourdieu, P. (1993) *Sociology in Question*. Translated by R. Nice. London: Sage.

Bourdieu, P. with Saint Martin, M. (1995) *The State Nobility: Elite Schools in the Field of Power*. Translated by L. C. Clough. Cambridge: Polity.

Bourdieu, P. (1999) Understanding, in P. Bourdieu et al. (eds) *The Weight of the World: Social Suffering in Contemporary Society*. Translated by P. P. Ferguson *et al.* Cambridge: Polity.

Bourdieu, P. (2000) *Pascalian Meditations*. Translated by R. Nice. Cambridge: Polity.

Bourdieu, P. (2004) *Science of Science and Reflexivity*. Translated by R. Nice. Cambridge: Polity.

Bourdieu, P. (2005) *The Social Structures of the Economy*. Translated by C. Turner. Cambridge: Polity.

Bourdieu, P. and Wacquant, L. J. (1992) *An Invitation to Reflexive Sociology*. Cambridge: Polity.

Bourdieu, P., Boltanski, L., Castel, R. and Chamboredon, J. C. (1990) *Photography: A Middle-brow Art*. Cambridge: Polity.

Bourdieu, P. et al. (1999) *The Weight of the World: Social Suffering in Contemporary Society*. Translated by P. P. Ferguson et al. Cambridge: Polity.

Bowker, G. C. and Star, S. L. (2002) *Sorting Things Out: Classification and its Consequences*. Cambridge, MA: MIT Press.

Brandon, P. and Lombardi, P. (2005) *Evaluating Sustainable Development in the Built Environment*. Oxford: Blackwell.

Bratton, J. (1992) *Japanization at Work: Managerial Studies for the 1990s*. London: Macmillan.

Brenner, N. (2004) *New State Spaces: Urban Governance and the Rescaling of Statehood*. Oxford: Oxford University Press.

Brewer, J. D. (2000) *Ethnography*. Buckingham: Open University Press.

British Sociological Association (1996) *Statement of Ethical Practice*. Durham: British Sociological Association.

Brooks, A. (2007) Reconceptualizing representation and identity, in T. Edwards (ed.) *Cultural Theory: Classical and Contemporary Positions*. London: Sage.

Brown, G. (1984) Accounts, meaning and causality, in G. Gilbert and P. Abell (eds) *Accounts and Action*. Aldershot: Gower.

Brown, G. and Harris, T. (1978) *The Social Origins of Depression: A Study of Psychiatric Depression in Women*. London: Tavistock.

Brückner, E. and Mayer, K. U. (1998) Collecting life history data: Experiences from the German life history study, in J. Z. Giele and G. H. Elder, Jr. (eds) *Methods of Life Course Research: Qualitative and Quantitative Approaches*. London: Sage.

Bruyn, S. T. (1966) *The Human Perspective in Sociology: The Methodology of Participant Observation*. Englewood Cliffs, NJ: Prentice-Hall.

Bryant, A. and Charmaz, K. (2010) Introduction, in A. Bryant and K. Charmaz (eds) *The Sage Handbook of Grounded Theory*, paperback edn. London: Sage.

Bryant, C. (1985) *Positivism in Social Theory and Research*. London: Macmillan.

Bryman, A. (1988a) *Quantity and Quality in Social Research*. London: Unwin Hyman.

Bryman, A. (ed.) (1988b) *Doing Research in Organizations*. London: Routledge.

Bryman, A. (1998) Quantitative and qualitative research strategies in knowing the social world, in T. May and M. Williams (eds) *Knowing the Social World*. Buckingham: Open University Press.

Bryson, J., Daniels, P., Henry, N. and Pollard, J. (eds) (2000) *Knowledge, Space, Economy*. London: Routledge.

Buchanan, D., Boddy, D. and McCalman, J. (1988) Getting in, getting on, getting out and getting back, in A. Bryman (ed.) *Doing Research in Organizations*. London: Routledge.

Bulmer, M. (ed.) (1979a) *Censuses, Surveys and Privacy*. London: Macmillan.

Bulmer, M. (1979b) Maintaining public confidence in quantitative social research, in M. Bulmer (ed.) *Censuses, Surveys and Privacy*. London: Macmillan.

Bulmer, M. (1982) *The Use of Social Research: Social Investigation in Public Policy-Making*. London: George Allen & Unwin.

Bulmer, M. (1984a) *The Chicago School of Sociology*. Chicago, IL: University of Chicago Press.

Bulmer, M. (1984b) Why don't sociologists make more use of official statistics?, in M. Bulmer (ed.) *Sociological Research Methods*, 2nd edn. London: Macmillan.

Bulmer, M. (1986a) The role of theory in applied social science research, in M. Bulmer with K. Banting, S. Blume, M. Carley and C. Weiss, *Social Science and Social Policy*. London: George Allen & Unwin.

Bulmer, M. (1986b) The use and abuse of social science, in M. Bulmer with K. Banting, S. Blume, M. Carley and C. Weiss, *Social Science and Social Policy*. London: George Allen & Unwin.

Burawoy, M., Blum, J., George, S., Gille, Z., Gowan, T., Haney, L., Klawiter, M., Lopez, S., Ó Riain, S. and Thayer, M. (2000) *Global Ethnography: Forces, Connections, and Imaginations in a Postmodern World*. Berkeley, CA: University of California Press.

Burgess, R. (1990) *In the Field: An Introduction to Field Research*. London: George Allen & Unwin.

Bury, M. and Holme, A. (1990) Researching very old people, in S. Peace (ed.) *Researching Social Gerontology: Concepts, Methods and Issues*. London: Sage.

Butler, A. (1994) Taking ourselves seriously: A feminist exploration into mental health and autobiography. Unpublished MA thesis, Department of Social Policy and Social Work, University of Plymouth.

Butler, D. and Stokes, D. (1969) *Political Change in Britain: Forces Shaping Electoral Choice*. London: Macmillan.

Byrne, D. (1998) *Complexity Theory and the Social Sciences*. London: Routledge.

Byrne, D. (2005) *Social Exclusion*. 2nd edn. Maidenhead: Open University Press.

Byrne, D. (2009) Case-based methods: Why we need them; what they are; how to do them, in D. Byrne and C. C. Ragin (eds) *The Sage Handbook of Case-Based Methods*. London: Sage.

Cain, M. (1990) Realist philosophy and standpoint epistemologies or feminist criminology as a successor science, in L. Gelsthorpe and A. Morris (eds) *Feminist Perspectives in Criminology*. Buckingham: Open University Press.

Calhoun, C. (1995) *Critical Social Theory: Culture, History and the Challenge of Difference*. Oxford: Blackwell.

Calvert, P. (1991) Using documentary sources, in G. Allan and C. Skinner (eds) *Handbook for Research Students in the Social Sciences*. London: Falmer.

Campbell, A. (1984) *The Girls in the Gang*. Oxford: Basil Blackwell.

Campbell, D. and Stanley, J. (1963) *Experimental and Quasi-experimental Designs for Research*. Chicago, IL: Rand McNally.

Caporaso, J. (2009) Is there a quantitative-qualitative divide in comparative politics? The case of process tracing, in T. Landmann and N. Robinson (eds) *The Sage Handbook of Comparative Politics*. London: Sage.

Caputi, J. (1987) *The Age of Sex Crime*. London: The Women's Press.

Caramani, D. (2009) *Introduction to the Comparative Method with Boolean Algebra*. Quantitative Applications in the Social Sciences Series, Volume 158. Beverly Hills, CA: Sage.

Carr-Hill, R. and Drew, D. (1988) Blacks, police and crime, in A. Bhat, R. Carr-Hill and S. Ohri (eds) *Britain's Black Population: A New Perspective*. Aldershot: Gower.

Carter, B. (2000) *Realism and Racism*. London: Routledge.

Carter, B. and New, C. (eds) (2004) *Making Realism Work: Realist Social Theory and Empirical Research*. London: Routledge.

Chalmers, A. F. (1999) *What is This Thing Called Science?*, 3rd edn. Buckingham: Open University Press.

Charlesworth, S. (2000) *A Phenomenology of Working Class Experience*. Cambridge: Cambridge University Press.

Chen, P. and Hinton, S. M. (1999) Realtime interviewing using the world wide web. *Sociological Research Online*, 4 (3): www.socresonline.org.uk/4/3/chen.html

Cicourel, A. (1964) *Method and Measurement in Sociology*. London: Macmillan.

Cicourel, A. (1976) *The Social Organisation of Juvenile Justice*, 2nd edn. London: Heinemann.

Clarke, A. with Dawson, R. (1999) *Evaluation Research: An Introduction to Principles, Methods and Practice*. London: Sage.

Clegg, S. R. (1989) *Frameworks of Power*. London: Sage.

Clifford, J. (1986) Introduction: Partial truths, in J. Clifford and G. Marcus (eds) *Writing Culture: The Poetics and Politics of Ethnography*. Berkeley, CA: University of California Press.

Clifford, J. and Marcus, G. (eds) (1986) *Writing Culture: The Poetics and Politics of Ethnography*. Berkeley, CA: University of California Press.

Clough, P. T. (1994) *Feminist Thought: Desire, Power, and Academic Discourse*. Oxford: Blackwell.

Cochrane, A. (2007) *Understanding Urban Policy: A Critical Approach*. Oxford: Blackwell.

Coffey, A. (1999) *The Ethnographic Self: Fieldwork and the Representation of Reality*. London: Sage.

Coffey, A. (2002) Ethnography and the self: Reflections and representations, in T. May (ed.) *Qualitative Research in Action*. London: Sage.

Cohen, G. A. (1984) *Karl Marx's Theory of History: A Defence*. Oxford: Oxford University Press.

Cohen, S. and Taylor, L. (1972) *Psychological Survival: The Experience of Long-Term Imprisonment*. Harmondsworth: Penguin.

Coleman, C. and Moynihan, J. (1996) *Understanding Crime Data: Haunted by the Dark Figure*. Buckingham: Open University Press.

Collier, A. (1994) *Critical Realism: An Introduction to Roy Bhaskar's Philosophy*. London: Verso.

Collins, P. H. (2000) *Black Feminist Thought: Knowledge, Consciousness, and the Politics of Empowerment*, 2nd edn. London: Routledge.

Cook, J. and Fonow, M. (1990) Knowledge and women's interests: Issues of epistemology and methodology in sociological research, in J. McCarl Nielsen (ed.) *Feminist Research Methods: Exemplary Readings in the Social Sciences*. London: Westview.

Cooper, B. (2005) Applying Ragin's crisp and fuzzy set QCA to large datasets: Social class and educational achievement in the National Child Development Study. *Sociological Research Online*, 10 (2): www.socresonline.org.uk/10/2/cooper.html

Cooper, G. (1999) The fear of unreason: Science wars and sociology. *Sociological Research Online*, 4 (3): www.socresonline.org.uk/4/3/cooper.html

Couper, M. P. (2008) *Designing Effective Web Surveys*. Cambridge: Cambridge University Press.

Crampton, J. W. (2007) Maps, race and Foucault: Eugenics and territorialization following World War I, in J. W. Crampton and S. Elden (eds) *Space, Knowledge and Power: Foucault and Geography*. Aldershot: Ashgate.

Crampton, J. W. and Elden, S. (eds) (2007) *Space, Knowledge and Power: Foucault and Geography*. Aldershot: Ashgate.

Croall, H. (1992) *White Collar Crime*. Buckingham: Open University Press.

Crow, G. (2004) Conceptualising state and society, in P. Kennett (ed.) *A Handbook of Comparative Social Policy*. Cheltenham: Edward Elgar.

Dale, A. (1999) Confidentiality of official statistics: An excuse for secrecy, in D. Dorling and S. Simpson (eds) *Statistics in Society: The Arithmetic of Politics*. London: Arnold.

Dale, A., Arber, S. and Procter, M. (1988) *Doing Secondary Analysis*. London: Unwin Hyman.

Dale, J. and Foster, P. (1986) *Feminists and State Welfare*. London: Routledge & Kegan Paul.

David, M. and Sutton, C. D. (2011) *Social Research: An Introduction*, 2nd edn. London: Sage.

Davies, P. M., Francis, P. and Jupp, V. (eds) (2010) *Doing Criminological Research*, 2nd edn. London: Sage.

Davis, A. (1981) *Women, Race and Class*. London: The Women's Press.

Dawkins, R. (2008) *The God Delusion*. New York: Mariner.

Dean, M. (1994) *Critical and Effective Histories: Foucault's Methods and Historical Sociology*. London: Routledge.

Dean, M. (1999) *Governmentality: Power and Rule in Modern Society*. London: Sage.

Dean, M. (2007) *Governing Societies: Political Perspectives on Domestic and International Rule*. Maidenhead: Open University Press.

Delanty, G. (2000) *Modernity and Postmodernity: Knowledge, Power and the Self*. London: Sage.

Denzin, N. K. (1978) *The Research Act in Sociology*. London: Butterworths.

Denzin, N. K. (1988) Blue velvet: Postmodern contradictions. *Theory, Culture and Society*, 5: 461–73.

Denzin, N. K. (1994) Postmodernism and deconstructionism, in D. R. Dickens and A. Fontana (eds) *Postmodernism and Social Inquiry*. London: UCL Press.

Desmond, J. (1998) Marketing and moral indifference, in M. Parker (ed.) *Ethics and Organizations*. London: Sage.

Deutsch, K. (1987) Prologue: Achievements and challenges in 2000 years of comparative research, in M. Dierkes, H. Weiler and A. Berthoin Antal (eds) *Comparative Policy Research: Learning from Experience*. Aldershot: Gower.

de Vaus, D. (1996) *Surveys in Social Research*, 4th edn. London: UCL Press.

de Vaus, D. (2002a) *Surveys in Social Research*, 5th edn. London: Routledge.

de Vaus, D. (2002b) *Analyzing Social Science Data: 50 Key Problems in Data Analysis*. London: Sage.

Dex, S. (ed.) (1991) *Life and Work History Analyses: Qualitative and Quantitative Developments*. London: Routledge.

Dey, I. (2010) Grounding categories, in A. Bryant and K. Charmaz (eds) *The Sage Handbook of Grounded Theory*, paperback edn. London: Sage.

Ditton, J. (1977) *Part-Time Crime: An Ethnography of Petty Crime*. London: Macmillan.

Dogan, M. (2004) The quantitative method in comparative research, in P. Kennett (ed.) *A Handbook of Comparative Social Policy*. Cheltenham: Edward Elgar.

Dolnicar, S., Laesser, C. and Matus, K. (2009) Online verses paper: Format effects in tourism surveys. *Journal of Travel Research*, 47 (3): 295–316.

Dopson, S. (2003) The potential of the case study method for organisational analysis. *Policy and Politics*, 31 (2): 217–26.

Dorling, D. and Simpson, S. (eds) (1999) *Statistics in Society: The Arithmetic of Politics*. London: Arnold.

Douglas, J. (1979) Living morality versus bureaucratic fiat, in C. Klockars and F. O'Connor (eds) *Deviance and Decency: The Ethics of Research with Human Subjects*. London: Sage.

Down, S. and Hughes, M. (2009) When the 'subject' and the 'researcher' speak together: Co-producing organizational ethnography, in S. Ybema, D. Yanow, H. Wels and F. Kamsteeg (eds) *Organizational Ethnography: Studying the Complexities of Everyday Life*. London: Sage.

Dreyfus, H. and Rabinow, P. (1982) *Michel Foucault: Beyond Structuralism and Hermeneutics*. Chicago, IL: University of Chicago Press.

Driver, E. (1989) Introduction, in E. Driver and A. Droisen (eds) *Child Sexual Abuse: Feminist Perspectives*. London: Macmillan.

du Gay, P. (1996) *Consumption and Identity at Work*. London: Sage.

Dunkerley, D. (1988) Historical methods and organizational analysis: The case of a naval dockyard, in A. Bryman (ed.) *Doing Research in Organizations*. London: Routledge.

Dunleavy, P. and Husbands, C. (1985) *British Democracy at the Crossroads: Voting and Party Competition in the 1980s*. London: George Allen & Unwin.

Durkheim, E. (1952) *Suicide*. London: Routledge & Kegan Paul.

Durkheim, E. (1964) *The Rules of Sociological Method*. Glencoe, IL: Free Press.

Easthope, A. and McGowan, K. (eds) (1992) *A Critical and Cultural Theory Reader*. Buckingham: Open University Press.

Eckstein, H. (1975) Case study and theory in political science, in F. Greenstein and N. Polsby (eds) *The Handbook of Political Science: Strategies of Inquiry, Volume 7*. London: Addison-Wesley.

Eco, U. (1979) *The Role of the Reader*. London: Hutchinson.

Eco, U. (1984) *Semiotics and the Philosophy of Language*. London: Macmillan.

Edwards, S. (1990) Provoking her own demise: From common assault to homicide, in J. Hanmer and M. Maynard (eds) *Women, Violence and Social Control*. London: Macmillan.

Eichler, M. (1988) *Nonsexist Research Methods: A Practical Guide*. London: Unwin Hyman.

Eichler, M. (1997) Feminist methodology. *Current Sociology*, 45 (2): 9–36.

Eisenhardt, K. (1989) Building theories from case study research. *Academy of Management Review*, 14 (4): 532–50.

Eisenhardt, K. and Graebner, M. (2007) Theory building from cases: Opportunities and challenges. *Academy of Management Journal*, 50 (1): 25–32.

Eldridge, J. (1986) Facets of 'relevance' in sociological research, in F. Heller (ed.) *The Use and Abuse of Social Science*. London: Sage.

Elias, N. (1987) *Involvement and Detachment*. Edited by M. Schrotter. Translated by E. Jephcott. Oxford: Blackwell.

Elliott, A. (1994) *Psychoanalytic Theory: An Introduction*. Oxford: Blackwell.

Ember, C. and Ember, R. (2009) *Cross-Cultural Research Methods*. Plymouth: AltaMira.

Emmet, D. (1966) *Rules, Roles and Relations*. London: Macmillan.

Emmet, E. R. (1981) *Learning to Philosophize*. Harmondsworth: Penguin.

Emmison, M. and Smith, P. (2000) *Researching the Visual: Images, Objects, Contexts and Interactions in Social and Cultural Inquiry*. London: Sage.

Equality and Human Rights Commission (2010) *Stop and Think: A Critical Review of the Stop and Search Powers in England and Wales*. Manchester: Equality and Human Rights Commission. Available at www.equalityhumanrights.com

Erickson, B. and Nosanchuk, T. (1992) *Understanding Data*, 2nd edn. Buckingham: Open University Press.

Ericson, R., Baranek, P. and Chan, J. (1987) *Visualizing Deviance: A Study of News Organization*. Milton Keynes: Open University Press.

Ericson, R., Baranek, P. and Chan, J. (1989) *Negotiating Control: A Study of News Sources*. Milton Keynes: Open University Press.

Ericson, R., Baranek, P. and Chan, J. (1991) *Representing Order: Crime, Law, and Justice in the News Media*. Buckingham: Open University Press.

Esping-Andersen, G. (1990) *The Three Worlds of Welfare Capitalism*. Cambridge: Polity.

Evans, G. (ed.) (1999) *The End of Class Politics? Class Voting in Comparative Context*. Oxford: Oxford University Press.

Evens, T. M. S and Handelman, D. (eds) (2006) *The Manchester School: Practice and Ethnographic Praxis in Anthropology*. Oxford: Berghahn.

Fahmy, E., Dorling, D., Rigby, J., Wheeler, B., Ballas, D., Thomas, B., Gordon, D. and Lupton, R. (2008) Poverty, wealth and place in Britain, 1968–2005. *Radical Statistics*, 97: 10–29.

Fairclough, N. (1995) *Critical Discourse Analysis: The Critical Study of Language*. London: Longman.

Fairclough, N. (2000) *New Labour, New Language?* London: Routledge.

Fairclough, N. (2003) *Analysing Discourse: Textual Analysis for Social Research*. London: Routledge.

Farrall, S., Jackson, J. and Gray, E. (2009) *Social Order and the Fear of Crime in Contemporary Times*. Oxford: Oxford University Press.

Farran, D. (1990) Analysing a photograph of Marilyn Monroe, in L. Stanley (ed.) *Feminist Praxis: Research, Theory and Epistemology in Feminist Sociology*. London: Routledge.

Fay, B. (1996) *Contemporary Philosophy of Social Science: A Multicultural Approach*. Oxford: Blackwell.

Fay, B. (2009) For science in the social sciences. *Philosophy of the Social Sciences*, 36 (2): 227–40.

Ferrari, V. (1990) Socio-legal concepts and their comparison, in E. Øyen (ed.) *Comparative Methodology*. London: Sage.

Festinger, L., Riecken, H. W. and Schachter, S. (1956) *When Prophecy Fails*. New York: Harper & Row.

Feyerabend, P. (1978) *Against Method*. London: Verso.

Field, A. (2009) *Discovering Statistics*, 3rd edn. London: Sage.

Fielding, J. and Gilbert, N. (2006) *Understanding Social Statistics*, 2nd edn. London: Sage.

Fielding, N. (1981) *The National Front*. London: Routledge & Kegan Paul.

Fielding, N. (1982) Observational research on the National Front, in M. Bulmer (ed.) *Social Research Ethics: An Examination of the Merits of a Covert Participation*. London: Macmillan.

Fielding, N. (ed.) (1988a) *Actions and Structure: Research Methods and Social Theory*. London: Sage.

Fielding, N. (1988b) *Joining Forces: Police Training, Socialization and Occupational Competence*. London: Routledge.

Fielding, N. (2002) Automating the ineffable: Qualitative software and the meaning of qualitative research, in T. May (ed.) *Qualitative Research: An International Guide to Issues in Practice*. London: Sage.

Fielding, N. and Fielding, J. (1986) *Linking Data: The Articulation of Quantitative and Qualitative Methods in Social Research*. London: Sage.

Fielding, N. and Lee, R. (eds) (1991) *Using Computers in Qualitative Research*. London: Sage.

Finch, J. (1984) It's great to have someone to talk to: The ethics and politics of interviewing women, in C. Bell and H. Roberts (eds) *Social Researching: Politics, Problems and Practice*. London: Routledge & Kegan Paul.

Fineman, S. and Gabriel, Y. (1996) *Experiencing Organizations*. London: Sage.

Fink, A. (1995) *How to Sample in Surveys*. Thousand Oaks, CA: Sage.

Fink, A. (2003) *How to Report on Surveys: The Survey Kit*, 2nd edn. London: Sage.

Fishman, P. (1990) Interaction: The work women do, in J. McCarl Nielsen (ed.) *Feminist Research Methods: Exemplary Readings in the Social Sciences*. London: Westview.

Fitz-Gibbon, C. and Lyons Morris, L. (1987) *How to Design a Program Evaluation*. London: Sage.

Flatley, J., Kershaw, C., Smith, K., Chaplin, R. and Moon, D. (2010) *Crime in England and Wales 2009/10: Findings from the British Crime Survey and Policy Recorded Crime*, 2nd edn. London: Home Office. Available at http://rds.homeoffice.gov.uk

Flyvbjerg, B. (2001) *Making Social Science Matter: Why Social Inquiry Fails and How it Can Succeed Again*. Translated by S. Sampson. Cambridge: Cambridge University Press.

Flyvbjerg, B. (2006) Five misunderstandings about case-study research. *Qualitative Inquiry*, 12 (2): 219–45.

Fontana, A. (1994) Ethnographic trends in the postmodern era, in D. R. Dickens and A. Fontana (eds) *Postmodernism and Social Inquiry*. London: UCL Press.

Fontana, A. and Frey, J. H. (1994) Interviewing: The art of science, in N. K. Denzin and Y. S. Lincoln (eds) *Handbook of Qualitative Research*. London: Sage.

Forster, N. (1994) The analysis of company documentation, in C. Cassell and G. Symon (eds) *Qualitative Methods in Organizational Research: A Practical Guide*. London: Sage.

Foucault, M. (1972) *The Archaeology of Knowledge*. Translated by A. M. Sheridan Smith. London: Routledge.

Foucault, M. (1977) *Discipline and Punish: The Birth of the Prison*. London: Allen Lane.

Foucault, M. (1980) *Power/Knowledge, Selected Interviews and Other Writings 1972–1977*. Edited by C. Gordon. Brighton: Harvester.

Foucault, M. (1989a) *The Archaeology of Knowledge* [originally published 1969]. Translated by A. M. Sheridan Smith. London: Routledge.

Foucault, M. (1989b) *Foucault Live: Collected Interviews 1961–1984*. Edited by E. Lotringer. Translated by J. Johnston. New York: Semiotext(e).

Foucault, M. (1991a) Questions of method, in G. Burchell, C. Gordon and P. Miller (eds) *The Foucault Effect: Studies in Governmentality*. London: Harvester Wheatsheaf.

Foucault, M. (1991b) *Remarks on Marx: Conversations with Duccio Trombadori*. Translated by R. J. Goldstein and J. Cascaito. New York: Semiotext(e).

Foucault, M. (2007) Question on geography, in J. W. Crampton and S. Elden (eds) *Space, Knowledge and Power: Foucault and Geography*. Aldershot: Ashgate.

Fowler, F. (1988) *Survey Research Methods*. London: Sage.

Fowler, F. (1995) *Improving Survey Questions: Design and Evaluation*. London: Sage.

Fowler, F. and Mangione, T. (1990) *Standardized Survey Interviewing: Minimizing Interviewer-Related Error*. London: Sage.

Franchet, Y. (2000) *Foreword: A presentation of eurostat*, http://ec.europa.eu/index_en.html

Franklin, A. (2010) *City Life*. London: Sage.

Fraser, N. (1989) *Unruly Practices: Power, Discourse and Gender in Contemporary Social Theory*. Cambridge: Polity.

Fraser, N. and Honneth, A. (2003). *Redistribution or Recognition: A Political-Philosophical Exchange*. London: Verso.

Frisby, D. (1984) *Georg Simmel*. London: Tavistock.

Fuller, S. (2000) *The Governance of Science: Ideology and the Future of the Open Society*. Buckingham: Open University Press.

Galesic, M., Tourangeau, R., Couper, M. P. and Conrad, F. G. (2008) Eye-tracking data: New insights on response order effects and other cognitive shortcuts in survey responding. *Public Opinion Quarterly*, 72 (5): 892–913.

Game, A. (1991) *Undoing the Social: Towards a Deconstructive Sociology*. Buckingham: Open University Press.

Gane, M. (ed.) (1993) *Baudrillard Live: Selected Interviews*. London: Routledge.

Garfinkel, H. (1967) *Studies in Ethnomethodology*. Englewood Cliffs, NJ: Prentice-Hall.

Geertz, C. (1973) Thick description, in C. Geertz (ed.) *The Interpretation of Cultures*. New York: Basic Books.

Gellner, E. (1974) The new idealism: Cause and meaning in the social sciences, in A. Giddens (ed.) *Positivism and Sociology*. London: Heinemann.

George, A. L. and Bennett, A. (2004) *Case Studies and Theory Development in the Social Sciences*. Cambridge, MA: Harvard University Press.

Gerring, J. (2004) What is a case study and what is it good for? *American Political Science Review*, 98 (2): 341–54.

Gerson, K. and Horowitz, R. (2002) Observation and interviewing: Options and choices in qualitative research, in T. May (ed.) *Qualitative Research in Action*. London: Sage.

Gerth, H. and Mills, C. W. (eds) (1948) *From Max Weber: Essays in Sociology*. London: Routledge & Kegan Paul.

Gibbons, M., Limoges, C., Nowotny, H., Schwartzmann, S., Scott, P. and Trow, M. (1994) *The New Production of Knowledge: The Dynamics of Science and Research in Contemporary Societies*. London: Sage.

Gibson-Graham, J. K. (1996) *The End of Capitalism (As We Knew It): A Feminist Critique of Political Economy*. Oxford: Blackwell.

Giddens, A. (1976) *New Rules of Sociological Method*. London: Hutchinson.

Giddens, A. (1979) *Central Problems in Social Theory*. London: Macmillan.

Giddens, A. (1984) *The Constitution of Society: Outline of the Theory of Structuration*. Cambridge: Polity.

Giddens, A. (1990) *The Consequences of Modernity*. Cambridge: Polity.

Giddens, A. (1996) *In Defence of Sociology: Essays, Interpretations and Rejoinders*. Cambridge: Polity.

Giddens, A. (2009) *The Politics of Climate Change*. Cambridge: Polity.

Giele, J. Z. and Elder, Jr., G. H. (eds) (1998) *Methods of Life Course Research: Qualitative and Quantitative Approaches*. London: Sage.

Gieryn, T. (1999) *Cultural Boundaries of Science: Credibility on the Line*. Chicago, IL: University of Chicago Press.

Gilbert, N. (1981) *Modelling Society: An Introduction to Loglinear Analysis for Social Researchers*. London: George Allen & Unwin.

Gilbert, N. (1993) *Analyzing Tabular Data: Loglinear and Logistic Models for Social Researchers*. London: UCL Press.

Gilbert, N. and Abell, P. (eds) (1984) *Accounts and Action*. Aldershot: Gower.

Gilbert, N. and Mulkay, M. (1984) *Opening Pandora's Box: A Sociological Analysis of Scientists' Discourse*. Cambridge: Cambridge University Press.

Gilbert, N. and Troitzsch, K. G. (1999) *Simulation for the Social Scientist*. Buckingham: Open University Press.

Ginn, J. and Duggard, P. (1994) Statistics: A gendered agenda. *Radical Statistics*, 58: 2–15.

Glaser, B. and Strauss, A. (1967) *The Discovery of Grounded Theory*. Chicago, IL: Aldine.

Gluckman, M. (1961) Ethnographic data in British social anthropology. *Sociological Review*, 9: 5–17.

Goffman, E. (1961) *Encounters: Two Studies in the Sociology of Interaction*. Harmondsworth: Penguin.

Goffman, E. (1968) *Asylums: Essays on the Social Situation of Mental Patients and Other Inmates* [originally published 1961]. Harmondsworth: Penguin.

Goffman, E. (1981) *Forms of Talk*. Philadelphia, PA: University of Pennsylvania Press.

Goffman, E. (1984) *The Presentation of Self in Everyday Life* [originally published 1959]. Harmondsworth: Penguin.

Gold, R. (1969) Roles in sociological field observation, in G. McCall and J. Simmons (eds) *Issues in Participant Observation: A Text and Reader*. London: Addison-Wesley.

Goldacre, B. (2008). *Bad Science*. London: Fourth Estate.

Golding, P. (1995) Public attitudes to social exclusion: Some problems of measurement and analysis, in R. Room (ed.) *Beyond the Threshold: The Measurement and Analysis of Social Exclusion*. Bristol: Policy Press.

Goldthorpe, J. (1984) The relevance of history to sociology, in M. Bulmer (ed.) *Sociological Research Methods*, 2nd edn. London: Macmillan.

Goldthorpe, J. (2000) *On Sociology: Numbers, Narratives, and the Integration of Research and Theory*. Oxford: Oxford University Press.

Gomm, R., Hammersley, M. and Foster, P. (2000) Case study and generalization, in R. Gomm, M. Hammersley and P. Foster (eds) *Case Study Method: Key Issues, Key Texts*. London: Sage.

Goode, W. J. and Hatt, P. K. (1952) *Methods in Social Research*. New York: McGraw-Hill.

Gorard, S. with Taylor, C. (2004) *Combining Methods in Educational and Social Research*. Maidenhead: Open University Press.

Gouldner, A. (1962) Anti-Minotaur: The myth of a value-free sociology. *Social Problems*, 9 (3): 199–213.

Gouldner, A. (1971) *The Coming Crisis in Western Sociology*. London: Heinemann.

Government Social Research Unit (2007) Why do social experiments? Experiments and quasi-experiments for evaluating government policies and programmes, in HM Treasury, *The Magenta Book: Guidance Notes for Policy Evaluation and Analysis*. London: HM Treasury.

Government Statisticians' Collective (1993) How official statistics are produced: Views from the inside [originally published 1979], in M. Hammersley (ed.) *Social Research: Philosophy, Politics and Practice*. London: Sage.

Graham, L. (1995) *On the Line at Subaru-Isuzu: The Japanese Model and the American Worker*. Ithaca, NY: Cornell University Press.

Gramsci, A. (2010) *Selections from the Prison Notebooks*. Edited and translated by Q. Hoare and G. Nowell Smith [originally published 1971]. New York: International Publishers.

Grant, A. and Wall, T. (2009) The neglected science and art of quasi-experimentation: Why-to, when-to and how-to advice for organisational researchers. *Organisational Research Methods*, 12 (4): 653–86.

Gravetter, F. J. and Wallnau, L. B. (2005) *Essentials of Statistics for the Behavioral Sciences*, 5th edn. Belmont, CA: Wadsworth.

Gray, A., Banks, S., Carpenter, J., Green, E. and May, T. (1999) *Professionalism and the Management of Local Authorities*. London: Improvement and Development Agency of the Local Government Association.

Greed, C. (1990) The professional and the personal: A study of women quantity surveyors, in L. Stanley (ed.) *Feminist Praxis: Research, Theory and Epistemology in Feminist Sociology*. London: Routledge.

Greenlaw, C. and Brown-Welty, S. (2009) A comparison of web-based and paper-based survey methods: Testing assumptions of survey mode and response cost. *Evaluation Review*, 33 (5): 464–80.

Greenwood, D. and Levin, M. (1998) *Introduction to Action Research: Social Research for Social Change*. London: Sage.

Griffith, A. I. (2006) Constructing single parent families for schooling: Discovering an institutional discourse, in D. E. Smith (ed.) *Institutional Ethnography as Practice*. Lanham, MD: Rowman & Littlefield.

Griffiths, M. (1995) *Feminisms and the Self: The Web of Identity*. London: Routledge.

Grimm, H. (2006) Entrepreneurship policy and regional economic growth: Exploring the link and theoretical implications, in B. Rihoux and H. Grimm, *Innovative Comparative Methods for Policy Analysis: Beyond the Qualitative–Quantitative Divide*. New York: Springer.

Grimshaw, A. (1973) Comparative sociology: In what ways different from other sociologies?, in M. Armer and A. Grimshaw (eds) *Comparative Social Research: Methodological Problems and Strategies*. London: Wiley.

Gross, M. and Krohn, W. (2005) Society as experiment: Sociological foundations for a self-experimental society. *History of the Human Sciences*, 18 (2): 63–86.

Grosz, E. (1994) Sexual difference and the problem of essentialism, in N. Schor and E. Weed (eds) *The Essential Difference*. Bloomington, IN: Indiana University Press.

Habermas, J. (1984) *Theory of Communicative Action. Volume 1: Reason and the Rationalization of Society*. Translated by T. McCarthy. Cambridge: Polity.

Habermas, J. (1987) *Theory of Communicative Action. Volume 2: Lifeworld and System: A Critique of Functionalist Reason.* Translated by T. McCarthy. Cambridge: Polity.

Habermas, J. (1989) *Knowledge and Human Interests* [originally published 1968]. Translated by J. J. Shapiro. Cambridge: Polity.

Habermas, J. (1990) *On the Logic of the Social Sciences* [originally published 1970]. Translated by S. W. Nicholsen and J. A. Stark. Cambridge: Polity.

Habermas, J. (1992) *Moral Consciousness and Communicative Action.* Translated by C. Lenhardt and S. Nicholsen. Introduction by T. McCarthy. Cambridge: Polity.

Habermas, J. (1994) *The Past as Future.* Interviews by M. Haller. Translated and edited by M. Pensky. Cambridge: Polity.

Habermas, J. (1996) *Between Facts and Norms: Contributions to a Discourse Theory of Law and Democracy.* Cambridge: Polity.

Habermas, J. (2003) *Truth and Justification.* Translated by B. Fultner. Cambridge: Polity.

Hacking, I. (1986) Making up people, in T. Heller, M. Sosna and D. Wellbery with A. Davidson, A. Swidler and I. Watt (eds) *Reconstructing Individualism: Autonomy, Individuality, and the Self in Western Thought.* Stanford, CA: Stanford University Press.

Hacking, I. (1999) *The Social Construction of What?* Cambridge, MA: Harvard University Press.

Hage, J. (ed.) (1994) *Formal Theory in Sociology: Opportunity or Pitfall?* New York: State University of New York Press.

Hakim, C. (1987) *Research Design.* London: George Allen & Unwin.

Hall, S. (1988) The toad in the garden: Thatcherism among the theorists, in C. Nelson and L. Grossberg (eds) *Marxism and the Interpretation of Culture.* London: Macmillan.

Hall, S., Cutcher, C., Jefferson, T. and Roberts, B. (1978) *Policing the Crisis: Mugging, the State and Law and Order.* London: Macmillan.

Hamel, J. with Dufour, S. and Fortin, D. (1993) *Case Study Methods.* English translation. London: Sage.

Hammersley, M. (1990a) *The Dilemma of Qualitative Method: Herbert Blumer and the Chicago Tradition.* London: Routledge.

Hammersley, M. (1990b) What's wrong with ethnography? The myth of theoretical description. *Sociology,* 24 (4): 597–615.

Hammersley, M. (1992) *What's Wrong with Ethnography? Methodological Explorations.* London: Routledge.

Hammersley, M. (1995) *The Politics of Social Research.* London: Sage.

Hammersley, M. (2000) *Taking Sides in Social Research: Essays in Partisanship and Bias.* London: Routledge.

Hammersley, M. (2001) On Michael Bassey's concept of the fuzzy generalisation. *Oxford Review of Education,* 27 (2): 219–25.

Hammersley, M. (2008) Causality as conundrum: The case of qualitative inquiry. *Methodological Innovations Online* 2 (3): http://erdt.plymouth.ac.uk/mionline/public_html/viewarticle.php?id=63

Hammersley, M. (2009) Why critical realism fails to justify critical social research. *Methodological Innovations Online*, 4 (2): www.pbs.plym.ac.uk/mi/index.html

Hammersley, M. and Atkinson, P. (1983) *Ethnography: Principles in Practice*. London: Routledge.

Hammersley, M. and Atkinson, P. (1995) *Ethnography: Principles in Practice*, 2nd edn. London: Routledge.

Hammersley, M. and Atkinson, P. (2007) *Ethnography: Principles in Practice*, 3rd edn. London: Routledge.

Haney, L. (2002) Negotiating power and expertise in the field, in T. May (ed.) *Qualitative Research in Action*. London: Sage.

Hansen, A. (1995) Using information technology to analyze newspaper content, in R. M. Lee (ed.) *Information Technology for the Social Scientist*. London: UCL Press.

Hantrais, L. (2004) Crossing cultural boundaries, in P. Kennett (ed.) *A Handbook of Comparative Social Policy*. Cheltenham: Edward Elgar.

Hantrais, L. and Mangen, S. (eds) (2007) *Cross-national Research Methodology and Practice*. London: Routledge.

Harding, S. (1987) Is there a feminist method?, in S. Harding (ed.) *Feminism and Methodology*. Bloomington, IN, and Milton Keynes: Indiana University Press and Open University Press.

Harding, S. (1991) *Whose Science? Whose Knowledge? Thinking from Women's Lives*. Buckingham: Open University Press.

Harding, S. (2006) *Science and Social Inequality: Feminist and Postcolonial Issues*. Urbana, IL: University of Illinois Press.

Harré, R. (1988) Accountability within a social order: The role of pronouns, in C. Antaki (ed.) *Analysing Everyday Explanation: A Casebook of Methods*. London: Sage.

Harré, R. (1993) *Social Being*, 2nd edn. Oxford: Blackwell.

Harré, R. (1998) *The Singular Self*. London: Sage.

Harré, R. and Moghaddam, F. (eds) (2003) *The Self and Others: Positioning Individuals and Groups in Personal, Political, and Cultural Contexts*. London: Praeger.

Hartley, J. (2004) Case study research, in C. Cassell and G. Symon (eds) *Essential Guide to Qualitative Methods in Organisational Research*. London: Sage.

Hartsock, N. (1987) The feminist standpoint: Developing the ground for a specifically historical materialism, in S. Harding (ed.) *Feminism and Methodology*. Bloomington, IN, and Milton Keynes: Indiana University Press and Open University Press.

Harvey, D. (2009) Complexity and case, in D. Byrne and C. C. Ragin (eds) *The Sage Handbook of Case-Based Methods*. London: Sage.

Harvey, D. (2010a) *A Companion to Marx's Capital*. London: Verso.

Harvey, D. (2010b) *The Enigma of Capital and the Crisis of Capitalism*. London: Profile Books.

Harvey, L. (1990) *Critical Social Research*. London: Unwin Hyman.

Haverland, M. (2010) If similarity is the challenge – congruence analysis should be part of the answer. *European Political Science*, 9 (1): 68–73.

Hawkins, D. (2009) Case studies, in T. Landmann and N. Robinson (eds) *The Sage Handbook of Comparative Politics*. London: Sage.

Hayden, P. and El-Ojeili, C. (2006) *Critical Theories of Globalization*. London: Macmillan.

Heath, C. (1981) The opening sequence in doctor–patient interaction, in P. Atkinson and C. Heath (eds) *Medical Work: Realities and Routines*. Aldershot: Gower.

Heath, C. (1988) Embarrassment and interactional organization, in P. Drew and A. Wootton (eds) *Erving Goffman: Exploring the Interaction Order*. Cambridge: Polity.

Heath, C. and Hindmarsh, J. (2002) Analysing social interaction: Talk, bodily conduct and the local environment, in T. May (ed.) *Qualitative Research: An International Guide to Issues in Practice*. London: Sage.

Heath, C., Hindmarsh, J. and Luff, P. (2010) *Video in Qualitative Research*. London: Sage.

Heelas, P., Lash, S. and Morris, P. (eds) (1996) *Detraditionalization: Critical Reflections on Authority and Identity*. Oxford: Blackwell.

Held, D. (1990) *Introduction to Critical Theory: Horkheimer to Habermas*. Cambridge: Polity.

Heller, A. and Fehér, F. (1988) *The Postmodern Political Condition*. Cambridge: Polity.

Henerson, M., Lyons Morris, L. and Fitz-Gibbon, C. (1987) *How to Measure Attitudes*. London: Sage.

Henriques, J., Hollway, W., Urwin, C., Venn, C. and Walkerdine, V. (1998) *Changing the Subject: Psychology, Social Regulation and Subjectivity*, revised edn. London: Routledge.

Heritage, J. (1984) *Garfinkel and Ethnomethodology*. Cambridge: Polity.

Heritage, J. (1997) Conversation analysis and institutional talk, in D. Silverman (ed.) *Qualitative Research: Theory, Method and Practice*. London: Sage.

Heron, J. (1996) *Co-operative Inquiry: Research into the Human Condition*. London: Sage.

Hertz, R. and Imber, J. B. (eds) (1995) *Studying Elites Using Qualitative Methods*. London: Sage.

Hesse-Biber, S. N. and Yaiser, M. L. (eds) (2004) *Feminist Perspectives on Social Research*. New York: Oxford University Press.

Hester, M., Kelly, L. and Radford, J. (eds) (1996) *Women, Violence and Male Power*. Buckingham: Open University Press.

Hewson, C., Yule, P., Laurent, D. and Vogel, C. (2003) *Internet Research Methods: A Practical Guide of the Social and Behavioural Sciences*. London: Sage.

Hey, V. (1997) *The Company She Keeps: An Ethnography of Girls' Friendship*. Buckingham: Open University Press.

Heyl, B. S. (2001) Ethnographic interviewing, in P. Atkinson, A. Coffey, S. Delamont, J. Lofland and L. Lofland (eds) *Handbook of Ethnography*. London: Sage.

Heynen, N. C., Kaika, M. and Swyngedouw, E. (eds) (2006) *In the Nature of Cities: Urban Political Ecology and the Politics of Urban Metabolism*. London: Routledge.

Hilgartner, S. (2006) Mapping systems and moral order: Constituting property in genome laboratories, in S. Jasanoff (ed.) *States of Knowledge: The Co-Production of Science and Social Order*. New York: Routledge.

Hindmarsh, J. (2008) Distributed video analysis in social research, in N. Fielding, R. M. Lee and G. Blank (eds) *The Sage Handbook of Online Research Methods*. London: Sage.

Hine, C. (2000) *Virtual Ethnography*. London: Sage.

Hirst, P. and Thompson, G. (1999) *Globalization in Question: The International Economy and the Possibilities of Governance*. 2nd edn. Cambridge: Polity.

Hobbs, D. and May, T. (eds) (1993) *Interpreting the Field: Accounts of Ethnography*. Oxford: Oxford University Press.

Hodson, M. and Marvin, S. (2009) Urban ecological security: A new urban paradigm? *International Journal of Urban and Regional Research*, 33 (1): 193–215.

Hodson, M. and Marvin, S. (2010) *World Cities and Climate Change: Producing Urban Ecological Security*. Maidenhead: McGraw-Hill.

Hoinville, G. and Jowell, R., in association with Airey, C., Brook, L., Courtenay, C. et al. (1987) *Survey Research Practice*. London: Heinemann.

Homan, R. (1991) *The Ethics of Social Research*. London: Longman.

Honneth, A. (1996) *The Struggle for Recognition: The Moral Grammar of Social Conflicts*. Translated by J. Anderson. Cambridge, MA: MIT Press.

Honneth, A. (2007) *Disrespect: The Normative Foundations of Critical Theory*. Cambridge: Polity.

Hood, R. (1992) *Race and Sentencing: A Study in the Crown Court*. Oxford: Clarendon.

Hopper, C. B. and Moore, J. (1990) Women in outlaw motorcycle gangs. *Journal of Contemporary Ethnography*, 18 (4): 363–87.

Horkheimer, M. (1972) *Critical Theory: Selected Essays*. Translated by M. J. O'Connell and others. New York: Herder & Herder.

Hörning, K., Gerhard, A. and Michailow, M. (1995) *Time Pioneers: Flexible Working Time and New Lifestyles*. Translated by A. Williams. Cambridge: Polity.

Hough, M. and Mayhew, P. (1983) *The British Crime Survey: First Report*. Home Office Research Study 76. London: HMSO.

Hough, M. and Mayhew, P. (1985) *Taking Account of Crime: Key Findings from the Second British Crime Survey*. Home Office Research Study 85. London: HMSO.

Houtkoop-Steenstra, H. (1993) Opening sequences in Dutch telephone conversations, in D. Boden and D. H. Zimmerman (eds) *Talk and Social Structure: Studies in Ethnomethodology and Conversation Analysis*. Cambridge: Polity.

Howe, K. (2004) A critique of experimentalism. *Qualitative Inquiry*, 10 (1): 42–61.

Huff, D. (1993) *How to Lie with Statistics*. Illustrations by I. Geis. New York: Norton.

Hughes, J. (1976) *Sociological Analysis*. London: Nelson.

Humm, M. (ed.) (1992) *Feminisms: A Reader*. London: Harvester Wheatsheaf.

Humm, M. (1995) *A Dictionary of Feminist Theory*, 2nd edn. London: Harvester Wheatsheaf.

Humphreys, L. (1970) *Tea Room Trade*. London: Duckworth.

Hurrell, A. (2005) The regional dimension in international relations theory, in M. Farrell, B. Hettne and L. van Langenhove (eds) *The Global Politics of Regionalism: Theory and Practice*. London: Pluto.

Husbands, C. (1981) The anti-quantitative bias in postwar British sociology, in P. Abrams, R. Deem, J. Finch and P. Rock (eds) *Practice and Progress: British Sociology 1950–1980*. London: George Allen & Unwin.

Hutchby, I. and Wooffitt, R. (2008) *Conversation Analysis*. 2nd edn. Cambridge: Polity.

Hutchinson, P., Read, R. and Sharrock, W. (2008) *There is No Such Thing as a Social Science: In Defence of Peter Winch*. Aldershot: Ashgate.

Inglehart, R. (1997) *Modernization and Postmodernization: Cultural, Economic and Political Change in 43 Societies*. Princeton, NJ: Princeton University Press.

Irvine, J., Miles, I. and Evans, I. (eds) (1979) *Demystifying Social Statistics*. London: Pluto.

Israel, M. and Hay, I. (2006) *Research Ethics for Social Scientists*. London: Sage.

Isserman, A. and Merrifield, J. (1987) Quasi-experimental control group methods for regional analysis: An application to an energy boomtown and growth pole theory. *Economic Geography*, 63 (1): 3–19.

Jackson, T. (2009) *Prosperity without Growth: Economics for a Finite Planet*. London: Earthscan.

Jaggar, A. (1983) *Feminist Politics and Human Nature*. Totowa, NJ: Rowman & Littlefield.

Jessop, B. (2004) Hollowing out the 'nation-state' and multi-level governance, in P. Kennett (ed.) *A Handbook of Comparative Social Policy*. Cheltenham: Edward Elgar.

Jick, T. (1979) Mixing qualitative and quantitative methods: Triangulation in action. *Administrative Science Quarterly*, 24: 602–11.

Johnson, T., Dandeker, C. and Ashworth, C. (1990) *The Structure of Social Theory*. London: Macmillan.

Jones, K. (2000) A regrettable oversight or a significant omission? Ethical considerations in quantitative research in education, in H. Simons and R. Usher (eds) *Situated Ethics in Educational Research*. London: Routledge.

Jones, A., Singer, L. and Magill, C. (2007) *Statistics on Race and the Criminal Justice System, 2006*. London: Ministry of Justice. Available at www.justice.gov.uk

Jordan-Zachery, J. S. (2009) *Black Women, Cultural Images, and Social Policy*. New York: Routledge.

Kaczmirek, L. (2008) Internet survey software tools, in N. Fielding, R. M. Lee and G. Blank (eds) *The Sage Handbook of Online Research Methods*. London: Sage.

Kamuf, P. (ed.) (1991) *A Derrida Reader: Between the Blinds*. London: Harvester Wheatsheaf.

Keat, R. and Urry, J. (1975) *Social Theory as Science*. London: Routledge & Kegan Paul.

Kelle, U. (ed.) (1995) *Computer-Aided Qualitative Data Analysis*. London: Sage.

Kelly, L. and Radford, J. (1987) The problem of men: Feminist perspectives on sexual violence, in P. Scraton (ed.) *Law, Order and the Authoritarian State*. Milton Keynes: Open University Press.

Kendall, G. and Wickham, G. (1999) *Using Foucault's Methods*. London: Sage.

Kennett, P. (2004) Constructing categories and data collection, in P. Kennett (ed.) *A Handbook of Comparative Social Policy*. Cheltenham: Edward Elgar.

Kent, R. (1981) *A History of British Empirical Sociology*. Aldershot: Gower.

Kidder, L. (1981) *Research Methods in Social Relations*, 4th edn. New York: Holt-Saunders.

Kimmel, A. (1988) *Ethics and Values in Applied Social Research*. London: Sage.

Kirk, J. and Miller, M. (1986) *Reliability and Validity in Qualitative Research*. London: Sage.

Kittel, B. (2006) A crazy methodology? On the limits of macroquantitative social science research. *International Sociology*, 21 (5): 647–77.

Kitzinger, J. and Barbour, R. S. (1999) Introduction: The challenge and promise of focus groups, in R. S. Barbour and J. Kitzinger (eds) *Developing Focus Group Research: Politics, Theory and Practice*. London: Sage.

Knorr-Cetina, K. (1999) *Epistemic Cultures: How the Sciences Make Knowledge*. Cambridge, MA: Harvard University Press.

Knorr-Cetina, K. and Cicourel, A. (eds) (1981) *Advances in Social Theory and Methodology: Towards an Integration of Micro and Macro Theories*. London: Routledge & Kegan Paul.

Kotamraju, N. P. (1999) The birth of web site design skills. *American Behavioural Scientist*, 43 (3): 464–74.

Kourany, J. A., Sterba, J. P. and Tong, R. (eds) (1999) *Feminist Philosophies: Problems, Theories and Applications*, 2nd edn. London: Prentice-Hall.

Kozinets, R. V. (2010) *Netnography: Doing Ethnographic Research Online*. London: Sage.

Kreuter, F. and Casas-Cordero, C. (2010) *Paradata Working Paper Series of the Council for Social and Economic Data* (RatSWD) April 2010. Available at www.ratswd.de/download/RatSWD_WP_2010/RatSWD_WP_136.pdf

Kuhn, T. (1970) *The Structure of Scientific Revolutions*. Chicago, IL: University of Chicago Press.

Kuhn, T. (1972) Scientific paradigms, in B. Barnes (ed.) *Sociology of Science: Selected Readings*. Harmondsworth: Penguin.

Kurtz, L. (1984) *Evaluating Chicago Sociology: A Guide to the Literature with an Annotated Bibliography*. Chicago, IL: University of Chicago Press.

Laclau, E. and Mouffe, C. (1985) *Hegemony and Socialist Strategy: Towards a Radical Democratic Politics*. London: Verso.

Lakatos, I. and Musgrave, A. (eds) (1970) *Criticism and the Growth of Knowledge*. Cambridge: Cambridge University Press.

Lamont, M. (2009) *How Professors Think: Inside the Curious World of Academic Judgement*. Cambridge, MA: Harvard University Press.

Landmann, T. and Robinson, N. (2009) *The Sage Handbook of Comparative Politics*. London: Sage.

Langan, M. and Ostner, I. (1991) Gender and welfare: Towards a comparative framework, in G. Room (ed.) *Towards a European Welfare State?* School for Advanced Urban Studies, Bristol: SAUS Publications.

Langer, R. and Beckman, S. (2005) Sensitive research topics: Netnography revisited. *Qualitative Market Research: An International Journal*, 8 (2): 189–203.

Lapiere, R. (1934) Attitudes versus actions. *Social Forces*, 13: 230–7.

Lash, S. (2002) *Critique of Information*. London: Sage.

Lash, S., Szerszynski, B. and Wynne, B. (eds) (1996) *Risk, Environment and Modernity: Towards a New Ecology*. London: Sage.

Lather, P. (2001) Postmodernism, post-structuralism and post (critical) ethnography: Of ruins, aporias and angels, in P. Atkinson, A. Coffey, S. Delamont, J. Lofland and L. Lofland (eds) *Handbook of Ethnography*. London: Sage.

Latour, B. (2004) *Politics of Nature: How to Bring the Sciences into Democracy*. Translated by C. Porter. Cambridge, MA: Harvard University Press.

Lavrakas, P. (1987) *Telephone Survey Methods: Sampling, Selection, and Supervision*. London: Sage.

Lawrence, P. (1988) In another country, in A. Bryman (ed.) *Doing Research in Organisations*. London: Routledge.

Layder, D. (1998) *Sociological Practice: Linking Theory and Social Research*. London: Sage.

Lee, R. M. (ed.) (1995) *Information Technology for the Social Scientist*. London: UCL Press.

Lee, R. M. (2000) *Unobtrusive Methods in Social Research*. Buckingham: Open University Press.

Lempert, L. B. (2010) Asking questions of the data: Memo writing in the grounded theory tradition, in A. Bryant and K. Charmaz (eds) *The Sage Handbook of Grounded Theory*, paperback edn. London: Sage.

Levi-Faur, D. (2006) Varieties of regulatory capitalism: Getting the most out of the comparative method. *Governance: An International Journal of Policy, Administration and Institutions*, 19 (3): 367–82.

Levitas, R. (1996) Fiddling while Britain burns? The 'measurement' of unemployment, in R. Levitas and W. Guy (eds) *Interpreting Official Statistics*. London: Routledge.

Levitas, R. and Guy, W. (eds) (1996) *Interpreting Official Statistics*. London: Routledge.

Lieblich, A., Tuval-Mashiach, R. and Zilber, T. (1998) *Narrative Research: Reading, Analysis, and Interpretation*. London: Sage.

Lijphart, A. (1971) Comparative politics and the comparative method. *American Political Science Review*, 65 (3): 682–93.

Livingstone, S. (2003) On the challenges of cross-national comparative media research. *European Journal of Communication*, 18 (4): 477–500.

Lofland, J. and Lofland, L. (1984) *Analysing Social Settings: A Guide to Qualitative Observation and Analysis*, 2nd edn. Belmont, CA: Wadsworth.

Longino, H. (1992) Can there be a feminist science?, in A. Garry and M. Pearsall (eds) *Women, Knowledge and Reality: Explorations in Feminist Philosophy*. London: Routledge.

Lorde, A. (1992) An open letter to Mary Daly, in M. Humm (ed.) *Feminism: A Reader*. London: Harvester Wheatsheaf.

Lukes, S. (1981) *Emile Durkheim: His Life and Work – A Historical and Critical Study*. Harmondsworth: Penguin.

Lukes, S. (1994) Some problems about rationality, in M. Martin and L. C. McIntyre (eds) *Readings in the Philosophy of Social Science*. Cambridge, MA: MIT Press.

Lyman, P. and Wakeford, N. (eds) (1999) Analyzing virtual societies: New directions in methodology. *American Behavioral Scientist*, 43 (3), special issue.

Lyon, D. (1999) *Postmodernity*, 2nd edn. Buckingham: Open University Press.

Lyon, D. (2001) *Surveillance Society: Monitoring Everyday Life*. Buckingham: Open University Press.

Lyotard, J. (1984) *The Postmodern Condition: A Report on Knowledge*. Manchester: Manchester University Press.

McDermott, R. (2002) Experimental methods in political science. *Annual Review of Political Science*, 5: 31–61.

MacDonald, B. and Walker, R. (1975) Case study and the social philosophy of educational research. *Cambridge Journal of Education*, 5 (1): 2–11.

McDonald, H. and Adam, S. (2003) A comparison of online and postal data collection methods in marketing research. *Marketing Intelligence and Planning*, 21 (2): 85–95.

McGivern, Y. (2006) *The Practice of Market and Social Research: An Introduction*, 2nd edn. Harlow: Pearson Education.

McKie, L. (2002) Engagement and evaluation in qualitative inquiry, in T. May (ed.) *Qualitative Research in Action*. London: Sage.

McKie, L. (2005) *Families, Violence and Social Change*. Maidenhead: Open University Press.

McKinlay, A. and Starkey, K. (eds) (1998) *Foucault, Management and Organization Theory*. London: Sage.

McLaughlin, E. (1991) Oppositional poverty: The quantitative/qualitative divide and other dichotomies. *Sociological Review*, 39 (2): 292–308.

McPherson, T. (1974) *Philosophy and Religious Belief*. London: Hutchinson.

Madsen, P. and Plunz, R. (eds) (2002) *The Urban Lifeworld: Formation, Perception, Representation*. London: Routledge.

Mahoney, J. (2003) Qualitative methodology and comparative politics. *Comparative Political Studies*, 40 (2): 122–44.

Mahoney, J. and Rueschemeyer, D. (eds) (2003) *Comparative Historical Analysis in the Social Sciences*. Cambridge: Cambridge University Press.

Malseed, J. (1987) Straw men: A note on Ann Oakley's treatment of textbook prescriptions for interviewing. *Sociology*, 21 (4): 629–31.

Mangen, S. (2004) 'Fit for purpose?' Qualitative methods in comparative social policy, in P. Kennett (ed.) *A Handbook of Comparative Social Policy*. Cheltenham: Edward Elgar.

Manis, J. (1976) *Analyzing Social Problems*. New York: Praeger.

Mann, C. and Stewart, F. (2000) *Internet Communication and Qualitative Research*. London: Sage.

Manning, P. (1987) *Semiotics and Fieldwork*. London: Sage.

Manning, P. (1988) Semiotics and social theory: The analysis of organizational beliefs, in N. Fielding (ed.) *Actions and Structure: Research Methods and Social Theory*. London: Sage.

Manning, P. (2001) Semiotics, semantics and ethnography, in P. Atkinson, A. Coffey, S. Delamont, J. Lofland and L. Lofland (eds) *Handbook of Ethnography*. London: Sage.

Marsh, C. (1979) Opinion polls: Social science or political manoeuvre?, in J. Irvine, I. Miles and J. Evans (eds) *Demystifying Social Statistics*. London: Pluto.

Marsh, C. (1982) *The Survey Method*. London: George Allen & Unwin.

Marsh, C. (1984) Problems with surveys: Method or epistemology?, in M. Bulmer (ed.) *Sociological Research Methods*, 2nd edn. London: Macmillan.

Marsh, C. and Gershuny, J. (1991) Handling work history data in standard statistical packages, in S. Dex (ed.) *Life and Work History Analyses: Qualitative and Quantitative Developments*. London: Routledge.

Marsh, I. and Melville, G. (2009) *Crime, Justice and the Media*. London: Routledge.

Marsh, R. (1967) *Comparative Sociology: A Codification of Cross-Societal Analysis*. New York: Harcourt & Brace.

Marshall, C. and Rossman, G. (1989) *Designing Qualitative Research*. London: Sage.

Mason, J. (2002) Qualitative interviewing: Asking, listening and interpreting, in T. May (ed.) *Qualitative Research in Action*. London: Sage.

Massey, D. (1995) *Spatial Divisions of Labour: Social Structures and the Geography of Production*, 2nd edn. London: Macmillan.

May, T. (1986) Neglected territory: Victims of car theft. Unpublished MSc thesis, Department of Sociology, University of Surrey.

May, T. (1991) *Probation: Politics, Policy and Practice*. Buckingham: Open University Press.

May, T. (1993) Feelings matter: Inverting the hidden equation, in D. Hobbs and T. May (eds) *Interpreting the Field: Accounts of Ethnography*. Oxford: Oxford University Press.

May, T. (1997) When theory fails? The history of American sociological research methods. *History of Human Sciences*, 10 (1): 163–71.

May, T. (1998a) Reflexivity in the age of reconstructive social science. *International Journal of Methodology: Theory and Practice*, 1 (1): 7–24.

May, T. (1998b) Reflections and reflexivity, in T. May and M. Williams (eds) *Knowing the Social World*. Buckingham: Open University Press.

May, T. (1999a) *Study Skills in Higher Education*. Salford: School of English, Sociology, Politics and Contemporary History, University of Salford.

May, T. (1999b) Reflexivity and sociological practice. *Sociological Research Online*, 4 (3): www.socresonline.org.uk/4/3/may.html

May, T. (ed.) (2002) *Qualitative Research in Action*. London: Sage.

May, T. (2003) Reflexive vigilance: Engagement, illumination, and development, in R. Harré and F. Moghaddam (eds) *The Self and Others: Positioning Individuals and Groups in Personal, Political, and Cultural Contexts*. London: Praeger.

May, T. (2004) Critical theory, in A. Bryman, M. Lewis-Beck and T. Futing Liao (eds) *Encyclopedia of Social Science Research Methods*. Thousand Oaks, CA: Sage.

May, T. (2005) Transformations in academic production: Context, content and consequences. *European Journal of Social Theory*, 8 (2): 193–209.

May, T. (2006a) The missing middle in methodology: Occupation cultures and institutional conditions. *Methodological Innovations Online*, 1 (1): www.methodologicalinnovations.org

May, T. (2006b) Transformative power: A study in human service organization, in H. Beynon and T. Nichols (eds) *Patterns of Work in the Post-Fordist Era, Volume 2*. Cheltenham: Edward Elgar.

May, T. (2007) Regulation, engagement and academic production, in A. Harding, A. Scott, S. Laske and C. Burtscher (eds) *Bright Satanic Mills: Universities, Regional Development and the Knowledge Economy*. Aldershot: Ashgate.

May, T. (2010) Contours in reflexivity: Commitment, criteria and change. *Methodological Innovations Online*, 5 (1): www.methodologicalinnovations.org

May, T. with Perry, B. (2011) *Social Research and Reflexivity: Content, Consequences and Context*. London: Sage.

May, T. and Landells, M. (1994) Administrative rationality and the delivery of social services: An organisation in flux. Paper delivered to the International Conference on Children, Family Life and Society, University of Plymouth, July.

May, T. and Marvin, S. (2009) Elected regional assemblies: Lessons for better policy making, in M. Sandford (ed.) *The Northern Veto*. Manchester: Manchester University Press.

May, T. and Perry, B. (2003) *Knowledge Capital: From Concept to Action*. Report for Contact Partnership of Greater Manchester Universities. Manchester.

May, T. and Perry, B. (2006) Cities, universities and the knowledge economy: Transformations in the image of the intangible. *Social Epistemology*, 20 (3–4): 259–82.

May, T. and Perry, B. (2010) *Implementing the Innovation Fund: Comparing Expectations and Practices*. Report to the Manchester Innovation Investment Fund Evaluation Group, National Endowment for Science, Technology and the Arts; Manchester City Council and the North-West Development Agency. Manchester, February.

May, T. and Powell, J. (2007) Michel Foucault, in T. Edwards (ed.) *Cultural Theory: Classical and Contemporary Positions*. London: Sage.

May, T. and Powell, J. (2008) *Situating Social Theory*. 2nd edn. Maidenhead: Open University Press.

May, T., Perry, B., Hodson, M. and Marvin, S. (2009) *Active Intermediaries in Effective Knowledge Exchange*. SURF Policy Briefing 1. Available at www.surf.salford.ac.uk

Maynard, M. (1998) Feminists' knowledge and the knowledge of feminisms: epistemology, theory, methodology and method, in T. May and M. Williams (eds) *Knowing the Social World*. Buckingham: Open University Press.

Mazzocchi, M. (2008) *Statistics for Marketing and Social Research*. London: Sage.

Merton, R. (1957) *Social Theory and Social Structure*. New York: Free Press.

Merton, R. and Kendal, P. (1946) The focused interview. *American Journal of Sociology*, 51: 541–57.

Merton, R., Fiske, M. and Kendall, P. (1990) *The Focused Interview: A Manual of Problem and Procedures* [originally published 1956], 2nd edn. New York: Free Press.

Meyers, D. T. (ed.) (1997) *Feminist Social Thought: A Reader*. London: Routledge.

Miller, G. (1997) Building bridges: The possibility of analytic dialogue between ethnography, conversation analysis and Foucault, in D. Silverman (ed.) *Qualitative Research: Theory, Method and Practice*. London: Sage.

Miller, J. and Glassner, B. (1997) The inside and outside: Finding realities in interviews, in D. Silverman (ed.) *Qualitative Research: Theory, Method and Practice*. London: Sage.

Mills, C. W. (1940) Situated accounts and vocabularies of motive. *American Sociological Review*, 6: 904–13.

Mills, C. W. (1959) *The Sociological Imagination*. New York: Oxford University Press.

Mills, M., van de Bunt, G. and de Bruijn, J. (2006) Comparative research: Persistent problems and promising solutions. *International Sociology*, 21 (5): 619–31.

Minkes, J. and Minkes, L. (2008) Introduction, in J. Minkes and L. Minkes (eds) *Corporate and White Collar Crime*. London: Sage.

Mirrlees-Black, C., Mayhew, P. and Percy, A. (1996) *The 1996 British Crime Survey: England and Wales*. London: HMSO.

Mirrlees-Black, C., Budd, T., Partridge, S. and Mayhew, P. (1998) *The 1998 British Crime Survey: England and Wales*. London: HMSO.

Mitchell, J. C. (1983) Case and situation analysis, reproduced in T. M. S. Evens and D. Handelman (eds) (2006) *The Manchester School: Practice and Ethnographic Praxis in Anthropology*. Oxford: Berghahn.

Mjoset, L. (2009) The contextualist approach to social science methodology, in D. Byrne and C. C. Ragin (eds) *The Sage Handbook of Case-Based Methods*. London: Sage.

Molina, O. and Rhodes, M. (2002) Corporatism: The past, present and future of a concept. *Annual Review of Political Sciences*, 5: 305–31.

Morrow, R. A. with Brown, D. D. (1994) *Critical Theory and Methodology*. London: Sage.

Moser, C. and Kalton, G. (1971) *Survey Methods in Social Investigation*, 2nd edn. Reprinted in 2004. Aldershot: Ashgate.

Moser, C. and Kalton, G. (1983) *Survey Methods in Social Investigation*, 2nd edn. London: Heinemann.

Mouffe, C. (2005). *On the Political*. London: Routledge.

Mounce, H. O. (1997) *The Two Pragmatisms: From Peirce to Rorty*. London: Routledge.

Moustakas, C. (1994) *Phenomenological Research Methods*. London: Sage.

Mullan, B. (1987) *Sociologists on Sociology*. London: Croom Helm.

Nagel, E. (1961) *The Structure of Science*. London: Routledge & Kegan Paul.

Nast, H. (1994) Women in the field: Critical feminist methodologies and theoretical perspectives. *Professional Geographer*, 46 (1): 54–66.

Newton, T. (1996) Agency and discourse: Recruiting consultants in a life insurance company. *Sociology*, 30 (4): 717–39.

Nichols, T. (1999) Industrial injury statistics, in D. Dorling and S. Simpson (eds) *Statistics in Society: The Arithmetic of Politics*. London: Arnold.

Norris, C. (1993) *The Truth about Postmodernism*. Oxford: Blackwell.

Oakley, A. (1979) *From Here to Maternity: Becoming a Mother*. Harmondsworth: Penguin.

Oakley, A. (1984) *Taking It Like a Woman*. London: Fontana.

Oakley, A. (1987) Comment on Malseed. *Sociology*, 21 (4): 632.

Oakley, A. (1990) Interviewing women: A contradiction in terms, in H. Roberts (ed.) *Doing Feminist Research*. London: Routledge & Kegan Paul.

Oakley, A. (1998) Gender, methodology and people's ways of knowing: Some problems with feminism and the paradigm debate in social science. *Sociology*, 32 (4): 707–31.

Oakley, A. (2000) *Experiments in Knowing: Gender and Method in the Social Sciences*. Cambridge: Polity.

Oakley, A. and Oakley, R. (1979) Sexism in official statistics, in J. Irvine, I. Miles and J. Evans (eds) *Demystifying Social Statistics*. London: Pluto.

Odih, P. (2007) *Gender and Work in Capitalist Economies*. Maidenhead: Open University Press.

OECD (2007) *Peer Review: A Tool for Co-operation and Change Policy Brief*. Paris: OECD.

O'Neill, J. (1995) *The Poverty of Postmodernism*. London: Routledge.

O'Neill, J., Holland, A. and Light, A. (2008) *Environmental Values*. London: Routledge.

Oppenheim, A. (1992) *Questionnaire Design, Interviewing and Attitude Measurement*. London: Pinter.

O'Reilly, J. (1996) Theoretical considerations in cross-national employment research, *Sociological Research Online*, 1 (1).

Ornstein, M. (1998) Survey research. *Current Sociology*, 46 (4): 1–135.

Outhwaite, W. (ed.) (1996) *The Habermas Reader*. Cambridge: Polity.

Owen, C. (1999) Government household surveys, in D. Dorling and S. Simpson (eds) *Statistics in Society: The Arithmetic of Politics*. London: Arnold.

Øyen, E. (ed.) (1990a) *Comparative Methodology*. London: Sage.

Øyen, E. (1990b) The imperfection of comparisons, in E. Øyen (ed.) *Comparative Methodology*. London: Sage.

Øyen, E. (2004) Living with imperfect comparisons, in P. Kennett (ed.) *A Handbook of Comparative Social Policy*. Cheltenham: Edward Elgar.

Padfield, M. and Procter, I. (1996) Effects of interviewer's gender on interviewing: A comparative inquiry. *Sociology*, 30 (2): 355–66.

Pahl, R. (1995) *After Success: Fin de Siècle Anxiety and Identity*. Cambridge: Polity.

Papineau, D. (1978) *For Science in the Social Sciences*. London: Macmillan.

Park, R. E. (1972) *The Crowd and the Public and Other Essays*. Edited by H. Elsner. Translated by C. Elsner. Chicago, IL: University of Chicago Press.

Pattillo-McCoy, M. (1999) *Black Picket Fences: Privilege and Peril among the Black Middle Class*. Chicago, IL: University of Chicago Press.

Pawson, R. (2006) *Evidence-based Policy: A Realist Perspective.* London: Sage.

Pawson, R. and Tilley, N. (1997) *Realistic Evaluation.* London: Sage.

Payne, G. and Williams, M. (2005) Generalisation in qualitative research. *Sociology,* 39 (2): 295–314.

Pearce, F. (1989) *The Radical Durkheim.* London: Unwin Hyman.

Pearce, F. and Woodiwiss, T. (2001) Reading Foucault as a realist, in J. López and G. Potter (eds) *After Postmodernism: An Introduction to Critical Realism.* London: Athlone.

Pearson, G. (1983) *Hooligan: A History of Respectable Fears.* London: Macmillan.

Pearson, G. (1993) Talking a good fight: Authenticity and distance in the ethnographer's craft, in D. Hobbs and T. May (eds) *Interpreting the Field: Accounts of Ethnography.* Oxford: Oxford University Press.

Penal Affairs Consortium (1996) *Race and Criminal Justice.* London: National Association for the Care and Resettlement of Offenders.

Pennings, P., Keman, H. and Kleinnijenhuis, J. (2009) Global comparative methods, in T. Landmann and N. Robinson (eds) *The Sage Handbook of Comparative Politics.* London: Sage.

Perry, B. (2007) The multi-level governance of science policy in England. *Regional Studies,* 41 (8): 1051–67.

Perry, B. (2008) Academic knowledge and urban development: Theory, policy and practice, in T. Yigitcanlar, K. Velibeyoglu and S. Baum (eds) *Knowledge-Based Urban Development: Planning and Applications in the Information Era.* London: IGI Global.

Perry, B. and May, T. (2006) Excellence, relevance and the university: The 'missing middle' in socio-economic engagement. *Journal of Higher Education in Africa,* 4 (3): 69–92.

Perry, B. and May, T. (eds) (2007) Governance, science policy and regions. *Regional Studies,* 41 (8), special issue.

Perry, B. and May, T. (2010) Urban knowledge exchange: Devilish dichotomies and active intermediation. *International Journal of Knowledge-Based Development,* 1 (1–2): 6–24.

Peters, S. (1998) Finding information on the World Wide Web. *Social Research Update,* 20: 1–4.

Phillips, C. (2009) Ethic inequalities: Another 10 years of the same?, in J. Hills, T. Sefton and K. Stewart (eds) *Towards a More Equal Society? Poverty, Inequality and Policy since 1997.* Bristol: Policy Press.

Phoenix, A. (1994) Practising feminist research: The intersection of gender and 'race' in the research process, in M. Maynard and J. Purvis (eds) *Researching Women's Lives from a Feminist Perspective.* London: Taylor & Francis.

Piekkari, R., Welch, C. and Paavilainen, E. (2009) The case study as disciplinary convention: Evidence from international business journals. *Organizational Research Methods,* 12 (3): 567–89.

Pinker, R. (1971) *Social Theory and Social Policy.* London: Heinemann.

Plano Clark, V. L. and Creswell, J. W. (2008) *The Mixed Methods Reader.* London: Sage.

Platt, J. (1981a) Evidence and proof in documentary research: 1 Some specific problems of documentary research. *Sociological Review,* 29 (1): 31–52.

Platt, J. (1981b) Evidence and proof in documentary research: 2 Some shared problems of documentary research. *Sociological Review*, 29 (1): 53–66.

Platt, J. (1992a) 'Case study' in American methodological thought. *Current Sociology*, 40: 17–48.

Platt, J. (1992b) Cases of cases . . . of cases, in C. C. Ragin and H. S. Becker (eds) *What is a Case? Exploring the Foundations of Social Inquiry*. Cambridge: Cambridge University Press.

Platt, J. (1996) *A History of Sociological Research Methods in America 1920–1960*. Cambridge: Cambridge University Press.

Plummer, K. (1990) *Documents of Life: An Introduction to the Problems and Literature of a Humanistic Method*. London: George Allen & Unwin.

Polsky, N. (1985) *Hustlers, Beats and Others*. Chicago, IL: University of Chicago Press.

Popper, K. R. (1959) *The Logic of Scientific Discovery*. London: Hutchinson.

Popper, K. R. (1970) The sociology of knowledge, in J. Curtis and J. Petras (eds) *The Sociology of Knowledge: A Reader*. London: Duckworth.

Porter, S. (1993) Critical realist ethnography: The case of racism and professionalism in a medical setting. *Sociology*, 27 (4): 591–609.

Porter, S. (2002) Critical realist ethnography, in T. May (ed.) *Qualitative Research in Action*. London: Sage.

Poster, M. (1990) *The Mode of Information: Poststructuralism and Social Context*. Cambridge: Polity.

Prior, L. (2003) *Using Documents in Social Research*. London: Sage.

Radford, J. (1990) Policing male violence – policing women, in J. Hanmer and M. Maynard (eds) *Women, Violence and Social Control*. London: Macmillan.

Radford, J. and Stanko, E. (1996) Violence against women and children: The contradictions of crime control under patriarchy, in M. Hester, L. Kelly and J. Radford (eds) *Women, Violence and Male Power*. Buckingham: Open University Press.

Ragin, C. C. (1987) *The Comparative Method: Moving Beyond Qualitative and Quantitative Strategies*. Berkeley, CA: University of California Press.

Ragin, C. C. (1991) Introduction: The problem of balancing discourses on cases and variables in comparative social research, in C. C. Ragin (ed.) *Issues and Alternatives in Comparative Social Research*. Leiden: E. J. Brill.

Ragin, C. C. (1992) Introduction: Cases of 'what is a case'?, in C. C. Ragin and H. S. Becker (eds) *What is a Case? Exploring the Foundations of Social Inquiry*. Cambridge: Cambridge University Press.

Ragin, C. C. (2000) *Fuzzy Set Social Science*. Chicago, IL: University of Chicago Press.

Ragin, C. C. (2009) Reflections on casing and case-oriented research, in D. Byrne and C. C. Ragin (eds) *The Sage Handbook of Case-Based Methods*. London: Sage.

Ragin, C. C. and Becker, H. S. (eds) (1992) *What is a Case? Exploring the Foundations of Social Inquiry*. Cambridge: Cambridge University Press.

Rallings, C. and Thrasher, M. (2009) The North-East referendum – the result and public reaction, in M. Sandford (ed.) *The Northern Veto*. Manchester: Manchester University Press.

Ratcliffe, P. (2004) *'Race', Ethnicity and Difference: Imagining the Inclusive Society*. Maidenhead: Open University Press.

Ravn, I. (1991) What should guide reality construction?, in F. Steier (ed.) *Research and Reflexivity*. London: Sage.

Reason, P. and Bradbury, H. (eds) (2001) *Handbook of Action Research: Participative Inquiry and Practice*. London: Sage.

Renfrew, C. and Bahn, P. (2008) *Archaeology: Theories, Methods and Practice*, 5th edn. London: Thames & Hudson.

Reynolds, T. (2002) Power in the research process: The relationship between black female researcher and black research participants, in T. May (ed.) *Qualitative Research: An International Guide to Issues in Practice*. London: Sage.

Ricoeur, P. (1982) *Hermeneutics and the Human Sciences*. Edited and translated by J. B. Thompson. Cambridge: Cambridge University Press.

Ricoeur, P. (1984) *Time and Narrative, Volume 1*. Translated by K. McLaughlin and D. Pellauer. Chicago, IL: University of Chicago Press.

Rihoux, B. and Grimm, H. (2006) *Innovative Comparative Methods for Policy Analysis: Beyond the Qualitative–Quantitative Divide*. New York: Springer.

Rihoux, B. and Ragin, C. (2008) *Configurational Comparative Methods: Qualitative Comparative Analysis (QCA) and Related Techniques (Applied Social Research Methods)*. London: Sage.

Riley, J., Cassidy, D. and Becker, J. (2009) *Statistics on Race and the Criminal Justice System 2007/8*. London: Ministry of Justice. Available at www.justice.gov.uk

Roberts, B. (2002) *Biographical Research*. Buckingham: Open University Press.

Roberts, H. (ed.) (1990) *Doing Feminist Research*. London: Routledge & Kegan Paul.

Rock, P. (1979) *The Making of Symbolic Interactionism*. London: Macmillan.

Rohwer, G. (2010) Qualitative comparative analysis: A discussion of interpretations, *European Sociological Review*, 19 July: 1–13.

Rojek, C. and Turner, B. (eds) (1993) *Forget Baudrillard?* London: Routledge.

Rorty, R. (1989) *Contingency, Irony and Solidarity*. Cambridge: Cambridge University Press.

Rose, D. and Sullivan, O. (1996) *Introducing Data Analysis for Social Scientists*, 2nd edn. Buckingham: Open University Press.

Rose, G. (2001) *Visual Methodologies: An Introduction to the Interpretation of Visual Materials*. London: Sage.

Rose, N. and Miller, P. (2008) *Governing the Present: Administering Economic, Social and Personal Life*. Cambridge: Polity.

Rose, R. (1991) Comparing forms of comparative analysis. *Political Studies*, 39 (3): 446–62.

Rosenberg, M. (1968) *The Logic of Survey Analysis*. New York: Basic Books.

Rosenberg, M. (1984) The meaning of relationships in social surveys, in M. Bulmer (ed.) *Sociological Research Methods*, 2nd edn. London: Macmillan.

Roseneil, S. (1993) Greenham revisited: Researching myself and my sisters, in D. Hobbs and T. May (eds) *Interpreting the Field: Accounts of Ethnography*. Oxford: Oxford University Press.

Rosenhan, D. (1982) On being sane in insane places, in M. Bulmer (ed.) *Social Research Ethics: An Examination of the Merits of Covert Participant Observation*. London: Macmillan.

Rowbotham, S. (1999) *Threads through Time: Writings on History and Autobiography*. Harmondsworth: Penguin.

Rowley, J. (2002) Using case studies in research. *Management Research News*, 25 (1): 16–27.

Ruddin, L. P. (2006) You can generalise stupid! Social scientists, Bent Flyvbjerg and case study methodology. *Qualitative Inquiry*, 12 (4): 797–812.

Rueschemeyer, D. (2003) Can one or a few cases yield theoretical gains?, in J. Mahoney and D. Rueschemeyer (eds) *Comparative Historical Analysis in the Social Sciences*. Cambridge: Cambridge University Press.

Russell, B. (1912) *Problems of Philosophy*. Oxford: Oxford University Press.

Said, E. (2004) *Power, Politics and Culture: Interviews with Edward W. Said*. Edited and introduced by G. Viswanathan. London: Bloomsbury.

Salmons, J. (2010) *Online Interviews in Real Time*. London: Sage.

Samuel, R. (1982) Local and oral history, in R. Burgess (ed.) *Field Research: A Sourcebook and Field Manual*. London: George Allen & Unwin.

Samuel, R. (1994) *Theatres of Memory, Volume 1: Past and Present in Contemporary Culture*. London: Verso.

Sánchez-Jankowski, M. (2002) Representation, responsibility and reliability in participant-observation, in T. May (ed.) *Qualitative Research in Action*. London: Sage.

Sandford, M. (ed.) (2009) *The Northern Veto*. Manchester: Manchester University Press.

Sayer, A. (1992) *Method in Social Science: A Realist Approach*, 2nd edn. London: Routledge.

Sayer, A. (2000) *Realism and Social Science*. London: Sage.

Schegloff, E. (1988) Goffman and the analysis of conversation, in P. Drew and A. Wootton (eds) *Erving Goffman: Exploring the Interaction Order*. Cambridge: Polity.

Scheuch, E. (1990) The development of comparative research: Towards causal explanations, in E. Øyen (ed.) *Comparative Methodology*. London: Sage.

Schram, S. and Caterino, B. (eds) (2006) *Making Political Science Matter: Debating Knowledge, Research, and Method*. New York: New York University Press.

Schuman, H. and Presser, S. (1996) *Questions and Answers in Attitude Surveys: Experiments on Question Form, Wording and Context*. London: Sage.

Schutz, A. (1979) Concept and theory formation in the social sciences, in J. Bynner and K. Stribley (eds) *Social Research: Principles and Procedures*. London: Longman.

Scott, J. (1990) *A Matter of Record: Documentary Sources in Social Research*. Cambridge: Polity.

Scott, J. and Alwin, D. (1998) Retrospective versus prospective measurement of life histories in longitudinal research, in J. Z. Giele and G. H. Elder, Jr. (eds) *Methods of Life Course Research: Qualitative and Quantitative Approaches*. London: Sage.

Scott, M. and Lyman, S. (1968) Accounts. *American Sociological Review*, 33 (1): 46–62.

Seale, C. (1999) *The Quality of Qualitative Research*. London: Sage.

Segert, A. and Zierke, I. (2000) The metamorphosis of *habitus* among East Germans, in P. Chamberlayne, J. Bornat and T. Wengraf (eds) *The Turn to Biographical Methods in Social Science: Comparative Issues and Examples*. London: Routledge.

Seidman, S. (2008) *Contested Knowledge: Social Theory Today*, 4th edn. Oxford: Wiley-Blackwell.

Shalev, M. (2007) Limits and alternatives to multiple regression in comparative analysis: A symposium of methodology in comparative research. *Comparative Social Research*, 24: 261–308.

Shallice, A. and Gordon, P. (1990) *Black People, White Justice? Race and the Criminal Justice System*. London: Runnymede Trust.

Sharrock, W. and Watson, R. (1988) Autonomy among social theories, in N. Fielding (ed.) *Actions and Structure: Research Methods and Social Theory*. London: Sage.

Shaw, C. (1930) *The Jack Roller: A Delinquent Boy's Own Story*. Chicago, IL: University of Chicago Press.

Shea, C. (2000) Don't talk to the humans: The crackdown on social science research. *Lingua Franca*, 10 (2): http://mailer.fsu.edu/~njumonvi/irb-article.htm

Sheehan, K. (2001) Email survey response rates: A review. *Journal of Computer-Mediated Communication*, 6: http://jcmc.indiana.edu/vol6/issue2/sheehan.html

Shipman, M. (1988) *The Limitations of Social Research*, 3rd edn. London: Longman.

Siggelkow, N. (2007) Persuasion with case studies. *Academy of Management Journal*, 50 (1): 20–4.

Silverman, D. (1985) *Qualitative Methodology and Sociology*. Aldershot: Gower.

Silverman, D. (1993) *Interpreting Qualitative Data: Methods for Analysing Talk, Text and Interaction*. London: Sage.

Silverman, D. (1998) *Harvey Sacks: Social Science and Conversation Analysis*. Cambridge: Polity.

Silverman, D. (2010) *Doing Qualitative Research: A Practical Handbook*. 3rd edn. London: Sage.

Simeoni, D. and Diani, M. (1995) The sociostylistics of life histories: Taking Jenny at her word(s). *Current Sociology*, 43 (2–3): 27–39.

Simmel, G. (1964) *The Sociology of Georg Simmel*. Translated, edited and introduced by K. H. Wolff [originally published 1950]. New York: Free Press.

Simons, H. (2009) *Case Study Research in Practice*. London: Sage.

Simons, H. and Usher, R. (eds) (2000) *Situated Ethics in Educational Research*. London: Routledge.

Singleton, A. (1999) Measuring international migration: The tools aren't up to the job, in D. Dorling and S. Simpson (eds) *Statistics in Society: The Arithmetic of Politics*. London: Arnold.

Skeggs, B. (1997) *Formations of Class and Gender: Becoming Respectable*. London: Sage.

Skeggs, B. (2001) Feminist ethnography, in P. Atkinson, A. Coffey, S. Delamont, J. Lofland and L. Lofland (eds) *Handbook of Ethnography*. London: Sage.

Skeggs, B. (2004) *Class, Self, Culture*. London: Routledge.

Slevin, J. (2000) *The Internet and Society*. Cambridge: Polity.

Smart, B. (1992) *Modern Conditions, Postmodern Controversies*. London: Routledge.

Smith, D. E. (1988) *The Everyday World as Problematic: A Feminist Sociology*. Milton Keynes: Open University Press.

Smith, D. E. (1993) *Texts, Facts and Femininity: Exploring the Relations of Ruling*. London: Routledge.

Smith, D. E. (1999) *Writing the Social: Critique, Theory and Investigations*. Toronto: Toronto University Press.

Smith, D. E. (2002) Institutional ethnography, in T. May (ed.) *Qualitative Research in Action*. London: Sage.

Smith, D. E. (2005). *Institutional Ethnography: A Sociology for People*. Oxford: Altamira.

Social and Community Planning Research (SCPR) (1981) Survey methods newsletter on open-ended questions. Autumn.

Søderbaum, F. (2009) Comparative regional integration and regionalism in T. Landmann and N. Robinson (eds) *The Sage Handbook of Comparative Politics*. London: Sage.

Sontag, S. (1978) *On Photography*. London: Allen Lane.

Sparks, R. (1992) *Television and the Drama of Crime: Moral Tales and the Place of Crime in Public Life*. Buckingham: Open University Press.

Spence, J. and Holland, P. (eds) (1991) *Family Snaps: The Meanings of Domestic Photography*. London: Virago.

Spender, D. (1982) *Women of Ideas (and What Men Have Done to Them)*. London: Ark.

Spradley, J. (1979) *The Ethnographic Interview*. New York: Holt, Rinehart & Winston.

Sprent, P. (1988) *Understanding Data*. Harmondsworth: Penguin.

Squires, P. (1990) *Anti-Social Policy: Welfare, Ideology and the Disciplinary State*. London: Harvester Wheatsheaf.

Stake, R. (1978) The case study method in social inquiry. *Educational Researcher*, 7 (2): 5–8.

Stake, R. (2000) Case studies, in N. Denzin and Y. Lincoln (eds) *Handbook of Qualitative Research*. 2nd edn. Thousand Oaks, CA: Sage.

Stake, R. (2005) Qualitative case studies, in N. Denzin and Y. Lincoln (eds) *The Sage Handbook of Qualitative Research*, 3rd edn. Thousand Oaks, CA: Sage.

Stam, R. and Shohat, E. (2009) Transnationalizing comparison: The uses and abuses of cross-cultural analogy. *New Literary History*, 40 (3): 473–99.

Stanko, B. (1990) When precaution is normal: A feminist critique of crime prevention, in L. Gelsthorpe and A. Morris (eds) *Feminist Perspectives in Criminology*. Buckingham: Open University Press.

Stanley, L. and Wise, S. (1993) *Breaking Out Again: Feminist Ontology and Epistemology*, 2nd edn. London: Routledge & Kegan Paul.

Stanley, L. and Wise, S. (2006) Putting it into practice: Using feminist fractured foundationalism in researching children in the concentration camps of the South African war. *Sociological Research Online*, 11 (1): www.socresonline. org.uk/11/1/stanley.html

Stehr, N. (2004) *The Governance of Knowledge*. New Brunswick, NJ: Transaction.

Stein, S. (1999) *Learning, Teaching and Researching on the Internet: A Practical Guide for Social Scientists*. London: Longman.

Stewart, D. and Shamdasani, P. (1990) *Focus Groups: Theory and Practice*. London: Sage.

Steyaert, C. and Bouwen, R. (1994) Group methods of organizational analysis, in C. Cassell and G. Symon (eds) *Qualitative Methods in Organizational Research: A Practical Guide*. London: Sage.

Stoker, G. (2010) Exploring the promise of experimentation in political science: Micro-foundational insights and policy relevance. *Political Studies*, 58: 300–19.

Strauss, A. (1978) *Negotiations, Varieties, Contexts, Processes and Social Order*. San Francisco, CA: Jossey-Bass.

Strauss, A. (1988) *Qualitative Analysis for Social Scientists*. Cambridge: Cambridge University Press.

Strauss, A. and Corbin, J. (1990) *Basics of Qualitative Research: Grounded Theory Procedures and Techniques*. London: Sage.

Sudman, S., Sirken, M. and Cowan, C. (1988) Sampling rare and elusive populations. *Science*, 240: 991–6.

Swank, D. (2007) What comparativists really do: A symposium of methodology in comparative research. *Comparative Social Research*, 24: 361–72.

Sydie, R. (1987) *Natural Women, Cultured Men: A Feminist Critique of Sociological Theory*. Milton Keynes: Open University Press.

Sykes, C. and Treleaven, L. (2009) Critical action research and organizational ethnography, in S. Ybema, D. Yanow, H. Wels and F. Kamsteeg (eds) *Organizational Ethnography: Studying the Complexities of Everyday Life*. London: Sage.

Tacq, J. (1997) *Multivariate Analysis and Techniques in Social Science Research*. London: Sage.

Tarafodi, R. (2010) Translation and cultural comparison: Some epistemological reflections. *Social and Personality Psychology Compass*, 4 (4): 227–37.

Tarling, R. (2009) *Statistical Modelling for Social Researchers: Principles and Practice*. London: Routledge.

Taylor, C. (1994) Neutrality in political science, in M. Martin and L. C. McIntyre (eds) *Readings in the Philosophy of Social Science*. Cambridge, MA: MIT Press.

Taylor, I. (ed.) (1990) *The Social Effects of Free Market Policies: An International Text*. London: Harvester Wheatsheaf.

Taylor, I., Walton, P. and Young, J. (1973) *The New Criminology: For a Social Theory of Deviance*. London: Routledge & Kegan Paul.

Temple, B. and Edwards, R. (2002) Interpreters/translators and cross-language research: Reflexivity and border crossings. *International Journal of Qualitative Methods*, 1 (2): 1–12.

Teune, H. (1990) Comparing countries: Lessons learned, in E. Øyen (ed.) *Comparative Methodology*. London: Sage.

Thayer, H. S. (1981) *Meaning and Action: A Critical History of Pragmatism*, 2nd edn. Indianapolis, IN: Hackett.

Thomas, R. (1996) Statistics as organizational products. *Sociological Research Online*, 1 (3).

Thompson, E. (1982) Anthropology and the discipline of historical context, in R. Burgess (ed.) *Field Research: A Sourcebook and Field Manual*. London: George Allen & Unwin.

Tight, M. (2010) The curious case of case study: A viewpoint. *International Journal of Social Research Methodology*, 13 (4): 329–39.

Titmuss, R. (1974) *Social Policy: An Introduction*. London: George Allen & Unwin.

Townsend, P. (1996) The struggle for independent statistics on poverty, in R. Levitas and W. Guy (eds) *Interpreting Official Statistics*. London: Routledge.

Turner, S. (2003) *Liberal Democracy 3.0. Civil Society in an Age of Experts*. London: Sage.

Van Maanen, J. (1978) On watching the watchers, in P. Manning and J. Van Maanen (eds) *Policing: A View for the Streets*. Santa Monica, CA: Goodyear.

Van Maanen, J. (1979) Reclaiming qualitative methods for organizational research: A preface. *Administrative Science Quarterly*, 24: 520–6.

Van Maanen, J. (1988) *Tales of the Field: On Writing Ethnography*. Chicago, IL: University of Chicago Press.

Van Wynsberghe, R. and Khan, S. (2007) Redefining case study. *International Journal of Qualitative Methods*, 6 (2): Article 6: www.ualberta.ca/~iiqm/backissues/6_2/vanwynsberghe.pdf

van Zijl, V. (1993) *A Guide to Local Housing Needs Assessment*. Coventry: Institute of Housing.

Vázquez, R. (2010) Re-imagining Gothenburg: Critical photography, in H. Holgersson, C. Thörn, H. Thörn and M. Wahlström (eds) *Researching Gothenburg: Essays on a Changing City*. Gothenburg: Glänta.

Vehovar, V. and Manfreda, K. L. (2008) Overview: Online surveys, in N. Fielding, R. M. Lee and G. Blank (eds) *The Sage Handbook of Online Research Methods*. London: Sage.

Verba, S. (1971) Cross-national survey research: The problem of credibility, in I. Vallier (ed.) *Comparative Methods in Sociology: Essays on Trends and Applications*. Los Angeles, CA: University of California Press.

Viinikka, S. (1989) Child sexual abuse and the law, in E. Driver and A. Droisen (eds) *Child Sexual Abuse: Feminist Perspectives*. London: Macmillan.

Walker, A. and Wong, C-K. (2004) The ethnocentric construction of the welfare state, in P. Kennett (ed.) *A Handbook of Comparative Social Policy*. Cheltenham: Edward Elgar.

Walton, C., Coyle, A. and Lyons, E. (2003) 'There you are man': Men's use of emotion discourses and their negotiation of emotional subject positions, in R. Harré and F. Moghaddam (eds) *The Self and Others: Positioning Individuals and Groups in Personal, Political, and Cultural Contexts*. London: Praeger.

Warwick, D. (1982) Tearoom trade: Means and ends in social research, in M. Bulmer (ed.) *Social Research Ethics: An Examination of the Merits of Covert Participation Observation*. London: Macmillan.

Warwick, D. and Pettigrew, T. (1983) Towards ethical guidelines for social science research in public policy, in D. Callahan and B. Jennings (eds) *Ethics, the Social Sciences, and Policy Analysis*. London: Plenum.

Waterton, C. and Wynne, B. (1999) Can focus groups access communist views?, in R. S. Barbour and J. Kitzinger (eds) *Developing Focus Group Research: Politics, Theory and Practice*. London: Sage.

Watson, R. (1997) Ethnomethodology and textual analysis, in D. Silverman (ed.) *Qualitative Research: Theory, Method and Practice*. London: Sage.

Watson, S. (2006) *City Publics: The (Dis)Enchantments of Urban Encounters*. London: Routledge.

Watson, T. J. (1994) *In Search of Management: Culture, Chaos and Control in Managerial Work*. London: Routledge.

Webb, E., Campbell, D., Schwartz, R. and Sechrest, L. (2000) *Unobtrusive Measures: Nonreactive Research in the Social Sciences*, revised edn [originally published 1966]. Thousand Oaks, CA: Sage.

Webb, S. (1990) Counter-arguments: An ethnographic look at women and class, in L. Stanley (ed.) *Feminist Praxis: Research, Theory and Epistemology in Feminist Sociology*. London: Routledge.

Weber, M. (1949) *The Methodology of the Social Sciences*. Glencoe, IL: Free Press.

Weber, M. (1964) *The Theory of Social and Economic Organization*. Translated by A. Henderson and T. Parsons. Edited with an introduction by T. Parsons. Glencoe, IL: Free Press.

Webster, C. (2007) *Understanding Race and Crime*. Maidenhead: Open University Press.

Wetherell, M. and Potter, J. (1988) Discourse analysis and the identification of interpretative repertoires, in C. Antaki (ed.) *Analysing Everyday Explanation: A Casebook of Methods*. London: Sage.

Whitehead, J. and McNiff, J. (2006) *Action Research Living Theory*. London: Sage.

Whyte, W. F. (1981) *Street Corner Society* [originally published 1943]. Chicago, IL: University of Chicago Press.

Whyte, W. F. (1984) *Learning from the Field: A Guide from Experience*. With the collaboration of Kathleen King Whyte. London: Sage.

Wilkinson, R. and Pickett, K. (2010) *The Spirit Level: Why Equality is Better for Everyone*. London: Penguin.

Williams, A. (1990) Reading feminism in fieldnotes, in L. Stanley (ed.) *Feminist Praxis: Research, Theory and Epistemology in Feminist Sociology*. London: Routledge.

Williams, B. (2002) *Truth and Truthfulness: An Essay in Genealogy*. Princeton, NJ: Princeton University Press.

Williams, M. (2000) *Science and Social Science: An Introduction*. London: Routledge.

Williams, M. and May, T. (1996) *Introduction to the Philosophy of Social Research*. London: UCL Press.

Williams, R. (1981) *Culture*. London: Fontana.

Williamson, J. (1987) *Consuming Passions: The Dynamics of Popular Culture*. London: Marion Boyars.

Willig, C. (ed.) (1999) *Applied Discourse Analysis: Social and Psychological Interventions*. Buckingham: Open University Press.

Willis, C. (1983) *The Use, Effectiveness and Impact of Police Stop and Search Powers*. London: Home Office Research Unit, Home Office.

Willis, P. (1977) *Learning to Labour: How Working Class Kids Get Working Class Jobs*. Farnborough: Saxon House.

Winch, P. (1990) *The Idea of a Social Science and its Relation to Philosophy*, 2nd edn [originally published 1958]. London: Routledge.

Wolcott, H. (1990) *Writing Up Qualitative Research*. London: Sage.

Worldwatch Institute (2010) *State of the World: Transforming Cultures from Consumerism to Sustainability*. New York: Norton.

Wynne, B. (1996) May the sheep safely graze? A reflexive view of the expert-lay knowledge divide, in S. Lash, B. Szerszynski and B. Wynne (eds) *Risk, Environment and Modernity: Towards a New Ecology*. London: Sage.

Ybema, S., Yanow, D., Wels, H. and Kamsteeg, F. (eds) (2009) *Organizational Ethnography: Studying the Complexities of Everyday Life*. London: Sage.

Yin, R. (1981) The case study crisis: Some answers. *Administrative Science Quarterly*, 26: 58–65.

Yin, R. (1994) *Case Study Research: Design and Methods*, 2nd edn. London: Sage.

Yin, R. (2009) *Case Study Research: Design and Methods*, 4th edn. Thousand Oaks, CA: Sage.

Young, A. (1990) *Femininity in Dissent*. London: Routledge.

Young, A. (1996) *Imagining Crime: Textual Outlaws and Criminal Conversations*. London: Sage.

Young, J. (1999) *The Exclusive Society: Social Exclusion, Crime and Difference in Late Modernity*. London: Sage.

Young, K. (1977) 'Values' in the policy process. *Policy and Politics*, 5 (3): 1–22.

Young, K. (1981) Discretion as an implementation problem, in M. Adler and S. Asquith (eds) *Discretion and Welfare*. London: Heinemann.

Yu, J. and Nijkamp, P. (2009) Methodological challenges and institutional barriers in the use of experimental method for the evaluation of business incubators: Lessons from the US, EU and China, in S. E. Cozzens and P. Catalan (eds) *Proceedings of the 2009 Atlanta Conference on Science and Innovation Policy*. Atlanta, GA, 2–3 October, pp. 1–9.

Zimmerman, D. (1974) Facts as practical accomplishment, in R. Turner (ed.) *Ethnomethodology*. Harmondsworth: Penguin.

Žižek, S. (2009) *First as Tragedy, Then as Farce*. London: Verso.

Žižek, S. (2010a) Joe Public v the volcano, *New Statesman*, 29 April.

Žižek, S. (2010b) *Living in the End Times*. London: Verso.

Author Index

Subject Index

THE GOOD RESEARCH GUIDE 4/E
For Small-scale Social Research
Projects

Martyn Denscombe

9780335241385 (Paperback)
2010

eBook also available

The Good Research Guide is a best-selling introductory book on the basics of social research. It provides practical and straightforward guidance for those who need to conduct small-scale research projects as part of their undergraduate, postgraduate or professional studies.

Key features:

- A clear, straightforward introduction to data collection methods and data analysis
- Jargon-free coverage of the key issues
- An attractive layout and user-friendly presentation
- Checklists to guide good practice

It is a valuable resource for anyone conducting social research including those in applied areas such as business studies, health studies, nursing, education, social work, policy studies, marketing, media studies and criminology.

www.openup.co.uk

OPEN UNIVERSITY PRESS
McGraw - Hill Education

GROUND RULES FOR SOCIAL RESEARCH 2/E
Guidelines for Good Practice

Martyn Denscombe

9780335233816 (Paperback)
2009

eBook also available

Ground Rules for Social Research is a user-friendly resource for people doing small-scale social research projects. It focuses on the key ideas and practices that underlie good research and provides clear guidelines to newcomers and experienced researchers alike.

Key features:

- The identification of 12 ground rules for good social research
- Checklists to help researchers evaluate their approach and avoid fundamental errors
- A clear and jargon-free style

The book is written for undergraduate, postgraduate and professional students in the social sciences, business studies, health studies, media studies and education who need to undertake research projects as part of their studies.

www.openup.co.uk

OPEN UNIVERSITY PRESS
McGraw - Hill Education

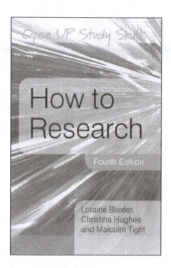

HOW TO RESEARCH 4/E

Loraine Blaxter, Christina Hughes
and Malcolm Tight

9780335238675 (Paperback)
2010

eBook also available

How to Research is a bestselling, practical book that reassures the
first time researcher by leading them systematically through the whole
research process; from the initial meetings with a supervisor to
critically evaluating their ideas, doing the research and finally writing
up the project.

Key features:

- Vignettes to help readers relate to research examples
- Additional coverage on literature reviews and mixed
  methodologies
- New material on changes in research ethics
- Detailed information on the use of diaries, internet ethnographies
  and visual methods

How to Research 4e is an ideal resource for the first-time researcher
doing a small-scale research project in the social sciences whether
they are at university or in the workplace. It supports its readers as
they develop their skills to become more experienced researchers.

www.openup.co.uk